The Political
Thought of
Hannah Arendt

The Political Thought of Hannah Arendt

by Michael G. Gottsegen

STATE UNIVERSITY OF NEW YORK PRESS

The author is grateful to the following publishers for kindly granting permission to reprint excerpts from their publications: Excerpts from THE HUMAN CONDITION, by Hannah Arendt, copyright © 1958 by Hannah Arendt, are reprinted by permission of The University of Chicago Press. Excerpts from LECTURES ON KANT'S POLITICAL PHIL-OSOPHY, by Hannah Arendt, edited by Ronald Beiner, copyright © 1982 by The University of Chicago, are reprinted by permission of The University of Chicago Press. Excerpts from MEN IN DARK TIMES, by Hannah Arendt, copyright © 1968 by Hannah Arendt, are reprinted by permission of Harcourt Brace & Company. Excerpts from THE ORIGINS OF TOTALITARIANISM, by Hannah Arendt, copyright © 1951 by Hannah Arendt and renewed in 1979 by Mary McCarthy West, are reprinted by permission of Harcourt Brace & Company. Excerpts from THE LIFE OF THE MIND: VOLUME ONE, THINKING, by Hannah Arendt, copyright © 1978 by Harcourt Brace & Company, are reprinted by permission of the publisher. Excerpts from THE LIFE OF THE MIND: VOLUME TWO, WILL-ING, by Hannah Arendt, copyright © 1978 by Harcourt Brace & Company, are reprinted by permission of the publisher. Excerpts from ON REVOLUTION, by Hannah Arendt, copyright © 1963 by Hannah Arendt, are used by permission of Viking Penguin, a division of Penguin Books USA Inc. Excerpts from BETWEEN PAST AND FUTURE, by Hannah Arendt, copyright © 1954, 1956, 1958, 1960 and 1961 by Hannah Arendt, are used by permission of Viking Penguin, a division of Penguin Books USA Inc.

Published by
State University of New York Press, Albany
© 1994 State University of New York
All rights reserved
Printed in the United States of America

For information, address State University of New York
Press, State University Plaza, Albany, N.Y., 12246

Production by Marilyn P. Semerad
Marketing by Bernadette LaManna

Library of Congress Cataloging-in-Publication Data
Gottsegen, Michael G., 1958–
    The political thought of Hannah Arendt / by Michael G. Gottsegen.
      p. cm.
    Includes bibliographical references and index.
    ISBN 0-7914-1729-8 (hard). — ISBN 0-7914-1730-1 (paper)
    1. Arendt, Hannah.   I. Title.
JC251.A74G68   1993
320.5'092—dc20   92–47131
                                       CIP
10 9 8 7 6 5 4 3 2 1

This book is dedicated
to my parents, Bob and Dorothy,
for their love, support,
and friendship.
And in memory of my grandmother,
Cele,
whom I came to know so well
and appreciate so completely
during the years in which
this labor was undertaken.

Contents

Preface

Several years ago I sat down with a Czech acquaintance of mine who was visiting New York from Prague. The "velvet revolution" had occurred only several months before and my interlocutor was filled with enthusiasm. For several hours he regaled me with stories of what had transpired during those extraordinary days in Prague. While his stories were in themselves quite transfixing, I was as much struck by the language with which he described the days of the revolution and the sweet taste of freedom: he spoke of the creation of public spaces where none had existed previously; he spoke of the joy that came with the opportunity to participate in common deliberations with his peers; and he spoke of how his sense of self had changed and deepened with each passing day of engagement in a struggle for what truly mattered.

The story he told sounded as if it could have been culled from the last chapter of Hannah Arendt's *On Revolution.* I asked him if he had ever read Hannah Arendt. Of course, he had not. Nonetheless, I thought it noteworthy that, though he had not read her work, he described his experience in the very idiom she used to describe the experience of "public happiness."

But this was what Arendt should have led me to expect. After all it had happened before: since 1776 there have arisen a succession of singular moments in which men and women have come to experience the public happiness that is tasted whenever people act in common. Had Arendt lived long enough to witness the fall of communism and the advent of democracy in Eastern Europe, she surely would have regarded it as yet another instance of that phenomenon which she had described so faithfully.

Arendt was painfully aware of the fact that the joys that are inherent in political participation are overlooked by most students of politics. Like most nonparticipants, they tend to construe participation as if it were only a means to ends that are external to the political process. As a result, the rewards that are internal to the process have been ignored and the sweetness of participation has gone unarticulated. But Arendt was determined to repair this oversight.

Indeed, almost alone amongst theorists in our generation, Hannah Arendt was acutely sensitive to this dimension of meaning, a fact that becomes all the more striking when it is recalled that she was hardly a participant herself. Nonetheless, she possessed the uncanny ability to articulate the experience of participation and to convey a feeling for its significance. But her interest lay not merely in phenomenal description. Rather, she hoped to instill a taste for the pleasure which she was so intent upon describing. After all, she might have reasoned, only an unarticulated pleasure can long remain unsought after.

Arendt also knew that it is hard to preserve and protect something, so long as our awareness and appreciation of it remains unarticulated. In this respect, history has proven particularly inhospitable to "public happiness" which has bloomed repeatedly only to be swept away as often, and, most often, before anybody understood or articulated what was at stake.

At the moment of this writing, it can still be said that "democracy is breaking out all over" and that the taste for "public happiness" continues to grow—not only in the East but in the West as well. In such a moment, and in the face of participatory democracy's always uncertain prospects, Hannah Arendt's works remain as timely as ever. For she helps us to "think what we are doing" and thus to understand what hangs in the balance. In placing my work on her work before the public, it is my hope that it will serve to deepen our understanding of Arendt's thought while heightening our sensitivity to the phenomenon of "public happiness" and to the conditions of its long continuance.

Acknowledgments

Over the years since I first began this project a number of individuals have been most helpful and encouraging. Despite their busy schedules Robert Amdur, Anita Mercier, and Cathy Sylvis each provided me with invaluable assistance at one time or another. Also deserving special thanks are the three anonymous readers who were selected by my publisher to review the manuscript. Together they helped me to avoid errors of various kinds. In addition, I would like to thank my father who closely read the manuscript and impressed upon me the importance of not writing so dryly and abstractly that the reader would tire of turning the pages. If I succeeded at all in this respect, it owes in large part to his repeated exhortations. I would also like to thank Clay Morgan, my editor at SUNY Press, for taking an interest in my project and for shepherding it through the publishing process in relatively short order.

Finally, I would like to thank my friends and family who helped to make an arduous task less so by providing me with warm support and hot meals. This book could not have been written without them.

List of Abbreviations

BPF	*Between Past and Future*
BPF/Pref	"Preface"
BPF/TMA	"Tradition and the Modern Age"
BPF/CH	"The Concept of History"
BPF/WA	"What Is Authority?"
BPF/WF	"What Is Freedom?"
BPF/CE	"The Crisis in Education"
BPF/CC	"The Crisis in Culture"
BPF/TP	"Truth and Politics"
CR	*Crises of the Republic*
EIJ	*Eichmann in Jerusalem: The Banality of Evil*
THC	*The Human Condition*
JP	*The Jew as Pariah*
LKPP	*Lectures on Kant's Political Philosophy*
LM	*The Life of the Mind* (in two volumes)
LMT	*Thinking* (LM: volume 1)
LMW	*Willing* (LM: volume 2)
MDT	*Men in Dark Times*
OR	*On Revolution*
OT	*The Origins of Totalitarianism*
RLR	"Reflections on Little Rock"
RV	*Rahel Varnhagen: The Life of a Jewish Woman*
UP	"Understanding and Politics"

Introduction

In this book we will trace the development of Hannah Arendt's mature political thought and demonstrate its organic coherence. In particular, our focus will be upon the range of works that span the years from 1958 to 1975, the years of Arendt's maximal productivity. The reason for undertaking this study can be simply stated: Viewed individually, the meaning of Arendt's works is oftentimes elusive and as a result misunderstandings of Arendt's works have proliferated. In the face of these interpretive difficulties, it would be fortunate if we could look to Arendt's broader project for guidance. However, because the broader logic that connects Arendt's works to one another remains obscure, the tendency among interpreters has been to interpret each work as if it were neither possible nor essential to situate it in relation to the whole of Arendt's oeuvre. Indeed, even those interpretations that treat the entire body of Arendt's work tend to interpret each particular text as if it were essentially self-contained. But the consequence of delimiting the interpretive approach in this way has been the proliferation of misunderstandings and of interpretive disagreements.

In effect, I challenge the view of those who have interpreted the parts of Arendt's oeuvre without sufficient cognizance of the whole. It is not that I deny that Arendt's oeuvre is riven and fissured in ways that ought to make one chary of imputing to it a cohesiveness that on the surface it seems to lack. Rather, over against the fractured foreground, I discern an overarching telos, an overarching project that makes the surface ruptures comprehensible and helps to clarify the internal ambiguities of the individual works. But the unity of Arendt's oeuvre is more than the unity of a project; in addition, beneath the heterogeneity of Arendt's topical concerns there exists a unitary conceptual framework and an encompassing categorial structure that remain relatively constant from one text to the next. In the course of this study both the underlying architectonic and the contours of Arendt's project will be clarified, as will the relationship between the two as it evolves in Arendt's successive works.

Those who are familiar with the chronology of Arendt's writings will already have been struck by the fact that by selecting 1958, the year of the publication of *The Human Condition*, as the point of demarcation between Arendt's mature project and what does not belong to it, I have placed *The Origins of Totalitarianism* (published in 1951) outside the parameters of this project and beyond the perimeter of the current study's field of focus. This is not an arbitrary decision.

I draw the line where I do because *The Origins of Totalitarianism* is largely concerned with a range of historical and sociological questions that do not directly figure in Arendt's subsequent writings. Moreover, to attend in detail to the contents of this particular work would take us too far afield from the main lines of our inquiry. It should not be inferred, however, that *The Origins of Totalitarianism* lies wholly beyond the range of our interest. Indeed, no full appreciation of Arendt's purpose in *The Human Condition*, and in the works that follow it, could be achieved without some appreciation for how Arendt's broader project relates to her conception of the mid-century European crisis, a conception that she fully develops in *The Origins of Totalitarianism* and nowhere else. And yet, in order to grasp what we need to know about Arendt's conception of this crisis, we do not need to lavish upon the work that discusses it the same intense scrutiny that we will bring to bear upon Arendt's later works. But attend to it, we must, and it is best to do so here at the outset. Let us begin, then, by surveying the context which transformed Hannah Arendt into a student of totalitarianism.

In 1929, at the age of twenty-three, Arendt had received her doctorate in philosophy. Though living amidst a politically turbulent period, Arendt herself was not fully engaged by the struggles of the moment. Her dissertation, a phenomenological study of Augustine's concept of love, stands aloof from the gathering storm. The interests of this protégée of Karl Jaspers and Martin Heidegger lay elsewhere. But things were about to change.

In Germany hard times were quickly becoming productive of ominous political developments. Politically motivated violence, xenophobia, and anti-Semitism were on the rise. And as larger and larger percentages of the electorate came to be persuaded that Germany's salvation lay in the appointment of a strong man capable of imposing order, the arguments of the National Socialists became more and more compelling to many. In such an environment aloofness from politics could offer no protection, especially if one happened to be Jewish. And as Arendt quickly learned, classical *Bildung* alone could not provide sufficient guidance in a world come unglued.

Banned from employment in Germany and fearing a quickly deteriorating political situation, Arendt took refuge in Paris. Seven years later, in May of 1940, Arendt was among the "enemy aliens" who were interned at Gurs on the order of the French government. From Gurs she escaped over the Pyrenees and, via Lisbon, to New York in May of 1941. She and so many more like her. And yet, when measured against the vast multitudes who found no means of escape, they were as a cup of water snatched from the sea. And they saw themselves as such.

Survival on such terms imposes burdens of its own, and debts that one way or another must be discharged. An offering must be made that one's soul might be granted reprieve. *The Origins of Totalitarianism* may be understood as constituting such an offering. Totalitarianism had brought the world to the edge of utter disaster. Corpses were piled high; human dignity and freedom were denied; the stability of the worldly frame was undermined; and the value of Western civilization was called into question. And what had happened in Germany and Russia could have happened elsewhere for, as Arendt would argue, totalitarianism had its roots in the very nature of modern society. That it not happen elsewhere, Arendt was driven to clarify the nature of the forces that conspired to produce the death camp as the ultimate symbol of our century. Inspiring Arendt is the hope that an understanding of the phenomenon might offer some protection against its recurrence.

At this juncture we are less interested in tracing the intricacies of Arendt's phenomenological analysis of totalitarianism than we are in highlighting those aspects of it which can help us to understand the relationship between the conception of the mid–century crisis that she develops in *The Origins of Totalitarianism* and the tenor of Arendt's subsequent work. Because Arendt's later work should be read as seeking, at least in part, to provide us with an understanding of the measures that will protect against a recrudescence of the totalitarian pathology, it is particularly important to focus upon those factors in Arendt's analysis of totalitarianism that she regards as most pathogenic. Of particular relevance from this perspective are Arendt's discussion of the masses whose conditions of life made them highly susceptible to the ideological appeal of the totalitarian movements and her discussion of worldlessness. Also of relevance are Arendt's analyses of the nature of ideological thinking and of the nature of its appeal.

The masses in question are the masses of modern society who brought the totalitarian movements to power.[1] In *The Origins of Totalitarianism* Arendt argues that the conditions of modern life have conspired to agglomerate the bulk of the population into a mass in which feelings of loneliness, meaninglessness, and anonymity correlate with real social isolation, worldlessness, and atomization.[2] One product of this situation has been a withering of the sense, so prominent since the Renaissance, of the self's significance as a primary center of value. More and more the self-image of the man in the mass has become that of being a small and superfluous cog in some vast inhuman machine. No end in himself is he, and he knows it. Small wonder then that this individual is unmoved by a bourgeois political rhetoric that takes his self-love and sense of self-interest for granted. Rather, as the leaders of the totalitarian movements well understood, the mass man will more readily respond to a politics that starts from the premise that the self by itself is a nullity, for such a politics speaks to the individual's everyday experience of life in mass society.[3]

Of course, it is not that the totalitarian movements proudly proclaim the insignificance of the individual; rather, by their insistence that a significant life can only be had by those who belong to the movement, they tacitly acknowledge the general vacuity of existence in the mass, albeit while promising a way out.[4] However, as Arendt hastens to point out, the redemption that these movements offer is unsatisfactory inasmuch as it fails to offer the individual any confirmation of the value of his unique self. Instead, movements which exhaustively define the individual as the instantiation of some shared group essence (as, for example, Aryan, or proletarian) encourage their members to find meaning and purpose by identifying completely with this supra-individual essence and with what the movement declares to be the group's role in world history.[5] As a result, the existential problem is not so much redressed as repressed, for—as Arendt observes—the self that feels itself to be glorified through participation in the movement is in fact being renounced. Of course this fact is hardly glimpsed by those who hope that participation in some movement will render their lives utterly significant. Apparently, only persons who already experience their lives as meaningful can fully appreciate the full extent of the self-renunciation that the ideologies of these movements impose. Alas, the conditions of mass society being what they are, millions have been ready to enlist behind the banners of movements that promise to liberate them from an awareness of their own superfluity.

Had Arendt been concerned with recommending corrective measures on the basis of this analysis—which she does not do in *The Origins of Totalitarianism* but arguably does do subsequently—the general directive is easy enough to infer. If a recrudescence of totalitarianism is to be avoided, by one means or another the conditions of mass society must be directly countered. If mass society bequeaths meaninglessness, then the sources of meaning must be uncovered and restored. If meaning and individuation are mutually entailing, then, the media by means of which the latter can be facilitated must be identified and institutionally buttressed. If mass society itself is the culprit and incapable of remedy, then, mass society itself must be disaggregated. Just what any one of these paths would concretely entail—and which one in particular Arendt will espouse as most likely to succeed—is a matter that can only become clear in the sequel. In

The Origins of Totalitarianism, however, her analysis takes us no further, at least insofar as this aspect of the problem is concerned.

Associated with Arendt's analysis of the experience of the masses of mass society—and ultimately of greater influence upon the orientation of Arendt's mature political thought—is the cognate concept of worldlessness.[6] Though I have already referred in passing to the worldlessness of the members of mass society, Arendt herself does not directly link her analysis of this concept to her reflections upon the condition of the masses of mass society. Instead, she develops this notion in relation to her consideration of the condition of statelessness, a condition into which German Jews and other victims of mass denaturalization were placed during the years preceding the outbreak of the Second World War.[7] That this concept is of broader relevance, and of particular relevance for understanding what ails the denizens of mass society, will become clear shortly.

In *The Origins of Totalitarianism* worldlessness is defined by Arendt as the condition of those persons who do not belong to a world in which they matter as individuals.[8] Objectively, it is a condition that is forced upon persons who are deprived of their political rights, for example, by forced denaturalization or tyranny. Subjectively, it is a condition that may overtake anyone who is effectively alienated from the public realm. Essentially, it is a condition of being deprived of "a place in the world which makes opinions significant and actions effective."[9] Worldless, then, is one whose words and deeds do not count. In other words, for one who has been placed in this condition what matters is not *who* one is—which can only be signified by one's words and deeds—but the ascriptive characteristics that identify *what* one is. In the eyes of the world, Arendt observes, such a person has become thing-like and as such is bereft of human dignity.[10] Aristotle, apprehending the essential link between human language, subjectivity, and responsibility, had defined man as the speaking animal; in light of this, Arendt observes that the stateless and effectively speechless alien is exiled from the human race.[11]

Having been a stateless Jewish refugee herself, Arendt is especially well placed to reflect upon the deeper implications of worldlessness. In the first instance, she stresses the sheer danger that comes with being thrown back on mere humanness.[12] And, as we have seen, she also shows how the stateless are reified and thus outwardly dehumanized by the communities that deny them the rights of membership. On a deeper level, however, Arendt wants to demonstrate how worldlessness itself works to undercut the very grip on reality of those who are deprived of "a place in the world which makes opinions significant and actions effective."[13] In this regard, Arendt starts from the observation that the stateless person has been cut off from connection with and responsibility for the common world.[14] By inference, then, the stateless person is also excluded from the discursive sharing of the world through which community is constituted. For one thing, this means that he who is worldless or stateless is deprived of community and its humanizing effects.[15] Since, by Arendt's description, participation in common discourse softens the hard edges of human otherness as it bequeaths the kind of common sense that facilitates mutual understanding, he who is thrown back upon a merely private life is denied all of these effects. As a result, the otherness of the alien—and in some sense we are all aliens but for the smoothing over of differences through social intercourse—remains unmodulated, while common sense, the common coin of common life, is not acquired.[16]

As I have already mentioned, Arendt does not directly relate her analysis of the worldlessness of the stateless to her consideration of the condition of the masses of mass society. Nonetheless, the affinity between the two situations, and between her characterizations of them both, is pronounced.[17] To begin with, it is apparent that the masses, like the stateless in this respect, are effectively deprived of "a place in the world which makes opinions significant and actions effective," albeit while retaining formal political rights. Like the stateless, then, they are effectively excluded from the public space and thrown back upon their private lives. And the price they pay, as a consequence of this exclusion from public life, is not dissimilar: they are deprived of the public experiences that develop individuality and, in their own eyes and in the eyes of the world, their identity becomes synonymous with the character of some relatively indiscriminate social category or class. In addition, they are deprived of the humanization that comes about through participation in the discourse of the world and are deprived of the common sense that is to be acquired through such participation. Moreover, as we shall see below, it is this very lack of common sense that permits the masses to respond so uncritically and so enthusiastically to the enticing appeal of totalitarian ideologies. It is, then, the worldlessness of the masses that makes them so great a threat to the world.[18]

Why the masses of modern society should fall prey to a kind of worldlessness that has so much in common with that experienced by stateless refugees is not a question that Arendt addresses directly. Nonetheless, it seems clear that effective political disenfranchisement (or exclusion from the political community) is the common denominator that links the two situations, although in one case it is de jure and in the other de facto. Whether in the latter case it is a consequence of social instability, social atomization, or the insubstantiality of modern political rights is harder to say. Though all three factors are likely to be involved, it is worth noting that Arendt points to social instability more frequently than she does to the other two. In particular, she singles out the industrial revolution, imperialism, and the modern dissolution of social and political institutions for unhinging the masses from the world and for preparing the way for the rise of totalitarian movements.[19] Apparently, masses rendered world-less and anxious by an unstable world that undermines common sense and eludes comprehension were drawn to totalitarian movements not only by the promise of "belonging," but by the promise of understanding as well.[20] From this we can infer that merely securing a place in the world for every citizen may not be enough to overcome the feelings of worldlessness and their destructive effects. It may also be necessary to insure that the world itself becomes a stable place. Either way, it is clear that any attempt to place the political order upon secure foundations will need to tackle worldlessness directly. Making sure that society provides its members with the means by which to develop an appreciation for their individuality is also important, but in light of Arendt's analysis of worldlessness it is clear that any solution which Arendt espouses will endeavor to address both problems at once.

The third aspect of Arendt's analysis of totalitarianism that will prove to be of great importance in our endeavor to assess the complex of motivations at the heart of her mature political philosophy comes to the fore in the third volume of *The Origins of Totalitarianism* and is discussed by Arendt under the rubric of ideological thinking. Under the first two headings, we have considered facets of modernity which Arendt singles out as particularly conducive to the advent of the totalitarian movements. Under the third heading, however, we are considering what on first glance appears to be not so much a facet of modernity as a dimension of the totalitarian movements themselves.[21]

In Arendt's analysis, ideological thinking and totalitarian thinking are one and the same.[22] In each case thought presents itself as an all-encompassing logic of the totality. All phenomena of present, past, and future are claimed to be perfectly knowable by one in possession of the ideological master key. Thus the ideologist becomes the scientist who alone among political players possesses access to the inmost truth of the social process. Such science, or the possession of such science, comes in turn to serve as the basis of the totalitarian party's claim of a right to rule. That the party must rule exclusively and dictatorially follows from its belief that it is the only element in society with the requisite knowledge. As truth is by its nature one, and the party that comprehends it is one, this party alone ought to wield political power.

Arendt's argument with ideological thinking and its implicit world view—an argument which she develops to some extent in *The Origins of Totalitarianism*—is comprised of two elements. First, Arendt contests the very possibility of totalizing knowledge.[23] For instance, the Marxist and Nazi claims to comprehension of the essential laws of the historical process are categorically rejected for their denial of the role of contingency and human freedom in shaping the course of historical becoming.[24] Anybody with common sense would surely know this denial to be false, Arendt avers. Thus, over against the ideologist's assertion of historical necessity and totalizing knowledge, Arendt asserts the ever unpredictable and yet most consequential interplay of contingency, an interplay which obviously precludes totalizing knowledge of the future.[25]

Secondly, Arendt contests the ideologist's claims to sole possession of the truth for its implicit rejection of a political process that presupposes the equal legitimacy of differing opinions.[26] According to the proponents of one ideological creed or another, the truth *(their* truth) is one, while opinion is inherently many. The former thus denies the legitimacy of the latter as it cannot help but regard multiplicity as synonymous with error. Thus, it can hardly be surprising that when totalitarian political movements come to power they proceed—in the name of truth of course—to silence all voices that are in disagreement with them. Hence Arendt's rejection of ideological thinking for being—both in theory and in practice—hostile to the elementary datum of human difference, which she is so concerned to protect, and hostile to the kind of politics that would foster rather than undercut the expression of this difference.

What begins, then, as a narrow quarrel with ideological thinking broadens into a consideration of the relation of truth to politics, a problematic of great concern to political philosophy since Plato placed it on the agenda.[27] Indeed, it is Plato who first argued that rule be exclusively vested in the hands of the philosophers because they alone had knowledge of ultimate truth, an argument not so far removed from that made by modern totalitarians on behalf of their own will to power.[28] Thus Arendt's argument against the latter must be construed as an argument against the former as well and by implication as an argument on behalf of the forms of popular government whose validity is implicitly denied by those who make political claims on behalf of the elites of knowledge. Of greater concern to Arendt, however, than the fate of democracy is the fate of human plurality, and of its expression, both of which are also called into question where monological conceptions of truth attain political primacy.

To declare the ideologists' conception of reality to be flawed and their claims to power to be misbegotten is hardly to set forth how political reality needs to be reconstructed if one wants to insure that the ideologists' appeal will fall upon deaf ears. Within *The Origins of Totalitarianism*, common sense is singled out as one factor that tends to protect against the ideologists' propagandistic appeals, and yet, common sense

presupposes a common world and a stable world both of which modernity has undermined. Revivifying common sense, then, entails much more
besides.[29] In addition, it should be pointed out that the critique of ideological thinking, and the critique of truth in politics that it entails, raise (but
do not answer) deep and troubling questions regarding the proper criterion of validity in politics. If not truth, then what? The sheer weight of
numbers? But why should the latter be regarded as less likely to become a
source of oppression? And in terms of an earlier thematic, one might ask
how well majoritarianism will conduce to the end of individuation that
Arendt is so concerned to foster. Again, my intent at this juncture is merely to signal how much remains to be clarified in the wake of *The Origins
of Totalitarianism*. In particular, I want to foreshadow Arendt's subsequent search for a new discursive logos of the public space that is capable
simultaneously of meeting the various criteria, and of overcoming the various problems that are foremost in *The Origins of Totalitarianism*.[30]

In *The Origins of Totalitarianism*, then, Arendt weaves together a
genealogical study of origins within a matrix of concepts and concerns
that includes those few elements canvased in this introduction. What
remains to be underscored is simply this: the factors already considered,
which are severally regarded by Arendt as *implicitly* destructive, on the
one hand, of human dignity, freedom, and individuality and, on the other
hand, of political community and of the world's stability, become *explicitly* and overwhelmingly destructive when they are brought into play by the
political action of the totalitarian movements.

Hitherto things had been bad and getting worse: slowly, gradually,
continuously. More and more, mass society degraded the individual; more
and more, the permanent instability of the modern age left the individual
in the midst of an increasingly anomic void; and more and more, forms of
ideological thinking were coming to the fore as common sense continued
to erode. But with the advent of the totalitarian movements, and even
more so with their coming to power, the conditions that spawned them
and the consequent degenerative and dehumanizing effects were, respectively, intensified and accelerated. Promises to the contrary notwithstanding, the effect of the totalitarian movements was to exacerbate rather than
to alleviate the conditions that brought them to power. What had once
been properly ranked among the unintended consequences of social
change now became a matter of conscious design as totalitarian movements set about the business of rendering individuals superfluous and
impermanence permanent under the cover of executing ideologically conceived laws of history.

That politics had been the medium by means of which the totalitarian movements had come to power, that politics had become the twentieth

century's chosen vehicle for bringing humanity to the brink of utter ruina-
tion and the world to the edge of annihilation made a profound impression upon Arendt who half-remembered and half-imagined another age in
which politics had constituted man's chief glory and the medium of his
highest achievement. Nonetheless, in the wake of the horrors of our age,
she might have chosen to abandon politics altogether, and yet Arendt
chose differently. As politics had degraded the species, so might it be the
means once again to its elevation.

It is Arendt's vision of a new and enhanced politics, a vision unfolded across the works written subsequent to *The Origins of Totalitarianism*,
that stands at the center of this inquiry. To redeem politics, humanity, and
the world by means of politics; or rather, to redeem politics, humanity,
and the world by means of a rhetorical vision of a redeemed politics that
might serve to inspire *her readers* to go forth and redeem politics by
means of political action: this is Arendt's true goal. And thus it becomes
our goal to apprehend the substance of this vision, and our duty to assess
the worth and the tenability of the emergent construct.

In this study, then, our aim will be to elucidate Arendt's comprehensive conception of political praxis. To achieve this end, it is necessary to
attend to the movement by which this conception develops through the
succession of her works. That a particular mode of political practice and a
particular form of political community might rescue man and his world
from the perils of the contemporary situation is a position articulated by
Arendt early in her career. Just how the appropriate form of politics and
polity ought to be conceived is, however, less clear, especially at the outset. As will be seen in the course of this explication, Arendt's conception is
always "on the way," and the revisions wrought along the way are most
significant.

In this text I will repeatedly refer to Arendt's comprehensive conception of politics as the "action-ideal." By this signification I do not mean to
imply that Arendt's conception is utopian, but rather I want to underscore
that, like an ideal, it functions more as a star by which Arendt steers than
as an object which once sighted is secured forthwith. The goal, in short,
is—at least in her early works—more readily seen than are the means by
which it is to be attained. In time, however, Arendt moves closer to her
goal as it becomes clearer to her what hitting the mark entails in all its
specificity.

Arendt's endeavor to articulate the nature of the action-ideal is best
comprehended as entailing two stratagems of clarification, and finally a
third which will be considered in due course. The first arises out of her
intuitive certitude that human dignity might be protected from the forces
arrayed against it by means of an existentially ennobling mode of political

action. In accordance with this approach, Arendt analyzes the fundamental structure of man's existential realization and conceptualizes a commensurate vision of political action. The second stratagem Arendt employs grows out of her belief that "world alienation"—a concept elaborated in *The Human Condition* that incorporates and deepens the idea of worldlessness that Arendt develops in *The Origins of Totalitarianism*—constitutes a threat to the common sense and historical continuity of the political communities—or worlds—within which we dwell. Out of this belief arises Arendt's mid- to late career endeavor to conceptualize: the nature of common sense, the nature of political continuity, the nature of the relationship between them, and the nature of the conceptual and institutional elements that secure this relationship within the world. As a further development of this second stratagem, Arendt endeavors to develop a more comprehensive conception of action which will facilitate the transcendence of world alienation by perpetually securing and resecuring the durability and continuity of a worldly frame which her original conception of action—were it realized—would have left at risk.

Though the action-ideal, by definition, contains both self-realizing and world-sustaining elements within a single community-constituting whole, when it comes to delineating the theoretical relationship between these two moments, how best to proceed is not always clear. In fact, as Arendt proceeds first from the one side and then from the other, we shall become ever more aware of the profound difficulties which attend what she aims to achieve. Elements on the one side will be seen to clash with elements on the other; conditions conducive to a mode of action that enables humanity to achieve the maximal degree of freedom and dignity will be seen to be potentially at odds with the conditions conducive to a modality of action keyed to a concern for overcoming world alienation and sustaining the lastingness of the worldly frame. What complicates Arendt's quest most of all is her insistence that both these ends be achieved by way of a single mode of political action that unfolds within a given public space. The liberal-democratic solution to this problematic, after all, has been to forgo the quest to achieve both ends simultaneously, let alone attempt to achieve them in the same sphere. From this standpoint, the private and social spheres are held to exist for the unfolding of selfhood, while the public space and the politics that unfolds within it are appointed to care only for the upkeep of the world.

For Arendt's part, the liberal-democratic solution of interest-group pluralism comes at too high a cost to the dignity and freedom of the individual, who in her view is left a radically diminished being by virtue of what amounts to his practical exclusion from the political sphere. Left only to a private life and to the pursuit of private interest within the sphere of civil society, our bourgeois is, in the first place—Arendt would note—a stunted specimen of humankind and, in the second place, a potential threat to the world on those occasions when he is driven to venture forth into the political realm. Of these two criticisms, however, it is the diminution of human stature and experience, which this solution entails, that concerns her more. Moreover, within this scheme, Arendt would argue, man is bereft of the existential fruits which follow from the substantive experience of political community: deprive a mature adult of this dimension of connection with his fellows and you deprive him of the only route out of the anomic despair and loneliness which Arendt sees as characterizing modern society.

This critique aside of what today is the preferred alternative, Arendt's problem remains. The liberal way out has prevailed not because it is ideal but because nothing else has come along that would be adequately pluralist and sufficiently stable. If Arendt would have us proceed in a different fashion, it is up to her to delineate a mode of political action that answers at once to the reality of human difference and to the need to insure an ordered world. If she can also show how a strong sense of political community might be imparted at the same time, then her proposal would surely merit the attention of all those liberals who are sensitive to the communitarian critique, but are fearful of what would happen to, for example, toleration, should we venture down the path these critics recommend.

In fact, after endeavoring to conceive the action-ideal—first from the side of her concern for human fulfillment and, then, from the side of her concern for overcoming world alienation by sustaining the continuity of the world—Arendt does point the way toward a synthesis.

Relatively late in her career, in writings which represent an alternative, though ultimately complementary, approach to the problem of overcoming world alienation, Arendt comes to pay close attention to the faculty of judgment and common sense in a manner that recalls her critique of ideological thinking in *The Origins of Totalitarianism*.[31] At issue once again, though this time more explicitly, is the conflict between a politics whose ultimate criterion of validity is truth and a politics whose ultimate criterion of validity is a consensus of opinion.

As we will see, in the writings that follow *The Origins of Totalitarianism*, and especially in *The Human Condition* and in her works of the late 1960s, what began as a critique of ideological rationality broadens to encompass most of the instrumentalizing and (neo-Cartesian) foundationalist conceptions of rationality that are espoused in the modern world. In these later writings, as a product of her effort to envision a politics capable of fostering the expression of selfhood, Arendt is led to argue that such instrumentalist and foundationalist conceptions of rationality are no less inimical to the manifestation of selfhood than the ideological conception she had pilloried so many years before. In a related train of thought, Arendt also observes that such conceptions of political rationality are intimately associated with the world alienation that she is equally intent upon overcoming.

It should come as no surprise, then, that Arendt is led, primarily in her work of the late 1960s and early 1970s, to search for a new conception of political judgment, and of political rationality, more generally, that would be capable of replacing the self-occluding and world-destabilizing conceptions that have been embraced by the modern age. The third stratagem aims, then, at the articulation of a new conception of political rationality but—as we shall see—it *begins* as an inquiry into the nature of the faculty of judgment and into the nature of the process whereby the members of a given group combine to render judgments in common. In Arendt's final writings, this analysis becomes the basis for rethinking the nature of action, a rethinking which—in contrast to her earlier conception of action—is fully cognizant of the relation between action and the moment of judgment that is contained within it.

Ultimately, Arendt seems to have hoped that a fresh conception of political rationality would emerge from the interstices of this analysis, a conception that would prove adequate to the two-sided demands of the action-ideal while constituting an alternative to the proto-totalitarian politics of truth. Unfortunately, Arendt would die before she was able to make clear to what degree this promise could have been fulfilled.

It is possible, however, to anticipate her theoretical trajectory and to apply what she had to tell us about the nature of political judgment to what she had already articulated regarding the nature of politics and polity. By doing this we can deduce a truly Arendtian vision of politics and political rationality which more closely approaches what had long eluded her, namely, a vision of a political community capable of fostering both world stability and individuating political participation on the broadest scale, a political community which would thereby enable Western humanity to attain the fulfillment of its Greek-originated political project. Such had long been Arendt's ideal, and, inasmuch as her last works do point the way, it seems incumbent upon us to unfold this vision as far as we can and to test it by her own criteria.

As intimated in the beginning of this introduction, the approach to Arendt's work to be undertaken here differs in kind from the approaches to her thought which have appeared thus far in the secondary literature. For the most part the commentators have focused their attention discretely either upon particular works or upon particular themes which figure in

either Arendt's or the commentator's eyes as meriting special consideration. Only a very few articles have appeared in which a serious attempt is
made to clarify the conceptual substrate which lies beneath the surface of
her work. And, of this latter group, none of the commentators has sought
to combine a synoptic conceptual elucidation with a genetic account of
where Arendt's various works stand in relation to the unfolding of this
underlying structure. The approach to be undertaken here attempts to fill
this lacuna.[32]

In the present study, my hope is to address Arendt's political thought
in a way which remains true to its own inner telos. At one level, this
means we will attend closely to the contours of Arendt's categorial distinctions. At another level, this means we shall seek to elucidate the implicit
conceptual framework within which Arendt's often seemingly arbitrary
distinctions make sense. Laying bare these fundamental relations will also
enable us to assess her underlying project and to situate her various writings in relation to it, as well as in relation to one another. In a paradoxical
way, then, we aim to take hold of Arendt's work in a manner that is at
once both organic and abstract. Above all, however, the current work
should be understood as endeavoring to trace the evolution of Arendt's
efforts to render the action-ideal realizable.

The text is divided into two parts. In chapter 1 which comprises the
first part, we shall consider the conceptual framework that underlies
Arendt's project and consider her first formulation of the action-ideal. We
will also begin to consider the potentially problematic relationship that
exists between the elements which comprise this ideal. In chapters 2 and
3, which comprise the second part, we shall consider Arendt's subsequent
reformulations of the action-ideal as she strives to secure the world's durability and to frame a post-totalitarian and post-Cartesian conception of
political rationality and common sense. Particularly in the third chapter, it
will be necessary to go beyond Arendt's own writings in order to fathom
how her exploration of judgment's nature might have figured within a
final reconception of the action-ideal. At issue will be whether such a
reconceptualization would have brought it much closer to realization.

Finally, a word about gender and style: Perhaps as a consequence of
the fact that the citizens of the polis were male, or perhaps as a consequence of the tradition within which she wrote, Arendt's use of the male
pronoun and the generic "man" or "men" is pervasive. From this it
should not be inferred that Arendt necessarily believes politics is an essentially male preserve. At the same time, it must be acknowledged that
Arendt's conception of political virtue does give prominence to a catalogue of putatively masculine qualities—in contrast to those which have
traditionally been denominated as feminine. Nonetheless, from her writ-

ings, I infer that Arendt would expect that women would come to manifest these traits as readily as do men if they were given the opportunity for full political participation.[33] Ultimately, then, for Arendt, the virtues of the political space are neither particularly male nor female, but are instead generically political and answer to human needs which, in her view, are not gender specific.[34] Since I believe that this is her view, I might have decided to translate Arendt's usage into nonsexist language on the assumption that this would neither distort nor attenuate her meaning. But for two reasons, this I could not in conscience do: On the one hand it is a matter of scholarly integrity. Simply put, Arendt's usage should be respected because it is her usage. On the other hand, Arendt's usage should be respected because, in the view of many, the relation between Arendt's particular usage and her assumptions about gender and virtue is quite problematic. From this perspective, to translate Arendt's diction into gender-neutral prose runs the risk of obscuring what some regard as the questionable assumptions that underlie her project. It seems to me, then, that the best solution is to follow Arendt's own usage both for the sake of scholarly integrity and in order that readers may come to their own opinion as to the implications of Arendt's diction. In choosing this option, I do so well aware of the fact that for some readers the result will appear overbearingly sexist and dated. This is not my intention.

Part One

The Original Formulation

Chapter One

Action and Human Existence

THE CONTOURS OF ACTION

In this chapter the focus of our attention will be upon the conception of political action which Arendt elaborates in her 1958 work, *The Human Condition*.[1] In this text, which constitutes the epicenter of Arendt's oeuvre, Arendt's interest reaches to both sides of the action-ideal, but her concern for political action as a mode of self-realization is foremost.[2] How this emphasis colors her conception will become clear as we proceed.

By way of preface, however, it is important to underscore that Arendt believes that political action has all but disappeared in the modern age, and where it still appears she believes it goes unrecognized or is misunderstood. In *The Human Condition* Arendt endeavors to correct this deficiency of understanding and strives to make her readers cognizant of the existential loss that the withering of the human capacity for action entails. By such means she hopes to kindle in her readers such appreciation for this capacity that they will be inspired to body it forth into the political realm.

But if Arendt is to achieve these ends she must first elucidate the nature of political action, and, in *The Human Condition*, Arendt pursues this objective by several stratagems. Her first is to map action's spatial coordinates by means of the distinction between the public realm and the private realm. At length, and with barely concealed normative intent, Arendt recovers the original Greek conception of this dichotomy and their high estimation of the public realm as the site of immortality-bestowing political action. In addition, Arendt employs the Greek conception to measure the shortcomings of the present age.

Arendt's second stratagem is to highlight the specificity of political action by contrasting it with labor and work, the two other components of the *vita activa*. To this end, Arendt elaborates phenomenological descriptions of each of these activities and does so in a manner which makes quite clear why she holds action to be the noblest of the three. Also, as part of her critique of the modern age, she tells the story of how action, which once held pride of place within the *vita activa*, fell from this position to be replaced first by work and more recently by labor. Arendt of course would like to see action restored to its prior prominence, and it is with this purpose in mind that Arendt's analysis is framed.

Our particular goal in this chapter will be to examine Arendt's baseline conceptions of political action and of political community as these are set forth in *The Human Condition*. But our angle of approach will differ from that which close fidelity to the surface contours of *The Human Condition* would suggest because our aim is to elucidate what lies below, and accounts for, the rather unusual topography of the surface. And thus, while the stratagems that Arendt herself employed in setting forth her conception of action will be canvased in some detail, this will only be done after the deeper logic of her account has been excavated.

But why, the reader may ask, need we seek to penetrate to the depths at all? What aspect of Arendt's own formulation is so problematic as to justify such "strategic" indirection? What is it, moreover, about the topography of the surface that is so "unusual" as to warrant such an approach?

To answer these questions, and to set the stage for the detailed analysis that is to follow, the general contours of the conceptions of action and polity that Arendt develops in *The Human Condition* ought to be considered:

At the center of the ideal polity envisioned by Arendt stands the public space where citizen and fellow citizen join together in action and are bound together by a concern for the common weal.[3] Institutionally, her ideal seems fairly akin to the New England town meetings of old. Conceptually, it is participatory democracy. Practically, it is face-to-face politics.

Political action is the main thing: it is for the sake of stepping forth from the darkness of the private into the light of the public that Arendt's ideal citizens live.[4] To act on behalf of, in common with, or before one's fellow citizens is held to constitute the consummation of an individual's existence. Through the word or deed spoken or done in full public view, the citizen is described as breaking free from obscurity and as actualizing his potentiality for public personhood. Moreover, as Arendt repeatedly underscores, such a citizen is well-placed to earn a great and lasting name should he act in a manner that commands the attention and affection of fellow citizens. Renown today creates the chance of renown tomorrow; and love of renown is regarded by Arendt as a worthy and authentic motive for political participation.[5] But more important to her than renown is individuation: by Arendt's measure, political action is more capable of making human plurality actual than is any other element of the *vita activa*; and, as one might infer from her analysis of totalitarianism's pre-conditions, this facet of action is accounted by her to be of great significance.

Surely, much that has been adumbrated in the preceding overview merits greater attention, but it is nonetheless arguable that nothing mentioned so far cries out for the discernment of some hidden architectonic principle that might bring order to a formulation whose inner logic hardly seems obscure. Indeed, if Arendt was nary more than a neo-civic-republican (albeit one of the first and most outspoken of the postwar period) or a garden-variety champion of participatory democracy, then there might be little reason to provide more than a descriptive account of her conception. What then is there to suggest that anything more is required?

Unconsidered thus far has been Arendt's conception of the specific content of the citizen's concern. We know the citizen to be public-spirited; and we know him to be bent upon attaining that kind of immortal fame which polities make available to those who perform great acts of service on behalf of the commonweal. But we do not know what kinds of issues in particular will elicit his advocacy or antipathy. Nor do we know what kinds of issues will properly be placed upon the public agenda. Of course, if Arendt merely passed over this matter in silence, it would hardly be appropriate to call attention to it. Indeed, one might have fairly assumed Arendt's indifference to the question and that no particular kinds of issues were ipso facto prohibited from receiving public consideration.

In fact, Arendt is far from silent on this point, and there is little doubt that many of her readers have found her comments regarding the range of issues that she would exclude from politics, as inherently antipolitical, to be most disturbing. For example, explicitly excluded by Arendt are economic questions—including the questions of the redistribution of wealth, of industrial relations, and of workplace democracy and discrimination. More generally, she calls into question the legitimacy of most of the issues that animate the politics of the modern state when she rails against the corruption of the public space by questions of what she calls "national housekeeping," which she depicts as entailing private, and thus antipolitical, concerns. In addition, she enunciates principles for determining the question of impermissible content that indicate to many that she would oppose as antipolitical whatever steps a polity might take to combat social discrimination against the members of social minorities. And if the exclusion of many issues is disturbing for its utter inexplicability, as disturbing is Arendt's seeming failure to articulate a clear criterion of inclusion. That much which one might assume to be the natural content of politics is rejected is apparent, but when so much has been purged, the question of what content remains becomes quite pressing. Yet regarding this matter, Arendt gives little guidance.

It is, then, Arendt's peculiar and heterodox conception of the issues that are legitimately topics of political debate that first signals the need to probe beneath the surface of the account she provides. Unless we do so, the rationale for exclusion will remain enigmatic, for on the textual surface these topical exclusions appear to be mere occasional and contingent utterances devoid of the theoretical necessity that only a subsurface, and structural, account can provide. Moreover, if we would endorse Arendt's conception of participatory democracy, then we must take seriously her reasons for (in effect) rejecting social democracy as incompatible with it. And if it is felt that she would have us divide what ought to be kept together, then it is necessary for us to discern and address the rationale that leads Arendt to posit their incompatibility.

As will become clear in the analysis to be unfolded in this chapter, Arendt's definition of certain issues as antipolitical, and her recommendation that these issues be excluded from political consideration, follows from theoretically prior formulations and valuations that reach to the heart of Arendt's political thought. Particularly entailed are her conceptions of freedom and individuation, and of their opposites. Also entailed are Arendt's conception of the public space and her conception of the temporally transcendent nature of the objects and concerns that are fit to appear within it. Only after close scrutiny of these concepts and of their interrelations will we be in a position to assess the validity of Arendt's case for the antipolitical nature of so many of the issues that constitute the substance of modern politics.

It must be stressed, however, that our mode of proceeding in this chapter owes only in part to our concern for "the content problem.'" Determinative to a far greater degree is our overarching objective of elucidating Arendt's conception of action, and the conviction that an exploration of the conceptual substrate that underlies it will produce the clearest comprehension of this conception and of the criteria of meaning and value which are entailed by it.

THE POLARITIES OF HUMAN EXISTENCE

As a general rule Arendt theorizes by dichotomizing. Almost always the concepts come on board the ark of theory in pairs. It is never freedom alone, but freedom *and* necessity. It is never the public alone, but the public *and* the private. The first term is defined by comparison and contrast with the second. Always the interrelations between the two are emphasized. Thus it becomes incumbent upon us to frame our analysis of the conceptual underpinnings of Arendt's conception of action with an eye to Arendt's own mode of conceptualization.

A moment ago I noted that the "content problem" pointed to a cluster of concepts which reach to the heart of Arendt's conception of action. In this section we will press our inquiry into the latter by focusing upon: the conceptual dichotomies that underlie it, the relations that exist between these pairs, and the relations that exist between these pairs and the various facets of Arendt's conception of action. Our focus upon these matters will also indicate why Arendt believes that a rejuvenated politics can raise humanity from its fallen condition.

As already noted, Arendt's conception of action is intimately related to her conceptions of freedom and individuation, and to her conceptions of temporal transcendence and of the public realm. And by inference we now know that the opposites of each of these conceptions are entailed as well. Accordingly we shall focus our attention upon the emergent dichotomies which underlie Arendt's conceptualization of the politically relevant aspects of the human condition, namely, freedom and necessity, uniqueness and uniformity, lasting and passing, and public and private.[6] Moreover, through our examination of these dyads we will uncover the foundations of a very particular vision of the human telos and of the vital role played by political action in enabling man to achieve it. Arendt's vision of political community as a community of actors will be considered as well.

From the outset, the reader ought to note that though these dichotomies constitute the essential underpinning of her thought, Arendt pays only scant and scattered attention to their origins in human experience.[7] Accordingly, as I present the dichotomies I shall seek to provide a better account of their origin than that which Arendt herself provides.

That she fails to account explicitly for the existential origin of her chief concepts and fails as well to argue for their adequacy is a significant shortcoming of her work that in the view of many severely undercuts the persuasive power of her analysis. By failing in this respect she leaves it to her readers to decide for or against her analysis on the basis of its intuitive appeal. To those for whom her analytic lacks such immediacy, she offers little by way of argument on its behalf.

Nonetheless, this arrogance of tone—for it is arrogance to present a set of new basal categories on a take it or leave it basis—while it may account for the distinctly mixed reception Arendt's work has received, cannot be reason to dismiss her analysis. That she fails to provide her reader with grounds does not make her arguments groundless. Indeed, the cogency of her basic analytic framework is such that it behooves her sympathetic critic to provide such an account of her categories as will explain why Arendt held them to constitute the fundamental ground for thinking about man and politics. As such an account, the following is in part interpretive, in part speculative, yet always hews as close as possible to Arendt's own account while seeking to be more expansive where she is terse and more systematic where she is epigrammatic.

Uniqueness and Uniformity

Our aim is to understand Arendt's conception of action and her reasons for holding action in such high esteem. In large measure the key to both follows from her conception of action as a medium which facilitates the actualization of human plurality or uniqueness.

At the conceptual level, this concern for the unique in man, and for the sites conducive to its manifestation, informs Arendt's analytic vision which, in consequence, discriminates assiduously between the unique and the uniform, between that which is particular to the individual and that which is common to the species. Traits, talents, virtues, as well as the activities and spaces where these become manifest are all brought under the scrutiny of this standpoint. At the level of value, man's project of achieving complete individuation translates into Arendt's valuation of all individuating factors, spheres, and spaces over those which render men similar.

Arendt most often treats human plurality as a datum, as something which is simply part of the human condition and, as such, need not be accounted for. On occasion, however, Arendt traces this datum to what she discerns as its roots in human natality.[8] In this vein, following Augustine, she describes birth as the entry into life of a singular and unrepeatable (and hence unique) individual.[9] What birth thus begins, Arendt depicts action as bringing to fruition, with action becoming a kind of second birth whereby the singular and unrepeatable individual enters into the world to manifest who he alone is.[10]

Apparently, though birth essentially individuates, it fails to do so existentially. Thus the uniqueness which Arendt depicts as an inalienable concomitant of birth is in fact a potentiality in need of existential actualization. Action and, more particularly, political action, are held by Arendt to constitute the sine qua non through which this actualization of inborn potential is to occur.[11] Conversely, then, as Arendt also maintains, one who is deprived of the opportunity to act is deprived of the opportunity to achieve this, and is thereby prevented from fulfilling a central aspect of the human telos.

What makes action so important is the fact that the essential uniqueness of each person, which action is said to make manifest, is opposed by forces which are quite capable of stymieing its manifestation, forces which Arendt characterizes as the biological and social aspects of human sameness.[12] The biological phenomena that attest to human sameness are quite familiar: death, in particular, is the great equalizer. All persons die, none can escape it. As measured against it, all differences between persons seem to pale. Moreover, as members of the same species our desires, needs, and life paths are necessarily similar. Sickness, suffering, pain, pleasure, hunger, love, and death are common to us all. As members of a given society, moreover, even our taste, opinions, and aspirations display that high degree of uniformity which Martin Heidegger so aptly characterized as the mentality of *das Man*, or the "they."[13] Nevertheless, be the elements arrayed against uniqueness ever so powerful, action is held by Arendt to be more powerful still and capable of triumphing over these individuality denying forces.[14]

Action is also singled out by Arendt for its capacity to facilitate the self's transcendence of those forces of role and functional differentiation that are the inevitable concomitants of social rationalization.[15] But for the kind of action which reveals a self that is both unitary and unique, Arendt believes that we would be imprisoned within forms of behavior that are completely subordinated to various social wholes and, as such, are quite contrary to the manifestation of the self's specific identity.

Thus, regarding the family, Arendt would argue that the possibilities of full self-display within it are eclipsed by the role-contingent norms that inevitably shape both behavior and perception as we take on the roles of husbands or wives, of fathers or mothers, or of sons or daughters—and behave, perceive, and are perceived according to our respective positions within the social whole of the family. Similarly, Arendt depicts the workplace as being analogously structured in accordance with the functional differentiation of employer and employee, and in accordance with the norms inherent in the shop floor division of labor.[16] Nor, in Arendt's account, is this subordination of self to role and norm diminished in the broader sphere of civil society which she regards as being even more conformist and less tolerant of individual difference.[17]

The problem for the self that would manifest itself as a unitary and unique personality can thus be described as a problem of both inward fragmentation and outward dispersion. Outwardly, the self wears as many masks as it has roles and functions, while inwardly its sense of identity is correspondingly fractured. If, as Arendt claims, the self comes to know itself in accordance with the ways in which it is known by others (that is, intersubjectively), then the self will come to know itself as an amalgam of masks devoid of a coherent center.[18] How, then, is this outward dispersion and inward fragmentation to be overcome? As one would expect—almost as a matter of definition—the answer is action, for action reveals the unitary and unique self that transcends the forces of biological and sociological uniformity.[19] And yet the question arises of where, and how, action can achieve this if all social interactions are overdetermined by role-playing and functionally rationalized behaviors. In response, Arendt would doubtless observe that there is one realm that is not thus overdetermined, namely, the political realm, and that it is in this realm of appearance that revelatory action finds its true home.[20]

By now the reader will have noticed that Arendt relies to some degree upon Heidegger's account of authenticity and its nemeses. It must be emphasized, however, that Arendt's analysis of natality distinguishes her account of human difference from that of Heidegger and other existentialists. For Heidegger, of course, it is the awareness that arises out of the individual's confrontation with the fact of his mortality that existentially differentiates him in all of his ultimate aloneness from the rest of humankind.[21] For Arendt, however, the authenticity thus obtained remains both essentially and existentially rooted not in mortality but in natality, for, as it is the latter that originally sends forth each person as unique, it is also the latter that makes possible the action, and more particularly the political action, which Arendt regards as the privileged vehicle of authentic self-disclosure. Mortality, as we shall see, figures in Arendt's account as that which impels men to achieve a preternatural lastingness; but it is the fact of their specific and unique natality that enables men to act in a way that stamps the individual's actions as unmistakably his own and unlike anybody else's.[22] The mere recoil from mortality cannot account for this.

At one level, the difference may seem to be a matter of taste: we are born alone and we die alone and in the course of our lives each of us

comes to grasp these twinned facts. Whether a theorist chooses to emphasize the one factor more than the other hardly seems to be decisive or significant. From an existentialist standpoint the consequences seem to be the
same: start from the one point or the other and one arrives at the reality
of human individuation and uniqueness. At most there might be a difference of tone.

From another perspective, however, the difference becomes more
significant. At issue is whether, at the most profound level, the differentiation of self from self is an originary or a derivative characteristic. For the
Heidegger of *Being and Time*, it is arguably the latter, dependent first
upon existential awakening and then upon the individual's stance as it
develops in light of an encounter with his ownmost possibility.[23] Not
Being but the individual wills the differentiation. From this perspective,
then, all persons arguably are essentially "the same."

For Arendt, however, while a confrontation with death as one's
ownmost possibility may cause one to become aware of one's unique destiny, the differentiation of self from self is primordial and marks every
individual from the moment of birth as the possessor of a unique telos
which may or may not be achieved in the course of his lifetime.[24] This difference is significant.

Once again following Heidegger, Arendt also maintains that entities—and human entities among them—are revealed through appearance;
they emerge from darkness into light in order to manifest their essence
before darkness covers them again.[25] But appearance presupposes a view-
er.[26] Thus he who would disclose his unique self through action does not
merely act; rather, he acts with and before other persons who are similarly
intent upon making an appearance.[27] Indeed, in Arendt's view, who a man
is in his singularity cannot be known, not even by the man himself, except
to the degree he attains concrete particularity as a man among men
through interaction with them.[28] Action, in other words, implies interaction, mutual revelation of mutual becoming, and mutual acknowledgment.[29] In short, action implies community.

Only in community, then, can men achieve the manifestation of who
they are. Yet, as has been intimated already, not every gathering of persons is such a community as might facilitate this process of comanifesta-
tion. Modern society, for example, is not such a community, not on
account of its size, but because of the behavioral conformity and uniformity which hold sway within it.[30] But it also fails to be such a community
because within it almost all interactions are private in the sense of being
one-on-one exchanges. Or, to frame the matter somewhat differently, in
society one never appears before the whole community; rather one

appears serially, before one person—and hence in one relational role—at a time.

By Arendt's definition, the community that enables those who belong to it to manifest their individuality through their interaction with one another is the political community. Indeed, politicality and the manifestation of plurality are synonymous for Arendt.[31] But what particularly facilitates this self-display is the fact that within the public space where the community gathers to discuss the affairs of the day, each citizen appears and speaks before all the rest who in turn bestow upon him the trans-subjective identity that corresponds with, and thus objectifies, his unique and unitary selfhood.[32] Thus by entering a properly constituted public space the citizen is able to overcome the limitations that inhere within that universe of interactions which are private, serial, or functional. Exactly how a community needs to be organized to achieve the aim of true politicality shall become clearer further on.

In theory, then, the public space allows the men who enter it to be known in all their specificity by virtue of the exposure they receive there. It would be a mistake to imagine, however, that the actor who stands before his peers is like some object that can be known all at once. In reality, this self-revelatory process unfolds in time and what the citizen reveals is a self that is always in the process of formation and manifestation.[33] It is a self that is revealed as a life, or more particularly, it is a self that is revealed *in* a life to the degree that it is a public life. It is not, however, a self that is merely unfolded before the spectators who record its self-related and self-determined contours. More than this it is a self that is shaped through its interactions with fellow actors and spectators.[34] Because the actions initiated by the others who inhabit the field of self-revelation are not to be known in advance, the nature and direction of the self's development, which is always responsive even when not reactive, cannot be known in advance either.[35] Thus Arendt's oft-repeated dicta that no man can be truly known until he has departed from the stage.[36]

It should be noted that Arendt celebrates the contingency which characterizes the realm of public action and interaction.[37] The actor, she observes, acts into a web of other actors who act and react as well.[38] The actor is not sovereign because those with whom he interacts are equally capable of action. The unpredictability of the first actor is matched by the unpredictability of the rest. Each in his spontaneity and uniqueness is capable of doing the unexpected and in doing so begins series of actions and reactions all along the web whose consequences are such as none can predict. Because men are free they can react and act in novel fashion, and the outcome of action, because it is always interaction, is forever in doubt.[39]

Nonetheless, it must be acknowledged that in taking this view Arendt goes too far sometimes, as if recoiling from an overextreme sense of life's radical contingency. That she tends to underestimate the degree to which, in normal periods, the consequences of action are foreseeable might be attributed to her having come to maturity during an epoch of instability and disintegration. Whatever the reason, the result is an overly radical formulation. The kernel of Arendt's insight, however, is sound. Absolute responsibility for consequences could be legitimately assigned only if the consequences of action are wholly predictable. But if, as Arendt suggests, the purchase price of such predictability entails the sacrifice of human freedom and plurality, then, surely the price is too high.

Thus one can see why Arendt feels it is necessary to shift our emphasis from the question of what is accomplished by some action to who is revealed by it as the crucial measure of value.[40] To esteem or disesteem the actor for the consequences of his action strikes her as wholly inappropriate for seldom is any particular outcome wholly attributable to one man's action. If the actor were to be judged by the consequences of his action which are such as wholly escape the actor/initiator, he would be wrongly praised or blamed for a result of which he was not the author.[41] Unless one aims to replace action with making and thus true politics with rule, such are the limits on the direct efficaciousness of action that Arendt says we must accept.[42]

In Arendt's estimation, then, sovereignty and plurality are forever at odds.[43] Man is free, but he is not sovereign. If he were granted sovereignty, plurality would be ruined, that is, one man's sovereignty would violate the plurality of the rest.[44]

But this loss of control is, by Arendt's measure, more than adequately compensated by what he receives in turn. It is man's lack of sovereignty and the consequent fact that he is an actor among actors that renders action heroic.[45] The actor, as we have seen, is not the author of events but at most their initiator. Once he has acted, a process that is boundless, unpredictable, and irreversible is set in motion.[46] He feels responsible for what he has begun, yet cannot see it through to the conclusion he desires. He acts and then suffers as the spectacle wrought by his hands goes awry.[47] However, if he is a man of courage and inmost nobility, he will not flee the field and retreat to the safe haven of obscurity, but will for the sake of his destiny push on, doing what he can and suffering what he must.[48]

Over the course of a lifetime spent in the public sphere every man is disclosed as a story of deeds done, words spoken, adversities suffered, and character revealed—a story that is authored by none and enacted, as it is interacted, in common with one's peers. If it be a record of achievement it owes much to the others by whose action it was carried through, but even if it is not, it is necessarily the story of a life and the record of how one man met—or failed to meet—the challenges of circumstance. Was he principled? Was he courageous? Was he an opportunist? In adversity was he strong or plaintive? Did he bare his back to bear the burdens of the hour, or did he shun the responsibilities which life places upon us all? Such questions of character are, in Arendt's view, the measure of man. But the answer, if it is going to reveal the individual's specific identity, must take the form of a story.[49]

Lasting and Passing

Our aim is to understand Arendt's conception of action and her reasons for holding action in such high esteem. As detailed in the previous section, in large measure, the key to both follows from the dichotomy of uniqueness and uniformity. As we have observed, in order that the latter may be overcome and the former manifest, Arendt conceives of action as that which gives birth to the public lives and stories through which human plurality is disclosed. But this is only one aspect of the account. In this section we turn our attention to a different aspect, namely, to the one which emanates from Arendt's reflections upon the political significance of mortality.

At the origin of Greek civilization Arendt discerns a recurrent existential motif from which arose the Greek obsession with temporal transcendence. The pivotal experience is that in which the individual authentically confronts the fact of his own mortality. Out of this confrontation there arises, dialectically, a Promethean will to persist in being, to overcome the futility of a fleeting existence, to become immortal somehow in some way.[50] Every age, if not every man, must grapple with this problem.[51] Arendt explains that for the early Greeks this dream of immortality was embodied in the immortality of the gods and in the hope that the doer of great deeds might attain to immortal fame.[52] For the early philosophers, by contrast, this hope was embodied in the notion that contemplation of the eternal eternalizes the soul of the one who contemplates.[53] Of these two paths, the former was clearly the one that led to the public square, a space that Arendt describes as one of "organized remembrance," a space that increases the chances that the doer of marvels could live on through collective memory.[54]

For the Christians, as Arendt—following Machiavelli and Rousseau—observes, the problems of mortality are cast in an altogether different light. Immortality is assured, only its tenor is in question. The political impetus is undercut.[55] In the current age, neither the hope of salvation nor the quest for personal immortality seems capable of motivating the mass of men. The impetus to greatness in word and deed is undermined in an age of mass anonymity in which instant, evanescent, top of the pop chart fame ("known by all today, remembered by none tomorrow") is all that is attainable. In the age of ideology, only the historical process is held to be immortal; at most, one might hope to play a small part in this ongoing process, at least touching and being touched by the everlasting, even though unable to achieve immortal fame thereby.[56]

On the basis of this insight into the cultural significance of the existential response to the problem of mortality, Arendt constructs one of her pivotal analytical distinctions. At a conceptual level, the experience of one's mortality vis à vis the durability of other things is used by Arendt to make her readers sensitive to the fact that the cosmos is composed of entities of varying duration; one becomes attentive, in other words, to the temporality of things.[57] At the level of value, the desire to persist in being is translated by her into the valuation of that which persists over that which evanesces all too quickly.[58] Between the lasting and the passing, she holds the lasting to be superior.

As a rule, Arendt heaps laurels upon the Greek conception while she is most critical of the modern responses to this existential concern; but it must be acknowledged that even the Greek political response has its limitations. We moderns are in a position to see just how short-lived immortal fame can be and thus cannot help but see its pursuit as vain and illusory. But one should not infer from this that the modern mind will find itself unalterably opposed to every conception that enables man to transcend his mortal condition. For example, it is clear that one component of man's desire for immortality is a desire for a life of significance to others. Man experiences dread before the prospect that his life will not have mattered, that he will have lived and died without his life having made a difference in the course of things. In order to overcome this dread man needs to establish a connection between himself and something that shall outlast his brief life. The desire for personal immortality is negated, raised, and preserved in the movement by which a man comes to see his own immortality as inherent in the potential immortality of that for the sake of which he ventures his own finite existence in action and advocacy.[59]

Admittedly, then, he hopes in vain who hopes to achieve immortal fame through the greatness of his words and deeds. At the same time, though the shortness of historical memory be not kind in this regard, Arendt in effect proposes that there is no greater spur to greatness than the desire to be deserving of this acclaim. Where, after all, will he who reasonably foresees no chance of being remembered ten minutes after he breathes his last—and gives not a care for the esteem in which he is held by posterity—find the inner resources to dare to be great?

Leaving aside, then, the question of whether the immortal fame craved by men is really attainable, Arendt asks instead what sort of man would be deserving of this honor if indeed it were bestowable at all. In reply, Arendt declares that the standard by which to measure such a man must be greatness: only that which is great is deserving of long remembrance. But what is meant by greatness?[60] Along what path ought man seek to exceed the commonplace? By what criterion are we to measure him: greatness of soul? of achievement? of consequence?

Arendt gives little direct guidance here. Indeed her references to greatness as the criterion of action are most enigmatic.[61] If the great and the long to be remembered are the same then one could as easily aim at being remembered for the greatness of one's criminality as for the greatness of one's virtue. Could Arendt mean to embrace such an amoral standard of action?[62] One point that counts against such a notion is the emphasis she places upon acclaim. He who would be accounted as great is said to seek acclaim—which is hardly equivalent to notoriety.[63] The question, however, still remains: what does Arendt mean by greatness, if she does not merely mean whatever is acclaimed in any particular time and place?

What Arendt means by greatness of action she never states in a direct manner. Luckily, however, she discusses greatness in the realm of aesthetics—which is suggestive of how we might understand it in this context. Thus in what follows we will seek to determine what Arendt means by greatness of men and of action by means of an interpretation based upon her discussion of greatness in art.[64]

As something which deserves to be saved from perishing, the humanly great can be likened to the work of art, and the greatness which makes a (man/deed) fit for long recollection can be likened to the beauty which makes an artwork worthy of long preservation. Such is the tack suggested by what Arendt has to say in *The Human Condition*, as well as by her discussion of art in *Between Past and Future*.[65]

As Arendt correctly observes, art objects are distinct from other objects in being taken from the realm of use in order to be preserved in perpetuity.[66] They are set aside because we find them to possess a beauty that far exceeds the commonplace and find their beauty to be such as we would like to see shine forever unto all generations. All other objects are judged primarily for their utility or function, as is appropriate to objects produced with such ends in mind. At the same time, these everyday objects share a vital aspect of their being in common with those objects produced as art objects: as objects they appear as objects, and though usually not designed with an eye to their appearance, they "cannot help being either beautiful, ugly, or something in between" for this quality of all objects is an inescapable concomitant of their appearing at all.[67] "Everything that is must appear and nothing can appear without a shape of its own; hence there is nothing which does not in some way transcend its functional use and its transcendence, its beauty, or ugliness is identical with appearing publicly and being seen."[68] And the world is tacitly aware of this fact, judging every object that appears within it, not only the art objects, for its "adequacy . . . to what it should look like" according to prevailing canons of aesthetic taste, criteria which have little to do with "mere usefulness."[69]

Similarly, the words and deeds, spoken and done, in pursuit of this or that worldly object or end, point in the direction of a dimension which transcends that which can be measured by the criteria of utility and consequence. Like all things in the world which, by virtue of possessing shapes, constitute appearances and are, as such, fittingly viewed from an aesthetic standpoint, so too do the actions of men, no matter what their worldly purpose, constitute symbolizations of character which are fittingly assessed for the magnitude of excellence, virtue, or beauty that they manifest.[70] As there are implicitly aesthetic norms governing our sense of what all objects should look like, so do we possess implicitly performative norms governing our sense of how men should appear. As it is pleasing to behold what exceeds the commonplace in the direction of great beauty, so too is it pleasing to behold what exceeds the commonplace in the direction of great virtue and bespeaks the presence of a superior person.[71]

That all objects appear does not make them all beautiful; that in all they do men reveal their characters does not make all characters pleasing to behold. The usual practice in matters of display, as Arendt would acknowledge, is to give less attention to that dimension of things that goes beyond use and function. It is in the nature of man to produce things that are more useful than beautiful and to comport himself more in accordance with the lowest standards of conduct than with the highest. Man in his activities of labor, work, and action may be so taken with his mundane ends as to overlook entirely the nonpurposive dimensions signified by a concern for beauty or excellence. But such a man, in Arendt's view, is not so free as he might be. If in all he did he kept one eye upon the ideal of beauty or upon the excellence he should strive to embody, his actions would be correspondingly uplifted into a realm of beauty and freedom.[72]

Helping to clarify this conception is Arendt's treatment of action in "What is Freedom?" an essay in which action is considered in terms of motives, goals, and principles.[73] To be sure, she notes, every deed or proposal has its motives and goals. Irrespective of whether one's endeavor be public or private, these it will surely have. Yet beyond these Arendt discerns a third element, necessarily present though varying in its degree of explicitness, namely the principle by which the act is inspired, and which in turn the act makes manifest in the world.

In the same way as the appearance of a thing or deed was said to transcend its mundane purpose or function, Arendt speaks of the principle of an action transcending the motives and goals which necessarily attend it as well. Also, analogously, it may be said that as all things appear and hence are potentially assessable for their beauty or ugliness, so too do all actions embody principles which may be thematized and assessed for their excellence and fittingness. In the principle—that is, in the principle that is immanent to a particular act—Arendt finds that which constitutes the specific ground of whatever meaning and whatever greatness a particular act contains.[74] Moreover, in Arendt's parlance, with regard to any given action, it may be said that the principle defines the idea, or the universal, "for the sake of [which]" an action is undertaken, as distinguished from the situation-specific "in order to" that pertains to the goal.

This distinction between "for the sake of" and "in order to" is crucial for Arendt inasmuch as it helps her to differentiate between the essence of an act and what an act accomplishes, and, by inference, to differentiate between "who" a man is and what he does. The former, or the dimension of character, is signified—albeit abstractly—by the principles that are manifest in any given deed as instances of virtue or of vice, whereas the latter pertains to an actor's ends and the question of whether he achieves them.[75] Obviously, the principles of action will be implicit in the actor's choice of ends as well, yet the import of Arendt's conception is to call attention to the performative manifestation of principle that occurs in *the way* ends are pursued. Thus she would insist that we clearly differentiate between the two, and that our assessment of action and actor give due consideration to both. Hence an action, or an actor, is not to be held "just" solely because justice is its, or his, end. Rather, it is more important for our assessment of either to know, irrespective of the end, whether it is pursued justly, that is, in a just fashion. Just*ly* done, then, would be acts done "for the sake of justice"; and acts thus done are done as a "just" person does them. Honorab*ly* done, by contrast, would be acts done "for the sake of honor"; and acts thus done are done as an honorable person does them. According to this conception, then, an actor could not act unjustly for the sake of justice though he might act unjustly "*in order to*" gain justice for himself or for another. In the latter case, the fact that he was willing to act unjustly says much about the nature of the deed and the doer. The character of the actor and his action, in other words, are to be read from the manner of the action more than from "what" it accomplishes—because it is the manner that truly expresses the action's principle.

Moreover, Arendt argues that it is the principle which imparts to an act its human significance, and timeless relevancy.[76] By contrast to the motives and goals which are exhausted in the realization of some end, Arendt declares that "the principle loses nothing in strength or validity through execution."[77] Confirming this notion is the fact that as the time, and hence the distance, between ourselves and a particular event increases, the event's power to hold our interest becomes altogether dependent upon whether or not we are capable of discerning in the event signs that some timelessly inspiring principle was immanently present in the original moment out of which the tale, and the imperative of its telling, arose.

Principle alone, however, does not make for the greatness that merits immortal fame. As intimated above, some principles make for notoriety; and so the principles for the sake of which the actor acts ought to be held in high esteem by that public whose acclaim is desired. But greatness also depends upon the worth of the actor's ends and upon the absolute magnitude of his act, a magnitude that is compounded of both the force of will manifested in the act and the measure of the obstacles which the actor has sought to overcome. Presumably, these considerations explain why Arendt regards courage as the foremost political virtue, for it alone enables the actor to act over against the obstacles, both inward and outward, that might deter another from acting in the same situation.[78] As Arendt observes, real courage is required of anyone who dares to depart from the comfortable obscurity of the private sphere in order to step forth into the brightly lit precincts of the political realm.[79] And where the objective risks attending, and the difficulties in the way of, a given action are large, even greater courage is required.

Thus far political action has been depicted as signifying a mode of activity that answers to the human aspirations of self-manifestation and immortalization. There is, however, a tension between these two ends in Arendt's formulation. Immortalization is understood in terms of acts of greatness, which in turn are understood in terms of the principles and virtues such acts are held to signify. But virtues and principles, being of a universal and typological nature, are ill-suited to convey the unique and unrepeatable nature of the actor.[80] How, then, can action be construed as both a medium of immortalization and a vehicle of self-manifestation?

To answer this question, it is necessary to differentiate between the criterion of greatness that the political realm lays upon the actor who would secure immortal fame and the aspiration of the actor to obtain the immortalization of who he uniquely is. In pursuit of the latter, the actor must meet the standard of the former, albeit that neither greatness per se, nor the virtue manifest in a single great action are capable of denoting the unique self of the actor. But in the course of a public life that includes many such actions, the actor will disclose a self which in its uniqueness and specificity transcends the generic virtues of character, and thus the principles, that such actions will also manifest. Thus the unique self that a life of action reveals is not to be conflated with a catalogue of traits and principles; rather, as observed in the preceding section of this chapter, Arendt conceives of the self as a singularity whose uniqueness can only be revealed *in*, and *as*, the narrative of its own public becoming. In sum, because uniqueness revealing and immortality bestowing stories are told only about the doers of great deeds, the actor must strive for greatness. But even as he thus strives, so much more than greatness is displayed.

Freedom and Necessity

At the beginning of this chapter it was suggested that attending to the dichotomies that underlie Arendt's conception of action would elucidate this conception while clarifying the "content problem." And yet to this point, though Arendt's conception of action has come into focus, the "content problem" remains unaddressed. By turning to the dichotomy of freedom and necessity, we shall overcome this lacuna quite directly.[81]

The third and most comprehensive of Arendt's essential binaries is the polarity of freedom and necessity. For Arendt, man is the being who is capable of willing the objectification of his uniqueness and of securing relative immortality thereby. In accordance with this capacity he encounters his world as a place in which it is possible for him to achieve these twin ends. In short, his encounter with the world assumes his freedom; it assumes his ability to will himself against that within himself which is not truly himself and against that which is not particular to his identity but is merely common to the species. It assumes man possesses this freedom at least up to a point, at least within certain limits.

Limits: Freedom traces its limit as it advances against that which opposes it, as it transcends what had before seemed to be its limit. By definition, the limit and essential antagonist of freedom is necessity.[82] Whether the primordial experience of necessity delineates the limit of freedom, or the primordial experience of freedom delineates the limits of necessity, does not matter for Arendt nearly as much as the fact that they mutually entail one another.

Necessity: The human animal is perhaps unique for foreseeing its own death, but like any other animal it does what it can to forestall it. In grasping his mortality man implicitly acknowledges the organic basis of his existence and the imperatives this animal substrate imposes upon him.

At the simplest level, these imperatives impress themselves upon him as necessity and must be addressed.[83] Instinct moves him, seems to necessitate him, leads him.

One might suppose that biological necessity would carry humankind along like all the other species: one generation following another, each coming and going with the cyclical uniformity of infinite repetition. But this lot has not befallen man. A willfulness born of human self-awareness and set against the natural impulses of the species seems to have insured that the members of the species would rebel against impulse-ordered happiness.[84] For reasons we cannot explore in detail here, Western man in particular has long refused to identify his essential being with his animal existence. Suffice it to say that from a very early age civilization sets for each of us the task of controlling ourselves, which in the first instance means learning to control our bodies. By these early efforts to achieve self-mastery we constitute, or become aware of, a will which is somehow not identical with the body which we are commanded to regulate, a will which henceforth will be the center of our sense of identity. The will which achieves mastery over the elemental forces of the body, a body which would necessitate one completely if not thus constrained, is a free will, a will free within the limits of its mastery.[85] This freedom, and the subjective pleasure taken in it, is the source of human dignity and pride.[86] This triumph over embodied necessity is of course only the first freedom, but it is as such the precondition of those free activities within which humans reveal their identities.

For Arendt, the territories conquered by the forces of freedom are never wholly secure. In man himself and in his political life, the forces of necessity remain strong even when occluded from vision by the radiance of a freedom whose victories are always precarious, always in need of being resecured. As both the horrors of our age, and the "bovine" existence of the masses make clear, the tendency of man to succumb to necessity remains strong. Vigilance on behalf of freedom remains essential always.

At the conceptual level, Arendt's interest in freedom, and its preconditions, translates into a multifaceted vision of man, the spaces of his lifeworld, and the nature of his activities, a vision which continuously discriminates between what belongs to freedom and what belongs to necessity.

At the level of value, Arendt is a partisan of freedom. Necessity by its very irrepressibility makes itself felt in every age. It needs no champions, though today it surely does not lack them. Freedom is a far more fragile flower, in need of all the support it can get. Arendt's writings are framed to provide such support.

Lasting and passing. Uniqueness and sameness. Freedom and necessity: three polar oppositions arising from the depths of man's condition and from the most basal levels of his life experience, three dyads at the root of every other distinction Arendt originates, constituting the substrate of her thought. Three, yet not even three, but one. One, refracted to discriminate three planes of analysis, three dimensions of concern which are indissolubly fused to constitute a single overarching bipolar conception of man in his world. On the one side are freedom, uniqueness, and permanence entailing one another in a way which we have yet to delineate fully; on the other side, likewise requiring coordinate elaboration, are necessity, uniformity, and evanescence. Ultimately, each of the terms takes its particular meaning from its relation to the rest. This does not mean, however, that each term, or even that each paired antithesis, plays as significant a role as the others in the course of Arendt's analysis. Freedom is Arendt's preeminent concern; and, as we shall see, the truly comprehensive binary—incorporating the other two as moments of its own elucidation—is the antithesis of freedom and necessity. We turn again to it now to unfold it in greater detail, and in the course of our close analysis Arendt's idiosyncratic solution to the "content problem" will become fully explicable.

Freedom: A Closer Look. For Arendt man is the animal born with the potential to become human. This is the most important fact about him. Man possesses an animal nature but is not identical with it; thus he is not a natural animal.[87] Rather, he is given to himself, not as himself, but in order to become what he wills himself to be and indeed, ultimately, to will more than himself. In a word, man is free. Unlike the other animals man is not necessitated in all he does, but he becomes the bearer of responsibility for what he does and for the kind of man he becomes because most all he does he does out of his freedom.[88] Whatever he does he could always have done otherwise, being free. Thus, even when he follows pure impulse and no act of will seems to be entailed, Arendt would hold—here obviously following Aristotle—that implicitly or silently his will willed that that inner impulse be followed. That he experienced no struggle of wills within him and acted reflexively without a moment's thought does not mean his will was not involved. As he acts, he wills and as he wills, he acts. Whatsoever he does, whosoever he is, through his freedom he is his author, and as such is rightly held accountable.

In taking this position, Arendt sets herself squarely against much that passes for wisdom in our era. Against the determinisms of (for example) psychology, sociology, and economics, Arendt insists upon attributing to man a maximum degree of responsibility for himself.[89] To her view, the "isms" of the age have become grandiose exculpatory schemas, which encourage irresponsibility and promote moral decline. She does not deny that these theories of necessary causation possess a certain truth but insists that they mistake a partial truth for the whole of it:[90]

On the one hand men are free to choose; on the other hand they do tend to choose in accordance with what various deterministic conceptions would predict. For Arendt this paradox is not an irreconcilable opposition. Persons, in their freedom, can choose to act in accordance with principles which oppose the promptings of their conditioned impulses—whether the conditioning ground be held to be biological, historical, psychological, or sociological makes no difference. That they only seldom resist these promptings does not mean that they are unable to do so. Statistics are of no relevance here, for even a single instance of the improbable exception to the rule proves the possibility of such exceptions and the reality of freedom. The problem with determinisms is not their truth per se but their tendency to make themselves ever more true as they fuse to constitute a Zeitgeist which encourages the seemingly necessitated behaviors which are in accordance with its credo.[91] In time there are fewer exceptions to the rule, in part, as a result of its widespread dissemination.

In Arendt's discussion of freedom, it should be noted that a certain ambiguity arises from her use of the term. On the one hand, when she has in mind man's essential nature, or the nature of his will, she writes of the freedom which is evident in what a man does whether it be in accordance with freely chosen principle or not. This freedom is predicated of what a man does, no matter what he does. It follows from the fact that what a man does he must will to do, and from the fact that what a man wills he could always have willed differently; in other words, as a matter of definition, the will wills freely.[92] In this sense, then, man is always free. From this standpoint, when necessity is contrasted with freedom, the point in so doing is to emphasize the difference between man and the other animals who in all they do are borne by impulse and are as such unfree.

In an altogether different sense, when treating of man himself and the uses he makes of the freedom inherent in his will, the predicates of freedom and necessity reappear, as Arendt endeavors to differentiate under these two rubrics the substantive grounds of the will's self-determination.[93]

As I noted above, man is the animal who, unlike every other animal, possesses the wherewithal not to act as impulse bids him. Man, through reflection, can deduce principles, ends, values which he can use to guide his will in its freedom. Man, in the world, is exposed to preexistent cultural norms and ideals which he can choose to make his own, letting them henceforth guide his action. At the same time, man is in the world with his

fellow man with whom he acts, interacts, deliberates, and comes to agreements regarding new projects, principles, and values which he pledges will
henceforth guide his action.[94] Together this ensemble of values and norms,
which either come to man in the world or are products of his own reflection, constitute principles of freedom according to which man may choose
to determine his will and his actions.[95]

Necessity: Biological and Rational. Still this tale of freedom is only
half the story. From the other side of our natures arises the constellation
of forces which Arendt denominates under the rubric of necessity, that is,
those forces which would automatically necessitate us to act as they command if we were not free. In the main, Arendt would categorize these
forces and impulsions, pejoratively, as belonging to our animal or lower
natures, but this is not true of them all. Most surprisingly, as we shall see
below, Arendt ranks among those elements of our nature which can in
certain conditions bear down upon the will with almost necessitating
force, the rational faculty itself. As compared with the elements of freedom, the elements of necessity often press upon the will with the greater
force, a force which most men by themselves would not be able to resist.
Yet because man is not alone, he is able to join with his fellows to form a
power strong enough to triumph over these forces that rise up within
him.[96]

Man—seeking to will himself and more than himself as manifestations of his freedom—is beset by forces of necessity which forever threaten
to submerge him, thus engaging him in a perpetual struggle. His nobility,
according to Arendt, comes through this struggle, and his dignity lies in
pursuing the unmarked path of freedom rather than the easy way of
necessity.[97] Only along the path of freedom can man come to himself and
attain, at the same time, to the depth of being which is at once the summit
of human possibility. But it is a hard road to travel.

Pressing against man's will to determine himself in freedom, and
arising out of his animal nature, are the impulses born of the biological
need for that which is biologically necessary for the maintenance of life.
Such impulses pose a continuous challenge to the will which, in cases
where they press with extreme urgency, most always succumbs. Extreme
hunger is but one example of such a force.[98]

Compassion is another example of a force which can be so over-
whelming as practically to necessitate the will. As men are driven to acts
of desperation by hunger, so too may men be driven by an excessive emo-
tion which coerces the will as if by necessity. Compassion figures large in
Arendt's catalogue of emotions which are potential dangers to freedom.[99]

More commonplace—and for Arendt's analysis more significant—is the pressure upon our wills of daily wants, needs, and desires which follow from our being desiring creatures living in a consumer society and craving by nature a certain animal-happiness.[100] Arendt, who is highly critical of Marx in most respects, would not dispute his contention that the satisfaction of need engenders new needs which press upon man with all the strength of the more primary needs that have been satisfied. There are ways to transcend the press of bionecessity, but satisfying each need as it arises is not one of them.[101] In Arendt's opinion, the reign of desire and bionecessity knows no natural limit and will grow in strength unless forcibly checked. Nor does the press of consumption facilitate that differentiation of self which man aspires to. Rather, consumption-oriented desires are inevitably leveling forces whose satisfaction mirrors in uniformity the species-wide invariance of these desires.[102] Especially in a consumer society where general affluence is a product of mass production, it is inevitable that increased consumption will be paralleled by a general leveling of differences in taste.[103]

For Arendt, a life governed by the desire to consume, on account of the essential insatiability of the latter, can only be subservient to necessity. Neither upscale nor high volume consumption will ever permit that differentiation of self which comes about only through freedom—a freedom which, in the first instance, is a freedom from the need to consume. Consumption and the desire to consume are inherently self-relating, moreover. Thus it is unlikely that they can facilitate the transcendence of elemental self-concern that entails the positing of something less evanescent than oneself as the object of one's concern.[104]

For Arendt, the tragedy of modern ease and abundance lies in our ability in the midst of plenty to ward off the experience of the unfulfillable needs, an experience which in the past led men to reconceive the quest for ultimate significance in transcendent terms.[105] Needs can make man aware of his freedom, but only by their being unmet.[106] Recall that in the last part of Plato's *Republic* the unfreedom of the despot is signified by his ability to satisfy his every need as it arises. Thus he is a slave to many masters, that is, to the many desires of his passing fancy. Never knowing the resistance of the limit, he is never impelled to transcend his runaway animality. For Arendt, such is the fate of most persons in our society of abundance.

The critique of lowly appetite and the disdain for the merely bodily which Arendt displays might seem to place her in that long line of Western thinkers who have, from the time of Plato, denigrated the animal nature while extolling the rational potency of man. Within this tradition man is understood as that hybrid creature whose stature rises or falls as the force of reason or appetite comes to prevail over his inward constitution. From this perspective, as man approaches the height of perfection, more and more of what he does will be subject to the rule of reason within him, and more and more of what he does will be brought into conformity with the one way of the true. For adherents of this tradition, the problem of man has been solved when man's appetite has been brought into accord with the reason that reasons rightly. Unfree, by contrast, is he who is in thrall to his desires. In reason, and by reason, man is made free.

These champions of reason do not worry that they are merely exchanging one master (desire) for another (reason). After all does one pity the acorn for being a slave to nature when, by virtue of a divine template, it is destined to be a tall oak? Of course not. But what is reason if not the means by which man may perceive the divine template which ought to be the model of his own growth? If all men were granted equal clarity of vision and equal strength of will then all could grow in accordance with this singular model of human perfection. To call such men slaves is surely to speak in riddles, and makes no sense at all.

Reason, a tyrant? Yes, says Arendt; it can be just that.[107] Like the primary instincts, reason bears down upon the will with almost compelling necessity.[108] The self-evidence of rational truth is coercive and the power of logic, from which this self-evidence derives, is even more so. For Arendt, the paradigmatic example of the inherently coercive nature of reason is the statement that $2+2=4$.[109] This equation brooks no dissent, suffers no qualification, calls forth no multiplicity of opinion. Rather, by the very structure of our rational faculty we are compelled to assent.[110]

In matters of action, almost as much as in matters of truth, the same coercive logic can be brought to bear but here it becomes destructive of freedom.[111] If one accepts the premises of an ideological or comprehensive metaphysical system then one is forced to accept the imperatives which follow with ineluctable necessity.[112] From axioms or propositions regarding what is true or real, propositions which the rational faculty finds compelling, logic may deduce imperatives which, bearing the imprimatur of the rational, seek to compel the assent and consequent deeds of the will.[113] If, for example, one accepts it as true that history is a war between the races in which inferior races are destroyed by those that are superior, and if one also accepts it as true that Jews or blacks are inferior peoples, then it requires no great logical acumen to deduce the imperative that it is necessary to exterminate these inferior races.[114] Otherwise, by my failure to act, I accuse myself of lacking the courage of my convictions and stand in contradiction with myself. By playing upon this fear of contradiction, the logic necessitated organon of human reason usurps its legitimate limits and comes to coerce the will, thus setting rationality in opposition to freedom.[115] That history is patently *not* wholly explicable as either racial struggle or as class warfare makes little difference to the will in thrall to some ideological vision of the whole. Embrace any vision of the Truth and the imperatives follow with ineluctable necessity.

In depicting the nature of the force which logic brings to bear upon the will, Arendt likens the force of logic to other elemental forces which well up within our bodies and impress themselves on our minds with necessitating power.[116] In this light, logic is viewed as an animal power, even if it is that animal power which distinguishes man from the other animal species.[117] As something common to the species, logic, in a formal sense, speaks in the same voice to all men, at most varying in volume.[118] Always its subject/object is the universal and its tone, accordingly impersonal even if only one man is listening. Were it to find the one truth it claims to seek and were all men to heed its voice then the result would be a uniformity of thought and deed which only a totalitarian could applaud.[119] For those who believe in the uniqueness of the individual—and for those who believe, with Arendt, that the will is the organ by which this uniqueness is to become manifest in the world—the specter of this reign of reason is sheer nightmare.

Like the other biodrives, reason lays a claim upon the will which it seeks to necessitate. If by nature the force which reason may bring to bear upon the will is weaker than the force brought to bear by those drives which man shares in common with the other species, Arendt argues that this inherent weakness has been compensated for, to an ever increasing degree, by the civilizational prejudice that esteems reason over the other drives and is forever seeking to install it as the will's sole commander. Arendt would not dispute the preference for reason over base animal instinct; nor, however, does she support its bid for unqualified rule over the will. For above reason's will to truth and uniformity, she values man's quest for individuation through freedom. But reason cannot be the specific ground of man's individuation because it is essentially invariant across the species and seeks to compel the will, thus undermining the freedom which she holds to be prerequisite to his self-determination. In light of these considerations, she includes reason among the necessitating forces which the will must resist.

The predicament of man, then, is to find himself opposed in his struggle for free self-determination by powerful adversarial forces which besiege him from within. Arendt groups these forces under the rubric of necessity which, as we have seen, she conceives as being of two basic types, bionecessity and rational necessity.[120] Man in his inward freedom is assailed by both. Man in his outward freedom, that is, man in the world, is assailed by them again. The configuration of forces within, prefigures the configuration of forces in the world at large. Nor, as we shall soon see, is this just a matter of happenstance.

Willing: *The Textual Evidence.* To this point I have for the most part proceeded synthetically in rendering coherent Arendt's scattered remarks regarding the interrelations between freedom and necessity. Arendt herself never called attention to the parallelism which is manifest in her understanding of organic and rational necessities in their essential relation to man's freedom. Each of these constructs stands by itself; each comes into focus in a different work. In *The Origins of Totalitarianism* her vision of rational necessity and of the coercive power of logic on the will emerges by way of her critique of the totalitarian elements present in ideological thinking.[121] With *The Human Condition*, however, the focus has shifted and we see for the first time an explicit conception of the conflict between freedom and necessity, though here it is bionecessity, as manifest in the imperatives which underlie the motions of civil society, which holds her gaze.[122] More striking to her than the coercive element at this point is another concomitant of bionecessity's reign, the leveling of human difference. It is only in the first part of *On Revolution* that the particularly coercive dimension of bionecessity emerges as a stressed theme.[123]

Only when we venture outside of her explicitly political writings do we come across a work wherein Arendt brings into conjunction these several types of necessity and their fundamental connection with the problem of human freedom:

It seems only fitting that an idea whose various lineaments had time and again occupied her attention throughout her life occupied her attention once again at its end. In *Willing (The Life of the Mind* vol. 2), a work completed only weeks before her death, Arendt at last found the occasion to pull together into a coherent construct her thoughts on the conceptual and inward foundations of freedom.

In *Willing* Arendt fathoms the peculiar "history" of this faculty, that is, the history of philosophical speculation about the will's nature, a faculty whose very existence, she tells us, has been in dispute since it was first asserted.[124] Given Arendt's phenomenological perspective, it is hardly surprising that she takes the existence of this faculty for granted; nor can it be surprising that she regards it as the inward agency of our freedom.[125] Our interest in *Willing* centers upon her endeavor to articulate the precise nature of the relation between the will's freedom and the forces of necessity which are arrayed against it. Arendt's own conception reaches its most complete articulation in the context of her encounter with the thought of Augustine and Duns Scotus.[126]

It was Paul who discovered the will in all its brokenness, but it is Augustine who reflected upon this discovery in a way which Arendt finds philosophically compelling. It was Augustine, after all, not Paul who, in *The City of God*, secures a place for the will within a philosophical psychology that had hitherto conceived the soul according to the opposition of reason and appetite.[127] For Augustine there was no doubt that Paul had made a genuine discovery; the will, he argued, could be reduced to neither appetite nor reason, nor could it be reduced to a simple vector sum of the two. For proof of this Augustine points to the rare yet decisive instance, not where reason and desire cancel each other out, but where their forces are united in urging some particular action which the man in whom these forces are as one vector nevertheless chooses to forego. By inference, Augustine deduces from this the existence of a faculty of choice, the will, which is neither reducible to, nor even necessarily submissive to, the other two elements. Arendt too is persuaded.

For Arendt the importance of Augustine, in this context, is not limited to his proof of the will's existence as a separate faculty set between reason and desire. Even more important than the fact of its existence is the fact from which its existence was inferred, namely, the fact of its freedom and of the freedom of man which comes through it. As the example evinced, it is through the will that man gains the freedom that makes him more than an automatic agent of the forces of reason and appetite which well up within him. Moreover, of these three faculties, it is only the will which is free. By contrast my rational faculty is compelled by logic and my desiring faculty is compelled by appetite. Thus it is only by virtue of the will's freedom—writes Arendt of Augustine's insight in words that well characterize her own view—that "I may say No to either the truth of reason or to the press of appetite [though I cannot do so] from the faculties themselves."[128] In contrast to man, a being that was wholly carnal or wholly rational could not be a free being.

The affinity between Arendt's thought and Augustine's is striking. In *Willing*, however, she seems to identify even more closely with the views of Duns Scotus. Recalling for us her own view, she cites Duns Scotus's opinion that "there is a difference between man's natural inclination to happiness and happiness as the *deliberately chosen* goal of one's life."[129] For Arendt, however, the true significance of this distinction between the will and mere inclination follows from the ability of the former to contravene and prevail against the latter. For the inherent freedom of the free will is such that "it is by no means impossible for man to discount happiness altogether in making his willed projects."[130] Such indeed is the very nature of the will—according to Duns Scotus—that it "freely designs ends that are pursued for their own sake and of this pursuance only the will is capable."[131] When, for example, the actor risks happiness (as well as life and limb) for the sake of justice or the commonweal this capacity becomes fully manifest.

But if in such instances the will is not determined by either reason or appetite what, then, is its determining ground? Or, is it to be maintained that the will's freedom militates against there being any determining ground at all—as if the presence of such were synonymous with unfreedom? Yet if this be so then the free will must be a radically arbitrary will, a random will such as only lunatics appear to possess. So far as one can tell there seems to be no reason why such a will will not prove wholly arbitrary or destructive. Indeed, from a certain point of view, the horror unleashed by the National Socialists may be understood as embodying such an errant will to power. That Arendt herself might have understood it as such is hinted at as she explores the reflections of Nietzsche and Heidegger on the nature of the will, reflections which eventually led them to reject the faculty altogether.[132] From within the will itself there seems to be no clear ground that might insure its positivity. Hence Arendt ends *The Life of The Mind: Willing* on a dark note, speaking of freedom as an "abyss" and as a "burden" to which we are apparently "doomed."[133] What, then, enables Arendt to avoid the path taken by Heidegger and Nietzsche, despite her strong sympathy for their point of view? What, in short, does Arendt envision to be the will's determining ground, assuming that by proclaiming the will free with respect to reason and appetite she does not propose to leave it entirely rudderless?

The ground would seem to be that pure particle of unique selfhood which lies deeper than the outer and inner conditioning forces which would conform the will in their image can reach.[134] Arendt is not very clear about this.[135] Rather, she emphasizes the spontaneity of the will which is neither arbitrary in its manifestation not reducible to the vectors, or vector sum, of reason, appetite, or socialization.[136] More definitively, in *The Origins of Totalitarianism*, Arendt links selfhood and spontaneity when she observes that the Nazis sought to obliterate the selfhood of concentration camp inmates by denying them any opportunity for spontaneous action.[137] To be deprived of the latter was to have the former destroyed. By tracing a connection between spontaneity and selfhood, moreover, it should be clear that the former is not meant to connote images of impulsive or lively behavior. Spontaneity, in Arendt's terminology, is hardly inimical to deliberation and choice. Indeed the one presupposes the other. One who acts spontaneously, then, is one who is one's own cause and as such one who transcends the forces that would otherwise be all-conditioning.[138] What one spontaneously does in one's freedom will manifest one's true self, that particle of uniqueness which is something deeper, more inward and more essential than all those sociological and biological factors which press toward uniformity.

Would it be accurate, then, to say that for Arendt the free will entails conformity to a law of self, albeit that this "law" can only become manifest where the forces of reason and appetite have been quelled? Such, indeed, is Arendt's conception, though the nature of this kernel of selfhood, or law of destiny, remains unclear. Sometimes it seems to be something inborn but inchoate and opaque, something of a deep structural yet protean tendency, that might be embodied in a range of life choices. Other times Arendt's emphasis lies more heavily upon the situations within which choices are framed and upon the conditioning impact of choices back upon the agent whose character is thus formed and reformed that in time it becomes a destiny. In either case, the core of self by means of which the will steers between the dictates of reason and appetite—a core that is manifest when the will displays the strength and depth that enables it to project its possibilities in an idiom not reducible to either reason or appetite—may be best understood as a configuration of ultimate value. The self's "weight" in the Augustinian sense, if you will. Or the Socratic *daemon*. When the will is guided by this and by this alone, the will is free and the individual's uniqueness is manifest. Such is the Arendtian criterion of "authenticity," albeit one that is more romantic than existentialist in cast.[139]

For Arendt, however, in contrast to Heidegger, Being is sometimes viewed as weighing-in on behalf of the individual's success in this undertaking, inasmuch as it is Being itself which bequeaths unto the individual—via natality—a specific potentiality given to him or her alone.[140] Indeed, in one formulation bearing upon this matter, Arendt goes so far as to speculate that Being risks the realization of its own earthly telos by making it dependent upon the actions of the human beings that it sends forth into the world.[141] By bequeathing unto each human being a unique potentiality, Being sows possibilities which if realized would constitute the realization of its own telos as well.[142]

Being itself, in Arendt's view, is progressive.[143] It wills change; it wills novelty and new beginnings. It wills the perpetual revitalization of all creation and so sends forth from its womb singular and unique beings whose very novelty signifies a capacity for authoring novel deeds which might keep the world from growing old.[144] Were every person alike then none could save the world from becoming rutted and ossified. Were every person alike then birth could hardly signify a new beginning or symbolize the possibility of the world's beginning anew.[145]

That Being is thus inclined, in Arendt's conception, is important, though it must be stressed that this fact alone hardly makes the task of the individual any easier than Heidegger estimated it to be. The path from potentiality to its actualization remains tortuous, and the telos allotted by Being to each person remains most obscure for the one who must struggle to achieve it. To liberate the pure kernel of potential selfhood from the flux of forces that would otherwise engulf it is, however, the task of the will in its freedom. For the will alone can bring forth the deeds which may actualize the self's ownmost potentiality and renew the world. But for the capacity of the will to stymie the forces that would otherwise necessitate it, neither of these intimately connected ends could be achieved. To reiterate, Arendt speaks only of possibilities. Though much hinges upon the outcome, there are no guarantees of success.

Some Implications. In the course of considering freedom and necessity it has become clear that this paired polarity comprehends the concerns of the other two. What frustrates man in his quest for duration and evanesces all too quickly is paradigmatically the biological, and hence the necessitated, aspect of existence. What endures, by contrast, must transcend the cyclical course of biological time and, as such, exists in freedom, that is, in freedom from the ruinous forces of necessity. Similarly, what frustrates man in his quest for complete individuation are those aspects of species-life that tend to impose upon men's lives an oppressive uniformity, that is, those aspects of species-life which Arendt denominates under the rubric of necessity. What individuates, by contrast, transcends these species-norms and frees itself from their necessitating and conformist tendencies.

In itself, freedom gives no specific content. Rather freedom, by making willing possible, is the precondition of all specific acts of will. In particular, man's freedom makes it possible for him to will a relation between himself and that which outlasts him, as it also makes possible the manifestation of his uniqueness. At the same time, knowing that freedom wills against necessity, we infer that the forces of necessity are opposed to the will that wills itself in relation to lasting things, and in relation to the attainment of uniqueness. In itself this should not be surprising. Animals, after all, who lack freedom and are wholly under the dictates of necessity, lack at the same time the wherewithal to will anything that might transcend the somatic level of species-being.

On a broader front, the impact of Arendt's conception of freedom and necessity is to be discerned most clearly in the way it permeates her thinking about political action: action and freedom are held to be coterminous, and necessity is held to be inimical to both. For the sake of the former elements, and for the sake of the individuation and immortalization they make possible, the latter element must be kept at bay. There persists some ambiguity, however, as to whether action is to be construed as the force that keeps necessity in check, or whether it is to be thought of as the beneficiary of necessity's having been constrained by other means. In the former vein, Arendt sometimes envisions men as gathering together and, by their joint action, triumphing over the forces of necessity that would necessitate them individually.[146] By such joint action freedom is created and necessity is overcome. Alternatively—and in what is the more prevalent conception—Arendt differentiates between a spatial realm of freedom and a spatial realm of necessity, and between free concerns and issues that necessitate: in this context, Arendt defines political action as the activity that transpires within the space of, and in relation to the concerns of, freedom. By inference, then, if the public realm is to be a site of action, none of the issues that necessitate can be objects of legitimate concern for the denizens of this realm.[147]

What this means concretely will become clear as we now train our attention upon Arendt's dichotomous conception of public and private realms, an antithesis of foremost prominence in Arendt's work and the recipient of much explicit attention from Arendt herself.[148] From our perspective, this dyad is especially striking in several respects. First, this dichotomy is almost perfectly isomorphic with the three dyads which have been singled out as implicit in Arendt's conception of action. Second, this dichotomy—unlike the three already discussed—signals a tangible structural principle whose ordering effect upon the real world of politics is plain to see. As such it serves to mediate between Arendt's conceptual world and the practical world of public affairs. By tethering the dream-world of concepts to the real-world distinctions of public and private, the practical implications of Arendt's work emerge in a form that is easier to grapple with.

PUBLIC AND PRIVATE: SPACES AND OBJECTS

The conceptual division between public and private is as all-encompassing as any Arendt employs. Strictly speaking, the division is spatial and is applied to the life-world as a whole which is divided into public and private spaces. As such, the dichotomy is essentially descriptive.[149] At the same time, however, Arendt deploys the dichotomy as an ideal criterion of allocation by which to determine what is *properly* public and *properly* private. At this normative level, public and private come to suggest not so much empirical spaces of variable content as much as the criteria which determine whether a given topic or activity properly belongs to one realm or to the other.[150] Thus it becomes possible to speak of appropriately private topics or activities, that is, topics or activities whose inherent nature befits them for the private realm, that inappropriately receive public attention. Indeed, as we will see, Arendt denominates a third sphere, "the social" or society, by the very hybrid notion just mentioned, namely that of properly private activities which have, contrary to their nature, entered the public realm.[151]

The public is also the lasting space, the lasting world (or polity) that is built by, and the home of, human acts.[152] For it is only an illusion that makes it seem that the public space, which precedes and succeeds the fleeting moment of our appearance within it, is naturally self-perpetuating. In reality, the long continuance of this space depends upon the efforts of those in every generation who make this continuance a matter of significant concern to themselves and, who by their efforts, secure the public world's viability unto each successive generation. And, of course, the actions that are undertaken for the sake of the polity's long perpetuation are in turn immortalized by it in expression of its appreciation.

At the descriptive-conceptual level, metaphors of illumination predominate in Arendt's differentiation of public and private realms—recalling our earlier discussion of uniformity and uniqueness and their relation to man's search for a lighted realm.[153] In what seems to be a metaphorical application of Heidegger's conception of truth (*alethia*) as "disclosedness," Arendt depicts the public realm as filled with the light of speech which illuminates all that appears within the realm; the private realm, by contrast, is depicted as an essentially mute sphere, a sphere of darkness, a hiding place, a place of privacy into which the light of the public does not—or should not—penetrate.[154] The public thus becomes the site of publicity, that illuminated clearing, that circle of light engendering discourse, at the edge of which darkness quickly closes in in all directions. Actors seek out this discursive light that is constituted by the attention of their fellow citizens in order that they may obtain that measure of discursive illumination which is the sine qua non of immortalization.

Also of great importance to Arendt are the epistemological implications that follow from this conception of the public realm as the realm of appearance: Arendt holds that what enters the public space achieves a heightened measure of reality through the attention it receives from all who are gathered there.[155] That public attention can make something real owes, in Arendt's opinion, to the supposition that only what appears and is spoken about is fully real.[156] But the reality that the public realm bestows owes, in this view, not to the mere fact of appearance, but to the fact that what receives this reality appears simultaneously to, and is spoken about by, many persons, each of whom occupies a different position and looks upon the phenomena from a different perspective—a differential of position and perspective that essentially correlates with human plurality.[157] Moreover, such discursive give-and-take, by constituting the reality of the public realm and the reality of the phenomena that appear within it, establishes the world as a *common* world even while it manifests the irreducible perspectival multiplicity of its denizens. Significantly, Arendt adds, the habit of such speech also imparts a *sense* for the reality of the world, a common sense that roots those who possess it in a shared reality that, by virtue of this common sense, makes sense.[158] By contrast, the private realm is unable to accomplish any of these things because, within a realm in which at most a very few perspectives are ever brought to bear, at best only an elusive and tenuous reality—and sense of reality—can be obtained. Worldlessness, then, is the condition of the private realm and worldless are those persons whose lives are wholly spent within its confines.

A Communal Space

As intimated in the previous paragraph, the public space is the site in which we are connected to one another as members of a *political* community.[159] What we experience in our privacy—or in the intimacy of the private realm that we share with a few at most—remains our private property and, by definition, cannot serve to relate us to those with whom we do not share this privacy. By contrast, what we experience in the public realm—or in relation to the objects which constitute the matters of concern in this realm—can connect us to our neighbors in a community as no private experience will ever do. Only by virtue of what is shared in the common realm of the public can we be said to share a world in common with one another at all:[160] such sharing is, in Arendtian parlance, thoroughly political.

To help illustrate this conception an optical metaphor is useful: Envision a theater in the round, a stage in the center illumined by a spotlight and an audience gathered about though hidden in darkness. What one man says to his neighbor may be known to them both, but veiled in darkness it remains a private affair. Only by what appears on the stage under the spotlight may all who are gathered be constituted as a community—assuming that those gathered around the stage attend to the action upon it while the drama unfolds.[161]

At the end of the drama, to return to the simile—imagine the house lights to come up and the audience, instead of departing homeward, to remain in place. Each now comes forward in turn in order to articulate his view of the evening's event. Inevitably, one speaker finds himself commenting upon the words of those who spoke previously as much as upon the event itself. In fact the discussion very quickly becomes the event with each person in attendance now playing, in alternation, the roles of actor and spectator, in turn revealing himself to all assembled and then becoming one to whom and through whom others are revealed. When such a process transpires in the public space, the public and the political realms are one, and—by Arendt's measure—things are as they should be.

In stark contrast is the community whose basis of bonding is some preexistent species essence common to all men everywhere. That men share a species likeness to one another may be the ultimate precondition of all community, but it is not a condition of the possibility of political community. If all men were exactly like one another, doubtless men, being social creatures, would live together in communities; but, in Arendt's view, it is only because men are at the same time *unlike* one another that they must constitute political communities, for only a political community is inherently cognizant of the individuality of each of its members.[162]

On the Public Character of Public Objects

The public space, then, is the realm within which political community is possible by virtue of the public discourse that appears in the light which is consubstantial with the space. It would be wrong to infer from this, however, that any issue or object of concern that appears within the public space can effectively serve to engender or perpetuate a community that would satisfy Arendt's criteria of politicality: in the first instance, it is necessary that any object of public attention that would suffice in this respect must be of concern to all who stand within the political or public space. Such, one might say, is the prerequisite of political community. And yet, as one might infer from our earlier discussion of freedom and necessity, more than this alone is required because not every issue that is of common concern will engender the manifestation of human difference that Arendt insists politicality equally demands. In *The Human Condition* Arendt emphasizes just this when she likens the world and its objects to a table which relates and *separates* all who are gathered around it, the table being such a thing that all who sit around it see what is on it from *different* perspectives.[163] For political community both elements are of importance: the issues upon the table must be truly common concerns, and they must be of such a nature as to relate those who are gathered around it *to* one another through their differences *from* one another.[164] What does not meet both of these criteria ought not to appear in public at all.

On these grounds, Arendt denies the legitimacy of those "political" issues that arise from the side of necessity because she is convinced that the discussion of such issues will block the manifestation of the actor's uniqueness, and that, as a result, his political positions will become reflexive articulations of needs he has in common with the rest of the species. Analogously, Arendt rejects the politics of the welfare state, or of "national housekeeping," as she calls it, and argues that such questions ought to be depoliticized and returned to the private realm (that is, to the sphere of necessity) where such issues truly belong, and where they will no longer be capable of ruining the public realm's raison d'être. Though common, and thus "table-like," in one respect, such questions cease to be "table-like" in another because the press of needs, which such questions presuppose and unleash, will tend to overwhelm the actor's freedom through which self-manifestation occurs.

In practical terms, the manifestation of self through freedom depends upon a movement of self-transcendence in which the self's quotidian and parochial concerns are overcome. To this end, Arendt insists that the issues of common concern must be of such a nature as will help the members of the polity, who are intent upon navigating the transit from necessity unto freedom, to make this move. Above all, this means that the issues of common concern must be *worldly* issues, that is, issues that bear upon the ongoing viability of a public world that is meant to last for generations. For such issues alone, inasmuch as they are bound up with the interests of a potentially immortal entity, require the actor who would make such issues his own to overcome that excessive concern for self-preservation and well-being that naturally characterizes all mortals.[165] In so doing, the actor steps beyond the press of egocentric necessity and enters into the inward realm of freedom that makes possible the outward manifestation of who he truly is.

One can discern here the basis for Arendt's belief that the most authentically political issues are those that encourage transcendence—and, we might add, those that constitute community—in two directions, one horizontal and one vertical, one synchronic and one diachronic. Along the synchronic axis, when an issue makes the requisite appeal, the natural propensity to care only for what is one's own may be overcome and replaced by a concern for what belongs to others as well; thus, in an expanding circle one's object of utmost concern may evolve from self to family to city to nation. Conversely, along the diachronic axis, the natural propensity to see in the length of one's days an inherent limit to the span of one's temporal concerns may be transcended once one has become sensitive to the specific temporality of the polity or public world, and its concerns.[166]

Admittedly, it is an "unnatural" point of view that encourages the citizen to act "unnaturally" on behalf of persons not yet born by championing in the here and now values, ways of life, and institutions which he hopes will be of value to them, even in the face of the knowledge that he may earn nothing but an expedited departure from this world in recompense for his endeavors.[167] For Arendt, however, this breaking away from the natural is most estimable because it constitutes a transit from necessity into freedom and from the species-uniform to the most supremely individuating.

It should be apparent that, in Arendt's view, there is an intimate association between the qualities of soul that a man displays and the objects, or issues, in reference to which they become manifest. The more self-transcendent and exalted the object of concern, the purer and more exalted will be the concomitant manifestation of self. Courage, for example, when it is displayed in defense of what is one's own is generally held to be less estimable than courage displayed in defense of some unprotected innocent with whom one has no connection whatsoever. And the courage that is manifested by one who is willing to lay down his life for the sake of his polity is accounted by Arendt to be greater still.[168] If the issues that engage the citizenry are to elicit the most excellent qualities of soul and the most complete revelation of self it follows, then, that these issues must be of sufficient magnitude for this task.

Already we have seen that Arendt would exclude from political discussion issues that are tied up with necessity because such issues fail to demand the transit from necessity unto freedom that Arendt regards as an indispensable element of action. We have also seen that an issue's fitness for public discussion depends upon its commonality, or synchronic breadth, and upon its diachronic reach as well. Comprehensively, then, the most essentially political issues will bear upon the polity's transgenerational identity or viability, will be of interest to all citizens, and will require the transcendence of the natural point of view which places self-interest ahead of all else. From this it follows that what does not meet these criteria ought to be kept from the public/political realm and consigned to the private sphere.

It should be noted, however, that while it is true, in general, that Arendt esteems the fittingly public over the fittingly private, and seems to argue that whatever possesses true worth ought to appear in the public where it will be permitted to shine, this is not always the case. Indeed, there are phenomena of the private sphere which Arendt holds to be of great worth which she readily acknowledges would be denatured and ruined were they made public and forced to submit to the procrustean transmogrification that publicity tends to effect upon things that ought not to be made public.[169] Love, for example, is inherently a tie between two persons and in its exclusivity it rises to its most perfect form.[170] Publicity, Arendt insists, would ruin love by insisting upon the unfairness of its exclusivity and by seeking to make it more inclusive, as if all possessed a right to share in it; but any attempt to share it or to make it conform with higher public principle would surely diminish it and diminish man in consequence.[171] Nor can love be said to last in the sense required of those activities or ends that appear in public. Unlike love, which is between two particular persons and has no future without them, neither a polis nor a properly political issue can be said to be tied to the lives of any particular generation of its citizens for it outlasts them all. Whatever, like love, sex, or dinner, is so tied to some particular group of living persons that it cannot be shared with others without being denatured in the process is unfit for publicity both because it will be ruined by it, and because such objects cannot make possible the two-dimensional transcendence which public objects ought to facilitate.

Where public and private things are in their proper places, Arendt believes that this division of the world into public and private spheres will serve to foster the appearance of glorious words and deeds in the public space, while protecting from exposure all that needs the darkness of intimacy to exist at all. The difficulty in achieving, or maintaining, this division stems from the fact that the forces of necessity, which are oriented to consumption, tend to be stronger than the will to freedom.[172] As a result, it is almost inevitable that men will seek to turn the public space into an extension of the private, seeking, for example, to make politics an extension of economics and bringing the maxims of bald self-interest to bear upon the whole of public life.[173]

In Arendt's view, the time for vigilance is before these forces have penetrated into the public realm. Once they have found a foothold there, it will be very hard to set things right again because the things that will then be appearing in the public, which will be private things really, will lack the capacity to call forth either the twofold movement of transcendence which makes one a partisan of the public interest or the great acts of virtue which only such partisanship can engender.[174] In the normal course of things, then, Arendt believes that it is imperative to maintain a hard and fast wall of separation between what is admitted into the public realm and what is not. How this is to be insured remains to be clarified.[175]

How the public and private articulate with the three dichotomies we have already explored ought by now to be quite clear. The public is the site of lastingness. Its objects, its concerns, and the world it constitutes all outlast the mortals whose only chance at, or taste of, immortality comes through their contact with it. By contrast, the private is the site of all that is evanescent—but not for that reason necessarily meaningless—in a man's life. If man were any other animal species he would have only a private life and leave no trace of himself. Generations would come and go noiselessly, in endlessly repetitive cycles of biological growth and decay, birth and death. It is the discontinuity of the public from the private life, the very unnaturalness of the former, as it were, that permits man a limited escape from the futility of a sheerly natural existence. Up from the realm of creaturely necessities man rises into a sphere of relative freedom where "unnatural" objects become the focus of his concern thus serving as a lever by which to free himself from thralldom to the forces of biological and egoistical necessity which by nature move him. By virtue of this pathway into freedom man is granted the possibility of being more than a cipher of species-life, of rising above the uniformity and obscurity which would have been his lot otherwise. In the light of the public space and in the course of a life in which man chooses to make its worldly objects his own, the citizen gains the wherewithal to rise to the heights of human greatness and to reveal a character uniquely his own.

THE NORMS OF PUBLIC ACTION

The community of those who act in concert and undertake their actions within the public space in reference to one another is, by Arendt's definition, a political community.[176] It is a *community* by virtue of the fact that its members participate in a common enterprise and thus share a common end which, at a minimum, Arendt would denote as the end of insuring the polity's continuance in time. But what makes it a *political* community is not the fact that its members share a common purpose, but the fact that it is a community bound together by speech, for it is shared speech which enables each member to develop and to manifest just who he is along the way.[177] Properly, all who are members of such a community will place a premium upon this moment of self-display and so attend to it almost as much as they do to the "political" matters at hand.

Arendt's conception of political community follows from her conception of action, entails the prior establishment of a public space, and presupposes the existence of common objects of communal concern. In large measure, the character of the community's political life follows from the premium placed upon intersubjective disclosure and the aspiration to greatness. Little has been said, however, of the political process itself or of the norms which, in Arendt's view, ought ideally to govern it. In truth, in

The Human Condition, Arendt hardly gives to these matters the attention they deserve. Thus, in *The Human Condition*, while taking great care to delineate many facets of political action, she addresses the question of how these citizens ought to interact with one another in the public space in a cursory way. Were the danger of flawed interaction between egos bent upon self-realization less self-evident, then this omission would be less frustrating.

Had Arendt passed over this matter in total silence our recourse would be unclear. Luckily, Arendt does provide her readers with a sufficient basis—albeit just barely—from which to deduce her view of the matter, at least in part. From within *The Human Condition*, then, I call the reader's attention to Arendt's conception of *isonomy* and to her cognate conception of *humanitas*.[178]

Isonomy

Isonomy, and the conception of political equality which Arendt derives from it, are of great importance in Arendt's conception of political community. Isonomy, or formal political equality, is in Arendt's view the formal condition which, more than any other, can help to insure that the political community is truly a community of action.

Where the legal structure of the polity renders all citizens political equals, as it presumably would in the Arendtian community, it secures to cach of thcm thc cqual right to step forth into the public space in a self-revelatory manner. More specifically, this means that every citizen possesses equal rights of public initiative and of public response to the initiatives of others. Only those whose rights are thus secured as the rights of political equals are positioned to engage in the one form of endeavor which bestows upon life the highest meaning. Such is the importance Arendt attributes to political equality; in her view, those denied it are denied all that makes life meaningful.[179]

By contrast, "rule," and hence the inegalitarian division of the citizen body into rulers and ruled, represents an assault upon, and a restriction of, this generic human capacity for action that isonomy is meant to protect.[180] Where there are rulers and ruled, or any formal divisions within the citizen body which might potentially dichotomize along such lines, it is Arendt's concern that those in a position to rule will, first, come to monopolize the right of initiating action, and, then, will come to dominate the field of action as well.

In light of this, it can hardly be surprising that Arendt espouses a radically participatory conception of direct democracy while refusing to countenance any system of representative government which, in the guise of the distinction between the representative and the represented, tends to reproduce the dichotomy of ruler and ruled.[181] For Arendt, proof of this equivalence is to be seen in the fact that within the system of representative government the largest part of the citizenry is, for all practical purposes, debarred from existentially meaningful political participation—just as it would be under more explicitly authoritarian forms of rule. Thus it is of hardly any importance, in her view, to grapple with the question of whether there are good reasons to esteem representative democracy over monarchical rule.[182] From Arendt's perspective the salient similarity that supports her assertion of their political parity is the fact that under either regime all but a fraction of the population is denied the chance to live truly political lives.[183] Simply put, in Arendt's opinion, where there is rule true politics dies.

"Rule," then (to recapitulate), signifies for Arendt an inequality in the rights of citizens to act which effectively insures that there will be less action and that fewer persons will be granted the possibility of acting in a politically, and hence in an existentially, meaningful way.[184] What the ruled do at the command, or behest, of the rulers does not count as action by Arendt's criterion. True action, according to the latter, partakes of mutuality and is premised upon a potential equality of spontaneity which the division between rulers and ruled precludes. Though political equality does not equalize absolutely, it can bring into existence equality enough to facilitate common action, and hence community, for all whose capacity for action is thus formally recognized. In sum, if only action redeems, and if action is only possible among political equals, then political equality ought to prevail. "Rule," to whatever degree it exists, diminishes action's prospects commensurately. Isonomy, then, is the watchword.

Humanitas *and Public Discourse*

Contrasting with isonomy which in essence signifies the formal criterion of political equality, *humanitas* is meant to be descriptive of the substantive spirit that must inform the community of political equals if it is truly to be a site of political action. For Arendt *humanitas* signifies primarily a willingness to share the world with one's fellow citizens.[185] The nature of this sharing is communicative; we share the world, and indeed constitute it as a world (as "reality"), by talking about it with one another.[186] By talking about it we humanize it and ourselves.[187] In the process we gather it and ourselves into a community which is ideally informed by a spirit of solidarity and by, what Arendt calls, political friendship, that is, a friendship that is grounded not in the sharing of selves in intimacy but in the sharing of the world at the distance which the world places between persons.[188]

From this vision of political community follow the virtues and norms of *humanitas* which include mutual respect among citizens, the willingness to forgive one another's unintentional trespasses, and tact, that is, a willingness to refrain from modes of speaking and doing which, for their lack of consideration for other members of the community, threaten to ruin civic solidarity and thus to undermine a crucial presupposition of common action.[189] Those whose communicative praxis most fully realizes these norms of civic discourse are, by Arendt's measure, most humane.[190]

Arendt's discussion of these virtues and norms is framed upon several levels. On the level just canvased, Arendt delineates the norms and virtues themselves. On another level, Arendt clarifies why these norms and virtues in particular are necessary if political action of the kind she espouses is to be continuously fostered. On a third level, Arendt traces the connection between these normative elements and the human faculties to which they correspond.

In arguing for the practical necessity of these normative elements, the desirability of constituting a political community that is maximally conducive to the continuous effusion of political action is presupposed. Arendt needs only to establish that the norm or virtue in question is properly conducive to this end or that the contrary norm or vice would constitute a certain hindrance. Thus, for example, having presupposed that the conditions for undistorted self-revelation are enhanced where the citizens are "with" yet neither "for" nor "against" one another in the public space, Arendt advocates solidarity as the virtue which sustains this condition of civic togetherness.[191] The virtues of tact and respect foster this same end by checking outbursts which might otherwise undermine the web of solidarity and fellow-feeling.

Similarly, for the sake of the long-term preservation of the public space as a site of action, Arendt emphasizes the functional importance of promise making, promise keeping, and forgiveness.[192] Action, as Arendt regularly observes, is inherently boundless, irreversible and unpredictable in its consequences.[193] Thus, the action that ought to sustain the public space might instead ruin it, or so damage the communal bonds, that no further action can be undertaken. The norms of promise making and promise keeping reduce this risk by bounding the range of action and by securing that modicum of predictability without which joint action would be impossible.[194] The virtue of forgiveness, by contrast, is espoused because it enables the citizenry to free themselves from the consequences of actions that might otherwise lock them into sterile cycles of action-bred reaction and mechanical vengeance.[195]

In this manner Arendt draws the connection between the norms and virtues she denominates under the rubric of *humanitas* and the maintenance of an action-oriented community. To will the end commits one to will the means. The imperative is less categorical than hypothetical.

So much then for the demonstration of the utility of *humanitas*. It remains for us to consider the relationship that Arendt posits between the normative elements and the human faculties to which they correspond. Before proceeding further, however, it ought to be noted that this derivation is not found in *The Human Condition*. Indeed, within that text, the normative elements are neither deduced or explicated, but are instead laconically adumbrated and sometimes merely implied. In pursuit of Arendt's derivation of these normative elements we must look to her other writings.

Of particular significance in this regard are Arendt's *Rahel Varnhagen: The Life of a Jewish Woman* and several of her essays, including both her "Politics and Understanding" and her "Philosophy and Politics." Among her later works the most important for helping to elucidate this derivation is her *Lectures on Kant's Political Philosophy* which will figure prominently in chapter 3 of this text. Since the views expressed in the last belong to a distinct period in the development of Arendt's thought our attention here will be confined to the earlier texts.

Insofar as Arendt undertakes to ground her conception of *humanitas* at all, she variously emphasizes either man's capacity for communication or his sociability, the latter grounding man's willingness to engage in communicative action, and the former establishing his capacity to do so.[196] Thus in *Rahel Varnhagen* Arendt presents solidarity, mutual respect, forbearance, and tact as virtues deriving from and sustained by man's inherent sociability, and depicts them as preserving the site of communal realization from the destruction that would otherwise be wrought by the forces of human difference and plurality.[197] Wanting to convey this conception to her readers, Arendt first makes them witness to Rahel's discovery of the vast chasm that yawns between one person and the next, that chasm born of human difference, which by the law of its own nature seems to grow wider with time.[198] But then the narrative reveals another and stronger force that presses in the opposite direction, the force of Rahel's need (and, by inference, the force of the self's need) to be known in all its specificity by the other.[199]

The sociability that overcomes human difference is hardly synonymous, then, with the gregariousness of those animal species whose members are identical to one another. Rather, Arendt singles out that form of sociability which can bind together beings who experience, in a strong way, their difference from one another, and can bind them together in a manner that is fully cognizant of this differentiation.[200] But Arendt also observes that, for two or more to be so bound, the social impulse must reach toward a kind of competency which goes beyond good feeling. Truly sociable humans, she makes clear, must be as skillful as they are gregarious, for it is only by means of skill that the impulse to know and to be known can attain fruition in all its specificity.[201] This is why Arendt hardly bothers in this context to consider the significance of the human equivalent of the herd instinct.[202] Instead, Arendt singles out the human capacity for mutual understanding as the means whereby community might be constituted among persons who, despite their essential differences, are capable of communicating to one another their judgments, thoughts, and feelings.[203]

From this standpoint, the virtues of *humanitas*—solidarity, mutual respect, tact, forbearance and openness to the other—are rightly construed as together signifying (where they are present) a *will* to participate in the process of mutual manifestation. The cognitive capacity which enables one person to understand the next is, however, under no necessity to be so directed. On the assumption that the intellect follows the will and that the will follows a prior interest, it can be observed that the relevant social interest—and thus the degree of willingness to be a party to the process of mutual manifestation—varies widely from one person to another.

Regulatively, however, the function of the normative aspects of *humanitas* does not vary at all. Only where these norms are generally manifest does there exist the possibility of a genuine human encounter. Only where my social relations are governed by these norms can I come to know the other and the other come to know me. Thus, inasmuch as we each have an interest in being known, and each have an interest in the other's abiding by these norms, the rule of reciprocity suggests that both of us ought to abide by them that we might both achieve our ends. In practice, however, the norm of perfect reciprocity will tend to be only imperfectly realized.

Though Arendt never explicitly undertakes to derive her conception of *humanitas* from the conception of action she develops in *The Human Condition*, it seems she might readily have done so. To this end, she could have proceeded by elucidating the implicit linkage between action, as a form of rational communication, and the norms of *humanitas*. The link between the latter terms had already been canvased by her in *Rahel Varnhagen*. Beyond the establishment of this link, she would only have needed to establish the essential identity between political action and other forms of communicative praxis—which also would have been easy enough for her to do.[204] Action, after all, is paradigmatically undertaken not only before others but with others as well. One citizen steps forward, speaks, appeals to his peers to do such and such for this and that reason, and in the process reveals himself—or, more to point, *communicates* himself and his opinions. That dissimilar beings may comprehend one another at all is really quite mysterious, yet such is the essence of action. What then constitutes the precondition of such an occurrence if not the same performative norms that enable communication generally. The norms of *humanitas*, then (for example, solidarity, mutual respect, tact, forbearance, and openness to the other), could have been presented by Arendt as articulating the normative presuppositions that are necessarily implicit in the intersubjective medium of the public space wherever and whenever action achieves its end.

In concluding this section, it should be noted that Arendt also sees in *humanitas* a set of norms that ought to hold not only within but *between* political communities as well.[205] As it is *humanitas* that enables us to live together with persons who differ from ourselves, Arendt would hope that *humanitas* might enable all the peoples of the earth to coexist in a peaceable fashion.[206] Of particular importance in this regard are the norms of respect and solidarity which Arendt would like to see extend from intra- to intercommunal relations.[207]

CONCLUSION

It will be recalled from the introduction that Arendt's conceptualization of the action-ideal was described as an evolving formulation which, over the years, passed through several distinct stages of articulation. Common to the various stages, however, is the basic architectonic structure delineated in this chapter. Uniqueness and uniformity, lasting and passing, and freedom and necessity together constitute an axiological matrix which is implicitly present throughout Arendt's oeuvre even when these terms do not appear.[208] Also implicitly present throughout is Arendt's dichotomy of public and private realms as well as her understanding of the normative relationship that holds between this conceptual pair and the dyads of value. It also follows, then, that the "content problem" continues as well.

In concluding this chapter, we must take a critical look at the "content problem" in order to ascertain whether there is any way of overcoming it which does not do great violence to Arendt's overarching conception of political life.

To begin with, it must be acknowledged that though the conception of action developed in *The Human Condition* is a multifaceted construct, in its dominant tonality it figures primarily as a vehicle for the manifestation of uniqueness. Most often, it is with this dimension in view that Arendt reflects upon how the public space ought to be constituted and upon what types of issues are appropriate for the deliberations which transpire within it.

Formally, Arendt's reflections on the problem of the content of politics are mediated by her dichotomizing dyads. At a conceptual level, having embraced uniqueness, freedom, and lastingness as the three value poles of the public (political) realm, she is led to see the three corollary poles of disvalue as lodged in the private (nonpolitical) realm. Consequently, Arendt concludes that the manifestation of uniqueness in the public sphere will be jeopardized so long as this sphere is "contaminated" by the stuff of species uniformity and biological necessity. In practice, then, Arendt would recommend that politics be purged of much of its traditionally mundane content which, in turn, she would banish to the extrapolitical spheres.

If uniqueness can only be purchased at so high a cost to what today we would consider to be the content of normal politics, it is certainly fair to ask whether it is worth the price. There is, for example, much that free enterprise leaves undone and much by way of social chaos and oppression that it would engender if left wholly unregulated. It is in the nature of modern political economy, moreover, to require that the government perform much ministration to matters of necessity. Arendt may bemoan this fact for being one of the reasons why modern political life is no longer conducive to greatness, but if the government were no longer to perform its "housekeeping" functions, it is not clear who would pick up the slack. Perhaps in ancient Greece the socioeconomic structure was such as to permit a healthy chasm to separate public and private realms, but today any movement in this direction would surely have ruinous consequences. To purchase the "good life" at such a cost to "mere life" would be most problematic—and certainly no broadly democratic polity would articulate such a preference.

For many of Arendt's readers the implications considered in the previous paragraph suffice to consign her theory to irrelevance. There is, however, much of merit in Arendt's analysis and hence my reluctance to adopt a dismissive stance. Instead, I would argue that it is possible to pare away what is most problematic while saving the substance of Arendt's construction from repudiation. In particular, I would argue that it is possible to save the underlying architectonic despite the fact that this same architectonic is responsible for Arendt's untenable rejection of so much of the content of modern politics.

What mars Arendt's deployment of an otherwise acute construct and, at the same time, accounts for Arendt's overly narrow conception of permissible political content is Arendt's failure to grasp the dialectical manner in which the poles of her various dichotomies are related to one another. As noted early in this chapter, Arendt tends to dichotomize, and this penchant for dichotomization enables her to erect a theoretical edifice of great breadth and depth. The problem with this approach, however, becomes manifest when this dichotomizing lens is turned upon reality and produces a conceptual checkerboard of white spaces and black. The grays, in other words, are washed away. Here is uniformity; there is uniqueness. Here is freedom; there is necessity. This is properly public; and that is properly private. Were this the actual character of the reality that is being described, then there would be no grounds for complaint. But it is not. In truth, where Arendt's schema would lead us to anticipate sharp contrasts, a mediating continuum is to be found. Only at the extremes—and the extremes are rare—do phenomena appear to belong strictly to one category or to its opposite. Yet even this is something of an illusion since, as will be argued below, the relationship between the poles is dialectical and mutually entailing. And thus within even a seemingly pure instance of freedom, a moment of necessity is to be found; as within a seemingly pure instance of uniqueness, a moment of uniformity can be discerned. Had Arendt understood the significance of her construction in this way, it is unlikely she would have thought to repair the world by erecting high walls between so-called matters of necessity and so-called matters of freedom. Moreover, she might have attended more closely to the implications that follow from the fact that the very act of making public what was previously private can serve to transform a thing of necessity into a thing of freedom, a transformational possibility that owes both to the dynamical power inherent in making public, and to the potentiality for becoming that is inherent in dialectical being.[209] Had Arendt grasped either of these points, she might have been less insistent upon purging politics of all concern for economic and social questions.[210]

So much then for a theoretical broadside: Arendt has been accused of being insufficiently dialectical in her approach, and it has been suggested that all of the problems that bedevil her construction would be alleviated were she to become more so. It is further alleged that the phenomena she purports to describe by means of her dichotomizing "either/or" can only be adequately described as "both/and." And yet to this point none of these claims have really been substantiated. To this end we must turn our attention to the most pivotal of Arendt's dichotomies, namely to that of freedom and necessity. Only an immanent critique of Arendt's conceptualization can serve to establish the cogency and utility of the theoretical broadside that has been leveled at her. Only an effective critique of the dichotomy of freedom and necessity will enable us to free Arendt's construct from the untenable consequences that follow from the overly sharp formulation of this dichotomy.

As already intimated, Arendt employs the distinction between freedom and necessity in a manner that tends to falsify human experience. As we have seen, Arendt treats these two categories as if they might be profitably employed to distinguish one kind of activity from another, and as if they rightly pertain to two different realms of human practice. Or, more precisely, we have seen that she uses the terms to differentiate a truly human, from a merely animal, sort of activity. What people share in common with "lower" animal life by virtue of their organic nature—for example, the need for, and hence the securing of, nourishment—she denominates as matters of necessity. Indeed, she goes so far as to include within this realm everything humans share with one another at the level of species-life. All else she denominates as matters of freedom. And, of course, matters of necessity properly belong to the private realm while matters of freedom alone are to be permitted entry into the public.

One problem with Arendt's utilization of these terms lies in the fact that, by dichotomizing so sharply, Arendt distorts the truth of human animality. Like an animal, man must eat. But whereas the animal eats in accordance with instinct—both in what it eats and in how it eats—the human does not. Only insofar as he eats because he must is a human's eating necessitated; but inasmuch as he chooses what to eat, and invents rituals regulating how and when to eat, he manifests a degree of freedom. Arendt's dichotomization seems to blind her to this alimentary and paradigmatic fact.[211]

Admittedly, the end of eating is not freely determined. Eating is not some spontaneous "idea" which arises out of human freedom; but how one eats and what one eats—inasmuch as it varies from culture to culture and from one person to the next—does entail the use of freedom and thus individuates as well. It is the same for most human ends. The end is usually given by nature, but the modality of its pursuit, by its very variety, manifests freedom and individuality.

Conversely, however, even those ends whose pursuit Arendt acknowledges to be the rightful stuff of politics are in large part derived from, if not given directly by, nature. Thus, that every polity seeks to secure its own preservation and the preservation of its members is an argument for regarding this end as a natural end.[212] Particular projects or policies that serve this end may arise from a contingent interplay of free wills and free minds, but if not for its being directly or indirectly given by nature, would this end be so readily undertaken by all polities?

There are perhaps some activities that appear to be ends in themselves and thus truly free ends.[213] Poetry, music, philosophy, and whatever else stands in no relation whatsoever to any practical end may be free in this way. Human self-display may be free in this sense as well, having no purpose beyond itself and existing solely for its own sake.[214] And yet one cannot be so sure that these higher activities are not born of natural—if not widely distributed—motives and impulses. That some people have a facility for these activities and others do not would seem to indicate a somatic and perhaps a necessitating basis as well.

Even more problematic, however, than the absolute dichotomization of freedom and necessity is the allied assumption that only matters of freedom and activities that are pursued as ends in themselves are capable of facilitating self-display. Indeed, it is Arendt's own observation that the "who" which gratuitously reveals itself can only reveal itself in relation to a "what" which the "who" transcends, a "what" (or "subject matter") that occasions its manifestation in the first place. Thus, in the political sphere, no less than in any other, a topic of some kind must be placed upon the table, for without something to talk about the self-disclosive interaction that Arendt wants so much to foster cannot occur. The question is just what matters these should be, and in particular whether there is a category of issues that is of such a nature as to make self-manifestation through freedom impossible. In Arendt's view, of course, matters of necessity are to be excluded for just this reason. And yet, I would ask why the "who" cannot transcend such a "what" as ably as it does any other kind of content?

Behind Arendt's wrongheaded handling of the "content problem" lies a failure to differentiate sufficiently between necessitating activities and the political discussion of these same activities. It should be noted, however, that in making this mistake Arendt neglected several of her own insights that should have kept her from so erring. First, she seems to overlook the far-reaching significance of her insight into the fact that the faculties of thought and speech enable humans to transcend those forces that necessitate animals and would necessitate men as well if they did not possess these faculties.[215] At the same time, she also seems to neglect the relevance of her observation that communities will often enable their members to prevail against forces of necessity that would otherwise necessitate them individually.[216] As a consequence, despite the fact that her own insights ought to have suggested otherwise, Arendt argues for the exclusion from public debate of issues that pertain to matters of necessity apparently because she felt that their necessitating aspect would determine the character of such issues' discussion.

Moreover, regarding the mundane issues Arendt would exclude from the political realm, in addition to disagreeing with her position that holds such matters to be inimical to individuating interaction, I would also note that such matters are by their nature more likely to encourage the political participation which is the sine qua non of self-revelatory action in the first place. In fact, it would seem that the "freest" ends, by virtue of their remoteness from matters of organic life and man's natural concerns, would make terribly poor political ends given how unlikely it is that they could ever come to be broadly shared.

It should be seen, then, that Arendt has gone wrong as a consequence of her overly dualistic employment of the conceptual antinomy of freedom and necessity. By inference, it should also be clear that modifications in our understanding of this dichotomy will reverberate throughout Arendt's entire conceptual edifice as a consequence of the centrality of freedom and necessity to the structure Arendt has erected. Thus, for example, if, as our analysis of various public and private activities suggests, freedom and necessity are to be found on both sides of the public-private divide, then transcendence and individuation must be attainable in both realms as well inasmuch as they are achievable through the freedom which belongs to both realms. Obviously, the *forms* of individuation and the *objects* of transcendence available within the private realm are not the same as those available in the public. Nor can the same type of community be created by virtue of the forms and objects which characterize individuation and transcendence within the private realm. Nor, in consequence, would I want to suggest that the dignity-bestowing power of the activities ongoing in this realm favorably compares with that of the activities ongoing in the public space. Thus I am quite ready to agree with Arendt's assertion that true greatness can only become manifest in the public realm because the activities of the private must remain small by comparison. Nonetheless, it must be seen that, given the necessary admixture of freedom and necessity, which follows from the composite nature of man himself, no possibility remains of emptying the public of man's "animal" concerns. Nor would we do well to try.

As by now has been amply demonstrated, it is easy enough to score points against Arendt's overly stark dichotomization of freedom and necessity, and against the consequences that follow from it. On this basis, moreover, we are quite ready to recommend that Arendt's content restrictions be set aside as untenable and to make this recommendation with complete assurance that self-manifestation will not be impeded thereby.

And yet, it might well be that we have dismissed the problem of necessity too readily. To this point, after all, we have critiqued Arendt's conceptualization of freedom and necessity without much attention to the nature of the practical concern that underlies it, a concern whose tenor is perhaps more substantively manifest in the other criteria she employs for determining the adequacy of an object for political debate. In particular, the reader will recall Arendt's emphasis upon the synchronic and diachronic transcendence that objects of political concern ought to engender. (Not only will the fate of a generation, but the destiny of the polity will ideally hang in the balance.) Also accorded prominence is Arendt's insistence that political action properly entails selfless dedication to the commonweal, and the inference that the most adequate political issues are those in which all members of the community share a common and equal interest. Thus, for example, on the basis of these substantive criteria, the fitness of such questions as that of war and peace to political debate depends not merely upon whether or not such questions are appropriate to a realm of freedom but upon whether or not the members of the polity potentially share a common and general interest in the outcome. The issues that most deserve to be allowed entry to the space of freedom, then, are those which place the citizens who are engaged in political debate on as close to an equal footing as possible vis à vis the subject under discussion.[217] Moreover, such issues are, as Arendt herself emphasizes, best suited to facilitate that self-manifestation which arises when members of the polity are together without being for or against one another. In sum, the political issues that meet these criteria are fit for entry into the space of freedom because such issues will enable those who are concerned with them to achieve that transcendence of self-concern that is synonymous with freedom and the basis of the self-display that freedom makes possible.

Measured against these substantive criteria of freedom, the exclusion from the public space of matters of necessity appears in a different light. Thus it becomes clear that the real danger posed by species-uniform animal necessities is not necessarily that these necessities will impose a uniqueness-denying uniformity upon the public realm. Rather, Arendt might more plausibly have been concerned that the politicization of such matters would have the effect of introducing into the polity a spirit of self-interested divisiveness which is likely to undercut that community of concern which she long held to be the sine qua non of any adequately self-revelatory politics. Such division of the community of citizens into competing interest groups, and the concomitant emergence of a "zero-sum" competitive mentality, would tend, in Arendt's view, to "ruin" politics by ruining that elementary "being together with, and neither for nor against" which is the precondition for insuring that a citizen's opinion will manifest "who" he is and not merely what he wants.[218] Arendt may also have feared that, with the introduction of such issues, a citizenry (now disaggregated into mutually antagonistic interest groups) would become engaged in the kind of conflict which highlights group differences while masking the uniqueness of the persons who are the members of these groups. Such fissures of the public space Arendt would counsel us to avoid.

The nature of necessity, then, for all its uniformity qua human need, is such that its entry into politics—at least on this side of some superabundant egalitarian utopia—may occasion a division of the polity along the lines of (for example) economic, racial, or gender differences. Moreover, as Arendt's characterization of class politics in *The Origins of Totalitarianism* makes clear, where such a politics prevails, the chances are minimal that more than the smallest handful of persons will ascend to the heights of self-actualizing participation. Though this view of the matter never explicitly appears in *The Human Condition*, that Arendt long continued to understand the issue as framed in this way may be inferred from her discussion in *On Revolution* of the transformation of "the social question" into a political issue during the French Revolution.[219]

Also, in support of this hypothesis as to Arendt's underlying concern, I would call the reader's attention to Arendt's analogous fears regarding the impact of cultural, racial, and religious differences on the prospects for a healthy political life. The problem with such group differences, where present within a single polity, lies—as in the case of class divisions—in the effect they will have of obscuring the distinctions between persons. These distinctions are, in Arendt's view, the only differences which are of true significance and, as such, deserving of being highlighted in a positive manner. Even if the political life of such a pluralistic polity does not resolve itself into intergroup conflict as Arendt would anticipate, the damage done by conspicuous difference will probably be present. Thus Arendt worries aloud on occasion that the Afro-American may never find a place of dignity in a polity whose members are predominantly white, on account of the fact that, in the eyes of his white audience, no Afro-American individuation will ever be seen.[220] And one can well imagine that Arendt might object to a feminist politics—which is not to say she would object to women participating in politics—on analogous grounds. Her great fear of such divisive issues, in other words, might be explicable as deriving from her anxiety that where such issues come to the fore individuals will be understood not in terms of their uniqueness but solely in terms of their group-specific qualities.[221] Such was the fate of the Jew within the Christian polities of Europe and the fate of the Afro-American in America. Given this conception of the pernicious consequences which group differences and group conflict can have upon what Arendt considers to be politics' most essential dimension, it is hardly surprising that she would seek to keep from the political arena those "species-uniform" or (more to point) group-specific concerns which prove to be so terribly divisive.

In this light, Arendt's reluctance to sanction the use of redistributive or antidiscriminatory politico-economic measures as a means of bringing about among the members of the polity that degree of effective political equality which, in her own view, is the indispensable precondition of a healthy political life is explicable but nonetheless paradoxical. Of course, it must be allowed that along the road to, for example, rough economic, racial, or sexual equality, the more powerful and the less powerful groups would be pitted against one another in a manner which, from Arendt's perspective, promises to be inimical to self-revelatory politics. But at the end of the tunnel it might be expected that the social or economic preconditions of genuine political community and true political action would emerge. That Arendt refuses to countenance such a politics is thus somewhat surprising. And yet Arendt's attitude might be explained as growing out of her familiarity with what she accounted to be the grim consequences that have attended every effort that has been made to solve the social question (or the problem of poverty) by political means.[222] Not only have such efforts proven incapable of solving the economic or social problem that engendered them; more damnable by far in Arendt's view is that wherever such efforts have been undertaken, the destruction of the public sphere and of all healthful political life has unfailingly followed. For Arendt, then, the introduction of economic or social questions into political life and the destruction of the political realm are directly correlated. And thus, while we might infer from Arendt's analysis that rough socioeconomic equality constitutes an extrapolitical precondition of true political community, Arendt herself remains unwilling to countenance any political discussion of economic or social questions—not even for the sake of rendering these issues finally apolitical because moot. For Arendt's taste, the risk is too great that too much else will be mooted besides.

Whatever her motivations and however realistic her fears, Arendt has excluded too much from politics. Perhaps she rightly calculates that the divisive politics of economic, racial, or sexual interest poses a dangerous challenge to the self-manifesting politics she so much esteems. The attempt to keep such issues out of politics has consequences, however, which are intolerable inasmuch as such an attempt will almost necessarily entail excluding from political life—in a de facto if not in a de jure manner—those segments of the population whose conditions of life conspire to insure that, if admitted, they would insist that such issues be placed on the agenda. Nor does it seem likely, even where such persons are excluded, that those who would be permitted entry into the public space would attend to matters of freedom alone. Indeed, it seems more reasonable to expect that, on account of the exclusion of "the many," "the few" will be required to spend much of their "free" time busily engaged in making those rather mundane calculations that are necessary if the status quo is to be preserved. (For example, minimum wage laws become necessary to insure that the poor do not become restless; laws or policies regulating the treatment of slaves become necessary to protect against slave rebellions; laws regulating birth control, marriage, and inheritance become necessary to keep women in their place.) That "ideal" action remains possible even in this kind of situation (as in the slave-sustained polis which Arendt idealizes) presumably owes to the fact that the common interest of the citizenry in (for example) the mode of production will protect against those differences of interest which divide the citizenry into blocs and thus undermine the conditions of self-manifestation.

Ideal action, if ever it seemed worth purchasing at such a price, does so no longer. Arendt, however, fearing the loss to the action potential of humanity—even if only to the talented tenth—is not so sure of this and remains, to the end, ambivalent regarding the policy implications which seem to follow from her anxious concern for action's fate in the modern world. Thus, in general, she seems willing to contemplate, if not always to countenance, all kinds of restrictions on political life for the sake of securing self-revelatory action's long-term future in the world.

As already noted, if in fact a choice had to be made between self-manifestation and other political goods, it is not likely that many would be willing to follow Arendt's lead in this matter. Too much of value would have to be sacrificed, and not merely governmental management of the economy.

In addition, it seems we would be forced to forgo that dimension of political life which turns the public space into the arena in which inter-*group* differences are articulated and at least to some extent are resolved. Such conflicts of interest—be they between religious, cultural, or economic groups—are endemic to social life, and to this point in history no arena but the public space has offered humanity the chance that such conflicts might be peaceably resolved and intergroup solidarity produced.

Ideally, of course, we should prefer a politics that can provide us with goods of both kinds, both those which Arendt esteems and those which politics currently provides. But with reference to this possibility, we have admitted that Arendt's fear that group interests will obscure self-manifestation is hardly groundless. It is nonetheless arguable that Arendt's fear is excessive and based upon an overly narrow conception of self-realization that is blind to the selfhood-constitutive dimensions that are present within the kind of politics she rejects.

One facet of self-realization, which Arendt overlooks entirely, is signified by the increase of self-understanding that political action often brings about. As Hannah Pitkin observes, if who I am may be defined, at least in part, by my loyalties, and if my growing awareness of these loyalties constitutes an increase in self-understanding, then participation in a process in which the real interests of real groups are at stake can make me more fully aware of who I am as my allegiances and sympathies are pulled this way and that in the face of a given issue.[223]

Nor does this process merely facilitate the growth of self-awareness. At the same time, on account of the imperative of political decision, I am often forced to choose, or to mediate, between loyalties which compete or conflict with one another. In either case, my choice, more than telling me who I am, will often have the effect of *changing* who I am, insofar as the shifting conception of my allegiances corresponds to an evolution of my own self-understanding.

Nor is it the case that a concern for the commonweal becomes unimportant amidst the politics of group conflict and division. Indeed, even within such a politics—no less than in Arendt's ideal politics—such a concern would figure as an important criterion, though no longer as the ground from which so much as the goal toward which the best citizen ought to strive in his civic deliberations. The best citizens, in other words, would still be those who make the public good their chief end and do their utmost to keep it in view. And freedom, on this view, comes to be understood not as inherent in one issue as distinguished from another, but as a quality of the citizen who overcomes his natural propensity to selfishness and transcends toward a primary concern for his community as synchronically and diachronically comprehended. Moreover, with Arendt, I would allow that in such moments of transcendence toward the common and the lasting, the citizen will manifest "who" he essentially is. No longer, however, is the path to the properly self-revelatory, disinterested, and publicly concerned standpoint eased by a predetermined range of subject matter that has been tested for its capacity to facilitate an easy passage from interest to disinterest.

Admittedly, under the aegis of the kind of politics that is being discussed, it will be harder for a citizen to adhere to this exalted perspective, especially when the magnitude of self- or group interest to be overcome is great. And, in fact, most members of the polity will neither rise, nor aspire to rise, to this level of public-spiritedness. But to note this is only to take cognizance of the fact that politics serves other ends besides that of fostering self-realization. First and foremost it serves to facilitate a process of strategic conflict by means of which important issues are resolved along the lines of relative force and self-interested compromise. Hence it ought not to come as any surprise that most members of a polity that is home to such a politics will behave in the rather predictable manner that such a politics entails; and yet, the more important point in this context is that some members will not. Nor, however, should this relative infrequency be troubling: as even Arendt would have to allow, greatness—by definition—is always rare.

Admittedly, against the background of this reality, an uncertain fate awaits those who do manage to transcend the pull of interest and rise to a standpoint that privileges the interests of the commonweal. What they achieve by way of enhanced self-actualization and self-understanding may not be paralleled by an equally enhanced self-*manifestation*. As Arendt's dynamic conception of the public space as a realm of appearance makes clear, what the actor can achieve by way of self-manifestation depends as much upon *how* he is *perceived* as upon *what* he does. And thus it must be acknowledged that where the disinterested passion of true citizenship is only infrequently manifest, citizens, who are in effect bred to the cynical belief that vice lurks behind every display of virtue, will likely be incapable of perceiving true citizenship even when it does appear before them.

That such a politics might undercut the dynamic grounds of self-manifestation—from the side of the actor as much as from the side of the spectator—ought not to blind us, however, to the fact that the existential achievement of one who does rise to the proper civic standpoint is not thereby diminished. Indeed, where the obstacles in the way of the ascent to this standpoint are increased, as they would be in the kind of politics that we are considering, the consequent existential achievement is all the greater, and, by Arendt's own criteria, those who do manage it ought to be considered great for having done so. That the conditions which would ideally assure them of applause are lacking ought hardly to matter.

In sum, then, I would accept, in broad outline, Arendt's characterization of the telos of the political space: Human dignity, freedom, and individuation are to be looked for in the political realm; self-transcendent self-display of a magnitude that makes such self-display synonymous with the attainment of greatness are to be looked for as well. Only Arendt's restrictive conception of permissible political content is rejected outright. The basis for her position on this point is sympathetically understood yet, in my view, it must be rejected nonetheless.

Part Two

Beyond World Alienation

Prelude

In chapter 1, I set forth, in the broadest terms, Arendt's overarching matrix of value. I elucidated the character of political action and attended to the vision of political community which, in *The Human Condition*, Arendt portrays as commensurate with it. In pointed criticism, I suggested that Arendt's conception of what alone ought to be regarded as the proper object of political concern was overly restrictive and fundamentally misguided. Were this weakness of Arendt's conception an absolutely necessary concomitant of her fundamental approach to politics, and hence incorrigible from within the parameters of Arendt's paradigm, then the worth of the whole would be placed in jeopardy. At the end of the last chapter, however, I argued that Arendt's conception of politics is flexible enough to enable us to escape from what seems most pernicious. Even a politics that is much concerned with questions of economic distribution or with other matters of necessity—as Arendt would describe them—need not undercut the self-revelatory and existential dimension of political action. Or so I argued against Arendt's view which, if put into practice, would surely vitiate what she hoped to invigorate and purify.

In beginning part two, however, it is important to observe that for all the urgency that has been attached to the "content problem," it is not a problem that arises for Arendt. Other weaknesses, or shortcomings, were apparent to her, and what they were can be inferred from the trajectory of her writings in the years following the completion of *The Human Condition*.[1] More important, however, to our overarching project of tracing the evolution of Arendt's conception of politics is the fact that as a result of her efforts to improve upon her original conception of action, a conception of action emerges that differs significantly from the one that emerged in *The Human Condition*.

The task in this introduction to the discussion of Arendt's later work, however, is not to detail the nature of the changes wrought in the original conception but rather to elucidate the basis for the shift in direction which the later work manifests.

In our discussion of action we saw that Arendt is of the opinion that the flourishing of action depends—among other things—upon the actors' feel for the lastingness of the world and upon their willingness to make the concerns of the public world their own. It was also intimated that in order to lead a public life citizens must possess the kind of common sense that conveys a feeling for the plurality of persons and for the public world's intersubjectively grounded objectivity and reality. But in the modern age, Arendt argues, both common sense and the kind of world orientation we have just adumbrated have broken down.[2]

Had we attended in detail to Arendt's comparative analysis of labor, work, and action we would have learned that the loss of common sense and worldliness—which in *The Origins of Totalitarianism* Arendt had linked to forces at work in mass society—is more particularly (and, perhaps, more fundamentally) associated with the triumph of "the laboring animal" who reigns supreme in the contemporary society of the jobholder.[3] To set forth Arendt's analysis in detail would lead us too far afield. Let it suffice, however, for us to note that, by Arendt's estimation, the conditions of the laboring life are inimical to worldliness and plurality. The nature of the labor process, she argues, presupposes the essential similarity, and hence the interchangeability, of all persons to a degree that strips those who labor under such conditions of the awareness of their own uniqueness and that of others.[4] Moreover, lacking this sense for human plurality, such persons are ill-equipped to acquire the common sense that presupposes such awareness and are likely to become easy prey for the ideologies to which those lacking common sense are most susceptible.[5] Arendt also insists that the laborer's life-activity is devoid of the experiences that impart an appreciation for enduring things and for what deserves to endure, both of which are, in her view, essential presuppositions of worldliness.[6] Finally, she defines mass society as the public realm which comes into existence when the preponderance of those who enter this realm are lacking worldliness, a feel for human plurality, and common sense.[7] It is such a society that has been constituted by the masses of jobholders who populate the public realm in the present day.

In *The Human Condition* the analysis of labor is followed by the analysis of work which in turn is followed by the analysis of action. Action, of course, is most esteemed by Arendt, and it is easy to infer from the logic of her presentation that she believes that *homo politicus* (that is, man qua political actor)—who has been eclipsed in the modern age first by *homo faber* and more recently by *animal laborans*—must be restored to the primacy that he truly deserves. But if our society is the society of the jobholder, and if the conditions of his quotidian existence operate to vitiate the presuppositions of plurality-manifesting and world-aware political action, then it becomes questionable whether the resuscitation of political action of the kind Arendt esteems is even possible.[8]

As if to underscore the difficulties that stand in the way of action's rejuvenation, in the final part of *The Human Condition* Arendt takes up once more the problem of modern man's worldlessness and lack of common sense, though this time approaching the problem both phenomenologically and in terms of its impact on the philosophical and social thought of the modern age.[9] In this section, Arendt proceeds by tracing the worldlessness of modern man to what she describes as "world alienation" and to the loss of common sense this has engendered.[10] Looking to the moment in which the modern age first dawned, Arendt observes that Galileo's discovery of the earth's rotation around the sun precipitated a crisis in the realm of thought, a crisis which ushered in the modern age as it deprived man of his faith in the ability of his senses to tell him what the world is like.[11] From this loss of trust in the evidence of the senses arose a search for new grounds of certainty, a search whose tenor and direction are most fully exemplified for Arendt by Descartes' recourse to introspection.[12]

Descartes, whom Arendt (following Heidegger) regards as the exemplary philosopher of the modern world, founded his new terra firma on the indubitable "*cogito ergo sum*," and by means of "clear and distinct ideas" was able to exit from his epistemological nightmare.[13] For Arendt, however, Descartes' solution is seriously flawed by the fact that it entails the abandonment of the world of common experience and common sense.[14] Hitherto, Arendt argues, reality had been intersubjectively constituted and guaranteed; the truth of one's perceptions was tested against the perceptions of others; what passed this test—the test of common sense, really—was held to be true and became part of common sense. By contrast, Descartes' truth is gleaned from the worldless data of introspection. From this perspective, the epistemological relevance of belonging to a common world is undercut as common sense is either replaced by private apperception or comes to be redefined in terms of mental processes (such as logic) that are common to all persons by virtue of their being human.[15]

For Arendt, the consequences that follow from the Cartesian shift are especially significant because they are so very much at odds with the epistemological preconditions of political action. In particular, Arendt is troubled by the fact that once common sense is redefined in terms of, for example, logic, truth can be pursued without any need for dialogue with others; she is also troubled by the fact that from this standpoint the relevance of human plurality to truth—a relevance that was implicitly upheld so long as truth had to be tested in discourse with others—is denied.[16] Moreover, she sees in the worldless solipsism that results once private apperception is made the measure of truth a solvent that makes for the disintegration of the common world's commonly validated reality.

The rise of Cartesian introspection is, however, only one of the momentous consequences that Arendt traces to Galileo's discovery. Of almost equal importance is the new process-conception of nature which is associated with the new science, a conception which in turn gives rise to the development of a new social science that looks upon the politico-historical world from a similarly process-oriented perspective.[17]

In Arendt's account of the emergence of this new perspective, Galileo figures only as a catalyst. Of greater significance is the fact that the new science, which develops in the wake of Galileo's discoveries, sought to get at the truth behind the appearances by means of experiments that were able to *produce* the phenomena which the old science had only been able to contemplate from without.[18] But that which was produced as an *effect* of an experiment was implicitly conceived of as the *product* of a process; and by analogy, nature, which for so long had been conceived of as a realm of final ends, was itself reconceived *first* as the product of a single overarching process, and eventually as a single unceasing process that sweeps away all finality.[19]

Arendt also emphasizes the importance of the fact that the new science had as its goal the construction of a unified field theory that might subsume under a simple set of quantifiable laws phenomena which—in accordance with the evidence of appearances—had been hitherto conceived of as qualitatively and ontically distinct.[20] This search for a universal science that might render explicable the nature of the underlying processes was, and continues to be, most evident in the field of physics; but, as Arendt observes, it was not long before the same theoretical standpoint and aspirations were brought to bear upon the phenomena of the politico-historical world as well.[21] Certainly this was the ambition of the social sciences, and of economics, in particular. And in the writings of Marx all of the gross particulars of world history are subsumed under the aegis of a single overarching process.[22]

As one would expect, Arendt is highly critical of the latter developments because she rightly regards the perspective that would reduce the play of appearances to an underlying law-governed process as inimical to the realities of human plurality, freedom, and action. What places action directly at risk is the fact that, from this perspective, the phenomenal reality of the world, of the common world, of the lasting world as that object on behalf of which citizens are urged to dedicate and even sacrifice their lives, is undermined as it is transformed into an effect of some overarching natural process. For that which denies the ontological specificity of the world removes the object which alone can call action into being. Hence, the basis for Arendt's repudiation of this development.

From Arendt's analysis of the modern age it follows that the resuscitation of action will require more than the creation of new public spaces. New spaces without a new ethos and a new logos will hardly be productive of the kind of action that Arendt so esteems. In particular, it is clear that world alienation, and the process-standpoint that denies both the value and the potential permanence of the world, must be overcome before men will be capable of acting again on its behalf. But how is this to be done?

In part it might be done by improving civic education, and by strengthening the cultural media and institutions that are capable of symbolizing a polity's potential immortality and of instilling a commitment to the realization of this potential. Indeed, we will see that Arendt pursues this approach in much of the work that follows *The Human Condition*. And yet, because world alienation also entails alienation from the public space (or epistemological field) within which citizens gather to speak and act, it should be clear that more than the world's object status must be secured if action is to be rendered tenable.

As we have seen, the world's status as a reality-bestowing space of appearance was ruined when the validity of the common sense that had facilitated the discursive sharing of this world was called into question by the new philosophy and the new science. For the space of appearance can bestow "reality" upon what appears within it only so long as "reality" is held to be the product of the varying perspectives and positions of those who speak and act within this epistemological field; but the common sense that guaranteed the truth (or validity) of this reality has been rejected by the modern age. This common sense (or community sense) which had served to connect unique individuals to one another through a common world has disappeared, and common sense has come to be redefined as a private and worldless sense. Clearly, then, the latter conception of common sense must be superseded, and some variant of the former revived, if action is to be resuscitated.

Just how Arendt would recommend that either of these things be accomplished is not made clear in *The Human Condition*. Indeed, one arrives at the end of the work unsure of the practical implications. In the final chapters Arendt has presented world alienation, the withering of common sense, and the rise of the process-standpoint as a cul de sac from which modernity seems unable to escape. What then is the practical significance of the conception of action that Arendt develops at the center of this work? Should we take the book's bleak conclusion to be indicative of a fundamental pessimism about action's future prospects?

Had Arendt wanted to impart to her readers a belief in the possibility of action's renewal, she should have pointed the way beyond the current situation and toward a strong conception of worldliness and toward a renewed "postmodern" conception of common sense that might sustain political action and the world. In *The Human Condition*, for reasons known to her alone, she does not do this. In the work that follows it, however, she does. Perhaps, in 1958, the path beyond the modern age that could make the world once again fit for action was not yet clear to her. But it is quite clear that in her subsequent work she places a good deal of emphasis upon just those elements of the earlier work which rendered its applicability most problematic.

In chapters 2 and 3, then, we will focus upon Arendt's efforts in the wake of *The Human Condition* to think through the nature and the renewal of worldliness, and the relationship between common sense and political action, efforts that become prominent in her work as she looks to facilitate the realization of the action-ideal in an age that in many ways is antithetical to such an undertaking. We will also attend to the further development of Arendt's conception of action that comes about as a result of the attention she pays to worldliness and common sense.

At the same time, on a level of lesser theoretical priority, we will want to ascertain whether Arendt's efforts to address the problem of world alienation make it possible for her to overcome other inadequacies of conceptualization that, while unrelated to those we have discussed so far, nonetheless call into question the practical tenability of the action-ideal. As I discuss below, in her first formulation of the action-ideal—perhaps as a consequence of the mighty emphasis she places upon the self-revelatory dimension of action—Arendt pays scant theoretical attention to the relationship between action and the world's long perpetuation. Given Arendt's sensitivity to the importance of the world's stability in *The Origins of Totalitarianism*, it is rather surprising to find that Arendt bequeaths to her readers a conception of action that places action's worldly house at risk. I would argue, however, that the course of her subsequent work indicates that she became aware of this shortcoming and sought to ameliorate it. In the second part of this work, tracing Arendt's endeavor of rectification will be our penultimate concern.

In the previous paragraph I suggested that in *The Human Condition* Arendt's emphasis upon action's self-revelatory function seems to engender a neglect of the relationship between action and the world's upkeep. One indication of this is the fact that for all the attention Arendt pays in

The Human Condition to the individual and to the *need* of each citizen to enter the political space, she pays strikingly little attention to what transpires within the public space once all the citizens have assembled there. Each citizen, we know, properly enters the public space with two ends: to disclose himself before his peers and to pursue the public good in common with them. But it remains unclear *how* these two potentially conflicting ends are to be pursued concurrently in a manner that insures the satisfaction of each. How, in short, are citizens and polities to navigate between the premium each citizen rightly places upon the revelation of his uniqueness and the need to sustain the continuity of the common world through common action? In *The Human Condition* this question is unaddressed.

Nor does Arendt explain how a polity framed along lines commensurate with the conception of action that she elaborates is to make decisions and achieve that consensus of opinion which the formation of state policy presupposes.[23] So attentive is Arendt, within *The Human Condition*, to the disclosive dimension of politics that she seems at times to have entirely forgotten that the polity has another role to play not as a world, but in the world. Indeed, within *The Human Condition* this side of things is almost completely overlooked. How her ideal polity will function as a state in a world of states in which action must be timely lest one's world be destroyed is never considered.[24]

Ideally, of course, the will to self-display will be fused with a will to do the public good in a manner which should insure that action does not degenerate into an agonal and egoistical free-for-all in which various actors promote policies for the sake of private gain and public acclaim in a manner that jeopardizes the long term viability of the polity. But how unlikely it is that such an ideal can be sustained over time is more than intuitively obvious.[25] Arendt's most cherished Athens was itself done in by such agonal egoism. That egos driven by the desire to achieve fame or power will be prone to conflict in ways that are less than conducive to the long-term health of the polity is sufficiently self-evident that Arendt should have explicated in greater detail how these foreseeable conflicts are to be resolved in a way commensurate with both the public good and the self-revelatory ideal. At the same time, it should be evident that short of developing a detailed conception of the political process, this matter could not be addressed within the parameters of the conception of action that Arendt delineates in *The Human Condition*. Fortunately, Arendt establishes a framework for developing a close-order conception of the political process in her later work.

But such a conception must do more than mediate between conflicting egos and the common good; in addition, such a conception must rationalize, and thus subsume, the seemingly inevitable conflict between man's quest for individuation and his need to live in a lasting frame, a conflict that is not addressed in *The Human Condition*. Where these two elements do not conflict this can only be because the actor pursues his individuation in a manner which does not lead him into conflict with the lasting frame of the world. But what exactly does this mean? There are after all many ways of expressing one's inmost essence that entail, at least in their first moment, the negation of that which is already. Especially when it is seen that the web of norms, values, and practices—or web of worldly common sense—which Arendt would have the citizen act to sustain is at least as much a part of the world as its material frame, it becomes clear that one does not need to be a bomb thrower to be a destroyer of worlds.[27] Words alone are sufficient to rent the fabric of the worldly web.

Indeed, one need not be a nihilist to find oneself in opposition to the world's continuous reproduction. Whoever would inscribe his name upon the honor roll of history, whoever would merely signify the uniqueness of his existence by the novelty and spontaneity of his words and deeds can be seen as an antagonist of what existed *in*—or as the world—before he arrived. Because the world is old and "wills" that the present and the future be merely its continuation, the individual, who is new and wills a future out of his natality, wills against the natural will of the world. He who would assert himself by destroying the world completely, and he who would insert himself by willing a new value or end, the one as much as the other, may, by their willing, undermine an essential aspect of what accounts for the continuity of the world.[28]

It is important to underscore that the threat to the world is posed not only by action that falls away from the ideal by willing mere material satisfaction or the sating of some animal need, but also by action of the highest, noblest, and most politically creative type: in *On Revolution* Arendt considers Jefferson's suggestion that there be a constitutional convention once in every generation in order that no generation of Americans be deprived of the thoroughly invigorating experience of action on the grandest scale.[29] In this impulse to wipe the slate clean in order to build afresh, Arendt perceives the natural bent of a "man of action" for the altogether new, and his natural antipathy for whatever is already of long-standing.[30] In part, it is an impulse to do again and to do better, but even more it is an urge to do differently—almost for the sake of novelty itself. While she acknowledges that this is the sort of action that men of action would naturally want to take, she cannot accept Jefferson's proposal as a wise one for it would collapse the framework of the world whose very durability makes it a vehicle of transcendence and a spur to action in the first place.[31] Apparently, Arendt had become aware that even action of the noblest sort and the continuity of the world may be at odds.

There is much in action, then, that makes it a potential nemesis of the public space, of common sense, and of the world. It may also be the mode of activity which answers to man's highest aspirations, but there seems to be little inherent within political action as it is conceived within *The Human Condition* to insure that it will be of the world-sustaining and commonsense-sustaining variety. Indeed, there is much to suggest the opposite, that is, that the drives harnessed by action may undermine the framework out of which it arose in the first place. Thus with every action there exists the risk that no further action will be possible in its wake. Within *The Human Condition*, however, such problems are not considered.

As intimated earlier in this section, it is my contention that Arendt's later work does in large measure address the problems to which my analysis of the shortcomings of *The Human Condition* has pointed. In particular, I would argue that Arendt rectifies most of the weaknesses inherent in her early conceptualization of the relation between action and the worldly frame and makes up for her original inattention to the related dimension of consensus formation. The latter, I would add, is most consequential for the former because it permits Arendt to conceptualize how the political process that produces consensus and continuity can at the same time enable the actor to achieve the manifestation of his uniqueness.

More important, however, is my contention that Arendt's late work ought to be understood both as the product of her effort to conceptualize the transcendence of world alienation and, by inference, as the product of her desire to escape the pessimistic implications we discerned in the last section of *The Human Condition*. As we have seen, world alienation and the breakdown of common sense are mutually entailing. If action is to renew the world and is itself to be renewed, then, a postmodern conception of the common sense that connects citizens to one another and enables them to share a common life and a common world is required. From the beginning of the modern age, however, the requisite common sense has been under assault and, by Arendt's estimation, today it is wholly lacking. In her later work Arendt seeks to provide the theoretical basis for its restoration, a restoration which if successful will also overcome world alienation as it renders her conception of political action tenable for our time.

With these purposes in mind, in chapters 2 and 3 we will focus upon the two rather divergent stratagems Arendt employs to this end. It will also be seen that these two stratagems also represent two stages in her endeavor to reconceptualize the relation between action and the world.[32] In the final analysis it will be seen that these stratagems (and stages) are indeed complementary, though perhaps only in the final analysis.

In chapter 2 we attend to works that are chronologically proximate to *The Human Condition*, works which represent Arendt's first effort to discern how we might escape the cul de sac of world alienation and release action's potential in the modern world. In these works, however, in a conceptual move at variance with what a reader of *The Human Condition* might expect, Arendt tackles the problem of world alienation without explicitly addressing the logically prior problem of reconstituting common sense. Notwithstanding the fact that in *The Human Condition* Arendt seemed to make the latter's restoration the sine qua non for overcoming the former, in most of the works that follow close in its wake she focuses upon, and champions the contemporary relevance of, the conceptual and institutional matrix (including tradition, authority, and culture) that had served to connect men to the common world before the advent of modern world alienation, as if the breakdown of common sense did not render future recourse to this matrix most problematic.[33] Ultimately, as part of this stratagem, Arendt counsels us to undertake the kind of epochal and world restorative action that might in a single instant restore this matrix and thereby overcome world alienation. In effect, she argues that such a revolution would restore that world-aware common sense which the healthy manifestation of political action presupposes. But this is only an inference, because in these works the problem of common sense in the modern age is hardly considered while instead Arendt focuses upon the problem of envisioning action in a manner commensurate with the long-term maintenance of the world's continuity.[34] Only our developmental approach to Arendt's work makes it clear that Arendt's broader purpose in these same texts is to think through the transcendence of world alienation and the resuscitation of common sense as well.

Arendt's second stratagem—that is, the "third way" of the introduction to part one—is much more straightforward and becomes the object of our attention in chapter 3. In that chapter we turn to those texts in which Arendt develops her analysis of common sense and political judgment, an analysis which—contrary to the opinion of some—seems to me to have been engendered by her belief that action's prospects in the contemporary world will remain dim until a post-Cartesian and post-Platonic conception of common sense is articulated. The approach taken in these works, because it directly counters the loss of common sense that Arendt so bemoans in *The Human Condition*, is the approach that our analysis of that text should have led us to anticipate. The case can also be made that, on a level of lesser theoretical priority, Arendt's analysis of judgment and common sense are born of her desire to redress her earlier neglect of the problems of the political process proper, that is, the problems of policy and consensus formation, and of political argument more generally. In chapter 3 we will attend to both of these aspects, and to certain questions that are brought to the fore by the works that are to be discussed in chapter 2 as well.

Chapter Two

Constituting A
Worldly Depth

THE ETHOS OF WORLDLINESS

Where world alienation and the attendant loss of common sense are present action will either wither or become monstrous. Because Arendt would have us avoid either outcome, she endeavors to determine how world alienation can be overcome. Chief among the means she discerns is the restoration of the world's stability and continuity. In the works to be considered in this chapter, we will explore the role that this insight plays in the period that follows the publication of *The Human Condition*.

Arendt had long been mindful of the relation between world alienation and the breakdown of worldly order and stability. In *The Origins of Totalitarianism*, for example, Arendt had traced the masses' totalitarian susceptibility to the breakdown of common sense—and thus, by implication, to the world alienation—that occurred under the impact of a world in flux and chaos. Ideological appeals could be successful, Arendt argues, only because, in an unreliable and disordered world, the masses had taken refuge in that worldless logical faculty to which ideology appeals. By inference, had the world been less disordered, world alienation would have been less pervasive and the consequences that followed from it would presumably have been less horrific.

World alienation and its relation to the loss of worldly order and stability also figure as matters of concern in *The Human Condition*. In that text Arendt makes clear that action only thrives when the public world is a stable and lasting world because where these attributes are lacking so too will be lacking the presuppositions of the actor's diachronic self-transcendence and the fixed standards of worth which properly guide those who seek immortalization. As our discussion of the last section of *The Human Condition* indicated, in a world of rapid change in which normative discontinuities proliferate, world alienation is not unnaturally the result, and flight from the insecurity of the world to the certainty of worldless mental processes is to be expected.[1]

While Arendt allots lexical priority in her discussion of the modern age to several discrete factors that she regards as uniquely implicated in the rise of modern world alienation, this ought not to blind us to the fact that world alienation can be precipitated as readily by the generic attributes of action. That Arendt herself understood this to be the case can be inferred from her observation that since antiquity most philosophers have repudiated action and retreated from the world of public affairs because they regarded action's boundlessness, unpredictability, and irreversibility as sources of the world's disorder.[2] In the prelude to part two, I only added to this litany by pointing out that the action-engendering imperative of self-disclosure might prove ruinous of the lasting frame of the world, and thus capable of precipitating alienation from the world, as well.

Ultimately, the root of the world's disorder, and of world alienation, is human plurality and the anarchic or unprecedented quality it imparts to every self-manifesting act. But the latter cannot be utterly sacrificed in the endeavor to bring about an end to world alienation for such a solution would deprive action of that which Arendt prizes most highly. Quite aware then—at least at the outset—of the fine line that must be tread when laying restrictions upon action for the sake of engendering future action, Arendt sets out in the period following *The Human Condition* to explore the conceptual bases of world stability and continuity. Clearly, her hope is that, by means of the institutional correlates of such concepts, world alienation can be overcome and conditions conducive to actions' renewed effluence might be secured. At the same time, however, because action itself—for the reasons considered in the previous paragraph—constitutes a chief source of the world's instability, Arendt also attends to the relation between action and the world's stability and focuses particularly upon ways of making action less of a threat to its own worldly preconditions.

That the actor and his deeds may prove destructive of the world's continuity or stability is a fact of no small importance; but of equal if not greater importance is the fact that the actor and his deeds are the source of whatever continuity and stability the world does possess. To clarify this paradox, and to set the stage for the analysis that is to follow, we would do well to reflect upon this relationship between the actor and the world.

In Arendt's work primacy is given in turn to action as the vehicle of the actor's self-realization and then to action as the means of the world's long perpetuation. The world figures in both accounts but in each it figures differently. In chapter 1 we explored what must be acknowledged as the dominant approach within Arendt's work. There we saw how, out of a meditation upon the substance of human fulfillment, Arendt derives a conception of the public world whereby it is made the site of human realization. Though the main point of emphasis throughout was upon man and his needs, we saw that Arendt conceived of the human telos in such a way that the relative autonomy of the world was never forgotten. Indeed, one of the cardinal elements in Arendt's conception of man was that his fulfillment is only possible through a self-overcoming which binds him to an object which is fundamentally other, an object which is either the world itself or provided by the world. Thus, in Arendt's view, the very nature of man is such that his self-realization requires that the world remain fundamentally autonomous, distinct, and alien. Only where this alterity is maintained can the movement of man from self-concern to world concern, a movement that Arendt sees as the precondition of human excellence and self-realization, come about. Where the autonomy of the world is wholly subordinated to man's self-concern, then, the road to transcendence is blocked and man is diminished.

Man, then, needs the world; he needs to participate in its common life; and he needs for its objects to be other than he would naturally give himself if he hopes to rise to the heights of his potential being. This is the lesson brought home by Arendt in *The Human Condition*, a lesson we canvased in chapter 1.

In Arendt's subsequent work, however, a shift of emphasis can be detected. Action is no longer considered exclusively in terms of self-realization. Because action that fails to secure the world's long perpetuation and stability can engender the kind of world alienation that ruins self-revelatory action, as well as the world, it becomes incumbent upon Arendt to focus upon the role of action as the agency of the world's continuous viability. As a result, action comes to be reconceived: though she continues to conceive of it as the medium of the actor's self-revelation, she also sees that action must either be conducive to the world's long duration or else undercut its own worldly presuppositions. At issue, then, for Arendt, in the works to be considered in this chapter, is the conceptualization of action as the vehicle of the world's interests. How, she asks, ought the right relationship between action and the world to be conceived? And, as importantly, she asks, how are action's tendencies that frequently make it the means of the world's corruption and dissolution to be overcome?

But for the actions of men there could be no world, no polis, no cultural construct. But for the specific efforts made by actors in every generation the world could not last. All that the world has been in the past, or will be in the future, has come about, or will come about, through the efforts of actors who, in every present, give the world their attention.[3] Yet the interests of men and the interests of the world are not necessarily the same. Nor can the world, even at a particular point in time, be equated with some specific group or generation, nor with their business.[4] What marks the chief difference between the world and its inhabitants is not so much their objects of concern, which may be the same if men choose to make what matters to the world matter to themselves. What marks the difference is not even the fact that the world comprises within itself a set of institutions, artifacts, and conceptual constructs which have no counterpart within the lives of men except insofar as they participate in the life of the world. Nor is the key distinction between what can be shared in common and what is necessarily a matter of self-concern.[5] All of these elements are comprised within the difference, but are themselves not the root of it.

What marks the difference between the world and its inhabitants as ontical, thoroughgoing, and fundamental arises out of the discontinuity in their respective experiences of time. As man's natural time sense follows from the brevity of his mortal existence, so too does the inherent time sense of the politico-cultural world follow from its presumptively long duration. On account of its potential immortality a polity may, in a sense, be said to dream, desire, and choose as no mere mortal can. Already generations are spanned by the reach of its memory, and limitless generations more are encompassed within its will to endure: a person of exceptional foresight may act with an eye to some point twenty or thirty years distant. Yet a nation that would act with analogously farsighted prudence often sets its sights upon goals that cannot be reached but in the course of several generations. Of course, it is always possible, and even likely, that any given polity and its citizens will refuse this long-term perspective and craft policy with a view to the short-term horizon instead. By Arendt's measure, however, to follow the latter path is to miss the mark. The polity will only be as it ought to be, and make available to its citizens the existential rewards that it ought to make available, when it lives and breathes according to the rhythms of designedly long duration. Such, Arendt declares, is the path that is commensurate with the polity's true nature.

Thus Arendt would have us view the world, and its common objects, as common not to a generation but to *generations*.[6] All who share in the life of the polity at any point in time are thus encompassed within its identity. Accordingly, when the polity acts, it ought to do so with a will to perpetuity. When it undertakes, for example, a public building program whose completion may be several generations hence, it should not hesitate as any mortal would before beginning a task of such magnitude. In choosing to set its sights on such a distant mark the polity acts not by a rule of self-sacrifice, but by the rule of destiny.

The essence of the world, then, is not the same as the essence of the men who are its denizens for a while. Nonetheless, unless the world proves able to marshall the resources and the will of the men who in every generation must be raised to full citizenship and to conscientious political stewardship then the world's essence, destiny, and, indeed, its very being shall be destroyed. For, as Arendt goes to great lengths to prove, the entities within the politico-historical universe are moved neither by laws of necessity, nor by hidden forces, nor by arcane determinisms that raise up and cast down men and nations. What happens within the realm of the politico-historical happens only by virtue of what men do or fail to do.[7]

Action is the mother of the historical which, in this instance, means that the polity's viability from day to day and year to year will depend not on the luminosity of its essence so much as upon the practical and caring action of its citizenry. In short, men are objectively responsible for the fate of the polity. It is a further inference, that follows from Arendt's analytic of action, that even those who sit on the sidelines and do nothing are accountable for what they fail to do.[8] When, in *The Human Condition*, Arendt inveighs against judging an action by its consequences she could hardly mean to pardon well-meaning political stupidity.[9] Rather she likely has in mind the situation where the would-be actor's presumption of his own *inconsequence* leads ostensibly well-meaning men to forgo action. They tell themselves that they would be risking their necks, their reputation, or their time in a hopeless cause which could not possibly succeed. Yet, if Arendt correctly understands the nature of action and the role of the contingent deed in precipitating the most unexpected results, then, this decision to sit on one's hands is a wholly misdirected form of prudence.[10]

Of every man it can be asked, "when the house was on fire, what did you do?" He who poured the gasoline; he who struck the match; he who did nothing to prevent it; and he who did not try to put it out—are all rightly held responsible for what occurred. Admittedly, one man may be unable to squelch a firestorm when it is raging, but had he been vigilant from the beginning, had he been paying attention when the arsonists first arrived, it is likely that the conflagration could have been prevented. In every generation, then, citizens of a polity are like night watchmen upon whose vigilance the integrity of the public house depends. Woe unto them, and woe unto the polity, if they doze off, for they may awaken within a house that has already become engulfed in flames.

It is lucky for the world that the ontical difference between it and the men upon whom it must rely for continuous superintendence seems to dovetail so nicely with the ideal of civic action which Arendt has identified as meeting man's deepest and most exalted needs. That this nexus between the highest interest of man and the long-standing interest of the world exists, even in theory, is a point of great importance for Arendt's project.

The problem of course, is that the real and the ideal are likely to remain apart unless some artifice is employed by which to narrow the gap. In general, the root of the difficulty stems from the fact that the ideal orientation and the real tendencies of action are often diametrically opposed. At the ideal point, man qua citizen would comprehend the public interest, take it for his own, and promote it with all the passion that by instinct he would bring to his private concerns.[11]

Specifying the ideal, however, is one thing; getting there is another. From one standpoint it appears that the heart of the problem is motivational. By nature most persons are not disposed to take an interest in politics and are even less concerned with the commonweal, let alone ready to sacrifice their own interests on behalf of it. Thus a major task faced by any polity which would constitute its political life on a broadly participatory foundation is to engender a will to participation and dedication to the commonweal. Arendt's own stratagems in this regard are clear enough. In *The Human Condition* and *On Revolution* her appeal on behalf of political participation is eudaemonistic. Elsewhere she appeals to conscience, the sense of duty, and the fear of shame as motives conducive to civic-minded political activity. We can infer that in an Arendtian polity the political socialization process would seek to enlist similar motives to this same end.[12]

At another level, however, it should be apparent that the problem is not entirely motivational. An active commitment—which ought to reign once the motivational problem has been overcome—must at the same time be an informed commitment, a commitment to a public interest that has been defined as comprising a specific constellation of values, principles, and process-norms. Had Arendt not so much emphasized the importance of maintaining political continuity—which might itself be defined as the

continuous transgenerational perpetuation of these selfsame values, principles, and process-norms—the cognitive/axiological dimension of political
socialization would have merited close attention, nonetheless, for being
the medium by means of which an informed commitment to the public
good is constituted. The premium placed upon the maintenance of long-
term political continuity only serves to redouble the significance of this
dimension inasmuch as it becomes vitally important to predestine the
tenor, direction, and consistency of public affairs. That the public space
within which the links of continuity are to be forged continues to be conceived of, by Arendt, as the site of self-revelation would seem to render
the task of political socialization absolutely indispensable, lest without it
the centrifugal forces of egoism break the polity apart. At the same time,
however, it should be observed that while Arendt still remains committed
to achieving both ends, the new emphasis upon political socialization
could quite readily come to undermine the viability of the self-revelatory
pole. Just how Arendt would have us comprehend and practically config-
ure the media of political socialization in light of her high estimation of
both of these goals is a matter with which we shall grapple throughout
this chapter.

In this chapter, in addition to our concern with substantive matters
of theory, we shall also be concerned to apprehend how the two works
that follow *The Human Condition* are to be understood in relation to it.
In particular, we want to know what, if anything, is substantively new
here. Some have seen *On Revolution*, for example, as but a colorful
retelling of *The Human Condition*, but is it no more than this? And what
of *Between Past and Future*, is its position between these two works significant? And if so, how so?

To understand the trajectory taken by Arendt's work in the period
that immediately follows *The Human Condition*, it is important to keep in
mind that the problem that she poses for herself, namely, that of securing
the polity's identity over time while overcoming world alienation, has several distinct components. First, there is the problem of getting citizens to
do—or to want to do—what they ought to do. This is very much a practical problem: How is a polity that places a premium upon political participation to insure a continuous concern for public affairs among the largest
part of the civic body? How is the polity to persuade its citizens that the
rewards of public life are at least as great as those enjoyed within the private and social spheres? Secondly, there is the problem which comes into
view when one looks beyond the *fact* of participation to the *quality* of
public action: Is it self-interested or public-spirited? Does it foster or
undermine the cohesion of the community? Is it pork-barrel or self-sacri-
ficing in its ethos? Thirdly, there is the problem which arises directly out

of the issue we have been concerned with in this chapter's introduction: Does the prevalent mode of public action advance the end of political continuity, that is, the long duration of the polity's essential identity?

From the perspective of her freshly ascendant world-concern, Arendt turns to explore the socio-political concepts and constructs by means of which these problems, problems of system-reproduction really, might be resolved. But first a word of warning: As we proceed, especially in the early part of the current chapter, it will appear that Arendt's concern for action, and, in particular, her concern for action as a vehicle of self-fulfillment, have been eclipsed as sociological and institutional issues come to the fore. Indeed, through much of this chapter, we will be attending to those problems of socialization and of political-identity formation which figure so large in *Between Past and Future*, the collection of essays which Arendt wrote in the wake of *The Human Condition*. That the occlusion of action is only temporary, however, will become apparent when late in this chapter we turn our attention to *On Revolution*, the successor to *Between Past and Future*.

At that point, it will become clear that the theoretical importance of *On Revolution* stems from the fact that in it Arendt weaves together the action-orientation of *The Human Condition* and the concern for the maintenance of political continuity which so much informs *Between Past and Future*. Just how the introduction of the latter dimension transforms the contours of the former will be of major concern when we come to consider *On Revolution* in detail. What makes the prospect of synthesis so interesting is that *ex hypothesi* such a synthesis could answer to the two-sided requirements of the action-ideal as *The Human Condition* alone did not.

Before turning our attention to *On Revolution*, however, it is necessary to focus upon the theoretical emphases of *Between Past and Future*. Already, in the introduction to this chapter, the forces making for political continuity have been generally canvased. A certain ethos, or orientation, of the citizenry has been singled out as the source from which this sought-for continuity might spring. In *Between Past and Future* Arendt aims to explore the objective structures and world-rooted concepts which, she would argue, constitute the means by which this continuity-engendering subjective orientation is to be forged. In addition, Arendt looks to certain institutional, and constitutional, elements—such as the U.S. Supreme Court, for example—which are capable of securing political continuity, even where the proper subjective orientation is to some degree lacking. In *Between Past and Future*, still with the goal of continuity in view, Arendt conceptualizes the nature of such factors; and since these elements come to play an important role in the balance struck in *On Revolution*, it will be necessary for us to attend to their consideration in *Between Past and Future* as well. Just how readily these institutional elements, in particular, can be squared with the action-orientation of *The Human Condition* is a problem whose analysis must be postponed until we come to deal critically with the synthesis proffered in *On Revolution*.

In turning from *The Human Condition* to *Between Past and Future* many readers are doubtless struck by one detail, the significance of which is perhaps nonetheless unclear. I refer to the shift from the Greek to the Roman paradigm. In *The Human Condition*, Arendt's exemplary historical prototype is Periclean Athens. The Greeks of that time and place are depicted by Arendt as having acted in, and comprehended, the public space in a manner very much akin to her own conception of what would constitute an ideal political life. In the wake of *The Human Condition*, however, as Arendt's concern for the world's continuity pressed to the fore, the Periclean polis qua paradigm could no longer suffice. The problem with the Periclean polis, and with the polis generally, from the standpoint of Arendt's newly ascendant concern, lay in its chronic instability and in its resultant inability to endure over time.[13] For the sake of stability and durability—the natural concomitants of political continuity—a different model became necessary. In the Roman political experience, and the set of concepts originated there, Arendt found just what she was looking for. Rome alone had solved the problems associated with the aspiration to long-term political continuity. Naturally, then, Arendt looks to the Roman experience for help in improving the prospect that her own ideal construct will possess this attribute. Moreover, since stability and continuity were maintained in the West only so long as the Roman conceptions of culture and authority remained tenable, it seems implicit that the West must look again to the Roman experience if it is to regain political stability and continuity. Accordingly, we begin by attending to these concepts, as they are depicted in *Between Past and Future* and *On Revolution*, where they grow out of Arendt's reflections upon select facets of the Roman political experience.

Before turning to Arendt's exploration of this terrain, a hermeneutic question must be addressed. At issue is whether Arendt's reflections upon the matrix of concepts which she identifies as the ground of Rome's long lastingness are intended by her to carry any practical weight. If, as Arendt occasionally suggests, the continuum of Western civilization has been irreparably ruptured by the events of the most recent period, then it becomes questionable whether it is even plausible to understand her as recommending that the problematics of the hour are to be resolved via recourse to a matrix of concepts which stands at the fountainhead of a repudiated tradition.

And yet, that the tradition is in ruins, might only mean that its self-evidence and easy currency have been lost. Might it not be Arendt's intent, then, to tell us that, in the current conjuncture, we have no choice but to seek out the originary ground of concepts whose significance is no longer clear, in order to see what might be uncovered and made serviceable again. To ascribe such a view to Arendt, moreover, would be more in keeping with her own mode of procedure generally, that is, a mode of procedure which looks to the world of the past for fragments that might be brought forward to revivify the political practices of the present.

What finally carries the day on behalf of this view of Arendt's practical intent—as will become clear late in this chapter—derives not from *Between Past and Future* but from *On Revolution*, the text which follows it in 1963. In this text, the practico-theoretical intent of which is clear, Arendt redeploys the constellation of Roman-originated concepts, originally elucidated in *Between Past and Future*, but to a different end than before. Here, the concepts which were merely explicated in *Between Past and Future* are enlisted as the essential means of insuring the long-term continuity and stability of the participatory political spaces which she espouses. Moreover, though she never refers in either text to *The Human Condition*, the nature of the revision implied in *Between Past and Future*, and made manifest in *On Revolution*, is clear: action by itself will not be self-sustaining over time unless it gives rise to those world-sustaining institutions which are the real-world equivalents of the concepts developed in *Between Past and Future*. In *Between Past and Future*, however, Arendt's approach to that web of concepts, which *once upon a time* constituted the roots of world stability, is analytical and, technically, noncommittal.

In what follows, then, we shall be guided in our discussion of the insights manifest in *Between Past and Future* by our understanding of Arendt's underlying intentions in pursuing these topics, an intention not fully realized until the writing of *On Revolution*.

INSURING THE PRIMACY OF THE ORIGIN

Arendt would have us aim to insure not that man will be a partisan of the world so much as a partisan of its continuity, for it is this that the world requires. Rome achieved this continuity and managed to impart an ethos capable of sustaining it. Its culture, its religion, its traditions, and its political institutions—especially the Senate—all played a part in this process.[14] Yet behind the apparent multiplicity of factors, Arendt discerns a single idea which each brought home to the citizenry in its own way. At the heart of Roman political culture was one idea, the primacy of the origin and of the principle of action that was said to be immanent within it.[15]

The Romans, Arendt tells us, held the birth of their city to be a divinely attended and eternally powerful moment. The beginning was felt to possess a paradigmatic status that made it a binding guide for all subsequent generations.[16] The old ways, the old families, and whatever else was hoary and hearkened back to the time of the founding, were accounted venerable.[17] Even as the time of the founding grew more and more remote, the citizenry sought to maintain its connection with the origin. In every new situation the sanction of the past was sought by seeking always for some guiding precedent.[18] By returning always to the past, and to the origin in particular, the Romans hoped to maintain their good fortune which, it was felt, could be lost if they extended the polity in ways incommensurate with the spirit of the founding.[19] In sum, Arendt suggests that the Roman attitude toward the origin was one of religious reverence.[20] In this context she notes that the English word "religion" comes from the Latin *religare* which means "to bind back."[21] Roman religiosity consisted of binding oneself back to the origin which was held to be authoritative.[22]

Even before turning to Rome and to the problematic of the world's continuity, Arendt—like Heidegger—had been fascinated with the idea of, and the power inherent in, beginnings.[23] Amidst her reflections on the nature of action she variously defined man as a "natal," and as "the beginner who is capable of making new beginnings."[24] Approvingly, she cited Augustine's statement that God created man in order that there be a beginning, and his further comment that God created man individually, unlike the animals whom he created as entire species, in order that every man be understood to be a new and unique beginning.[25] In the same vein she associates action and freedom with novelty and beginnings.

The subject of these past musings was, of course, not beginnings per se, and even less the beginnings of politics, but rather man's inherent capacity to begin. Insofar as man is the beginner of cities, as well as of himself, man's capacity for beginnings looms as the origin of origins. To that degree, to discourse on the beginnings of cities and upon the actions of men is to discourse upon the same thing. There is one important difference to note. Whereas man's capacity for action bespeaks a capacity for sending off into the world beginnings as multifarious as man's projects are various, the subject under discussion now is not this potential plurality but the power that may emanate from just one beginning in particular when men are led to orient themselves by it.[26] Whether this change of emphasis ought to be held significant is a matter we shall have occasion to meditate upon later.[27] For the moment, however, it is of more importance for us to see what lessons Arendt draws from her reflections upon the structure of the Roman experience of the world.

Arendt's concern for origins, and for their central role in constituting a people's sense of its collective identity and purpose, leads her to attend to the problematics of cultural creation and cultural transmission by means of which the origin—which in itself is but a single evanescent flash in the ongoing time continuum—becomes imbued with the character of a perpetually living, and *authoritative*, moment. Hence Arendt's attention to storytelling, culture, and education.

Of Storytelling and the Roots of Cultural Self-Understanding

For Arendt, as we have seen, polities achieve their being, or, at least in retrospect, come to understand themselves as having received their being, through some unique, collectively shared event which in retrospect comes to be seen as a *beginning*. Presumably, the experience of the beginning will strongly mark the generation of the founding and, in addition to imparting to it a sense of collective identity and common destiny, it will likely give to it a strong sense of a "before" and an "after," a sense that something new and distinctly different has begun. Yet it might be the case that this awareness dawns only slowly or *inchoately*. It may even be the case that the generation of the founding grasps that something new has begun only in retrospect and long after an event which, looking back, they come to understand as having constituted a new beginning.

For the beginning to assume its paradigmatic status it must be worked up into the transmissible form that collectivity defining stories are made of. For members of the front generation, however, the problem of cultural transmission does not arise in the same way as it does for their descendants. Because they actually participated in the constitutive event, members of the front generation have an immediate access to the beginning that none who follow after them can ever know. For this reason, it is a unique responsibility that is borne by those who stand at the origin, for it is they alone who are well situated to articulate and transmit that story which, when told to future generations, will answer not only the question of where they come from but, implicitly, will answer the questions of who they are and of where they are going as well.[28]

Over the course of time a people will tell at least as many stories about itself as there are critical junctures in its history. However, of all the stories that a people will ever come to tell, the story of their origin will remain, in Arendt's opinion, most important of all.[29] In the face of that event which marks both an end as well as a beginning, the responsibility of the storytellers is particularly weighty. Over time, the story they tell, through its telling and retelling will come to constitute the identity of the people whose genesis it relates. The story's heroes, and the principles for which they stand, will become exemplary, and in every age youths will be exhorted to be like them.[30] The sense of national mission and national destiny, as it is depicted as having been understood by those present at the founding, will be appealed to as normative.[31]

More generally, Arendt would emphasize the fact that those publicists who stand at the beginning of a national political tradition bequeath, both to the future and to their contemporaries, a conceptual lexicon and a grammar of basic political experience that will, to a large degree, delimit the nation's vocabulary of political self-understanding and a good part of its common sense.[32] That this task of transforming unarticulated collective experience into articulated collective self-understanding is performed by *all* those bards who employ their linguistic craft upon the material of a nation's political life is true. What differentiates the storyteller of the beginning from those who follow afterwards is the greater likelihood that the former will delimit the hermeneutic horizon within which the latter will work.

Strictly speaking, Arendt's concern with cultural production is not new. In *The Human Condition* Arendt focuses on the storytellers and historians whose tale-telling alone is capable of bestowing upon the actor that immortality which he so desires[33]. It will be recalled that Homer and Thucydides figure in that text as the paradigmatic bestowers of immortal fame.[34] It should be noted, however, that in *The Human Condition* Arendt does not trace any connection between the memorializing activity of the artists and the mechanism of cultural reproduction. In *The Human Condition* the artist figures only as the ideal spectator who, by the retrospective judgment he manifests in his work, bestows definitive meaning upon the event.[35] But the significance of his story as one of the more important means by which the lastingness of the polity is insured, receives no attention.

Stories alone, however, while a necessary condition for transmitting the originary event into every subsequent age as a living bequest and lodestone, are not of themselves capable of insuring this. What else is required becomes clear in the preface to *Between Past and Future* as Arendt reflects upon Rene Char's 1946 recollection of his wartime service in the Resistance.[36] What strikes Char, less than a year after the war's end, is how difficult it is to preserve the memory of the wartime experience, given his lack of a language adequate to the contours of the experience. Wrongly, Char imagines that the lack of a language with which to keep his memories intact owes to the sheer unprecedentedness of the experience enjoyed by the members of the Resistance. But to Arendt's view, the experience recounted by the members of the Resistance has much in common with the experiences of "public happiness" that Greeks, Romans, Americans, and even the French had known at earlier points in their history. In short, the experiences in question are not unprecedented at all. That Char experiences them as such points, then, not to their unprecedentedness, but to what Arendt describes as a failure of collective memory and of cultural transmission.[37]

Narrative reification alone is not enough; this is but the first precondition of cultural transmissibility. As important is the second precondition: the cultural continuity that stories of the origin makes possible will only come to exist if the story either originates, or finds a place within, a living tradition which alone can insure the availability of what is past to a present which stands at ever further remove. That Char and his confreres lacked the language by which to stabilize their memories owed then to the fact that no living cultural stream carried the stories of earlier instances of public happiness to their ears. So far as these former members of the Resistance were concerned, the earlier instances might just as well have never occurred.

Reflecting on this matter, Arendt observes that the contemporaneity of past and present which culture properly engenders stands upon a twofold basis. First, of course, there are the stories themselves. But, second, and just as important, these stories must become elements within a living cultural tradition.

For the first precondition to hold it is only necessary that there be persons present at the edges of the events, as it were, who are capable of thinking through what has happened, thus providing events with, what Arendt calls, their "thinking completion."[38]

For the second precondition to hold, it is necessary that poets, storytellers, and thinkers stand in a living and reciprocal relationship to a living culture.[39] If the reflective articulations of experience produced by the artisans of culture are to be of general significance for the spiritual life of a people, not only must these products remain rooted in the soil of popular experience, but more importantly they must be made to reenter the ground from which they first emerged.[40] Through a cultural feedback loop it is absolutely essential that the clarifying articulations of collective experience reenter the collective mind whose articulation they are meant to be. Only thus will the products of culture be saved from being epiphenomenal to the culture and be made instead to serve as formative components of the citizenry's collective self-understanding. Only by means of such a loop can the interpretations of experience arrived at by the cultural producers become paradigmatic for the population at large, both prefiguring the categories of their worldly understanding and engendering certain idealized types of action.

Put in this way, it may appear that the storytellers are able to over-determine the direction and tenor of action. Were action incapable of transcending what conditions it, this impression would be most cogent. Against this view, however, it is necessary to recall Arendt's conception of action as an irrepressible and ineluctable root of novelty. Even where the cultural conditioning of the agent is extensive, action will tend to escape the relatively narrow parameters of a future conceived as nothing but a mechanical extrapolation from the past.[41]

Rather than rigidly binding action, then, Arendt would suggest that the cultural feedback loop has the effect of *guiding* action and its interpre-tation in such a way as to facilitate, in periods of normal politics, that all-important sense for the long-term continuity of the world which action by its very novelty would otherwise threaten quite directly. Prospectively, the web of stories that comprise a living tradition will tend to orient the novel deeds toward somewhat familiar and prelegitimated ends. Retrospectively, each new story, which unites the novel with the already known, functions to bind the event which has ruptured the time continuum back into the diachronic matrix of the world. In Arendt's view this function is of great significance, even if the resulting sense of continuity is more illusory than real.[42] Apparently, it is the perception of continuity as much as the fact that constitutes the polis as an object for the sake of which citizens are willing to live and die in every generation. Hence, the vital role that is played by the rightly framed story.

Finally, it should be underscored that Arendt's view of the relation between the artifacts of a culture and that culture's living reality is premised upon a notion that has become problematic in our own age. Arendt's view presupposes a public space wherein a people discursively participate in those kinds of collective and public experiences which by their very nature cry out for public interpretation. Without such a discur-sively constituted public space, even outwardly shared experiences will remain private inasmuch as they are undergone mutely and individually. Many may experience similar feelings as a consequence of living in similar situations, but for the most part, though perhaps homologous, these expe-riences are not discursively shared. In such a situation the novelists of society or of the private life may find a ready market, but there will be lit-tle need for the kind of storytelling which Arendt has in mind, the story-telling that is keyed to the activities of the public sphere and is composed with an eye to the articulation and continuous revitalization of an ongoing public life.[43] Nor will the conditions exist which enable the authors of such works to test the validity of their insights by the criterion of whether the public for whom they are written regards them as being authentically illuminating.

Of Culture and Cultural Mediation

Arendt's attention to stories arose from her concern for the origin and for the problematics of insuring that action be made compatible with the multigenerational continuity of the polis. The oft-told tales of a nation's political beginnings seemed, in her view, to constitute a primary vehicle for the socialization of each successive generation, a socialization that in turn could be sufficient to secure the polity's long-term continuity.[44] Upon reflection, however, Arendt grasped that stories alone could not facilitate the desired end. Stories that lacked a place in a living tradition were unread stories.[45] Hence the importance Arendt comes to ascribe to tradition as the agent making for cultural continuity.

The underlying concern, of course, is with political continuity not with cultural continuity nor with tradition per se. In the texts under consideration, however, Arendt contends that political continuity is built upon pre- and extrapolitical foundations, and, in particular, upon the extrapolitical grounds of culture and education.[46]

As has been already observed, in the period following the completion of *The Human Condition*, Arendt's primary concern shifted from the self-revelatory to the world-sustaining side of the action ideal. In simplest terms, the new focus was upon those mechanisms of socialization by means of which the citizens would be led to enter politics as partisans of the public weal and to define the public weal in terms of institutional and ideational continuity.[47] For reasons already explored in ample detail, Arendt regarded the continuity of the polity's substantive identity to be of utmost importance.

That culture becomes so important to Arendt at this point—especially in *Between Past and Future*—is readily explained in light of the way Arendt conceives of it. For Arendt, culture signifies at once the objective elements of culture—for example, the stories, artworks and values which putatively hail from the past and from the origin in particular—and the subjective orientation of the individual which arises through exposure to these value-laden elements.[48] Thus culture refers as much to the objects of culture as to the "taste" or attitude engendered by thoroughgoing exposure to these objects.

For Arendt, the objective dimension of culture is necessarily weighted toward the past.[49] In any age much is created, many works of culture, many stories and, in short, much evanescent scree. Only time will tell what will last, what will withstand the test of time. The cultural legacy of a nation will be comprised of just those works, stories, and values that have withstood this test. On one view, it might be argued that this test is of a physical nature: monuments crumble, texts molder and are lost. On another view—and this much closer to Arendt's—it might be argued that to a very large degree what passes the test of time does so because successive generations have chosen to insure that thus and thus be protected, preserved, and transmitted as a living legacy.[50] But for this decision to single out, preserve, and transmit, the objects would not and could not long survive.[51]

What the past hands down to the present will tend to be transmitted as a unified whole. No matter which realm of cultural endeavor one considers, this will be observed to be true. What accounts for this unity of value in the ensemble of cultural objects is the unity of criteria according to which the objects have been adjudged to be worthy of cultural transmission. That most stories, paintings, and sonatas fail to find a place in the pantheon of immortal works is oblique testimony to the operation of certain criteria of discrimination. Just how these criteria are determined, and how these criteria are applied, is beyond the scope of this chapter. Suffice it to say that such criteria do exist and that the "heritage of ages" is comprised of works which meet such criteria. Such, Arendt would argue, is the very nature of a tradition.[52] What conforms to the tradition's criteria of worth and value is gathered up into its arms and transmitted across the ages. What fails to meet its implicit standards is left to be covered over by the sands of time. Objectively, then, the works that comprise a given tradition will be seen to share certain things in common. A tradition is constituted by privileging these aspects over the more idiosyncratic elements.[53]

That a tradition is broader than the selection of works which achieve true prominence within it, is seen by Arendt as indicative of the fact that within a tradition certain works, or stories, will be singled out as "great," exemplary, or paradigmatic.[54] The "great books," for example, are not merely considered to be so for being instances of certain values esteemed by the tradition. Rather, their greatness stems from the fact that these books represent these values in a paradigmatic manner. The "great," as I observed in the last chapter, is held to be so for transcending what is average in the direction of perfection. Those works which any given culture singles out for being "great" or "classic" or "exemplary" will come to constitute for it a canon, an objectified representation of the culture's very essence. When it comes to transmitting the cultural values from one generation to the next, these works will likely play a vital role.[55]

So much then for the *objective* dimension of culture. Subjectively, however, to *stand* in a tradition and to *participate* in a given culture is to be socialized in accordance with the values for which the tradition stands. Where the cultural matter is poetic or musical, the values implicitly imparted will be values relevant to poetry or music. Where the cultural matter is political—or to speak more precisely, where the cultural matter is comprised of stories about central, identity-constituting moments of a people's political history—the values implicitly imparted will be values which, in the view of the tradition, ought to stand at the center of political life.

Patriotism, commitment to the commonweal, the desire to dedicate one's life to the values for which one's forebears gave their own—such is the harvest to be reaped should cultural conditioning operate to the proper end. Where stories find their place in a living tradition and the tradition is made a vital force in the lives of a citizen body, this should be the outcome. Admittedly, it is easy to envision a political culture which operates to sustain different kinds of values than those just enumerated. Given Arendt's own conception of politics, however, it is clear what kinds of values she would hope that the national political culture would manage to impart.

As already observed, every culture will possess some quasi-objective criterion of excellence by which great works will be distinguished from the rest. Tutelage in the ways of one's culture will properly entail being exposed to the works which meet or surpass this standard.[56] In the first instance such exposure constitutes a means of explicit socialization. This we have just explored. In addition, however, Arendt wants us to become aware of the implicit socialization which follows from the nature of what it means to be exposed to a living tradition, a dimension of implicit socialization which will be operative irrespective of the character of the explicitly privileged value mix.

Of any living cultural tradition two very important things can be said, both of which have already been hinted at previously. On the one hand, a tradition—or more particularly the ensemble of paradigmatic or exemplary instances or works which are held to embody its essence—most fully constitutes, as it were, a template for those who would achieve a similarly enduring excellence. Greatness, it is hoped, will breed greatness. And once harnessed, the spirit of emulation—which by Arendt's measure is a force of no small significance—should call forth "the best" from those who have been bred to the task of achieving such excellence for themselves.[57] More to point, when the tradition is functioning properly, those individuals who are especially motivated by "an authentic concern for immortality" should find in the timeless works of their culture evidence that they too may escape oblivion through the achievement of greatness in their works and deeds. Of course, the greatness that is aspired to is culturally specific, but from Arendt's perspective this is a virtue. Indeed, on account of it—and this is Arendt's second point—the individual who has internalized a given ensemble of cultural standards or values (and strives to meet or realize them) will necessarily act in a manner that is conducive to the perpetuation of cultural continuity as well. What the individual does for his own sake will thus come to redound to the benefit of the world, and thus the potential for radical cultural discontinuity will be in large measure overcome.

In truth, to inherit such a tradition is at once to apprehend both its antiquity and its contemporaneity. On the one hand, it is "from Sinai" and, on the other hand, it is as contemporary as the latest *halakhic* responsa. A tradition, in other words, may *objectively* comprehend a vast span of time; subjectively, however, to receive a tradition as one's inheritance is to apprehend its perpetual contemporaneity as well.

We have already called attention to the importance that Arendt attaches to the fact that what comes down to us through hundreds or even thousands of years as a bequest from generations long dead does so as a consequence of the decisions made by each successive generation to transmit what it had received.[58] Thus far, however, this transmission from one generation to the next has been presented as if it only occurs because enough members of the up-and-coming generation choose to ride the tradition's values as a vehicle along the way to the earthly immortality of fame. But this analysis, which explains how the perpetuation of the tradition and its values is produced as an unintended consequence of human striving, tells only one part of the story. In addition Arendt calls our attention to the fact that in large measure the transmission of a tradition from one generation to the next is brought about through the efforts of those individuals who consciously endeavor to secure this very end.[59]

Implicitly, the tradition itself envisions its recipients in every age as its continuators. The past, as it were, thus seeks to obligate the present. The more generations to have met this obligation previously, the weightier the responsibility upon the current generation. The more links in the chain of transmission to have been forged already, the more consequential seems the decision by any present or future generation to break the chain by refusing to transmit what it has received. Assuming that successive generations have striven and sacrificed on behalf of the tradition and its values, the generation that chooses not to transmit, by implication, denies the value or validity of the tradition and of the sacrifices made on its behalf.[60] Nor is it only the past generations which are deprived thereby.

Substituting "polity" for "tradition"—as Arendt (does and) wants us to do—makes clear how much is at stake.[61] For the polity (or tradition) that preexists and ought to outlast us is the object par excellence on behalf of which self-transcending endeavor is paradigmatically undertaken. Break the chain of culturo-political transmission that raises evanescent generations into eternity and you shatter the most tangible representation of the human world's enduring character. Sever the cord that has long bound the ages together and you deprive present and future generations of the means of transcendence. Not only is the value of past sacrifice retroactively degraded, but the path of future sacrifice is proleptically nullified. Consequently, Arendt recommends due deference toward the inheritance of ages that paves over the gap between past and future, and makes transcendence possible.[62]

That traditions possess intrinsic value and a value that increases with every new link in the generational chain has been acutely perceived by those in every age who have decided to make themselves continuators not in order to gain a lasting name for themselves but because they perceive the continuation of the tradition to be in itself good.[63]

According to Arendt, though every culture that desires to perpetuate itself ought to inculcate such an ethos of preservation and continuation, the Greeks never managed to do so.[64] In her essay "The Crisis in Culture," in which Arendt makes this observation, Arendt may be seen as implicitly acknowledging a limitation that was inherent in her original conception of action. Earlier, I noted that the world suffered as a result of action's tendency to devour its offspring, a tendency that arose from the inability of man qua actor to appreciate the principle of preservation.[65] What was critically alleged of action by this reader, Arendt is now heard to allege of Greece in contrast to Rome. The Greeks, she says, knew how to create beautiful things, but they did not know how to care for what they created.[66] They had a strong aesthetic sense, but did not take care to preserve what they found beautiful. The Romans, by contrast, had a much less developed aesthetic sense; what they did have, however, was an instinct for preservation.[67] They knew how to take care of things, how to nurture what was young and fragile, and how to protect what was old and venerable.

Both nurture and preservation are implied, according to Arendt, in the Roman conception of culture which, she notes, comes from the Latin *colere* meaning "to cultivate," as in the cultivation of land.[68] What one cultivates will bear fruit, but note, the fruit does not come at once. Cultivation implies an ongoing process of caring, nurturing, protecting, and preserving even more than it implies harvesting.[69] Cultivation also implies upkeep; one hopes that what one has cultivated will last, that one's trees will bear fruit in every season, so one undertakes to insure that they will.

By extension, we might note, one can be taught to care as much for what others have cultivated, especially if one finds oneself to be the recipient of the fruits of another's cultivating care. Bearing in mind that an olive tree, for example, can bear fruit for over four hundred years, one who fathoms even one-tenth of how much loving cultivation has been poured into each tree may come to care as much for the trees as if he had planted them himself. Even where one is not the direct recipient (as by inheritance) one may still come to take an attitude of loving care toward those things which have been the recipient of much loving care in the past.

An English Garden, similarly, is a fragile thing brought to full bloom only after the longest period of cultivation; but even then it is neither hearty nor naturally self-perpetuating. Neglect it for a season and it is overgrown; neglect it for a few and it becomes near impossible to bring it back to its glory. Though someone may take no joy in such things, is it inconceivable to imagine that one who found himself the chance owner of such a garden might—out of appreciation for the generations-long periods of continuous cultivation, and out of an appreciation for the relationship between continuous cultivation and the long-term vitality of the garden— undertake to keep it in best health for the sake of those dead and those unborn? Such is, according to Arendt, the attitude that will rightly come to inform one's relation to the things of the world and to the world as a whole when citizens, by right tutelage in culture, come to grasp their role as trustees for the generations.

Though much of the time Arendt speaks of culture in only the most general way, it is important to note that she also singles out the political dimension of culture as meriting special emphasis. In choosing to emphasize the political dimension of culture Arendt signals her fierce antipathy for that apolitical variety of *Bildung* which predominated in the Germany of her youth.[70] Upon no other group does she heap such scorn as she does upon those who combine high culture with a disdain for the lowly political affairs of the world.[71] By Arendt's definition, such men as would forsake the public space for the sake of inward cultivation, or for a life of the arts, are hardly cultivated. Rather, they display what, paraphrasing Pericles, she derides as an immoderate love of the beautiful or an immoderate taste for philosophy, which in Arendt's neo-Greek parlance makes them more men of barbarian effeminacy than men of true cultivation.[72]

True cultivation, as Arendt never tired of reiterating, possesses a strong political dimension.[73] No one of true cultivation would display a reckless and self-centered disregard for the affairs of the world. In the end, the stability of the political world is the foundation of all good things. One of true cultivation will understand this and will grasp that it is through the medium of meeting one's political responsibilities that the perpetuation of high culture is assured. The twentieth century has made only too clear that it is no longer possible to live a life of refinement in secure isolation from politics. If one would perpetuate the possibility of refinement then one must meet one's political responsibilities as well.

As Arendt understands the nature of culture and its inherent worldliness, the right exposure to the classics alone ought to impel one to do one's part to uphold the frame of the world. At the same time as if to underscore the particularist aspect of this duty, Arendt emphasizes that specifically nationalist dimension of culture which is dedicated to the commemoration of great words and deeds spoken and done on behalf of one's nation.[74]

As culture at the broadest level extends itself across time and space as a self-identical tradition, so too does the narrower political culture of a particular polity.[75] On first glance this might be disputed by pointing to the institutions of power which maintain a polity's identity over time by means of a monopoly on the legitimate use of force. Arendt would argue that appearances are in this case deceiving, and that this argument confuses power with authority as it reduces both to force.[76] Wherever true identity is maintained over time, this owes not so much to institutional power and even less to brute force; rather, it follows from the structure of authority as it operates on objective and subjective levels.

We have explored Arendt's conception of culture as it stands in relation to both the production of culture and its natural ground, namely, the soil of collective experience. In the main our purview has been limited, however, to conceptualizing how these elements might interact at the highest level of public life. Guiding us throughout has been a point of view which seeks to understand how culture and authority directly affect, and are affected in turn by, the political life of a public space in which adult citizens are regularly gathered.

Of equal concern to Arendt, however, is the way in which authority and culture ought to be brought to bear upon those members of the community who have not yet reached the age of political maturity. It has been, after all, our concern in following Arendt down this path to trace her study of those mechanisms which once upon a time combined, and might combine again, to insure that an appropriately patriotic and worldly ethos would be implanted in the hearts of a polity's members. Thus, it can hardly be surprising that among the topics which engaged Arendt's interest as bearing on this concern is the question of how best to impart to youths the perspective which will be most conducive to what she would regard as a healthy political life.

Of Civics and Education

Newcomers, children of the present, with both eyes trained upon the future, we are born. Subjectively, we know of no past prior to our emergence; our own experience encompasses only the narrowest swath of time. Yet we belong to a socio-cultural entity, or "world," that outlasts us all. It existed before our arrival and will remain after our departure. It is a transgenerational entity whose every present arises out of its past and goes forward into its future.

Man is born between past and future. His "world" receives him, shapes him, and in turn is shaped by him. What he makes of *it* depends in large part upon what it makes of him. Much, in short, depends upon education, that is, upon how and upon what one generation teaches the next.[77] Moreover, as Plato observed, to any given form of political regime there corresponds a single curriculum which will insure the regime's continuous reproduction. When this correspondence breaks down, political instability will be the predictable result. It pays, then, to be mindful of this relationship when making changes in the field of education. What we teach our children will likely have political consequences of the first magnitude.

Education comes to play a pivotal role in Arendt's work at the same time that her general emphasis shifts from action to world.[78] Only proper education can insure that the average citizen approaches the ideal. Only proper education can insure that in his political judgment the citizen will undertake to uphold those standards which make for the ennoblement of the public realm: as the errant propensities of the actor must be countered by the sound judgment of the spectator, so must the potential for unsound judgment by the spectator be countered by the principles imparted by right education. Education, then, serves for ballast in Arendt's ship of state.[79]

In what has been dubbed Arendtian politics, citizens are expected to measure themselves against the great men of the past. The old ones, the founders, are axiomatically accounted to be the better ones, the *maiores*, the greater ones who are alone worth emulating.[80] The time of the origin is accounted a purer time. Then, men risked all for the sake of honor and country as men of today are capable of doing only by virtue of calling those hoary exemplars and that timeless time to mind. Yet it is by no means the natural bent of mind to range backwards over all time whenever one encounters a present challenge; and even if one does possess such a tendency, the range of an untutored mind is necessarily quite limited and can hardly be expected to forage a past which lies beyond its experience. Only where an individual's historical memory has been completely stocked with the requisite precedents and personages, and only where the proper deference toward the past has been inculcated, will there be any chance that he will orient himself in politics by the light of the past. If this orientation is to predominate, as Arendt would like to see, it must be imparted to citizens before they arrive at the age of political maturity; its communication is not the task of politics so much as it is the task of the prepolitical activity of education.

Into the future, then, by means of attention to the past. Is this an odd notion or is it most wise? By one account the paramount need is to equip the youth of today with the practical skills that will be necessary in the world of tomorrow. Especially in a world that changes as fast as ours, it is argued, there is little point in conveying knowledge which quickly becomes obsolete; and inasmuch as the past is held to be no guide to a present which is ever so different from it, the conveyance of historical awareness seems to be of little importance. Nor, according to the ideology of progress, should the past be seen as being in any way exemplary. Better to teach math, sciences, modern languages, and computer skills than history, ancient languages, and literature.

From Arendt's standpoint, however, a skill-oriented pedagogy which does not undertake at the same time to bind men to their past, and thus to their world, constitutes a danger to that very world of which the proponents of "relevant" skills believe themselves to be so mindful. More important to Arendt than the imparting of skills is the imparting of an ethos of worldliness and world-concern which the teaching of skills alone will not serve to inculcate.[82] For Arendt the most pressing pedagogic problem is not a lack of skill, but a lack of world-concern and a lack of the diachronic awareness which can insure that action will hew to a line commensurate with man's need to maintain the world's continuity.

For Arendt, being unprepared to meet the challenges of the future has altogether different connotations than it has for the futurists. For Arendt, he is unprepared who is ready to meet the challenges of the future boldly without regard for past or precedent; indeed, he who would confront them thus meets them without the slightest comprehension of what is at stake. It is not that the citizen who lacks a proper grounding in the past will be unable to act. What is in question is whether such untutored action will be commensurate with a world whose continuity is potentially ventured by every action men undertake.

Arendt's approach to solving the pedagogic problem begins, then, with her insight into the multigenerational lastingness of the *res publica*.[83] By nature, as we have observed, man is oriented toward a future which he regards as his own, and for the sake of which he acts. Through education, however, he may be oriented to a past which is not so much his own as it is the world's, though he may, by the very process of studying it, come to identify with it, thus making it his own. Where education has been most successful this identification will be most complete and the brevity of a man's personal history will be supplemented by the longevity of a collective or national history. As a result the citizen's projects should cease to be wholly self-reflexive in their structure and should arise instead from a personal identity that has been securely grounded upon a collective destiny.

For generations the way to this end was a curriculum steeped in the classics of Western art, literature, and philosophy, whose very transmission across the millennia symbolized the very essence of worldliness. By a process of osmosis, through contact with these texts, fresh born youths were transformed into cultured individuals whose impulses, sentiments, and ideas were hewn into accordance with the ethos these texts exemplify.[84]

Even within Arendt's politicized conception of *Bildung,* no doubt the Occidental classics would still find a place. Of greater importance, however, would be those texts which serve to impart to youths a familiarity with their own national political culture.

Thus, in the same way as one comes to identify with the ongoing entity called Western Civilization by becoming intimate with its greatest monuments, one would come to identify with the ongoing project called America through the study of its past.[85] In neither case should this effort be undertaken with detachment and a "mere" historical interest. The aim is not to impart knowledge for its own sake.[86] In each case the tradition must be conveyed under the rubric of "this is who you are," (for example) an American who rises to his full stature when he acts as an American, that is, as Washington, Jefferson, or Lincoln would have done under whatever circumstances befell them. Much emphasis will be placed upon the moment of the founding, upon its heroes, and upon its guiding principles in order to impart a sense for the ongoing primacy of these principles and for the continuous relevance of the heroes who should be presented as exemplars of the virtues which the nation would have its citizens personify.[87] Because a world is only as strong as the most recent link in the chain of generations, the perpetual inculcation of this ethos is indispensable to the nation's long-term vitality.

Where civic education is most successful, an attitude of reverence will extend from the moment of the founding, and its heroes, to one's country's political institutions, habits, and principles.[88] Arendt points to American reverence for the U.S. Constitution as a case in point.[89] To this day the founders, the founding, and the foundations that were laid (that is, the Constitution itself) are regarded as authoritative by most Americans, and by the members of the political institutions which came into existence as a result of the great event. So strong is the authority of the origin over all that has come after it that we allow the Supreme Court to strike down as invalid any laws of Congress which it regards as incommensurate with the spirit of the founding. Only a people whose cultural orientation had made it so enthusiastically submissive to the moment of its founding could ever cede such power to a body whose very purpose is to insure continuity with the original principles.

What must be underscored in this context is that Arendt does not look to such institutions of formal authority as if they could substitute for what elsewhere she suggests is an imperative need to inculcate a certain deference toward the past on the part of the citizenry as a whole. Rather, she perceives these institutions as complementing and indeed as presupposing the inculcation of this deferential orientation. They may serve to strengthen but cannot replace nor even exercise any authority at all where the ethos which accounts for compliance does not already exist as a result of a sustained educational endeavor. In America, in short, the authority of the Supreme Court rests upon the authority of the U.S. Constitution but the authority of the Constitution rests in turn upon the reverence of the people for it, a reverence which must be fostered in the hearts of each successive generation if the spirit of the beginning is continuously to prevail.[90]

Where such a curriculum is in place, not just one citizen but many of them might come to share in a past-oriented and community-minded common sense which would necessarily serve as a common framework for their common action.[91] The cultivated taste and commitment of one man may be a good thing in itself and good for the man whose life is enhanced by it, but this is not Arendt's main concern. Her hopes are for the enhancement of our public life, and to this end she reasons that the upbringing of our youths ought to be guided by an understanding of the fact that the orientation towards the world which they receive in school will markedly, if not decisively, shape their orientation towards political action. For better or worse, what children are taught in the classroom they will carry with them into the world. To a very large degree it will color what they will later think of as plain common sense, that is, that unadorned and deceptively natural collective wisdom by which a people charts its common destiny.[92]

Thus far we have attended to Arendt's various analytic forays as she sought, in the period subsequent to the writing of *The Human Condition*, to understand what enables a given culturo-political order, or world, to perpetuate its identity through time. Hence her attention to the origin and to the tales of the origin which transmit its force and guidance to future generations. Hence her attention to culture and tradition as the media by means of which the forces of continuity are transmitted into every present. Hence her attention to education as the primary vehicle of cultural conditioning. On the surface, then, these analyses have been united by the overarching concern for discerning the mechanism whereby the world's identity is forged and maintained. From this angle, the several factors seem to be so many means to a common end.

From a broader perspective, however, a deeper connection can be observed. In one way or another each of the elements we have scrutinized bears upon the problem of authority, and upon the question of its proper extent and nature. The problem of securing the primacy of the origin, in other words, might be construed as a problem of securing the *authority* of the origin. Culture and education, thus considered, appear to be means of establishing this authority. The tradition which runs from past to present thus becomes marked as an authoritative tradition. The end of political continuity presupposes, in other words, the authoritativeness of that which is to be continued and may entail the specification of the authorities by means of which this continuity is to be secured.

The concept of authority and a consideration of how it bears upon the cultural questions we have been discussing in this chapter come center stage in Arendt's essay on the modern derogation of authority which, not surprisingly, is to be found in *Between Past and Future*.[93] In this essay Arendt seeks to differentiate the nature of authority from seemingly kindred concepts, and, as is her usual bent, proceeds by seeking out the historical and etymological roots of the concept. Throughout the essay, despite the pretense of having none but an analytical interest, one senses Arendt's underlying pragmatic concern. Authority has evaporated: how is it to be restored? Hence the need to probe its specific nature and to uncover its roots. Hence the need to elucidate just how the nature of authority and the soil of culture mutually articulate: Will a crisis in the one necessarily reflect a crisis in the other? Can one be viable where the other has broken down? Does one have conceptual priority? Pragmatically, how is the condition of each to be repaired? Need both be repaired in order to secure political continuity over against the forces of modernity on the one hand and errant action on the other?

The Roman Roots of Authority

By conventional definition authority may be understood as a relationship between one who has authority, that is, the "power to require and receive submission," and the one who obediently submits to it.[94] What this definition fails to provide, however, is any explanation of what gives to one the power to command and to the other the inclination to submit. Is it strength on the one side and fear on the other? Or does the latter comply willingly because he regards the claim of the former to be legitimate? And if legitimate, then upon what grounds? Arendt's meditation upon the

Roman experience provides answers to these questions which reveal what she sees to be the indispensability of authority to world stability.[95]

Scrutiny of the Roman case reveals to Arendt that those with authority did not wield authority by virtue of force, nor by virtue of persuasion, but by virtue of a relationship between themselves and the origin.[96] Those with authority did not assert their authority as if they were themselves the origin of it, but instead asserted it on behalf of those men, or principles of the past, from whom their right to claim authority in the present was held to stem.[97] Those who accepted the legitimacy of this claim, and displayed the virtue of free obedience in relation to those making it, would ideally do so, then, not out of subservience to these men in particular, but out of a prior acceptance of the normativity of the past for the present. Thus every assertion of authority in the present could be viewed as signifying, in the same moment, an assertion of the authority of the past for the present; and, conversely, every free act of submission to authority in the present could be viewed as a free act of submission, not merely to the authorities of the present, but to the authority of the past as well. So long as the commitment to the past embodied in this relationship remained genuine, that is, so long as it did not degenerate into mere rhetorical pretence, one could expect therefore that the presence of a Roman-like concept of authority within a polity would prove to be a powerful agent for intergenerational historical continuity.

How strong the relationship was between the Roman concept of authority and the belief in the normativity of the past for the present can be seen in the etymology of *auctoritas*, the Latin word for authority, which derives from *augere*, meaning "to augment." Arendt explains that those in authority were, by virtue of their prior connection with the founders of the polity, members of an elite empowered to authorize all augmentations to the foundations of the city.[99] Thus, in Rome, the senators whose senatorial seats were received by inheritance were esteemed and granted authority because of their bloodline descent from the founders whose original claim to authority owed to having participated in the founding itself.[100] Through the senators "the imprimatur of the founders" could be bestowed upon augmentations to the foundations made necessary by changes in time and circumstance, an imprimatur only bestowed where the augmentation was commensurate with the underlying principle of the origin. The assumption was that those who were linked by blood to the founders of the city would countenance only those changes or additions to the original constitution that were wholly commensurate with it. Strictly speaking, only such changes or additions truly count as augmentations. To undercut or transmogrify is scarcely to augment.

Given the paramount position of the Senate qua authority, it is no wonder that the spirit of Roman politics was profoundly conservative.[101] Change, Arendt suggests, was never accepted willy-nilly. Always attention was paid to the maintenance of continuity. To stay in an unbroken line with the past was, as Arendt describes it, a Roman obsession.[102] Always they sought continuous guidance from the past as they went forward into the future.

The necessary consequence of this orientation was traditionalism in politics. "The uninterrupted continuity of this augmentation and of its inherent authority could come about only through tradition, that is through the handing down, through an unbroken line of successors, of the principle established in the beginning."[103] Out of this tradition-creating, origin-centered, and authority-enhancing attitude arose the Roman attitude of *pietas* which combined pious remembrance with a will to conserve the past while going forward into the future.[104]

In succession we have considered Arendt's treatment of origins, stories, culture, education, and authority. Our aim throughout has been to explicate the factors that enable a given world to maintain its identity over time. Had we wanted to bring authority to prominence at the outset, we only needed to observe that the continuity Arendt wants to secure is built upon the continuous maintenance of the authority of the origin for all subsequent time. The formulation, telling, and retelling of stories; the constitution of an origin-centered tradition; and the inter-generational transmission of culture by means of education together constitute the means whereby the authority of the origin is realized in every successive present.[105] Hence the stories, the tradition, and the culture are denominated as authoritative as well by virtue of their connection with the origin.

Authority, thus conceived, has no connection with physical coercion. As was observed in the discussion of Arendt's views of education, though the diachronic root of authority will always remain the origin, the synchronic base lies in the properly cultivated hearts and minds of the citizenry. The authoritative is authoritative because the citizens' regard makes it so.

Admittedly, to this point, Arendt's analysis of authority has manifest neither concreteness nor practical pith. Indeed, as was observed early in this chapter, this shortcoming is generally characteristic of the essays that are gathered together in *Between Past and Future*. That the analysis of authority does come to have practical relevance in Arendt's later work becomes most apparent in *On Revolution*, a text whose pragmatic thrust is unambiguous. Let it suffice for the moment to observe (since we will attend to *On Revolution* in greater detail shortly) that in the later work the concept of authority and the matrix of ancillary concepts by which it is sustained recur in a more particularized and more normative guise.[106] Thus authority in general becomes the authority that emanates from the moment of the polity's founding, an authority that becomes particularized as a set of authoritative principles and stabilized by means of an authoritative constitution which is the concrete product of the founding.[107] Together, the founding, the principles, and the constitution which pays homage to both are envisioned by Arendt as constituting the authoritative and normative roots of the people's political existence.[108] Still more indicative of the way in which Arendt comes to concretize her conception of authority is her conception of the political and constitutional traditions which she envisions as flowing out from the origin into all successive time. Rendering the American experience prototypical in this regard (as in many others which will be discussed further on) Arendt endorses the role played by the Supreme Court as the official guardian and authorized interpreter of the U.S. Constitution in every age.[109] Thus, as a consequence of its continuous interpretive task, there would grow up an authoritative constitutional tradition which, like a red thread, would run from age to age as a force making for political continuity.[110] Such would be the effect to be wrought, not by the workings of authority in general, but by the effect of one authority in particular, albeit in conjunction with the less particularized authoritative elements already mentioned.

Thus we see that the path from authority in general to authorities and political authorities in particular is easily traversed. In passing, however, we would note that one need not travel as far along this road as Arendt wants to lead us in *On Revolution*. It is possible, for example, to envision an unstratified collectivity which possesses an authoritative political culture but lacks any formally, or even informally, constituted body that has been authorized to represent itself as authoritative for the whole community. Along such lines one might even envision a polity with a political culture like that of the United States in many ways but without a Supreme Court and the arguably antidemocratic conception of authority implicit in its functioning. Just why one might choose to take issue with Arendt's readiness to erect a Supreme Court-like body in her ideal polity will become clearer further on and, especially, in this chapter's conclusion. In particular, we shall have to consider how the presence of such a body would impinge upon the collectivity- and self-expressive pole of the action-ideal.

ON REVOLUTION: A MOMENT OF SYNTHESIS

Before exploring the contours of this synthesis, lest there be any confusion regarding the relationship between the claims we are making and the text we are interpreting, a few things must be said about the text itself. The chief point that needs to be made is this: though we will be (and have been) reading *On Revolution* with the aim of elucidating Arendt's "intermediate" conceptualization of the action-ideal, it is not Arendt's conscious purpose in this text to update *The Human Condition* in the way our analysis may seem to presuppose. Instead, as one would imagine, revolutions and the principles that guide them are her primary concerns. Structurally, the text is organized around the contrast Arendt develops between the American and French revolutions.

Not surprisingly, Arendt's criteria of successful revolution are essentially twofold. On the one hand, success is measured by the extent to which a revolution establishes sites for popular civic action: the greater the success of the revolution, the greater will be the number of citizens who, in the wake of it, regularly experience the joys of public happiness."[111] On the other hand, success is gauged by whether or not a revolution gives birth to a stable and enduring polity.[112] Of the two criteria of value, Arendt regards the former as primary; but in practical terms, she makes clear that both are necessary.

It should also be pointed out that, of the two revolutions, the American Revolution comes closest to meeting Arendt's criteria of success, and Arendt makes clear her great admiration for the achievement of "the founding fathers."[113] At the same time, she discusses the U.S. Constitution in a way that makes it possible for us to infer how it would have to be modified before it could receive her complete approval.[114] Helping to elucidate the nature of the required modifications is *On Revolution*'s final chapter in which Arendt discusses the participatory councils that have briefly emerged as sites of public happiness in the shadows of almost every revolution since 1789. Between the qualified praise Arendt gives to the U.S. Constitution and her celebration of the participatory councils, the operative political ideal of *On Revolution* can be inferred.

In important respects, the ideal polity that emerges from the interstices of this text is akin to the American Republic. Its design is federal and at its center one would likely find an arrangement of governmental branches like that envisioned in the U.S. Constitution.[115] Authority flows from the polity's origin, is vested in the constitution, and finds voice in the present through an organ like the Supreme Court. The people revere their constitution, respect its authority, and endeavor to maintain political continuity.

In one crucial respect, however, the ideal envisioned within *On Revolution* departs from the American design: in order to increase the amount of political participation and the extent of public happiness, Arendt would reframe the links between the federal and local levels of government.[116]

Like Jefferson, Arendt believes that the founders of the republic had erred when they failed to anchor the federal constitutional order upon the townships and parishes.[117] By her measure, the consequence of this failure was the devitalization of local political life and the loss of civic spirit as politics quickly became the business of a few.[118] To reverse this trend, Arendt revives Jefferson's proposal for directly incorporating the smallest units of self-government, the precincts and wards, into the federal system.[119] Following Jefferson, Arendt proposes a multi-tiered arrangement whereby deliberative assemblies on the precinct level would become the primary public spaces and the basic units of self-government.[120] Between the local precinct meeting and the national legislative assembly an ascending series of progressively more encompassing representative bodies would be established, each of which would elect members to the body immediately above it.[121] Finally, to insure the practical impact of such changes Arendt would do away with popular suffrage.[122] Instead, political participation in the fora on a given level would become the basis for determining one's eligibility to elect, or to be elected as, a representative to the next higher level. Thus Arendt's ideal would improve upon the American political order by grafting to it a multi-tiered system of popular citizens' councils.[123] Admittedly, Arendt does not pause to discuss details, but the basic thrust of her conception is clear. The political order must be framed to make sure that the joys of political action can be broadly shared.

From the beginning of this chapter, we have been looking toward the moment when close examination of *On Revolution* would indicate the nature of the synthesis to be achieved between the emphases of *The Human Condition* and the concerns of *Between Past and Future*. In the prelude to part two, I called attention to the one-sidedness of the conception of action delineated in *The Human Condition*. As we know, the action-ideal proper contains both self-revelatory and world-sustaining poles, and yet the conception of action articulated in *The Human Condition* was seen to be insufficiently attentive to the latter. Just whether or not Arendt was fully aware of this weakness cannot be answered with any certainty. What is certain is that in the period following the writing of *The Human Condition*, Arendt turned her attention to the matters upon which we have focused in this chapter, matters which answer to the lacunae of *The Human Condition*. What suggests that this shift of focus was more than a matter of happenstance is the fact that the concerns first manifested in the essays collected in *Between Past and Future* reappear in *On Revolution*, a text that in every other respect parallels the orientation of *The Human Condition*. In consequence, *On Revolution*—which on the surface appears to be a popularization of *The Human Condition*—constitutes instead a synthesis of the self-revelatory orientation of *The Human Condi-*

tion and the continuity-fostering elements so prominent in *Between Past and Future*. That the synthesis remains problematic in certain respects must be acknowledged, but this is not to deny that it constitutes a significant step forward. Before attending to the shortcomings, however, the configuration of the synthesis must be considered:

Continuous with the structure of the earlier of the two works is Arendt's recapitulation of many of the themes discussed in the first chapter. Specifically stressed from *The Human Condition* are the emphases upon the existential supremacy of political action, public freedom, and public happiness.[124] While more attention is paid to the sheer pleasure of participation than in *The Human Condition*, Arendt still emphasizes the self-revelatory and agonal dimensions of participation, here considering it under the rubrics of "the passion for distinction" and "the desire to excel."[125] Conversely, Arendt, as was her wont in *The Human Condition*, pillories the private life, private freedom, and private happiness.[126]

At a still deeper level, though unmistakably permeating the entire text, one senses the presence of the underlying valuational antitheses whose exploration figured so prominently in chapter 1. Of the three, the polarity of freedom and necessity figures most prominently, that of lasting and passing somewhat less so, and that of uniqueness and uniformity more by way of implication than by way of explicit reference.[127] In sum, most of what assumed significance under the aegis of the conception of action developed in *The Human Condition* remains of great importance within *On Revolution*.

If this continuity with *The Human Condition* is hardly surprising, the continuities with *Between Past and Future* are much more so given Arendt's refusal in the latter text to consider the question of whether the concepts explored in this chapter ought to be understood as means of resolving certain problems of modernity. In *On Revolution* not only does Arendt recapitulate her earlier analyses of culture, authority, and tradition, but she places her discussion of these themes in such a context as to make it unequivocally clear that she regards these elements as means for remedying "the current crisis."[128]

At the nexus then, between *The Human Condition* and *Between Past and Future*, Arendt sketches her vision of a polity whose political life unites the action dimension of the former and the world-strengthening elements of the latter. It is a polity born of revolution; and the moment of revolutionary experience figures both as a collectivity-constituting crucible and as the foundation of a public space wherein action of the type depicted in *The Human Condition* might flourish. No longer, however, will the untempered potentiality of action war against the fragile boundaries of the public space, for these will have been strengthened by the inculcation of an ethos which will insure that all action is undertaken with an eye toward the principles of the origin and with a heart committed to the maintenance of continuity.

Ideally, this ethos will arise out of the revolutionary experience, or, more precisely, as a corollary to the collective self-understanding that has been forged through this experience, and through the transmission of its authoritative interpretation. The net result, if all unfolds as Arendt desires, will be a polity that unites public freedom and durability, the existential achievements of action and long-term continuity.

The object upon which Arendt's hopes are focused in *On Revolution* is the constitution in all its various significations from the document itself to the way of life it fosters.[129] In *On Revolution* the constitution figures primarily as that agreement which secures and delimits, respectively, the lastingness and the extent of the public space as the site of public action.[130] That those who have joined together in common action choose to draft a constitution represents for Arendt a symbolization of their willingness to preserve a space within which their action potential can be experienced again and again.[131] It is only fitting that those who have once tasted the joys of collective action establish a constitution in order that they might partake of such an experience more regularly. That "secondary" or extrapolitical benefits may accrue to those who are joined in a scheme of political cooperation hardly receives Arendt's notice.

Strikingly, Arendt's conception of the constitution contains within itself elements drawn from *The Human Condition* and *Between Past and Future* to such a degree as to make the balance struck between them quite representative of the synthesis she endeavors to achieve in the text of *On Revolution* as a whole. From the side of *The Human Condition*, Arendt takes the telos for the sake of which the constitution is drafted, namely the end of constituting a public space as a home for action. In stipulating membership qualifications and in delineating the framework of political relationships, the constitution serves the end of clearing and demarcating a space for action. In addition, Arendt's conception of the constitution as a kind of covenant that is entered into in order to secure the continuous effluence of public action hearkens back to the morality internal to action that Arendt elaborates in *The Human Condition*.[132] There, it will be recalled, she refers to man's ability to make and keep promises as the essential means whereby action's boundlessness, on the one hand, and its unpredictability, on the other, may be checked.[133] There, with no mention of constitutions, she refers to the web of promises which renders the public space durable and its members reliable.[134] There, however, it is a matter of little note. Here it undergirds her conception of the constitution as born of a horizontal covenant, and plays a crucial role.

In passing, the reader should also note the interesting use Arendt makes of traditional contract theory. True to one strand of this tradition, in *On Revolution* she depicts the constitution as a mutual compact entered into for the sake of the benefits which are expected to be derived from the association. For the sake of these benefits, the members of the association agree to be bound by decision norms such as majority rule which are instituted to secure the smooth functioning and longevity of the association. Where Arendt departs from more traditional conceptions of the contract is in her view of its purpose. Unlike so many (for example, Hobbes and Locke) who have understood the scheme of social cooperation as one that is entered into for the sake of the private benefits which will flow to the members, Arendt envisions the mutual covenanting as taking place for the sake of the benefits which will flow to each in the course of participating in a common public life. That some might covenant merely to assure themselves security of life, liberty, and property receives no mention. For Arendt, covenanting and constitution making become matters of theoretical interest only insofar as the people who are doing the covenanting and constitution making are doing so with the intention of constituting a space within which public happiness, and not private security, is to be enjoyed. The latter may follow as well, but that it might is not a subject which concerns Arendt.

That a direct line can be traced between Arendt's early emphasis upon promising and her understanding of the nature of a constitution says much on behalf of the continuity in her thought which links *The Human Condition* and *On Revolution*.[135] At the same time, it is quite clear that, in Arendt's view, as it is developed in *On Revolution*, there is much more to a constitution than the notion of mutual promising entails. What plays into Arendt's conception, in addition, are a set of concepts which she develops in *Between Past and Future*, concepts already canvased throughout this chapter. Chief among the concepts enlisted to this end is Arendt's understanding of the origin and of the authority of that which remains tied to it.

Thus the concept of the constitution qua agreement is transmuted into the notion of the constitution qua foundation.[136] Think of it this way: out of the origin comes the constitution; but for generations subsequent to the first, the constitution *is* the origin.[137] From this point of view, action, the father of all beginnings, has brought forth the constitution as the repository for its essence, or principle, which will henceforth be the force behind all that is done in congruence with the constitution's form.[138] In other words, the constitution properly serves to insure that what flows out of the moment of the founding will be stamped by the spirit, or principle, which was present in the beginning and was breathed into the constitution as the principle of its life. Thus the constitution, by shaping all subsequent action, secures continuity.

Also prominent in *On Revolution* is the notion which holds that the constitution, because it bears within itself the spirit of the founding, is the objective ground from which all legitimate authority derives.[139] As envisioned by Arendt, the constitution will properly become the focal point of an origin-oriented cultural tradition which will in turn enhance the prospect that the actions undertaken in every present will remain commensurate with the principles embodied in the constitution itself.[140] Within a culture built upon such a foundation, the constitution will be venerated with the effect of making the citizenry perpetually mindful of the principles for which the nation stands and to which all action appropriately refers.[141]

Within *On Revolution*, Arendt's conception of the constitution rests as a jewel within its setting, flanked on all sides by a conception of the political process and a conception of the political culture whose guiding perspective was delineated at the center of this chapter. In the discussion of Arendt's view of education, I commented upon the centrality which she accords to the teaching of civics through "monumental" history. That this orientation colors the relevant sections of *On Revolution* can hardly be surprising.

Of crucial importance as well within *On Revolution* is the highly sympathetic and quite complimentary attitude Arendt takes towards such authoritarian institutions as the Roman Senate and the U.S. Supreme Court.[142] As previously indicated, Arendt affords to these institutions the privileged role of being the living voice of the origin in every present. On account of this exalted function alone the constitution and its principles are assured of being a vital presence in every present, yet the position Arendt grants them assures much more. Not only do these institutions insure that the present will remain mindful of a past which might otherwise be forgotten, but by the nature of their keystone-in-the-arch position the authorized interpreters and augmenters of the foundation are given an almost absolute right to insure that continuity is maintained. For all the truth in the earlier discussed notion which pointed out that the Supreme Court, for example, lacks any power but that of its authority (which is the authority of the past concentrated into a single point, an authority ultimately contingent upon the attitude toward the past of the citizenry as a whole), Arendt would grant the court vast power over the citizenry's deliberations by vesting the former with the right of declaring legislative actions unconstitutional. Ideally, of course, the general affection for the past will be of a strength sufficient to insure that the legislative body of the citizenry undertakes to pass no such legislation as would warrant the use of this ultimate sanction. In the final instance, however, the court would have in its hands the means by which to insure that continuity is maintained. From the evidence of *On Revolution* it appears reasonable to conclude that Arendt would accept such an institutional device as a moment within her paradigmatic political order.[143]

In sum, we find that Arendt has brought together all those means of insuring continuity which I have traced to her growing concern for the worldly pole of the action ideal. Where the public space is framed in the manner she suggests, it is her hope that its permanence will be secured; through the generations the constitution will emit a guiding light capable of insuring that long-term stability and continuity are attained without sacrificing public freedom in the process. "Self-revelatory political action not incommensurate with long-term continuity," might be the operative slogan of an ideal Arendtian regime in which the citizenry is filled with participatory civic zeal and inspired by the principles which the continuous prominence of the constitution—a prominence ultimately guaranteed by some Supreme Court-like organ—inspires.

With *On Revolution*, then, it would seem Arendt has accomplished the goal of uniting what had hitherto seemed destined to fly apart. The self-revelatory orientation of *The Human Condition* and the world-concern of *Between Past and Future*, which at first glance appear to be unmediable antitheses, have been brought into a single construct seemingly full of promise.

CREATING A NEW TRADITION OUT OF A REVOLUTIONARY MOMENT

As is well known, Arendt was of the opinion that with the advent of totalitarianism the cord which had long bound the past to the future had been irreparably severed.[144] In particular, the Occidental tradition which had remained viable from the fall of the Roman Empire and the rise of the Western Church to the beginning of the modern age, by Arendt's measure, is no longer so.[145] Just when the proliferating discontinuities between the conceptual world of the tradition and the realities of everyday experience reached critical mass is hard for Arendt to pinpoint exactly. The age of exploration, the rise of science, the growth of secularism, and the rise of mass industrial society each contributed to the incipient crisis in what had been the medieval world view.[146] Slowly the heart of the Occidental tradition had been burned out, but with totalitarianism, Arendt argues, even the husk was thrown away.[147] In our post-totalitarian epoch the ruins of what once stood so serene and sure exercise a fascination but alas, as

Arendt tells us, there is no going home again. The root experiences upon which the tradition had once been grounded, Arendt argues, are either inaccessible or lacking in self-evidence.[148] Neither faith in reason, nor faith in revelation, nor faith in the agreement of one with the other accords with modern man's experience of the world. The old compass is broken; the old truths prove no guide to our current experience.

Assuming for argument's sake that Arendt's conception of the break between the past and present is plausible, it becomes clear as well that by Arendt's own reckoning the existential loss is profound. If there is no tradition binding past to future and man to both, then the individual is bereft of the means of transcendence and of self-realization as well. Cultural traditions, in other words, do more than effect the objective continuity of the cultural and political worlds. Subjectively considered, tradition imparts to the individuals who live within it a matrix of ends and values from which lives of meaningfulness are constructed. Bereft of tradition, the threat of nihilism and anomie impinges.

Against this background, Arendt's work can be understood as comprising both an analysis of the problem and an attempt to fashion the lineaments of a solution. The former has already been elucidated. The latter is quite clear as well: Arendt would have us bring a living tradition into existence, a tradition which would, among other things, give prominence to the "building blocks" of meaningfulness that were discussed in chapter 1. Before concluding this chapter, then, we would do well to consider the nature of the new tradition Arendt espouses. In particular, we shall concentrate upon the rather peculiar notion of inventing a tradition out of whole cloth: how can one conscientiously set out to constitute a "new" tradition, a tradition whose very novelty would seem to undercut its aspiration to being traditional?[149] That Arendt would constitute a new tradition does seem to be apparent, but so too are the paradoxes such an undertaking entails.

On behalf of this notion one might argue that the cumulative effect of *The Human Condition* and *On Revolution* attests to Arendt's desire to call such a tradition into being. In *The Human Condition* Arendt sets forth the existential structure of the political experience which she refers to generically as "action." Notably, she takes as evidence for the experiential substantiation of her conception, fragments from the extra-philosophical historical and literary records of Greece. Paradoxically, because this part of the Greek experience never entered the philosophical tradition, in Arendt's view, it has been spared the fate of repudiation which has befallen most of the contents of that tradition.[150] Thus, even from the far-side of the collapse of metaphysics, she feels secure in anchoring her new culture of politics upon it.

In *On Revolution*, among other things, Arendt can be understood as gathering together further instances of phenomena which are existentially akin to that which she describes in *The Human Condition*.[151] Thus her stories of Roman and of early American experience allow her to flesh out the paradigmatic experience which she denominates as "public happiness"; and while she makes no reference at all in this text to the Greek political experience, the family resemblances are easily seen. In addition, as if to underscore the universality of "public happiness" and of man's desire to attain it, Arendt traces the manifestations of this "lost tradition" as they appear in, for example, the Paris Commune, the Soviets of 1917, and the workers councils of Hungary in 1956.[152]

When these two works, *On Revolution* and *The Human Condition*, are juxtaposed, it can be seen that Arendt herself has performed the role which, as noted above, she ascribes to the storyteller, and to the best kind of political thinker who, in her view, must be a storyteller as well: out of a sustained meditation upon a certain kind of political experience, Arendt deduces a conceptual structure which, she believes, best illuminates the existential reality at its heart. Through this conceptual web, a web which seems to be implicit in each of the episodes she narrates, Arendt in effect constructs a literary genre, and, perhaps the basis for a tradition.

In themselves, however, these moments do not constitute a tradition because—and this is a fact which Arendt finds most remarkable—each instance was an isolated event. Aside from certain aspects of self-conscious repetition which characterize the relationship between the Roman and American experiences, Arendt regards the eruptions of public freedom that she records not as the upwelling of a tradition that prefigures and precipitates its own moments of repetition but as singular manifestations of the human desire to live a life of public happiness. Indeed, the independence of these events might be said to justify Arendt's treating what some might regard as historically contingent instances as an "existential" of general human significance.[153] And yet, at the same time, Arendt very distinctly bemoans the fact that no traditions arose to conceptualize and to narrate the stories of these events which are for her so filled with meaning and importance.[154] Had such traditions arisen to transmit the tale by the telling—and this is certainly Arendt's view—such phenomena as these stories relate would have been manifest much more frequently.[155]

In Arendt's work, however, such a tradition is at long last constituted. But is this enough to insure that action of the most heroic and awesome variety will be manifest with regularity? Were the tradition of Arendt's literary invention a living tradition, we could expect the answer to be yes. Such is the kind of productivity Arendt herself has led us to anticipate from a living tradition. Does much hinge then upon the distinction between a literary and a living tradition? Apparently much does. It is not that the two are never found together but rather that on occasion they are not. A thriving culture may manifest its vitality on both the theoretical (read: literary) and practical planes. A dead culture may leave behind only a literary testament. Between the two is the idea which aspires to inspire both theory and practice, the idea which wants to be a seed from which will grow a living tradition and a living culture. Not every such seed takes root; where it does not, only the literary husk survives as a reminder. A literary construct that wants to be a seed, this, then, is what Arendt bequeaths to us.

A seed that would be a sapling; but of all such aspirations it can be said that much depends on the soil and upon its prior preparation. How then would Arendt advise us to prepare the soil? How, in short, does she envision the movement from theory to practice, from books to life?

In truth, Arendt never directly spells out her answer to our problem, though the answer is implicit in *On Revolution*. It will be recalled that, in *Between Past and Future*, Arendt responds negatively, or at best noncommittally, to the question of whether the Roman-rooted concepts upon which she focuses can serve as the means to the solution of our contemporary crisis. Several possible reasons for Arendt's position were discussed. The most important of these is Arendt's insight into the organic connection which links the vitality of a conceptual vocabulary to the question of whether this language speaks to the matrix of a people's common experience. Since the experience of the modern age hardly conforms to the categories of Arendt's ideal political culture, she can hardly advocate the direct adoption of her Weltanschauung since it would lack authentic roots in the soil of life. Thus it becomes clear why in *Between Past and Future* Arendt would exhort her readers to abide in "the gap" while warning them against taking cover in the arms of some conceptual tradition which no longer connects with the experiential ground.

In *On Revolution*, however, Arendt moves beyond this position as she articulates, at least by implication, a vision of the path by means of which the roseate conceptual landscape of *The Human Condition* might become the symbolic world of a living people. What *On Revolution* receives from *Between Past and Future* constitutes a large part of the "how" dimension which *The Human Condition* altogether lacked. Yet what *Between Past and Future* contributes pertains much more to preserving the spirit of the beginning than to the beginning itself. New in *On Revolution*, however, is a vision of the beginning and attention to how it is made. What makes this so important, of course, is that it is only by means of a new (and revolutionary) beginning that the "tradition" of public happiness, which Arendt would bestow, can become a matter of lived experience and thus saved from existential irrelevance.

The problem, then, is that of providing authentic and experiential roots for a literary "tradition" which is discontinuous with political life as it is lived anywhere in the modern world. The solution implicit in *On Revolution* is clear: a living tradition can be engendered only by means of the kind of political revolution that gathers an entire people into its movement, and constitutes for it that kind of collective experience which, in retrospect, is understood as having reconstituted the community through a common beginning.

Simply put, then, Arendt is now willing to advocate the revolutionary reshaping of the experiential common ground in such a way as would facilitate the coming into being of a common political culture of the type she espouses.

Out of such a new beginning, and out of the interpretative process which takes hold of it, Arendt would hope that there might germinate an authoritative cultural tradition which would in turn shape that common sense of the community out of which, in every present, action arises. Should the orientation toward the origin which Arendt espouses take hold within this culture then one could expect that action would henceforth be undertaken in such a way as to strengthen the authority of the past in every present. Over time the mechanism should become self-perpetuating and the cultural categories of perception should operate in every present to prefigure a modality of action congruent with the principles immanent in the new beginning.

CONCLUSION

By a leap of collective action, then, we are asked to overcome world alienation, escape from the philosophical perplexities of modern solipsism, and transcend the groundlessness of modern politics. Out of this new beginning it is hoped that there will arise the stories, structures, and spaces that connect men to the world and to one another. In consequence, men who previously took their bearings from a worldless kind of private sense will henceforth be guided by a common sense that is rooted in a shared world and will make decisions that accord with the mode of validity such a common sense presupposes.

In effect, by such means, Arendt proposes to solve the problem of world alienation while avoiding the difficulties that a direct confrontation with the Cartesian dissolution of worldly common sense would entail. And yet, given the nature and extent of modern world alienation, it is questionable whether the requisite leap of action is even possible. It is also unclear why we should not expect that the intellectual forces that have engendered modern world alienation before will not engender it again by attacking the validity of the new common sense and the presuppositions of its authority. For both of these reasons, even in the wake of all she has accomplished in the works considered in this chapter, it is still incumbent upon Arendt to articulate a post-Cartesian conception of common sense that is fully cognizant of the epistemological presuppositions of the modern age. Indeed, only upon such grounds can the tenability of the return to Roman foundations that Arendt espouses be established. Small wonder, then, that Arendt's second stratagem gives way, in the works we will be considering in the next chapter, to her third, that is, to an explicit conceptualization of a postmodern conception of common sense.

Before turning to those works, however, it is necessary for us to thematize certain problematic implications that follow from the changes that have been wrought in Arendt's conception of action in the movement from *The Human Condition* to *On Revolution*. At the same time, by so doing, we will be bringing into full focus the cluster of concerns that will be of penultimate interest to us in the next chapter.[156]

In the first chapter, we focused upon Arendt's conception of political action as it had been conceived from the perspective of Arendt's concern for man's attainment of his telos. In this chapter, Arendt's concern for this particular facet of action has been much less in evidence as we have focused upon her efforts to conceptualize the transcendence of world alienation and the relationship between action and the maintenance of the world's perdurance. It should be seen, however, that the shift of emphasis has been from one element of the action ideal to another equally indispensable component. Action is properly as much the vehicle of the one as of the other, and only attains to the ideal when it serves both these ends simultaneously. But for the actions of men which must repeatedly secure it in every present, the continuity of the world could not be maintained; but for the continuity of the world, men would lack a site of, and a spur to, uniqueness-revealing action in the first place.

That both of these elements are mutually entailing, and are mutually entailed by Arendt's conception of action, should not obscure the fact, however, that the prime object of concern has shifted from the self-revelatory to the world-sustaining pole of action. In consequence, a conception of action has emerged which in certain ways is quite at variance with the conception of action articulated in the first chapter. Conspicuously attenuated is the emphasis which Arendt had hitherto placed upon political participation as the uniquely tenable vehicle of self-definition.

Though Arendt continues in *On Revolution* to emphasize the participatory dimension of public life, because this participation unfolds within a framework guided by its own imperative of self-reproduction, the range of self-actualizing activity is necessarily bounded more narrowly than before: On the one hand, the role allotted to mechanisms of cultural reproduction must engender the concern that the possibilities of authentic self-display may be squelched as a consequence of the self's being excessively "normalized" in the course of the socialization process. On the other hand, the power allotted to such extrapolitical authorities as the Supreme Court, and to the constitution generally, raises the specter of the frustration of the collective process from without. At issue, with respect to this last point, is not only the question of whether the citizenry will be blocked from the enthralling experience of collectively authoring the wholly novel; more significantly, there arises the theoretical question of whether such a conception of authority, as Arendt has introduced, is at all compatible with her paradigmatic definition of the political space as a space informed by political equality and isonomy. Might not the role she allots to authority have the effect of reintroducing the distinction between rulers and ruled which in *The Human Condition* she had been so concerned to eradicate?

Assuming that a form of political action adequate to the end of insuring the world's continuity could be brought into being by means of the elements delineated in this chapter, we want to know whether this type of action would be adequate to the end of man's actualizing his uniqueness. To achieve the former without the latter hardly suffices. Any conception of politics deserving of Arendt's approbation must surely satisfy both these criteria.

In the prelude to part two, I observed that man's desire to achieve full manifestation of his uniqueness might give rise to a kind of action capable of destroying the world's frame, or at the least, of ruining its continuity. Since that point, I have traced a movement of reflective recoil which begins from the side of a world whose lastingness must be secured by the actor lest it—and action generally—be destroyed by him. To this end we have canvased Arendt's efforts in *Between Past and Future* and *On Revolution* to identify that ensemble of concepts and institutions which is capable of instilling the appropriate orientation, that ensemble which is capable of insuring that all action will be commensurate with the world's continuity.

What must be asked, however, is how action's self-revealing pole fares after this shoring up of the pole which had hitherto been at risk: Can appropriately worlding action be appropriately self-revealing as well? Or, more to the point, does Arendt achieve this result through the structures discussed in this chapter?

The problem with revolutionary action, it will be recalled, lies in the fact that it undermines the world's continuity. At the same time, however, more than any other mode of action it offers those who participate in it the opportunity of revealing themselves in all their unmistakable individuality while bringing a new polity into being. Certainly, founding action provides the occasion for self-display of the most heroic variety. We might also anticipate that times of political crisis will be equally conducive to the revelation of character.

But can the same be said of the action which serves the end not of new creation, nor of heroic defense, but of mere world-perpetuation? What occasion does action of this sort provide for the display of a citizen's uniqueness? Moreover, if there is a connection between human uniqueness and man's capacity to do or to begin the novel, then how is the former quality, which was hitherto held to be the ground of action, to be manifest in a type of action which is blocked from doing or beginning anything in an unprecedented fashion whenever it is possible to follow a precedent? In short, we must ask once again, whether the action that aims at continuity can, at the same time, be the miracle working faculty which brings individuals to fullest individuation, and novelty into the world.

By the measure of revolutionary action world-sustaining action certainly seems to fall flat. Action of the world-sustaining variety would likely offer the joys of public happiness to those who choose to participate in it, but it is hard to see how action that aspires to continuity with the past can at the same time offer an opportunity for that sort of heroic self-manifestation that accompanies action of the world-creating variety. Indeed, by the criterion of founding action, action of the world-sustaining kind will often appear as if there was nothing more to it than a merely conditioned type of behavior that attests more to the character of the agencies of indoctrination than to the individual character of the one performing the acts. As such, action would be at once bereft of its actor-revealing and community-constituting capacity.

In *On Revolution*, the text in which the world-sustaining factors come to the fore in a most systematic fashion, Arendt herself seems to be painfully aware of the fact that the requirements of world-preservation may entail the diminution of action's existential significance.[157] In effect, she acknowledges that the men of revolution are men of action more than those living in noncritical periods can ever be. But the world itself can ill afford the effusion of such action on a continuous basis.[158] Rather, such pure moments of action must give birth to political structures whose very permanence necessarily entails setting certain limits to action's inherent boundlessness. Henceforth, action must become a hybrid of world-sustaining and actor-revealing elements, a hybrid which only rarely shall give rise to those extraordinary moments which occur when all impediments are removed and action's inherent potentiality blazes forth freely.

Jefferson, as mentioned earlier, grasped this fact and was unwilling to accept it. He recommended continuous revolution for the sake of continuous and unimpeded action. How can one generation which has known the joys of revolutionary action seek to deprive another of the same, he asked. Arendt grants him his point, but refuses to accept his solution. The world's continuity is too important a value to be squandered as it would be if Jefferson's proposal were accepted.[159] Action must be brought down to earth and constrained in order that the world might be sustained over time by means of a controlled summoning of action's potentiality.

Only in crisis situations can action's capacity to author infinite new beginnings and novel deeds be set free. At all other times, Arendt apparently would have the actor hearken back to one beginning in particular. No more does Arendt laud the actor who prides himself on his ability to author new beginnings out of his own infinite originality and potentiality. Rather, the new hero is he who looks back before he acts and takes his cue from the way things have been done before. In this light, it is perhaps significant that, in *On Revolution*, Arendt speaks not so much of self-revelation but of "public happiness" instead. These pleasures may not be the same.

At stake here is more than the possibility of individual existential attainment. The factors which render this facet of political action problematic, in the same instant, impede the citizenry's ongoing quest for *collective* self-definition, a quest which in *The Human Condition* was greatly facilitated by the conditions of political equality and isonomy.[160] What adversely affects this latter telos, in particular, is not so much the ascendancy of the past per se, but its ascendancy through the mouths of those authorities to whom Arendt grants what amounts to a veto power over the polity's collective deliberations whenever these stray too far from the former's sense of appropriate bounds. While granting that such entities as the Supreme Court can play an essential role as agents of continuity, it must still be seen that to afford to any element of the political structure such potential power over against the collective deliberations of the citizenry has the effect of incorporating into the body of the polity a hierarchical differentiation very much akin to the kind which Arendt so assiduously criticizes in *The Human Condition.*

In *The Human Condition*, it will be recalled, Arendt critiques mainstream political philosophy from Plato onwards as carrying within itself an antipolitical bias, a bias evidenced most clearly in its continuing effort to replace politics with rule.[161] From this perspective, the antipathy of most philosophers towards politics is born of their preference for order, predictability, and the quiet life over the disorder, contingency, and passion of political existence.[162] As a consequence, the political philosophers—who, on occasion, have also had reason to fear for their lives at the hands of the mob—have articulated one rationale after another on behalf of what, in Arendt's view, is a thoroughly antipolitical politics. As testament to this reading of the tradition, Arendt refers to a long line of proposals whose effect would be to vest political power in the hands of a select elite, and concomitantly, would have the effect of replacing political equality with hierarchy, and isonomy with the division of the citizenry into rulers and ruled.[163]

That the public space will be a more turbulent and less predictable place on account of isonomy and political equality is, in *The Human Condition*, freely acknowledged by Arendt who accepts it as a price well worth paying for the sake of the gain that would come of it.[164] Even in *Between Past and Future*, in the context of Arendt's first discussion of authority, she clearly notes its problematic status within a political order in which it would constitute an affront to the concept of political equality.[165] While she is willing to accept the importance of attaching, in a general way, the status of authority to the past for the present, she shows herself extremely reluctant to grant authority to any particular political elements.[166]

In "The Crisis in Education," for example, though she emphasizes the importance of imparting to children a general sense for the authoritativeness of the world, its ways, and the past from which it arises, she is very careful to vest authority only with parents and teachers.[167] In this same essay, without even a hint of qualification, Arendt insists that the limits of legitimate authority are bounded by the borders of the prepolitical realm.[168] According to the position Arendt articulates at that time, when authorities set themselves up over against the political realm, the citizens are thereby reduced to children or slaves, and, for obvious reasons, Arendt refuses to countenance such an affront to the dignity of political life.[169] As in *The Human Condition*, Arendt shows herself unwilling to sanction any mechanisms which would undercut political equality and divide the citizenry into rulers and ruled.

With *On Revolution*, however, Arendt's restraint seems to dissipate under the pressure of her concern for securing permanence. In this text she is quite ready to accept the role of an organ like the Supreme Court or Roman Senate as a means of securing a modicum of world continuity. Without so much as acknowledging the volte-face her solution seems to entail, by accepting such a constitutional device Arendt gives her readers a basis for concluding that she prizes continuity more than either the freedom of the collective process or the political equality whose subordination her choice seems to necessitate. That in fact Arendt does esteem self-revelation more than continuity and would like most of all to hit upon a conception of action conducive to both does not vitiate the objections that have been raised.[170] One can only imagine that Arendt herself would no longer be pleased with this solution in the face of these criticisms.[171]

A further objection to the approach that has been canvased in this chapter turns not on the potential for the suppression of individual self-display nor on the potential for the suppression of the collective process, but on the potential for the suppression of political subcultures. Particularly threatened by the hegemonic cultural tradition that Arendt espouses are alternative, counter- and non-hegemonic traditions and the collective self-expression of the constituencies that sustain, and are sustained by, them. Whether these minority traditions are so for positing heterodox interpretations of the meaning of the origin or for positing master narratives that are utterly incompatible with the hegemonic narrative hardly matters. Where the mechanisms of social reproduction are smoothly functioning, the danger exists that, in the quest for a unitary public culture, these alternative cultures will be politically suppressed.[172]

Unfortunately, because the multiculturalist challenge to the construct developed in this chapter remains peripheral to Arendt's understanding of the problematic aspects of the action ideal, Arendt never addresses it directly.[173] Thus if we would discern how Arendt would respond to this challenge, we must infer her response from the evolution of her later work as it bears on the problematic relationship between self-display and the preservation of world-continuity.[174] This will be one of our tasks in the next chapter.

In the face of these points of criticism, the viability of the action-ideal must be called into question. Can it find a place within the framework of "normal" politics? If Arendt is correct in her estimation of the importance of the constituents of the action-ideal, then man (qua actor) requires an enduring world as much as he requires a variety of action that will enable him to manifest his inborn uniqueness before others. Because both needs are equally primordial and equally essential, there can be no solution that would do away with the one for the sake of the other. To this point, however, how these seemingly antithetical, yet equally indispensable, imperatives might be brought together has not been made clear. What has been made clear is that any politics or any conception of the political process which privileges the one imperative at the expense of the other will be found lacking and one-sided from the standpoint which acknowledges the importance of both. Each partial view must be canceled, raised, and incorporated within a single paradigm of politics. Synthesis demands not negation, but sublation. Neither pole can be overlooked; at the heart of what seems to be an irreconcilable opposition a moment of practical and conceptual mediation must be found.

Because Arendt was undone by death before she was able to articulate this "third way" in politics, we shall never know just how she would have worked it out. What we do know is that the conceptualization of political judgment and common sense would have likely played a very large part in its formulation because it was in the course of her meditations upon political judgment and common sense that she discovered a means of mediating between the conflicting imperatives that flowed from the competing elements in her conception of politics.[175] Even in those few writings which she leaves to us it can be seen that, as a result of her reflections upon the nature of judgment and common sense, she was moving toward a new conception of action that included within itself a world-sustaining, as well as a self-expressive, component.[176]

Thus judgment and common sense come to the fore as Arendt endeavors to mediate between the contrary emphases of *The Human Condition* and *On Revolution*. At the same time, the turn to judgment and common sense enables Arendt to compensate for her earlier neglect of the dynamics of the political process and of consensus formation, albeit that Arendt's conceptualization of this process in the wake of the works canvased in this chapter necessarily differs from that which the emphases of *The Human Condition* alone would have likely entailed.[177] Most important of all, however, Arendt's turn to judgment and common sense signifies her intention to formulate a post-Cartesian and postmodern conception of judgment and common sense, an intention that corresponds to a need that is as much extant at the end of *On Revolution* as it was at the end of *The Human Condition*.[178] And of the magnitude of this need there should be no doubt. Indeed, as we inferred from the last section of *The Human Condition*, the theoretical adequacy of Arendt's conception of a postmodern politics hangs in the balance.

Unfortunately, none of these matters are worked out fully, nor does Arendt ever fully explicate how what she has to say about judgment and common sense relates to her earlier discussions of politics from either of the standpoints which are implicitly superseded by this new emphasis. What I propose to do in the third chapter, then, is to explore Arendt's work on judgment and common sense, and to situate it with respect to what has come before in order that we might critically analyze whether Arendt's "third way" could have succeeded.

Chapter Three

The Rectification of the Action-Ideal: Judgment, Common Sense, and a New Logos of Politics

TOWARD JUDGMENT

From the beginning of this text our primary concern has been to trace the emergence and subsequent development of Arendt's conception of political action. In the first chapter, the self-revelatory telos at the heart of this conception was elucidated. In the second chapter, we attended to the changes wrought in the original conception as Arendt's recognition of action's world-sustaining function came to the fore. In this chapter our focus shifts again as we turn to Arendt's late work on judgment and common sense and to the final stage in the development of Arendt's conception of action that this work entails. Significantly, our attention to this body of work will also provide us with the opportunity to examine how Arendt envisions the transcendence of the Cartesian epistemological cul de sac of the modern age which, by Arendt's own report, looms as a mighty obstacle in the way of the realization of her conception of action. As it was the breakdown of common sense and the advent of the new epistemology of the modern age that undermined action's viability, it stands to reason that action's future prospects depend upon the articulation of a

postmodern conception of common sense and upon a defense of its epistemological presuppositions.[1] Arendt seeks to provide both and we shall
attend to her efforts in this chapter.

Already we have established that for Arendt the viability of her conception of political action presupposes the transcendence of world alienation. But we have also seen that if action is to secure its telos, it is equally
important that the common sense which overcomes world alienation does
so in a manner that respects the dignity of human difference and the validity of the world view that arises out of the welter of perspectival heterogeneity. From Arendt's perspective, of course, the latter stipulation is
implicit in the former. Because the worldly (or political) reality of the
things that appear within the world (or realm of appearance) is defined by
Arendt as comprising the full variety of aspects that are manifest to the
persons who are gathered there, the transcendence of world alienation
necessarily entails respect for human plurality. Nonetheless, such matters
of definition notwithstanding, our criticism of *On Revolution* suggests
that at times these criteria fail to hang together as Arendt presupposes
they do. A completely adequate conception of common sense, however,
must satisfy them both.

We have also seen that the neo-Cartesian "common sense" of the
modern age—which Arendt depicts as an introspective private sense and
thus not really as a common sense at all—clearly fails to meet these criteria and for this reason cannot possibly serve as a foundation for the conception of political action that Arendt develops in *The Human Condition*,
let alone for the conception she develops subsequently. On similar
grounds, Arendt rejects the "common sense" that brought totalitarian ideologies to the fore as well. Neither can the conception implicit in *On Revolution* be accepted as adequate to the requirements that Arendt delineates. We turn to Arendt's later writings on judgment and common sense
in the hope, then, that we shall be able to uncover an adequate conception. This is of foremost concern in this chapter: the possibility of the realization of Arendt's—or of any other postmodern—conception of political
action hangs in the balance.

As we begin our search for a more adequate conception of judgment
and common sense, it is important to keep in mind that 'adequacy' at this
stage in the development of Arendt's work is as much defined in terms of
Arendt's late conception of political action as it is in terms of the requirements of a post-Cartesian conception of common sense. As we have seen,
as a result of the movement of thought manifest in the works that were
considered in chapter 2, action, which was initially defined essentially in
terms of self-actualization, has been redefined as sustaining the world as
well. Inadequate, then, would be any conception of judgment and com-

mon sense that is not compatible with the simultaneous realization of both of these ends.

We are already familiar with the difficulties that attended Arendt's earlier efforts to conceptualize a mode of action that is capable of meeting these twin criteria. In each case, failure vis à vis one criterion was the price paid for success vis à vis the other. In turning our attention to Arendt's work on judgment and common sense we want particularly to ascertain whether this work, and the close-order conceptualization of the political process that it makes possible, can facilitate the elusive end of satisfying them both concurrently. To the degree that it can facilitate this end, we will want also to clarify the nature of the changes in Arendt's conception of action that the late work on judgment and common sense entails.

That judgment comes to occupy an increasingly important position in Arendt's later work has been noted by many.[2] Strikingly, however, this "turn" to judgment is often depicted as embodying a turning *away* from her lifelong concern with political action.[3] While it is right to note the importance of retrospective historical judgment in Arendt's later thought, to oppose this emphasis to either Arendt's "early" concern with action or her "middle-period" concern with an action-oriented variety of judgment—as Ronald Beiner has done—distorts the overarching unity of her thought and misses the significance of her "late" work on judgment for an understanding of her "early" work on action.

Already in this text judgment has come to the fore on several occasions. In chapter 1, in the course of unfolding Arendt's conception of action, the symbiotic relationship between actor and spectator was thematized. There we saw that the actor sought out the public space not merely for the sake of acting *with* his peers but for the sake of acting *before* those who might applaud him as well. What went unrecognized then but becomes apparent in light of our current concern is that this conception of the actor's telos makes him dependent upon the *judgment* of the spectator.[4]

In chapter 2, judgment was again a matter of interest, though not the judgment of the citizen who renders his verdict upon the spectacle which unfolds before him. Rather, the spectator became the storyteller, the one who looks back upon the now-completed event in order to save it through interpretation and reification. But what are such stories if not judgments rendered in narrative form?

It can be presupposed that judgments of the two kinds enumerated in the above paragraphs are related to one another, and that a comprehensive theory of the role of judgment in political life will account for both of these variants individually and in their relation to one another. More important, in the present context, however, is a third mode of judgment, this one not directed towards time past but towards time future.

This mode of judgment which, for purposes of reference, I will designate as political judgment proper, is prospective in its temporal stance, deliberative in its nature, and collective in its way of proceeding. When I suggested at the end of the last chapter that Arendt's conception of judgment might contain the means by which to overcome the obstacles which have stood in the way of the action-ideal's adequate conceptualization, I did so with this dimension of judgment in mind.

In fact, as shall become clearer below, these three aspects of judgment are intimately connected with one another both in practice (inasmuch as each mode will be seen to make reference to the others) and in conception, inasmuch as each mode will be seen to operate according to procedures inherent in the other two as well.

With reference to political judgment proper, the reader may notice that much of what has just been ascribed to political judgment was ascribed in chapter 1 to action, at least by implication. What, after all, is political action if not a collective process whereby the future is determined? What goes on in the public space if not collective deliberations with the aim of securing the public weal?

That such observations are, indeed, to the point should not obscure one other fact: In *The Human Condition* and in *On Revolution* these facets of political action—implicit in the concept of action as they may be—receive almost no attention. Instead, in *The Human Condition*, for example, while Arendt discusses action's existential achievement, she scarcely attends to the dynamics of the collective process through which these benefits are to be secured.[5] Nor are these matters attended to in much greater detail in *On Revolution*.[6] Had she done so, she would have had to consider those aspects of political action which are more precisely comprehended as exercises of political judgment. This route, of course, was not taken. In consequence, action appears as an undifferentiated essence at the one pole of a dichotomy. At the other pole, sits the spectator, or the agent of authority, as the only one, according to this schema, who is to exercise judgment. Thus within the framework of these texts, the moment of judgment inherent in action is obscured while judgment and action are implicitly dichotomized and spatially projected onto the political landscape in such a way as to enjoy little beyond an external and contingent complementarity.

One matter of great concern to Arendt in *The Human Condition* is the existential significance of human speech.[7] Speech, it will be recalled, is that which alone can truly manifest *who* the actor is.[8] But because of an almost total lack of concern for the political process itself, Arendt never considers what differentiates political speech from other kinds of talk. Thus, we read too much of the deed-like quality of fine words but not enough about what occasions their being spoken. Because Arendt seeks to direct our attention away from *what* such words accomplish to *"whom"* such words reveal, she becomes inattentive to the rhetorical functions of speech which are practically synonymous with their politicality. Thus throughout *The Human Condition* there is little to be found that might intimate that he who acts before his peers by speaking, speaks *on behalf of* this or that, and acts by opining, arguing, and by seeking to persuade: clearly, each of these acts of political, or deliberative, speech requires that the actor exercise political judgment of some kind, for without the display of such judgment he would be incapable of influencing the course of the collective deliberations. Nor, presumably, would the actor be capable of arriving at a sound opinion of his own if he wholly lacked this capacity for making political judgments. Obvious as this all may be, it is equally clear that within the body of *The Human Condition* Arendt never attends to these matters.

From our discussion thus far one might reasonably infer that Arendt only became mindful of the relationship between action and judgment late in life. Ironically, this is hardly the case. Though she scarcely considers this relationship in either *The Human Condition* or *On Revolution*, she had done so in several essays written in earlier years, and in one essay written in the period between the composition of these major works she depicts this relationship in a manner which is strongly suggestive of the course that her future deliberations would take.[9] Had her own sense of purpose in either *The Human Condition* or *On Revolution* required that she attend to the deliberative process in greater detail, it is likely that Arendt's partially developed conception would have come to the fore at that time. Instead, the idealism and existential atomism which characterize her account of action in *The Human Condition* apparently conspired to insure that she would touch lightly upon matters which, had she delved into them more deeply, would have entailed a discussion of political judgment proper. That judgment is all but neglected in *On Revolution* as well is harder to account for given the putative role of judgment in the maintenance of continuity.[10] Nonetheless, the fact that judgment is largely overlooked remains. Had the case been otherwise, Arendt's construct might have been protected from difficulties which to this point are still unmastered, difficulties which can only be addressed by means of a developed conception of political judgment.

As already outlined, our aims in this chapter are varied. They range from the clarification of action's post-Cartesian epistemological presuppositions to the articulation of a conception of the political process as a whole that will facilitate the simultaneous achievement of action's double telos. But necessarily prior to the attainment of these aims is the task of elucidating Arendt's mature conception of judgment and common sense. It is to this task that we now turn.

The steps of our inquiry will be as follows: First, we will review the development of Arendt's conception of judgment and its commonsense foundations; second, we will explore the changes that are wrought in Arendt's conception of the political landscape and in her conception of action when the late work on judgment and common sense is brought to bear upon them both; and third, we will examine whether the newly emergent conception of action enables us to reconceptualize and resolve the problems extant at the end of chapter 2. At that point we will be in a position to determine whether this avenue of approach has facilitated the achievement of Arendt's broader aims.

ON THE RELATIONSHIP OF JUDGMENT TO COMMON SENSE: THE GENEALOGY OF A CONCEPTION

In this section the evolution of Arendt's conceptions of judgment and common sense will be traced from her earliest work to her latest. Proceeding in this manner, I will lay the foundations for what might otherwise seem to be an excessively speculative rendering of Arendt's appropriation of Kant's conception of judgment. As shall be seen presently, Arendt's most sustained analyses of judgment are to be found among her minor works.[11] Moreover, the most important source, her posthumously published lecture notes for a course on Kant's political philosophy are written in such a way as to leave quite unclear how much of what she says should be taken as evidence of her own views and how much ought to be taken as her rendering of Kant's. Not surprisingly, this situation has already had ramifications upon the secondary literature as one thread or another emergent from this text has been seized upon as ostensibly indicative of the direction Arendt's work would have been taken had she not been undone by so untimely a death. In such a context interpretive caution is to be advised. Hence the need to ground one's interpretation of this important text upon those that precede it, and especially upon those within which the problem of judgment is discussed.

In particular, for reasons that will only become clear when we come to Arendt's discussion of Kant, it is necessary to attend not only to Arendt's evolving conception of judgment, but to her conception of the relationship between judgment and common sense as well. That Arendt always conceives the two in tandem will prove to be of great significance.

The Early Period

As I noted in the introduction, Arendt's analysis of political judgment and her search for a new and human-plurality validating logos of politics unfolds against the background of her ever-broadening critique of ideological thinking. The devotees of ideological thinking had, of course, made war upon human plurality and, in this respect, reminded Arendt of all those Platonists, neo-Platonists, and twisted pseudo-Platonists who had ever declared war upon human difference in the name of the one truth.[12] And thus, after Arendt comes to the conclusion that the antipolitical root of totalitarian evil and the antipolitical root of Platonic politics are one and the same, Arendt's critique of ideological thinking first broadens, and then shifts, to become a critique of political (pseudo- and neo-) Platonisms generally.[13] In the name of truth, politics had become destructive of that which politics ought properly to foster; in defense of human plurality, truth and the politics that would place truth in power were to be opposed.

Thus, from *The Origins of Totalitarianism* through *Thinking*, Arendt allies herself with those moderns who have endeavored to undermine all metaphysical pretensions to absolute truth and universality.[14] For Arendt, however, the significance of the critique lies in its ability to clear an epistemological space within which the manifestation of human difference as the irreducible content of politics can be protected against all who would oppose or replace it with the metaphysically grounded politics of truth. And, in light of the position staked out by Arendt in *The Human Condition* and *On Revolution*, it ought also to be noted that Arendt's defense of the political space as a site for the articulation of human plurality is mounted against those who would undercut this process in the name of the material well-being of the many as well.

To assert the primacy of the logos of self-disclosure, and the primacy of a political process that conduces to this same end—as it welds consensus from the welter of difference—is, however, hardly to delineate the shape of this logos or to articulate just how this process itself ought to be conceived. And thus Arendt's reader is led to ask whether her critique of the logos of truth-in-power ever gives way to an alternative conception. It is, then, with an eye to arriving at an understanding of Arendt's alternative that we must proceed.

As previously noted, *The Origins of Totalitarianism* better conveys Arendt's early grasp of the problems inherent in the modern conception of politics than it does a sense for wherein the solution lies. The specter of truth in power, and of its necessitating and coercive logicality, is well depicted, but the alternative is only vaguely intimated. The totalitarian's logical assault upon human difference and spontaneity is well documented but the means of escaping from such logical necessity is hardly developed. Of course, as noted at the outset, in *The Origins of Totalitarianism* Arendt does not aim to go beyond the subject matter posited by the book's title. The alternative vision is developed only subsequently, and indeed it constitutes the substance of Arendt's mature political thought just as it has constituted the substance of this text thus far.

At this point, however, my concern is not with Arendt's response to totalitarianism in general, but rather with tracing the contours of Arendt's evolving endeavor to articulate an alternative to ideological thinking. At immediate issue is whether the intimations of such an alternative can be discerned within *The Origins of Totalitarianism*, and whether from such intimations (if they are in fact present) one might infer the direction Arendt will take when she comes to the task of articulating her conception of the kind of rationality that is appropriate to the nature of the political space.

When considered from this perspective, one hitherto unmentioned and seemingly unexceptional aspect of Arendt's analysis takes on new meaning. At once it is noted that, as a foil to the bête noire of ideological thinking, Arendt has counterpoised "common sense," albeit without developing the concept fully.[15] Thus in *The Origins of Totalitarianism* Arendt is seen to trace the rise of ideologies to the breakdown of common sense.[16] As Arendt proceeds to explain why this is so, it becomes clear that, in her view, only those lacking in common sense could ever come to find the ideological construction of reality to be at all plausible.[17] Though the ideologist "knows" all history to be the systematic and wholly consistent product of inexorable historical laws, in Arendt's opinion, those who possess common sense know better.[18]

In particular, Arendt looks to common sense to provide one with a "realistic" feel for the role of accident and freedom in determining the course of events.[19] To one who possesses a feel for the way the world works, that which is overly consistent, like the all-too-perfect alibi, seems to be more likely a lie than the truth.[20] Only one who lacked such a feel could fall prey to such totalizing fictions as the ideologists peddle. Ultimately, Arendt's description of action's inherent boundlessness, unpredictability, and irreversibility can be seen as relating this aspect of common sense to her broader conception of action.

One matter of importance which any theory which would ground judgment in common sense must address has to do with the nature of this common sense: To whom is it common? To everyone, by virtue of being human? Or to some group in particular? And if only to the latter, then, on what basis? Already in *The Origins of Totalitarianism*, Arendt implicitly characterizes common sense as a community sense belonging to members of a community as a consequence of their shared activity.[21] Thus common sense is contrasted with those ideologies which are embraced by those whose communal connections have dissolved.[22] In a parallel manner, Arendt distinguishes between a common sense which is common by virtue of shared experience and one which is common to men by virtue of their being Homo sapiens who happen to possess the same logical capacity and perceptual equipment.[23] This distinction corresponds to the distinction which Arendt will later draw between the *sensus communis*, or community sense, and such a common sense as logic which is common to all men by virtue of their rational faculty.[24] Common sense of the sort being praised in *The Origins of Totalitarianism* is of the former variety, while ideology relies upon the common mental capacity signified by common sense of the latter.

In her 1953 "Understanding and Politics" Arendt returns to this notion of common sense qua community sense, rendering explicit and developing further the ramifications of what was implicit in her earlier formulation. In *The Origins of Totalitarianism*, after all, it is not clear whether the common sense of one community is likely to differ from the common sense of another. One of its components, an empirical feel for the formative impact of contingent events upon the fabric of the historical web, would presumably be available to anybody anywhere who attended to the way things actually happen in life. The other component, which emerges only through the contrast with the isolation which characterizes those who fall prey to ideology, might also be available to anyone anywhere. Only in this essay, however, does Arendt make unequivocally clear that the common sense of one community will differ from the common sense of another.[26]

Common sense, says Arendt in this essay, is that body of preunderstandings which are shared by members of a community and unite them as such.[27] These preunderstandings constitute a kind of common language whose roots are a common culture, a concrete collective life, and the learning which integrates a person into both of these frameworks. While one part of this common language will include a feel for the role of contingency in human affairs, another part will be much more time and place specific. Arendt points to this latter component in particular as equipping citizens to make common sense of their common world as they must do on the way to common action.[28]

Thus it is a language that makes special reference to features of a common life and reference as well to what are commonly perceived as threats to the same. It is a language which enables the citizen who stands before the community to speak of (for example) freedom and tyranny and to be understood. As such it is a language which enables the citizen to exercise his judgment in a publicly comprehensible fashion. In a formulation crucial for our effort to trace the development of Arendt's thought, she describes common sense as that implicitly shared language out of which judgment arises and to which it always returns.[29]

In this same essay, Arendt articulates the conceptual basis for the feedback loop between retrospective judgment and action which figured so prominently in chapter 2. To this end, Arendt traces both the judgment antecedent to action and the retrospective interpretation of past action to the conceptual web which comprises the heart of common sense. It is for this reason that the proposal for action which does not strike roots in this common ground necessarily falls on deaf ears; and this is why the action which unfolds in ways which fail to conform to common sense expectations remains quite literally beyond comprehension. In the wake of such events, it is the role of the theorist and storyteller to assess the meaning of the novel happening by mediating between it and the framework of common understanding, even if the latter must be stretched or partially revamped in order to take it into account.[30] The consequence of such theoretical activity will be the continuous replenishment and perpetual revitalization of a common sense whose adequacy to reality is thus secured.[31]

Conversely, where a people's common sense is vitiated and out of touch with the reality it once adequately described, this will be manifest, Arendt declares, as an inability to judge.[32] But what can it mean to say that someone lacks this ability? Certainly it cannot mean that he ceases to discriminate one thing from another; nor can it mean that the person ceases to prefer one thing to another. Rather what Arendt signals here is her conviction that judgment is only exercised rightly when it is a judgment commensurate with common sense. It is as if Arendt were to distinguish between taste and Taste. By nature we can all be said to possess the former, but only by virtue of common sense—which we may or may not possess—can we be said to possess the latter.[33]

Implicit here is a notion that Arendt will make much of in the future. By this notion, over against the infinite proliferation of incommensurable subjectivities, there exists for those with access to common sense, the capacity to manifest good or sound judgment, that is, judgment from such a general or intersubjective standpoint as will facilitate the reaching of common agreement. That common sense, or the body of preunderstandings which it encompasses, can make available such a standpoint to men who are otherwise quite unlike one another is for Arendt a most remarkable thing.[34] Through this standpoint alone does the world of men become a common world, a world in which a collective life is possible.

Rising to the standpoint of common sense, it should be noted, does not guarantee that agreement will always follow with respect to whatever issue is before the community, but it does make agreement much more likely by virtue of its bounding the range of potential disagreement. On the one hand, this range is bounded by the relatively limited number of concepts of clear public standing. On the other hand, this range is bounded by the conventions delimiting what shall be deemed a valid argument or a good reason, conventions which in Arendt's view always form a part of common sense and facilitate the resolution of the disputes which arise on its public terrain. The former may be understood as demarcating the playing field, the latter as defining the rules of the game; between the two, persons who would otherwise have nothing at all in common and no clear way of communicating their opinions—let alone of persuading others to make them their own—are given the means of doing so. For Arendt, the political significance is clear: that people have the capacity to render judgments which abstract from their particularity in such a way as to embody the community sense, proves that they are capable of rendering public judgments on behalf of the public interest and of reaching agreements with respect to the same. The significance of this early insight for her later work is evident.

As important as the question of *how* this standpoint is to be reached is the question of *why* citizens should strive to attain it. Arendt's answer to this latter question is most fully detailed in her *Lectures on Kant's Political Philosophy*. Suffice it to say at this point that, in Arendt's view, such an orientation of the citizenry is the precondition of the community's remaining intact over time. Unless the largest part of its members seek out, and are prepared to defer to, this general standpoint, then, in Arendt's view, the public space will wither and the benefits it bestows upon those who appear within it will be lost. This much was implicit after all in the discussion of the constitution at the end of chapter 2. In her *Lectures on Kant's Political Philosophy*, however, Arendt goes further, and argues that the citizen's willingness to subordinate his opinion to that of the community as a whole, and his willingness to commit himself in advance to abide by the outcome of a process whose end is the determination of the community's sense (as it bears upon any given issue), constitutes the essence of his humanity.[35] Thus humanity comes to be defined as that ensemble of attributes which befits us for a common life in the common realm which we share with our fellows. If we would be fully human, our humanity requires that we adopt this standpoint when we are engaged in common deliberation with our peers.

Before unfolding this conception in further detail, we must attend to what Arendt sets forth in *The Human Condition*, a text which, as we have noted, fails to address the matters under discussion in a direct, or substantive, way. That it is important for us to attend to *The Human Condition* in this context, nonetheless, owes to the fact that in light of what Arendt sets forth in this text we are better positioned to understand the relationship between her "early" and "late" reflections on the nature of judgment and its normative criteria, reflections which are "early" or "late" vis à vis this, the central text, of Arendt's oeuvre.

The Middle Period

Judgment and The Human Condition. The reader will recall from our discussion of the last section of *The Human Condition* that the realization of Arendt's conception of political action was held to depend upon the transcendence of world alienation and thus upon the articulation of a post-Cartesian conception of common sense that might serve as the medium of this transcendence. The reader will also recall that, despite the importance imputed to the articulation of this post-Cartesian conception, Arendt does not even begin to frame it in *The Human Condition*. This inattention was itself somewhat surprising when it was first noted, but it surely becomes even more so when we find that Arendt had been engaged by this matter prior to the publication of *The Human Condition*. If before, then, why not in the latter text as well?

Equally striking, in light of Arendt's attention to judgment and common sense in the work that precedes *The Human Condition*, is her failure to articulate a positive conception of the relationship between judgment and common sense in the context of her discussion of action and human plurality. Instead, her comments in this regard are merely critical as she makes clear her determination to keep the political space free from forms of rationality that she perceives as being insensitive to human difference. One manifestation of this determination is Arendt's critique of the plurality-inimical consequences of both the modern "process-standpoint" and of modern utilitarianism, a critique developed in part 6 of *The Human Condition* and considered at length under the rubric of necessity in chapter 1 of the current text.[36] On similar grounds Arendt also pillories what she describes as the Platonic, and neo-Platonic, "politics of making" or "politics of *techne*" according to which politics is conceived as being instrumental to the attainment of some extrapolitical end.[37] Whether this end be the actualization of the laws of history, the institutional realization of some metaphysical truth, or the greatest happiness of the greatest number makes no difference. The proponents of such ends have instrumentalized politics and have adopted a standpoint at odds with the human plurality that, by its very nature, gets in the way of the direct attainment of these ends.[38] Thus, sooner or later, the instrumentalists in politics are bound to oppose the politics of self-manifestation and human difference that Arendt wants so much to foster. By inference, then, it becomes clear that the new logos of a redeemed and redeeming politics will be antithetical to the instrumentalizing politics of making and of truth, as it will be to ideological thinking. Nonetheless, it remains the case that in *The Human Condition* the positive shape of this new logos, that is neither "a" nor "b" nor "c," is not considered.

This does not mean, however, that so far as judgment and common sense are concerned, *The Human Condition* is wholly devoid of positive significance. Indeed much can be inferred from Arendt's positive conception of action. In particular, it seems reasonable to regard the criteria of right action as elements of common sense.[39] Among these criteria, *humanitas* would no doubt be foremost, followed perhaps by those criteria which are concomitants of Arendt's aestheticization of political action and are meant to insure that deeds will be done and judged in accordance with that measure of greatness which alone befits whatever attains it for immortal fame. Presumably, the stories which, according to Arendt, every actor aspires to have written about himself would prove to be essential vehicles for the continuous inculcation of these norms and of common sense generally.[40]

Before turning away from *The Human Condition*, it is necessary to attend to another aspect of Arendt's conception of action that will come to be of great significance in the subsequent development of her conception of judgment and common sense. I refer to Arendt's conception of the actor-spectator relationship which achieves its implicit centrality within Arendt's account through the notion that action takes place within a realm of appearance.

In turning to consider this relationship, it must be noted that though the dynamic of the actor-spectator relationship is given initial prominence in Arendt's account of action, it fails to play the substantive role in *The Human Condition* that it comes to play in her later work.[41] In turning to it, then, I want only to explore the problem of its stunted development and then to examine how it might have been utilized had Arendt chosen to do so. To substantiate the latter, I will refer to Arendt's conceptualization of actor-spectator relations in "The Crisis in Culture" and in *Thinking.*[42] The importance of this train of thought will, I trust, become clear in the sequel.

Actor-Spectator Relations: A Path Untaken. In *The Human Condition* Arendt likens political action to theatrical performance. And yet, when it comes to unpacking the full significance of this analogy, Arendt falls short as she seems to succumb to that suspension of disbelief which, in a theater, enables an audience to pretend that the actors upon the stage do not know that they are performers at all. It is of course a matter of dramatic convention that most plays present themselves as if they were not plays but life itself; and thus the actors upon the stage interact with one another as if unaware that an audience is present. The play, though hardly real, pretends to be such, while the audience pretends to be invisible viewers not of something being performed for their sake, but of life itself.

Assuming the play to be a veritable slice of life, one might draw conclusions from it about life itself, as if the structure of the play were not largely determined by its dramatic form. In a similar way, Arendt, having indicated the play-like status of the performance, proceeds, perhaps without full cognizance, to bracket this awareness as if she could, by so doing, observe action itself; thus she blinds herself to the degree to which what appears to be inherent in "the play" is inherent only by virtue of the consciousness, which never leaves the actors minds, that an audience is watching. Thus Arendt becomes insufficiently sensitive to the fact that the norms which govern the action upon the stage are upheld by the expectations, conventions, and norms of the assembled spectators.

Accordingly, when Arendt is seeking to make comprehensible her insistence that action be judged not for its consequences, but for the quality of the characters who are revealed in the course of an event, a judgment of persons which she equates with the judgment of art, she emphasizes the action/actor side of the analogy much more than the spectator pole—as if beauty and virtue were entities in themselves which could be considered without reference to the subject who perceives them. How the beauty of an artwork is akin to the virtue of a man receives more attention by far than does the implicit assertion which holds that the point of view which knows how to attend to the one is akin to the point of view which knows how to attend to the other.

Perhaps, as a consequence of treating the object side first and deriving, as it were, the analogy at the subject pole from this, within *The Human Condition* Arendt never fully addresses the problematic of how actors and spectators, who by nature are inclined to attend to less ethereal matters, are to acquire this concern for beauty and virtue in the first place. Her castigation of those who attend to the affairs of the world with a materialistic and self-concerned utilitarianism hardly substitutes for explaining in closer detail how a higher "point of view" is to be attained.

Perhaps, because action's own potential for errancy is not brought into focus within *The Human Condition*, the potential role of the spectator in checking this slide remains unexplored. As a result, at no point within this text does Arendt meditate upon the role of the spectator, or upon the nature of the faculty of judgment which the spectator exercises, both of which she attends to subsequently.[43]

Had Arendt undertaken to address the problem of errant action from within the framework she elaborates in *The Human Condition*, she would have likely begun by calling attention to the fact that errant action occurs within a public space or upon a public stage and thus *in plain sight* before a throng of assembled spectators whose role, in this case, would be to signal their disapproval of that which appears before them.[44] Be action most foul or fair, presumably, the spectators will note it, and the estimation of those acting before them will rise or fall accordingly. On the assumption that the actor is concerned with his standing before the spectators—an assumption Arendt makes, and one which presumably holds at least within a representative democracy—then the spectators are in a position to play an important role as a check upon any variety of action that might displease them.[45]

Ultimately, as Arendt makes clear in *Thinking*, the relationship between actors and spectators should be symbiotic and mutually conditioning.[46] The taste of the spectators, as presupposed by the actors, should shape their action. Action in turn, over time, should shape the standards by which it is judged. Yet at any particular point in time the taste of the spectator looms as a relatively constant criterion, making it a potential force for continuity in contrast to the ever shifting winds which blow across the field of action—winds that vary in direction and intensity with every change in circumstance or personality.[47] Acculturation might be described as just that process whereby the norms of spectatorship come to be implanted.[48]

In Arendt's early work the primacy of action is unqualified; yet, as we have seen, it is likely that action will, under the impact of diverse influences, fail to hew to the Arendtian ideal. When Arendt turns to reconsider the actor-spectator relationship in the work following *The Human Condition*, one can imagine she does this in part because she sees in it a means by which action might be kept to its proper way.[49] But it should also be seen that inasmuch as this relationship depends upon norms of political judgment that are simultaneously shared, substantive, and contingent, the closer scrutiny of this relationship will also offer Arendt a basis for developing that democratic and postfoundationalist conception of political judgment and common sense that we know her to have been seeking.

Opposing the fecundity of what might have been, however, is the relative paucity of Arendt's own references within *The Human Condition* to the dynamic I have elucidated. Only in her subsequent work does this conception come to the fore. Yet even if this dynamic did not become important in Arendt's subsequent work, we would be justified in treating

The Human Condition in the context of our current concerns if only
because the influence that this work has on all that follows it is so strong,
even where only implicit. Nor is it the case, however, that following *The
Human Condition*, the earlier conceptions of judgment and common sense
are simply reasserted. Rather, when they reappear they are incorporated
within a framework that has been definitively shaped by the conception of
action Arendt delineates in *The Human Condition*. Particularly suggestive
of this influence is the fact that, henceforth, Arendt's reflections on judgment and common sense will always be conceived within parameters
which follow from the division of the public space between the actors who
are intent upon achieving fame and the spectators who alone possess the
power to bestow it.

Following *The Human Condition* Arendt's thought proceeds along
three paths which would have likely coalesced had Arendt lived to draw
the strands into their natural nexus. The first path leads from *The Human
Condition* through *Between Past and Future* to *On Revolution* and manifests Arendt's concern with overcoming world alienation and with securing the world's continuity by the means considered in chapter 2. The second leads from *The Human Condition* through *Between Past and Future*
to the *Lectures on Kant's Political Philosophy* and entails the direct evolution of Arendt's conception of *spectator* judgment. The third leads from
The Human Condition through "Truth and Politics" to the *Lectures on
Kant's Political Philosophy* and traces the evolution of Arendt's conception of the *actors'* prospective judgment, a conception that is strongly
influenced by Arendt's developing conception of spectator judgment. My
goal in what remains of this section is to review each of these strands in
turn and to point the way toward their ultimate synthesis.[50]

On Revolution *and Authority*. The first line of march out of *The
Human Condition* led to the works discussed in chapter 2 and was occasioned not so much by a concern for seeking out a new logos of political
judgment as by a concern for overcoming world alienation and for securing the continuity and stability of the world's frame against action's
propensity to render these things most problematic. At the same time, it
would not be inappropriate to observe that what was discussed in the last
chapter as making for the continuity and stability of the world might also
be characterized as conditioning a people's *common sense* in such a way
as to insure that their *collective judgment* operated in a continuity and sta-
bility-preserving manner.

Considered in light of Arendt's overarching project, it made sense to
regard the movement of thought that is manifest in several of the essays of
Between Past and Future and in *On Revolution* as emanating from

Arendt's world-concern, for surely it was this pole which was being reinforced as a result. Now, however, we are in a position to see that within the realm configured by the actor-spectator dichotomy the source of the desired effect might more plausibly come about through the office of the spectator than through that of the actor. Though actors too would be bred upon virtue imparting tales, it is hardly certain that such an education would be sufficient to offset the inherent propensity of action to author novel, and hence continuity disruptive, deeds. Far more reliable, because likely to be less affected by the passions of the moment, are the spectators whose education in the spirit of the regime and in the importance of its preservation might serve to check an otherwise errant course of action.[51] Formally, of course, there is no reason why the judgment of the spectators would be more conservative than that of the actors, given that both actors and spectators have been bred upon the same diet of common sense. And yet our exploration of the implicit dynamics of the actor-spectator relationship makes clear why each might tend to exercise its judgment in generically different ways.

Had Arendt, in *On Revolution*, been more mindful of the spectator pole's specificity, I believe she would have more closely considered the nature of the difference between the judgment of the actor and the judgment of the spectator. In fact, Arendt's neglect of the spectator's specificity keeps her from looking to his vantage point to provide ballast for the ship of state. Nor, however, does she trust the outcome completely to the beneficent agency of a past-oriented culture and education. Instead, much hinges upon the authorities in whom Arendt would invest the responsibility for insuring the long-term maintenance of continuity. In a different context, we explored the magnitude of the injury done to the ideal of isonomy by this reliance upon authority. More important, in the context of our current concerns, is the light which Arendt's conception of authority sheds upon her evolving conception of judgment.

To grasp the significance of Arendt's reflections upon authority, what was stated in the above paragraph must be reformulated slightly. In particular, the statement holding that Arendt neglects the specificity of the role of the spectator and has recourse to authority instead must be qualified. In fact, Arendt has not neglected the *function* of the spectator; rather she has overlooked the role potentially exercised by that *gathering* of spectators who surround the site of action, and who, through the articulation of their opinions, are able to influence what transpires on the stage before them. The paradox is only apparent: spectatorship can be considered and the realm of spectators ignored by reposing the function elsewhere. That Arendt has done this becomes clear when Arendt's conception of authority is examined from this perspective.

That the role of authority is to act as the definitive ideal spectator is first indicated by the fact that, in *On Revolution*, the spectator pole of the actor-spectator dyad drops from sight while the functions imputed to the spectator in our analysis of *The Human Condition* are now exercised by the agents of authority.[52] Thus it becomes the role of authority to act as a check upon the errant propensities of action, and, in particular, to act as a check upon its tendency to shatter continuity by innovations which are either incommensurate with original principles, too rapidly introduced, or both.[53] Also indicative of the correlation between authority and the role of the spectator is Arendt's emphasis upon the relative disinterest of the authorities whose only proper interest lies in insuring the upkeep of the realm's standards.[54] That such disinterest is proper to the spectator as well is a point which, in different contexts, Arendt makes repeatedly.

Once this correlation has been established, it is possible to read the relationship in the other direction and thus to explore what light Arendt's treatment of the judgment exercised by paradigmatic authority sheds upon what is implicitly a conception of the judgment exercised by the spectator.[55] In this connection, the process whereby authority mediates between past and future by means of the check it exerts upon the present becomes most important. At issue is not whether or not this is its role, but exactly how this role is played.

In *On Revolution*, Arendt singles out the Supreme Court as exemplifying her conception of authority for both its explicit past-relatedness and its continuity-sustaining role in every present.[56] The Supreme Court exercises its authority whenever it acts to insure that the actions undertaken in the present remain congruent with the principles embodied in the originary moment or document. How it actually manages this feat merits greater attention than Arendt accords it.

Close attention to the procedure of the Court and to the nature of the judgment it exercises suggests that it performs its function by means of a double hermeneutic movement which combines attributes of both retrospective and present-oriented varieties of judgment. Given a particularly hard case of questionable constitutionality, the jurist, like the retrospective judge or storyteller, paradigmatically proceeds, in the first moment, by looking back toward the origin and to the authoritative precedents arising from it in search of the significance or meaning of the principle which is at issue. In the second moment, the judge must assess the case before him for its congruence with the principle which his past-oriented hermeneutic deduction proffered. In practice, of course, this clean analytical differentiation of moments is hardly as clear-cut as it is in theory. In practice, one would assume that the relationship between the two moments is more of a dialectical and ongoing back and forth, the net effect of which will be to insure that the assessments of both the principle in question and the case at hand are continuously interdependent. In other words, it is in the very nature of such judgments that the past will be interpreted in light of the present and the present assessed in light of the past. But it is hardly possible to say with a priori certainty which of these moments will, in any given case, take precedence.

By analogy, then, we might understand the nature of spectator judgment as proceeding in similar fashion, though grounding its judgments not upon a fixed body of law but rather upon the principles implicit in the stories which comprise a major component of common sense. Note also that, as in fact a jurist's relationship to a constitution/origin is mediated by precedents and received judicial doctrines, a spectator's relationship to the origin is similarly mediated by past tellings of the tale and by the chain of successive origin-interpreting events.

It remains the case, however, that this extrapolatory movement is not traced by Arendt in any of the texts we have considered thus far.[57] Nor does her analysis of the workings of authority, as illuminating as it is of the logos guiding the judgment of the spectator, provide us with any sense of how this double hermeneutic movement articulates with the plurality of the spectators or authorities (for example, the members of the Supreme Court) who are engaged in the process. How differences of opinion within the body of spectators—or within the body of actors—might be resolved has hardly been addressed because within the texts attended to thus far this problem does not arise at all. That Arendt could fail to address this aspect of the political situation which in *The Human Condition* she had deemed to be of its very essence is odd. One might cite her own words against her and suggest that not even world-continuity can be secured by a political logos which fails to take due cognizance of human plurality as an irreducible given. That such a politics would hardly satisfy what Arendt describes as the self-expressive dimension of political life goes almost without saying.

There is, then, much in the works discussed in chapter 2 that keeps us from accepting the train of thought which culminated in *On Revolution* as adequate to Arendt's own theoretical aspirations. In critical review of this moment in her enterprise, besides calling attention to her retreat from isonomy to authority, we have now noted both her inadequate attention to the spectator pole and her relative neglect of plurality and of its propensity for manifestation. For the sake of insuring continuity much would seem to have been sacrificed. And yet, as intimated in our analysis, *On Revolution* points beyond itself.

We turn, then, to the second and third paths which go forth from *The Human Condition* in the hope that Arendt will equip us with the means by which to rectify the shortcomings which our analysis of *On Revolution* identified. In addition, we still look for her to provide us with an adequate account of political judgment proper as exercised by the actor among, and with, his peers. We also seek an account of the process of spectatorship which is true to both the influence of spectatorship upon the realm of action and to the human plurality of the spectators themselves. Finally, we will want to see whether Arendt manages to frame a path beyond Cartesian worldlessness and to construct that post-Cartesian conception of the *sensus communis* that we have been awaiting since the end of *The Human Condition*. To a large degree we will find just what we are looking for, but to glean it we will have to proceed methodically.

Central to the second and third paths is Arendt's endeavor to envision a process whereby the differences of individual judgment, that are themselves reflective of human plurality, can be mediated without recourse to fixed or eternal, external criteria. The roots of Arendt's quest in this regard can be traced to her critique of ideological thinking in *The Origins of Totalitarianism*. In the forthcoming section, however, we shall focus not upon the roots but upon the branches as our attention is turned toward Arendt's maturing formulation of the problem and her most elaborate attempt at its solution, formulations which emerge from the midst of Arendt's reflections on Kant's conception of judgment. Before turning to Arendt's lectures on Kant however, it behooves us to attend to an ensemble of three works, two of which well indicate that Arendt was already looking to Kant's conception of judgment to help her shape her conception of the political process several years before delivering her lectures on Kant.[58]

For present purposes, the reasons for attending to these works are twofold. Firstly, doing so will help to buttress my claim as to the legitimacy of regarding certain ideas developed by Arendt in the Kant lectures as elements of her own (and not merely of Kant's) political philosophy. Secondly, and more importantly, a glance at these works will enable us to arrive at a closer formulation of the precise problematic that Arendt was grappling with as she prepared her lectures on Kant.

The Maturation of a Conception

"*The Crisis in Culture*." "The Crisis in Culture" provides us with the first public evidence of Arendt's insight into the political relevance of Kant's "Critique of Aesthetic Judgment." This evidence comes not in the first half of this essay which is concerned with the fate of culture in mass society, but in the second half when Arendt's attention shifts from cultural artifacts to the *cultura animi* of the spectator who appreciates and knows how to care for these public objects.[59] In the essay's relevant section, Arendt starts off by suggesting that the *cultura animi* is synonymous with "taste." Having posited this equivalence, Arendt turns to Kant's critique of taste which Kant frames as "a critique of the judgment of the beautiful that is exercised by the spectator."[60] For Arendt, however, it is not this move but the next one which really matters.

Arendt's next move is to assert that the aesthetic judgment of the spectator and the political judgment of the spectator/citizen are essentially the same. Of course, Kant himself never suggested that there was any connection between the two, and preferred to ground his own conception of politics on practical reason and moral judgment. Nonetheless, this is the claim Arendt wants to make, and it rests on two arguments. First, Arendt argues for the phenomenal equivalence of art objects on the one hand and the words and deeds of political actors on the other. Both, she suggests, are phenomena of the realm of appearance; both only achieve the fullness of their being when they belong to the public world; and, for those who look on from the spectators' gallery, both signify the temporal transcendence of the public realm itself.[61] Second, Arendt argues for the direct equivalence of the modes of aesthetic and political judgment by demonstrating, via recourse to Kant's analytic, that the former is mindful of the opinions of others and mindful of the common world in an essentially political way.[62]

As will be considered at greater length further on, Kant does not claim that every judgment of taste possesses general validity. Indeed, he would allow that most do not. Rather, it is his aim to identify the conditions under which such general validity can be legitimately claimed. In this context, I would note that Arendt's orientation toward political opinion parallels Kant's conception of taste in both respects.

Were the validity of aesthetic judgments the same as that of logical judgments then the criterion of validity would be that of logical self-evidence. Instead, Kant claims, the criterion of validity is the enlightened sensibility that would be common to most persons if they each undertook to look upon the object from a disinterested point of view. Or, in Arendt's paraphrase, judgment's validity rests on "the potential agreement of others" that is possible once one's judgment has been liberated from the "'subjective private conditions,' . . . [or] idiosyncracies, which naturally determine the outlook of each individual in his privacy."[63] Similarly, Arendt argues, if politics were about questions of truth and falsity then logical self-evidence would be the criterion of political validity, but instead politics ultimately concerns matters to which the criteria of truth and falsity do not apply. In this epistemological situation, Arendt discerns in

Kant's recommendation of disinterestedness a basis for securing agreements on nonuniversal and nonultimate grounds.

To the end of purging away the dross of idiosyncracy, and for the sake of arriving at generality, Kant recommends that people give up their naturally excessive preference for their own points of view and engage in what Arendt describes as "representative thinking," that is, in a process whereby one endeavors to look upon the object from the perspectives of others, that one may thereby come to acquire and judge from an impartial and "enlarged mentality."[64] The extent of the validity that such judgments possess is in turn, as Arendt observes, a function of this very process: "Its claims to validity can never extend further than the others in whose place the judging person has put himself for his considerations."[65] As we shall see, Arendt will come to define the process of formulating political judgments in the same idiom, as a matter of engaging in representative thinking and of arriving at judgments of a similarly situated validity.

In sum, what leads Arendt to regard Kant's conception of aesthetic judgment as a direct analogue of political judgment is her sense that, in effect, he had demarcated a paradigm for conceiving of a process in which human plurality is given and agreements nonetheless remain possible. The conceptual keys to this process are disinterest and impartiality. In Kant's usage, these terms are practically synonymous; in Arendt's usage, however, they are not.

For Arendt, the meaning of disinterest recalls the dichotomy of freedom and necessity, and is tied up with her conception of the spectator who "attends the games seeking neither gain nor fame."[66] The spectator is thus disinterested because he has transcended the press of utilitarian necessity and can enjoy the spectacle for its own sake. Or, to put the matter more politically, because he does not come to the public square with the hope of personal gain, his "interest in the world is purely "disinterested"" and he is free to "judge the world in its appearance and in its worldliness."[67] And for Arendt, this is no small thing. For, by the exercise of his judgment, the attentive spectator determines how the world will look and sound. Disinterest is so essential, then, because only disinterested judgment will serve to maintain that worldliness of the world that Arendt defines in terms of the world's permanence and in terms of the world's being a site for the display of that alone which deserves permanence. The disinterested judge, in other words, looks out upon the spectacle of the world and asks himself not what is good for himself, nor what is good for others, but what is appropriate for the world.[68]

Disinterestedness, then, is the sine qua non which signifies that one has placed the world before all else. In Arendt's view this is the essential political attitude. The normativity of impartiality, by contrast, follows from the fact that however one answers the question, "What is appropriate for the world?" one can never do more than offer one's own opinion. And one opinion will surely differ from the next, because, if Arendt is correct, where political judgments are entailed there is neither true nor false and so no logico-mechanical method can prevail here against the natural welter of perspectival heterogeneity. Indeed, even among those who have attained the appropriate disinterestedness, in any given instance, there will likely be a wide range of opinions because where there is no neutral method that all can apply to produce identical judgments, it is inevitable that human plurality will make its presence felt.

It is, then, because there is no objective reason to privilege and prefer one's own disinterested (yet, nonetheless, perspectival) opinion to another's that Arendt advocates impartiality as the path to generality and to potential agreement. Were enough of the citizens of a given polity to display the willingness to engage in "representative thinking"—which itself is evidence of the desire to achieve impartiality—Arendt would hope that an "enlarged mentality" would take hold on a sufficiently broad scale to facilitate the emergence of intersubjectively valid political agreements. As Arendt notes, *peitho*, or persuasion, is the noncoercive rhetorical midwife of such agreements that is called for where logic is irrelevant and violence is forbidden.[69]

Perhaps the most striking thing about "The Crisis in Culture" is not the close manner in which it anticipates the substance of the views Arendt will develop in her lectures on Kant almost ten years later. Rather, what is most surprising is the fact that this text, which addresses problems that are unaddressed in *The Human Condition* and become even more problematic in *On Revolution*, was written after the one and before the other. Why it had no influence upon the latter when such an influence would have likely been salutary is inexplicable. Apparently its time had not yet come. In the wake of *On Revolution*, however, as if she were now aware of a redoubled need, Arendt does return to the themes that she had developed in the second half of this essay.

"Truth and Politics." In part three of her 1967 "Truth and Politics" Arendt returns to the themes of "The Crisis in Culture" and takes a significant step in the direction of articulating a world-rooted, postmodern, and post-Cartesian conception of politics. In this essay, Arendt also clarifies what she perceives to be the essential antagonism between truth and politics in a manner that cuts through to the core of the epistemological issue that underlies her opposition to both the politics born of ideological thinking and the instrumentalizing "politics of making."[70] Thus, in the course of this essay, what Arendt first depicts as an antagonism between truth and politics is soon revealed to be an antagonism between truth and opinion, and an antagonism between those who espouse a politics of truth's attainment and institutionalization, and those who defend a politics of consensus formation and democratic validity that is incapable of attaining the certitude that a truth-centered politics wants to provide.[71] That Arendt takes the side of opinion in this argument is hardly surprising. More striking is her claim that the politics of truth is intrinsically antipolitical, a claim that is based upon her own conception of the essential relationship between politics and human plurality. From this perspective, what marks the search for truth, and truth itself, as antipolitical is its mode of asserting validity.[72] Whereas politics in its search for consensus is properly mindful, and at least tacitly respectful, of the various perspectives of the citizens whose support must be garnered, truth, in Arendt's view, does not play this game. Truth is blunt, factical, non-perspectival, and coercive in its appeal to logical self-evidence.[73] Truth, moreover—for Plato as much as for Descartes (and Arendt has both in mind)—is vouchsafed as "truth" to the individual only insofar as, qua knower, it is grasped by him individually as truth. Ten thousand voices arrayed on one side or the other, in other words, does not make "true" even if it does make for the establishment of policy.

More significant than Arendt's characterization of truth, however, is her characterization of the political process and her assessment of its specific validity.[74] In particular—contra Plato and Descartes—Arendt makes clear, as she had intimated in "The Crisis in Culture," that the logos of politics can only be that which is appropriate to a realm of opinion.[75] Thus the realm of politics and the realm of opinion are once again held to be coextensive. Within this realm, the criterion of validity, Arendt continues, is not truth but consensus.[76]

Again, the contrast with truth is foremost. The pursuit of truth is a solitary business:[77] since no vote can be determinative of it, where "the many" are gathered the aim cannot be truth but must instead be consensus. That "the many" are gathered may also be understood as implying that the search for consensus, and the logos of politics which is synonymous with it, unfold within a community, that is, within a political community. So far as the truth itself is concerned, since it can only be appropriated by each knower individually, one can infer that in Arendt's view the communal dimension of the search for truth is relatively inessential to the end that is being sought.[78] A politics without a community is, by contrast, inconceivable.

That the political process properly has much to do with the logos of opinion and little to do with the logos of truth is further indicated, in Arendt's view, by the fate that overtakes metaphysical truths when they are introduced into the political realm and are thereby transformed into simple opinions.[79] No longer self-evident universals, extrapolitical truths are thrown into competition with other opinions for citizen-supporters and rhetorically polished advocates. Indicative of this change in the status of metaphysical propositions once they have been translated into the terms of political validity are Thomas Jefferson's words in the Declaration of Independence.

Thus, writing of Jefferson's "*we hold* these truths to be self-evident," Arendt calls attention to the fact that Jefferson does not merely indicate that such and such truths *are* self-evidently true.[80] Rather, by noting that "*we* hold" these truths, Jefferson shows that in politics the status of these truths *for us* depends not upon their self-evidence or intrinsic truth, but upon the fact that we hold them.[81] By her citation of this example Arendt would have her reader grasp that in the political sphere, because it is a realm of opinion, validity presupposes not self-evidence or logic but a consensus of opinion on behalf of that which is accounted valid, a consensus of opinion which in itself can be presumed to have come into being over against the interplay of differences.[82]

As already mentioned, our chief reason for attending to this essay at this juncture is because it serves to indicate the tenor of Arendt's neo-Kantian conception of political judgment and serves to clarify the problematic that Arendt will grapple with in her lectures on Kant. At issue is the question of how to characterize a search for consensus that is not reducible to a search for truth. That there is more to this process than securing a mere show of hands is apparent, but how is this process to be described?

Picking up themes first explored in the second part of "The Crisis in Culture," Arendt has recourse to Kant's "Critique of Aesthetic Judgment" as she endeavors to conceptualize a mode of judgment that is oriented not towards the determination of truth but towards the production of a consensus of opinion. Once again she equates aesthetic and political judgment, and equates the process of generating a consensus concerning the beautiful with the process of attaining a consensus regarding what a given polity ought to do.[83]

The substance of Arendt's Kantian borrowing was considered in the last section and will be considered in close detail when we turn to Arendt's lectures on Kant's political philosophy. For the moment, I want only to call the reader's attention to a few of the Kantian elements which are brought to the fore in "Truth and Politics." Foremost among these is Arendt's neo-Kantian notion that aesthetic/political judgment properly entails what she calls "representative thinking," and describes in this essay as a kind of "discursive running, as it were, from place to place, from one part of the world to another, through all kinds of conflicting views, until it finally ascends from these particularities to some kind of generality."[84] As in "The Crisis in Culture," the purpose of representative thinking is held to be the attainment of an impartial or "enlarged mentality" from which a consensus of opinion might be readily forged.[85] Once more Arendt acknowledges that many, if not most, members of a given judging community will fail to let go of their partiality for their own opinion (and interest); nonetheless, she maintains that the telos of political judgment requires that one do so.[86] Just why one must do so is not discussed, however. Also unaddressed within "Truth and Politics" is the question of what makes either consensus or an enlarged mentality the desideratum of the realm of opinion in the first place.

More troubling still is Arendt's failure to specify what reason there is for believing that the various perspectives that are to be integrated within an enlarged mentality will not be incommensurable, or utterly contradictory, thus making it impossible to attain an all encompassing or general standpoint. Even among those who attain the requisite degree of impartiality and disinterestedness and have thus shed their natural partiality for their own party or section, it is easy enough to imagine that differences of opinion will continue to persist. How in such cases—and one can be sure they will not be uncommon—is a consensus to be reached? To what principles, if any, might an appeal be made? And in light of the concerns foremost in the previous chapter, one might ask what is to guarantee that where a consensus is obtained it will in fact be productive of that modicum of world-continuity which Arendt regards as existentially indispensable.

It is to be hoped that several of these shortcomings might be overcome by means of a more extensive elaboration of Arendt's reading of Kant's categories. More essentially, one can envision that the remaining lacunae might be filled were Arendt to bring her Kantian moment into contact with the conception of common sense whose development was traced in the earlier sections of this chapter. That Kant himself looked to common sense, or to the *sensus communis*, as he calls it in the *Critique of Judgement*, to serve as the ground of potential agreement between members of a given judging community would seem to buttress this intuition. Ironically, though, in "Truth and Politics" Arendt pays no attention to the role Kant allots to common sense in his Third Critique. Nor did she pay sufficient attention to it in "The Crisis in Culture." In her lectures on Kant's political philosophy, however, as if she had become cognizant of the importance of what she had previously overlooked, Arendt does focus upon Kant's conception of the *sensus communis* and upon its role as the ground of a potential consensus of opinion. It is, then, to Arendt's lectures on Kant's political philosophy that we will have to turn both in order to explore Arendt's most expansive testimony to her appropriation of Kant and in order to explore the manner in which Arendt brings together Kant's conception of the *sensus communis* and her own. But before taking this step, we must attend to one other text which also bears a strong Kantian imprint in order that the stage will be fully set.

Thinking: *Judging, and Common Sense.* In *The Life of the Mind* Arendt differentiates between the faculties of thinking, willing, and judging, which together comprise the life of the mind. Each faculty has its own objects and operates in accordance with its own particular nature. Arendt's analysis begins with thinking and proceeds to willing; as we have noted, Arendt died just after she had begun to set down her analysis of judgment. We have assumed, however, that the tenor of the unwritten section can be inferred by situating the conception of political judgment that Arendt develops in her lectures on Kant in relation to her other writings on judgment and common sense. In turning to *Thinking*, then, although the text is not specifically framed with an eye to judgment, we want to ascertain whether Arendt sheds any light upon it, even by indirection. We also want to attend to Arendt's continuing effort to refute Cartesian solipsism and world alienation, an effort that achieves greater thematic prominence in this text than in any other.

As Arendt observes, the differentiation of mental faculties was not always perceived in the past. Prior to Paul, for example, the will was not clearly distinguished from the other faculties. And it is only with Kant that the difference between judgment and thinking and the internal distinctions within each of these faculties become fully clarified.[87] From our perspective, however, more important than the distinctions themselves are their implications for politics.

In our discussion of "Truth and Politics," we saw the importance Arendt imputes to the distinction between a politics that is grounded upon truths that are thought to be absolute and unequivocal and a politics grounded upon an irreducible plurality of opinion. To constitute politics on Arendtian grounds the legitimacy of the former conception must be overthrown and the latter validated. In *Thinking* Arendt takes a further step in this direction via her appropriation of Kant's distinction between knowing (*Verstand*) and thinking (*Vernunft*), the former being oriented toward the determination of truth (both factual and logical) and the latter being oriented toward the comprehension of meaning.[88] In elucidating the significance of this dichotomy, Arendt emphasizes that knowing aims at cognition and that cognitions are either true or false; she also notes that thinking, by contrast, aims at meaning and that meanings are neither true nor false.[89] Knowing, she continues, tells us what is or is not the case, and he who possesses the surer method and greater brain power will be more capable of knowing than he who lacks these things.[90] Thinking, by contrast, engenders in us our ideas and clarifies the meaning of these ideas, yielding ideas and meanings that, once again, are neither true nor false.[91] God, freedom and immortality are three such ideas, but Arendt extends Kant's list to include the vast range of ideas by which we bring meaning to our lives. Beauty, goodness, justice, courage, and right are only a few examples drawn from that endless list of ideas that are neither true nor false but nonetheless quite meaningful.[92]

In distinguishing meaning and truth in the way she does, it should be clear that Arendt means to oppose the conflation of the two and, more particularly, the antipolitical consequences of this conflation that mar Platonic and neo-Cartesian political thought.[93] For those who believe that politics is a field for the application (or realization) of "clear and distinct" (or true) ideas, which only the few are capable of discerning, will inevitably be led to conceive of politics as a mode of autocratic poesis. If, by contrast, politics be conceived as a realm in which meanings that are neither true nor false are at stake, the rationale for an antipluralist politics is undercut since there is no privileged position for the determination of meaning. Meanings, then, can only be instances of *dokei moi* ("it seems to me"), or matters of opinion, in other words. There is, in short, no Archimedean standpoint, no privileged Platonic perspective, and no indubitable Cartesian method that can fairly trump the interplay of opinion and opinion.

In leaping to consider the political implications of the distinction between truth and meaning, we have in fact elided the crucial distinction between the faculties of thinking and judging and their respective domains. Thinking, in Arendt's words, deals with invisibles and generalities. Judgment, by contrast, is always the judgment of particulars.[94] It is judgment and not thinking, then, that pertains directly to politics because the latter is a field of particularity. This does not mean that judging and thinking are unrelated faculties. Indeed, judgment pertains as much to thought things (that is, to concepts) as it does to the field of particulars, inasmuch as it is judgment's function to mediate between them both. Judgment is analogous to thinking, moreover, in being divided into two modes, that is, into the modes of determinative and reflective judgment, a distinction which to some extent parallels that drawn between *Verstand* and *Vernunft*.

That there are two modes of judgment follows from the fact that the mediation between the universal and the particular can proceed from the former to the latter or from the latter to the former. Determinative judgments are those which proceed from a thought thing (that is, from a general concept or universal principle) and designate the particulars which are to be subsumed under the general term. Reflective judgments, by contrast, are those which proceed from a given particular to the discovery of a general concept or universal principle under which the particular may be subsumed. It is the latter mode of judgment which enables me to judge the meaning of some particular "x" that is there before me. It enables me to pass from the particular in front of me to the universal and declare: "*This* is right." "*This* is just." "*This* is beautiful." Such judgments are of limited validity, however, for, as Arendt notes, there are neither necessary rules nor sure methods for making them.[95] Such judgments, furthermore, are not cognitions and for that reason are neither true nor false. Rather they are judgments of meaning, instances of *dokei moi* in two respects: first, because they are judgments of meaning; and second, because, without objective rules or methods to guide the one who judges, something ineluctably subjective will cling to every exercise of reflective judgment. Such judgments, finally, are, in Arendt's view, the kinds of judgments at the center of political life.[96]

Had Arendt only established the equation between the political sphere and the sphere of *dokei moi* ("it seems to me"), she could have justly claimed victory in her attempt to take back the realm of the political from the clutches of those who would ruin politics by imposing truth from above. But this alone would not protect the political realm from the nomadic solipsism that has come to permeate it now that only the introspective turn survives from the original Cartesian quest for ultimate foundations. To the latter end, Arendt proceeds by taking up the challenge she framed for herself at the end of *The Human Condition*, namely, the challenge of directly countering the validity of the Cartesian project of achieving self-certainty through the retreat to introspection.

Descartes had withdrawn from the realm of untrustworthy appearances in order to find an indubitable foundation upon which to ground reality. Upon the "*cogito, ergo sum*" he built his fortress, securing reality upon solipsistic foundations. It is this latter move that Arendt questions. Relying upon Husserl's insight into the intentional structure of consciousness, Arendt calls our attention to the irreducible subjectivity of all "objective" perceptions.[97] Objects appear to us, in other words, in the mode of *dokei moi*, that is, in the mode of it-seems-to-me, and, as such, in a mode that is perpetually prey to error and illusion.[98] Of course, Descartes would escape from the shifting sands of subjectivity by taking refuge in the ostensible objectivity of pure thought. But Arendt casts doubt upon whether such a refuge really exists.[99] Indeed, by her emphasis upon the intentional structure of consciousness, Arendt helps us to see that the perceptions of the mind's eye are no less tainted by the "it-seems-to-me" than are the perceptions of one's real eyes. For this reason Arendt rejects Descartes' project as misguided.

As importantly, Arendt rejects Descartes' repudiation of common sense, arguing to the contrary that common sense alone possesses the wherewithal to free us from the limitations that follow from the inherent subjectivity of perception.[100] What the cogitations of the self-enclosed thinking ego are unable to guarantee, she argues, can be assured more adequately by common sense and commonsense reasoning.[101]

In particular, Descartes had sought to guarantee the independent existence of his ego—and the independent existence of the world beyond his ego—by recourse to the experiences of the thinking ego, but in this he was mistaken. "The subjectivity of the it-seems-to-me," which Descartes sought to remedy by recourse to introspection, "is remedied by the fact that the same object also appears to others though its mode of appearance may be different."[102] Common sense tells us to check our perceptions of things against the perceptions of others and tells us that only those perceptual objects that can be intersubjectively validated are to be granted the status of reality.[103]

On the face of things, it may appear that modern science—since the discoveries of Galileo—has pursued its quest for truth by rejecting common sense and commonsense reasoning. Arendt disagrees and argues that though the new science does not place much trust in the evidence of our unaided senses, it retains its attachment to sense evidence and continues to rely upon commonsense reasoning, albeit of a highly refined kind.[104] Even in the field of subatomic physics, Arendt observes, despite the esotericism of the theory and the sophistication of the experimental equipment, the ultimate criterion of validity remains the evidence of the senses and the intersubjective confirmation of the results.[105] Thus, even at their most recondite, scientists remain attached to the world of appearances and to a form of commonsense reasoning that enables them to transcend the solipsistic myopia of the "it-seems-to-me."

In light of the distinction Arendt draws between cognition and meaning, and given Arendt's conception of politics as a field of meaning, it cannot be uncritically assumed that what holds true for science (that is, the transcendence of self-enclosed rationalism and of solipsism more generally) will hold true for politics. As Arendt forcefully argues, thinking (*Vernunft*), in its quest for meaning, transcends common sense and common sense reasoning as knowing (*Verstand*), in its quest for cognition, does not. By inference, then, the validity of thinking cannot depend upon an intersubjective criterion as knowing does. Thinking, then, would seem to be inescapably mired in *dokei moi* as knowing and cognition are not.

In Arendt's view, what saves politics from the abyss of nomadic solipsism that would seem to follow from the disjuncture between thinking and common sense is the fact that though politics is about meaning, the mental faculty that governs the political realm is reflective judgment and not thought. Just what difference this makes will only become fully clarified in the next part of this chapter when we turn to Arendt's lectures on Kant's political philosophy and in particular to her analysis of Kant's *Critique of Judgment*. For the moment let it suffice for us to note the following:

By Arendt's description, thinking is a solitary business, but reflective judgment proceeds with reference to a community and with reference to common opinion. Like thinking, reflective judgment also begins with *dokei moi*, but, unlike thinking, reflective judgment—even the reflective judgment of meaning—seeks and may obtain a degree of intersubjective validation that necessarily eludes thinking. It may do this because, in the moments of its formulation and persuasive articulation, reflective judgment appeals to common opinion, that is, to the *sensus communis* as thinking never does.[106] In other words, even as one judges for oneself, one also judges as a member of a given community and properly endeavors to frame judgments that can gain the agreement or approval of this community. Precisely how the reflective judgment proceeds in this matter will be taken up in the next section.

From the foregoing description of how the reflective judgment operates, it may appear that it has much in common with scientific judgment. After all, each seems to be grounded upon common sense and each seems to escape from solipsism and secure intersubjective validity on this basis. This appearance is, however, largely deceptive and arises from a conflation of the two kinds of common sense that Arendt so carefully distinguishes in *The Human Condition*:

It will be recalled from *The Human Condition* that Arendt differentiates between *Gemeinsinn*, or the community sense, proper, and *gesunder Menschenverstand*, or "common human understanding." By the latter term, Arendt singles out such worldless human capacities as logic and the harmonious interworking of the five senses which compel us by their self-evidence, claim universal and necessary validity, and are essential to the cognition of truth.[107] By the former term, Arendt signifies the sense that enables us to communicate with one another and to thereby share our opinions and validate our perceptions. *Gemeinsinn* refers both to the communicative capacity itself and to the common opinions that arise from its exercise. Moreover, the validity of the latter is contingent and limited to the range of interlocutors who have exercised their communicative capacities together.

Had Arendt claimed that scientific inquiry depends solely upon "common human understanding" and that, by contrast, the political process relies upon the workings of *Gemeinsinn,* or the community sense proper, the contrast would be clear. It could then be said that while both science and politics rely upon common sense, they rely upon different kinds of common sense and so arrive at judgments of contrasting validity. In fact Arendt would largely agree with this formulation for it comes close to capturing the gist of her conception.[108] What renders Arendt's account of these distinctions in *Thinking* relatively opaque is Arendt's inchoate post-Kuhnian awareness that scientific knowledge is in fact built upon common sense of both kinds: it is essentially a product of "common human understanding" but it is also the product of cooperative human endeavor and communicative praxis. On the basis of the former, scientists claim universal validity for their understanding; and yet, the recurrent paradigm shifts attest to the communally constituted and limited validity of these same claims.

For these reasons, Arendt is led in *Thinking* to emphasize the contrast between the respective object domains of science and politics as being largely determinative of the difference between the specific validity that is possible in each of these fields. Once again the dichotomy between truth and meaning becomes probative as Arendt contrasts the grounded and independently verifiable nature of the former with the groundless and merely potentially sharable nature of the latter. It is, then, because meanings have no empirical and independently verifiable existence but exist only subjectively and intersubjectively that *Gemeinsinn* assumes much greater prominence in the political than in the scientific realm. The surprising thing is Arendt's claim that, by virtue of the workings of the *Gemeinsinn,* intersubjectively shared—and to that extent valid—judgments of meaning can be regularly achieved. As we will see more concretely when we attend to the Kant lectures, this claim provides the foundation for a conception of politics that steers clear of the Scylla and Charybdis of rationalist monism and solipsistic fragmentation. Just how it manages to do this without at the same time occluding the manifestation of plurality is something we will be particularly concerned to assess.

In bringing this section to a close, I want only to call attention to one of the more salient differences between the scientific mode of cognitive judgment and the political mode of meaning-oriented reflective judgment. The difference is one of motivation. Appeals to common sense and to the community of opinion in the context of scientific disputes are self-evidently motivated by cognitive and practical interests. Less clear, however, and scarcely considered in *Thinking* or in the two Kantian essays that we have scrutinized, is the nature of the interest that could motivate the judging individual to prefer impartiality and *shared* meaning to partiality for his own point of view and for idiosyncratic personal meaning. Arendt does make reference to man's existential need for meaning, an interest in meaning that motivates thinking, but the interest in shared meaning and impartiality that motivates judging is hardly reducible to it.[109] In an earlier section, we suggested that Arendt believes that such shared and impartial judgments are the sine qua non of the polity's long enduring as a site of mutual and reciprocal self-revelation; from this perspective, the interest in shared judgment and the interest in the polity's long duration are synonymous. In her lectures on Kant's political philosophy, Arendt points to the human interest in sociability as an additional factor. In *Thinking*, however, the problem of motivation goes unexplored. It nonetheless remains an important problem because it is one thing to specify the nature of a faculty and quite another to indicate why we ought to expect humans to regularly exercise it.

As is doubtless apparent by now, *Thinking* hardly provides us with a full account of judging. Indeed it neither provides us with a more adequate conception of judging than Arendt provides in "The Crisis in Culture" or "Truth and Politics," nor does it address the aporias of the latter essay that were enumerated at the end of the last section. And yet this is slight criticism when we recall that *Thinking* is not meant to be an account of judging but only the prelude to such an account. For this we must turn to Arendt's lectures on Kant, which we shall do presently. In ending this section, however, this much must be underscored: What *Thinking* does demonstrate is that Arendt's reflections upon judgment are intimately associated with her continuing endeavor to think through the transcendence of Cartesian solipsism.

THE KANT LECTURES AND THEIR SIGNIFICANCE

The text of central significance from this moment forward is Arendt's *Lectures on Kant's Political Philosophy*.[110] Before turning to the text itself, however, a few facts must be placed before the reader. First, as noted already, what we have before us in this text suffers from all the ambiguities of being an interpretation even before I add to these those born of my own interpretative gloss. In this connection, what is most striking are not Arendt's brazen misconstructions of Kant's meaning, of which there are only a few, so much as the way in which Arendt has thematically organized his political thought in order to make it address the lacunae of her own. That at times this amounts to an almost willful distortion of his intent can be seen most clearly in Arendt's decision to place not the *Critique of Practical Reason* but the "Critique of Aesthetic Judgment" at the center of her exposition of Kant's political philosophy. That for Kant the latter was without any relevance to politics is for Arendt of little consequence. That, as it turns out, the "third critique" is much more congenial to her own political vision than the "second critique" is hardly surprising. The "third," moreover, is readily turned in a direction that marks a further stage of development in her own theory.

That Arendt departs from Kant's conception of judgment at a crucial point will become clear as we proceed. This difference aside—and it is not even clear that Arendt grasped its full significance—it is easy to see why Arendt found Kant's analytic of aesthetic judgment so highly serviceable.

In the "Critique of Aesthetic Judgment" Kant analyzes the nature and preconditions of the spectator's judgment of the artwork. For Kant, what makes such judgments problematic is their implicit claim to universal validity. In Kant's view, one who judges "x" as being beautiful implicitly demands that everybody assent to his opinion. Yet, asks Kant, on what basis can this demand be made? If such judgments were arrived at by logical inference, then the claim to universal validity would be no more problematic than the similar claim made on behalf of the equation that $2+2=4$. Aesthetic judgments appeal, however, not to logic but to feeling. How then, asks Kant, can the assumption of agreement be allowed, given how much the taste of one man differs from that of another? In his effort to master these problems, Kant looks to the discursive process by which agreements in matters of taste are reached, and finds that differences of aesthetic opinion are mediated and resolved by reference to a kind of common sense which he denotes as the *sensus communis*.[112]

Why Arendt might find such a conception appealing is immediately clear. First, from the side of the object, Kant's problematic hearkens back to Arendt's aesthetics of action. Second, from the side of the judging subject, Kant's problematic has obvious affinities with Arendt's notion that a politics of freedom (and meaning) cannot be grounded upon appeals to logic or truth.[113] Third, in privileging the *sensus communis* as the ground of appeal for the resolution of aesthetic differences, Kant's view points in the direction of Arendt's analogous notion that differences of political opinion are to be mediated by appeals not to reason, but to common sense.[114] More generally, it is clear that Kant's mode of approach to aesthetics might also provide Arendt with a vehicle for addressing the problem of spectator judgment which, prior to this point, has not received adequate conceptualization.[115] That, contrary to much opinion, the process-conception which Arendt derives from Kant's account of the aesthetic judgment exercised by the spectator might prove to be of equal relevance for her endeavor to work out the nature of the judgment exercised by the actor will only become clear once Kant's conception of spectator judgment has been fully delineated.[116] It will also be seen that Arendt's Kantian meditations enable her to elucidate the contours of the actor-spectator symbiosis.[117]

In defense of the proposition that in presenting Arendt's readings of Kant's conception of judgment one can adequately differentiate between those aspects which Arendt takes over and makes her own, and those which she does not, I would note the following. First, as previously noted, there are points at which Arendt's interpretation of Kant veers so far from the plain intent of Kant's words that it becomes quite apparent that Arendt is endeavoring to draw Kant into her own conceptual orbit and thus to turn his words to her own advantage as she endeavors to formulate a conception of political judgment. Here, the test of consistency with Arendt's prior theoretical commitments serves as a benchmark for determining which idiosyncratic interpretive moves ought to be imputed to Arendt's own positive conception of judgment and which ought not to be. A second, and more substantive, check on erroneous imputation, however, is the fact that in "The Crisis in Culture" and "Truth and Politics"— the latter of which is roughly contemporaneous with Arendt's preparation of her Kant lectures—Arendt turns to Kant's analytic of aesthetic judgment in order to delineate her own conception of the judgment executed by actors and spectators.[118] Indeed section two of "The Crisis in Culture" and section three of "Truth and Politics" together read as if they were a précis of that part of the Kant lectures which pertains to the judgment of the spectator.[119] Thus, while reading Arendt's lectures on Kant, we will keep one eye trained upon these essays in which Arendt's borrowing from Kant is explicit in order to provide ourselves with a sure criterion of legitimate imputation.[120] Finally, as an additional and irrefutable aid, there are Arendt's own statements of agreement or disagreement (as the case may be) with one or another of the arguments or insights that she attributes to Kant.

In turn, then, we shall review Arendt's rendering of Kant's conception of aesthetic judgment before exploring precisely how she modifies this conception in order to depict the judgment of political actors which I have denoted as political judgment proper.

Mediating Differences of Taste: The Judging Spectator and the Sensus Communis

For Kant, as for Arendt, it was clear that all persons judge. Yet what struck him most was the fact that when a man says (for example) "this is beautiful," he does not mean "this is beautiful to *me*." Rather he claims, at least implicitly, that what seems to him to be beautiful is beautiful in itself and must therefore be acknowledged as such by any other observer.[122] What, asks Kant, is the basis for such a claim? Can such a claim be made at all?

Of course what flies in the face of such a claim to universality is the claim which holds otherwise.[123] What one person holds to be beautiful, another holds to be hardly so. Between the two, assuming the claim of each to be implicitly universalizing, how is the difference of opinion to be overcome? Are such conflicting claims mediable or must it be concluded that in matters of taste or opinion to each his own?[124]

That such questions as these—and the problematic from which they stem—are of potential relevance for a conception of the political process is apparent. Differences of opinion are, in Arendt's view, the lifeblood of politics.[125] Especially where a premium is placed upon the revelation of particularity, differences of opinion will be sure to arise. How to mediate among a welter of conflicting opinions in order to arrive at a consensus on behalf of a particular policy: that is the political question par excellence, albeit one scarcely touched upon by Arendt in *The Human Condition*.

For Arendt, the differences of taste that concern Kant are analogous to differences of opinion more generally.[126] Were it a question of truth or falsehood then logical proofs could carry the day.[127] Instead, assuming that each of the parties to a dispute wants to gain the assent of the others to his opinion and implicitly pledges himself to persuade or to be persuaded, a different type of appeal must be made. For Kant, as for Arendt, *peitho*, the logos of persuasion with respect to matters of opinion, operates by means of appeals that are mediated as appeals to that which connects persons who might otherwise remain locked in wholly self-enclosed and incommensurable subjectivities.[128]

Kant does not deny that we each possess our own private taste.[129] Yet in addition to this sense, which by definition is nonsharable, he would insist that we possess as well a sense which befits us for membership in a community, a public sense, the *sensus communis*.[130] Because it is the latter alone which each man may share with his neighbor, it is to the latter that appeals must be made whenever one man seeks the agreement of another.[131]

Admittedly, the need to seek agreement in matters of aesthetics may seem less than compelling. In reference to such questions we may prefer to let a hundred flowers bloom. In principle, however, Kant's conception proves useful inasmuch as it enables Arendt to conceptualize the basis upon which differences of opinion may be resolved when they arise within the political realm, a realm in which differences are sure to arise and in which—in Arendt's view at least—the need to pursue a consensus is plain.[132]

In our analysis of *Thinking* we noted that Arendt failed to indicate the specific nature of the human interest that might be able to motivate individual citizens to forsake their attachment to their own opinion and to prefer sharable opinions instead. In her lectures on Kant's conception of judgment, the rationale and the relevant human interest are more clearly delineated.

The ideal itself is clear: whoever is most humane and most fitted to a communal existence will be one who in his discursive praxis seeks the agreement of his peers and is prepared to abide by their collective judgment even when he disagrees. The reasons given for this by Arendt are several.

Among the most elementary is the fact that, as Kant emphasizes, humans are sociable and communicative beings who as such are motivated to act in a manner that will maximize the extent of their communicative being together.[133] To wit, not only do they seek to share their opinions with one another, but they seek as well to cultivate that impartial standpoint in their common discourse that will serve to maintain the cohesion and longevity of their association.[134] Second, as if translating this almost anthropological notion into her own idiom, Arendt notes that actors who would reap the rewards of appearing in public have an interest in maintaining the public realm's good health and the good of the political association which is synonymous with it. The articulation of sharable opinions and the pursuit of the agreement of one's fellow citizens are then to be understood as means to these ends. In other words, the long preservation of the public space, and of the rewards flowing from it, requires that this attitude be taken. Third, and here we enter new terrain, there is an incipient notion afoot within the *Lectures on Kant's Political Philosophy*—and within "The Crisis in Culture" as well—which would justify the orientation toward agreement in terms of the existential of "being in a *common world*," which refers to the particular community (or polis) within which one lives.[135]

As an existential orientation, the perspective Arendt develops may be understood as deriving from the insight which grasps that a polis, or public space, which by rights of citizenship persons are entitled to enter, belongs to no group of citizens in particular, but to all equally insofar as they are equally intent upon appearing within it.[136] Political equality might be conceived as formally corresponding to this existential equality of men vis à vis the realm of appearance which, in its generic sense, we may be said to enter at birth and to exit at death.

This last point sheds additional light on Arendt's conception of the world's commonality as it calls to mind the importance she attributes to its multigenerational lastingness, and hence to its multigenerational commonality.[137] In this respect, what was said negatively of persons holds true for generations. As no citizen has a right to privilege himself before other citizens where matters of the world are concerned, so too may it be said that no generation has a right to regard the commonweal as if it were something of concern to itself alone. Reversed, this means that the polis belongs equally to all its citizens—past, present, and future—and must be treated accordingly.[138]

When this comprehensive conception of the world's commonality is joined to Arendt's conception of the political realm as ordered by the logos of opinion, a particular ethos or worldly orientation is seen to follow, one implicit in the *Lectures on Kant's Political Philosophy*. From this standpoint, the question of why one ought to seek to look upon issues from the communal, or public, perspective may be answered directly: because the world belongs to all citizens (past, present, and future), and to no group of citizens any more than to the rest, each citizen ought to strive to look upon all questions facing the polity from a commensurately self-, and even generationally, transcendent standpoint.[139] In Arendt's view, it follows from this that in our political deliberations we ought to demonstrate a willingness to let go of our own partiality for ourselves, and for our opinions (which for existential reasons we must nonetheless articulate), and seek instead to think from the standpoint of the commonweal.[140] Our aim in deliberation, then, ought to be the articulation of sharable opinions, and we ought to manifest a flexibility of mind in order that we might together arrive at such positions as can be widely shared. Generality, and transcendence of all private and partial perspectives, in Arendt's view, corresponds with and follows as an imperative from the fact that the world is common to all.[141] In politics as in taste—because the world and not ourselves is what we are concerned with—egoism is to be overcome.[142] Or, to frame this same imperative in a more eudaemonistic manner: great are the existential rewards which come through the process by which we transcend the limitations of our private perspectives and rise to the general standpoint of the community as a whole.[143]

It is with an eye, then, to conceptualizing how the citizen may attain to this exalted perspective that Arendt has recourse, in the Kant lectures, to Kant's conception of the norms which are meant to facilitate the movement from one-sided subjectivity to an intersubjective, and thus sharable, standpoint.[144] To this same end, as in "The Crisis in Culture" and in "Truth and Politics," Arendt appropriates Kant's conceptualization of how best to purge judgments and opinions of the traces of mere privacy which mar them by coloring them with bias and partiality.[145] More particularly, Arendt again recommends "representative thinking" as the quasi-Kantian mode of reflection that should be adopted by the judicious citizen who, quite properly, will want to consider sympathetically the opinions of his fellow citizens (regarding any given issue) before framing his own opinion.[146] In these same lectures Arendt also relies upon Kant's formulation to help her make explicit for the first time that the net result of such "travelling," or "visiting by means of the imagination," should be the extirpation of bias and the triumph of common sense.[147]

Arguably more important than the triumph of common sense, however, is that which this triumph would make possible. For Kant, writing of aesthetic judgment, it is the ascension to the vantage of common sense that enables those who make this ascent to reach common agreement in their judgments of beauty. In effect reasoning by analogy, Arendt proposes that shared political judgments could be secured in a similar fashion, that is, if the members of the polity would commit themselves to order their collective deliberations in accordance with the norms that facilitate the ascendancy of common sense. At the end of the day, in other words, the discursive back and forth of political life should produce the great desideratum of consensus.[148]

Had we been attending to Kant's critique of aesthetic judgment *rather* than to Arendt's interpretation of it, it would have become quite clear by now that for Kant the common sense which comes to the fore through representative thinking is common by virtue of the fact that the inner law-governed sense for beauty is the same for all Homo sapiens once the individual's idiosyncratic impurities have been purged away.[149] Thus for Kant each man can become the representative of all men even with respect to something as noncognitive and nonobjective as the judgment of the beautiful. But would Arendt agree?

To this point, it would certainly appear that Arendt has followed Kant's conception of judgment most faithfully. By analogy with Kant's conception of the mediation of aesthetic differences, she would have us envision citizens endeavoring to realize the Kantian ideals of disinterest and impartiality as together they deliberate upon the question of wherein lies the public good. Yet where Kant would have us abide by these process norms in order to render a pure judgment grounded upon a common *inner* sense—which we all possess by virtue of being human—Arendt would have us follow them in order to render a judgment which is pure by virtue of its relationship to a common sense which we possess as members of a particular community.[150] The difference is most significant.

A Critical Distance

For Arendt, the common sense of each member of the community is the community sense of all because these persons share a concrete, historically conditioned life together.[151] They share a common sense by virtue of that web of preunderstandings which participants in a common culture pick up along the road to maturity. In conjunction with this web of preunderstandings, the Kantian process norms should ideally insure that when judging, the citizen's culturally and historically contingent common, or public, sense will prevail over his private preferences.[152]

Had Arendt sought to render this departure from Kant explicit she might have done so by noting how her previously developed conception of common sense would bear upon the Kantian conception of aesthetic judgment. For Kant, a judgment of beauty—after the dross of bias and partiality are shorn away—is pure to the extent that one's judgment is uncontaminated by historically, or otherwise heteronomous, conditioning factors. For Arendt, by contrast, it follows that a pure aesthetic judgment is one that could be justified by appeals to what would *in effect* be an acquired and historically contingent common aesthetic.[153] For Kant that which "pleases in the imagination" ought to please all men irrespective of time and place and hence without reference to learned rules or past models.[154] For Arendt, however, it seems fair to imagine that before the court of aesthetic appeals recourse would be had not to laws of perception, but to past works, shared models, and an artistic tradition—all of which are historically conditioned phenomena. Thus an argument on behalf of the beauty of "x" would likely entail an endeavor to trace the ways in which the beauty of "x" is like those works singled out by tradition "y" as embodying the essence of beauty.

What Arendt seems to overlook in her appropriation of Kant's conception is the essentialist universalism which leads Kant to an altogether different view of human plurality, and of the worth of the differences of opinion that it engenders, than she would ever countenance. For Kant, stated baldly, human plurality—when viewed from the ideal judging standpoint—is a source of error.[155] The aim of "representative thinking" is, then, to purge judgment of human dross, bias, and perspectival distortion. The goal is to attain and to judge from the *purely* human standpoint, a standpoint which bears a strong family resemblance to the universal standpoint of the pure rational being of Kantian aprioristic ethics. The goal, in other words, is aesthetic autonomy with the Kantian sense of autonomy very much underscored. From such a standpoint, the function of debate and discussion is only critical. Ideally, it would be unnecessary and all persons would arrive at the same judgments on account of their being grounded upon that faculty which is the same for all judging persons.

For Arendt, of course, such an ideal would hardly be desirable. The value she places upon the manifestation of human plurality would be undercut. For Arendt, differences of opinion are neither error nor dross but a healthful manifestation of human plurality. No doubt she regards it as humankind's good fortune as well that the culturally contingent common sense, which any given people shares, is not of so monistic a nature as to obviate completely the chance that those who share it will continuously differ over how it applies in any particular case. Appeals to common sense figure prominently as a basis for seeking agreement, but not, as in Kant's conception, because the common sense to which one appeals is something common to all persons by virtue of their being human. Rather, it figures as a third term, as something "out there" in the public domain, as it were, to which all members of a given culture can refer as a ground of a possible—but by no means necessary—agreement. Not that agreement is *empirically* necessary in Kant's view either, but given his understanding of the nature of the *sensus communis,* where agreement is not reached this could only be because of a degree of frowardness or gross heteronomy which keeps individuals from rising to the pure standpoint which we all carry within ourselves. For Arendt, however, no such pure standpoint exists, nor would it be at all desirable if it did, for the existential loss would be too great. For Arendt, common sense—qua community sense—assumes such an important role, not because it is rooted in the fundamental likeness of one person to the next, but rather because it makes possible communication and, on occasion, even agreement between persons who are otherwise—and in all that is most significant—not alike at all.[156]

Similarly indicative of the distance between Kant's conception of judgment and the way in which Arendt appropriates it, is the use she makes of his analysis of perception and exemplary validity.[157] In *The Critique of Pure Reason,* as is well known, Kant asks how perception in accordance with concepts or ideas is possible. How is it, for instance, that no person of sane mind ever mistakes a triangle for a circle? How is it, moreover, that some brute sensory input from the world could have ever been denominated as a triangle in the first place? And how is it possible that we all know what a triangle is and seldom differ with one another when it comes to identifying them in the material world? For Kant the answers to these questions, like the questions themselves, entail a consideration of species-wide uniformities.

More to point, what intrigues Kant is the problem of accounting for those elements of experience which are invariant across the species. By contrast, the problem of accounting for intergroup differences of perception or understanding does not figure for him as an object of inquiry. Thus when discussing the workings of the cognitive or reflective judgment it does not occur to Kant to query why the members of one culture employ these capacities in a way that differs from the way the members of another culture might employ them. As I have already observed regarding the universalizing thrust of his analysis of aesthetic judgment, so too with respect to his analysis of the structures of perception and understanding. Presumably, if one were seeking to model a conception of political judgment along the lines suggested by either of Kant's critiques one would attempt to frame a similarly universalizing conception. And yet, as we know, this is hardly Arendt's intent, and thus it should come as no surprise that Arendt turns Kant's analytic in a direction that adds credence to a conception of political discourse and political judgment that is rooted in a web of norms, values, and principles that are contingently interwoven and spatiotemporally localized. In short, Kant's analytic is employed by Arendt to show how and why it is that the *sensus communis* which grounds political life cannot be the universal substrate that Kant's own employment of the concept would entail.

Between Judgment and the Sensus Communis: The Role of Concepts and Examples

Though I did not attend so much to this fact in particular when first considering the nature of common sense, it was implicit that common sense operated to "organize" the manifold of experience by shaping both comprehension and the attitude towards that which was comprehended. Endeavoring to clarify how it does this, Arendt turns her attention to Kant's "First Critique," and in particular to his remarks about cognition and judgment.[158] Judgment, and in particular reflective judgment, is something of a generic category. Included within it—and thus accounting for Arendt's interest—are, as we noted in discussing *Thinking*, value judgments generally, what Arendt denominates as spectator judgment, and what I have described as political judgment proper.

Setting the stage for the forthcoming discussion, Arendt observes that between the concepts which are implanted within us and the intuitions of sense received from the world outside, there is need of a faculty which will correctly align the two. It is judgment that enables us to do this.[159]

Following Kant, Arendt distinguishes cognition from (reflective) judgment.[160] It is the former that enables us to identify the intuitions we receive by way of the material senses; it enables us to say "this is a ball . . .

a rock . . . a house . . ."[161] The latter, by contrast, enables us to "perceive" ideas by way of material hints of their presence.[162] Thus though there is no material thing called justice or honor or virtue, we are able to describe a man or his deeds as just, honorable, or virtuous by the use of reflective judgment. But precisely how does this judgment work?

According to Kant cognition works by aligning concepts of the understanding with intuitions of sense by means of schemata of the imagination.[163] These schemata are inner blueprints, as it were, one corresponding to each concept, which delineate the distinguishing marks by which an object in the world may be automatically correlated with the concept which denotes it.[164] Thus it is by means of such schemata that we are able to identify a given material object as "x" and not "y." In an analogous fashion, Kant describes the (reflective) judgment, as mediating between the inner world of ideas and the outer world of sense, but whereas the cognition relies upon schemata of the imagination to facilitate this mediation, the (reflective) judgment has recourse to a stock of examples given originally by either education or experience and stored away in the memory for this purpose.[165] Examples, as Arendt is fond of quoting Kant as saying, are the go-carts of judgment.[166]

As the schema corresponding to the concept of a triangle enables us to identify "closed, three sided, two-dimensional figures" as triangles, so too do the examples corresponding to the concept of courage enable us to distinguish a courageous act from one that is not. The example, in other words, marks out the paradigmatic traits which correspond with the real-world entity that deserves to bear the name. Because we have examples of (for example) the just man, the courageous man, and the righteous man we are able, via the workings of the reflective judgment, to say of the man who stands before us that he is just or unjust, courageous or cowardly, righteous or unrighteous. Without such examples we could not say.[167]

As Arendt traces the workings of the reflective judgment, she emphasizes, in particular, the role of these examples in the very act of judging.[168] Examples, are not merely important for *teaching* the concept in question, which we then employ as the criterion of our judgment. Rather, the example comes to be the very criterion of judgment as it comes to shape our perception.[169] As we do not generally see three-sided figures but see triangles, we do not generally see deeds of such and such spatiotemporal aspect and then adjudge them to be just; rather, we "see" justice. He who has only the idea will be unable to see in accordance with it; but he who possesses the example that corresponds to the idea shall see in accordance with it.[170] He will see deeds of justice and acts of charity in the same way as he sees stones and trees. No ratiocination will be necessary to see them.

From a truly Kantian perspective, the significance of the foregoing analysis is global. In exploring the linguistic and conceptual web by which mental and material worlds are joined, Kant in effect explicates the substrate that makes possible understanding, communication, and discourse, generally. Indeed, it might be argued that the political significance of this epistemological analysis lies in the indirect support it could give to the ideal of an all-encompassing linguistic community of humankind within which all manner of mutual understanding could be facilitated. For Arendt, however, the most significant implications are highly particularistic. What Kant has established with respect to the relations between language and perception generally, applies in Arendt's view to languages in their particularity and ought to be understood as sharply differentiating one linguistic community from another. Of special significance in helping her to buttress this perspective is Arendt's understanding of the relationship between the ideas and examples which undergird the reflective judgment's functioning and comprise a large proportion of that body of pre-understandings which Arendt denominates under the rubric of common sense.

What leads Arendt in a direction contrary to Kant's is that, whereas he is much more concerned with the status and nature of the *ideas* utilized by the reflective judgment, she is much more concerned with the role played by *examples*. Thus, in a given instance, Kant is more likely to be struck by the status of "justice" as a linguistic universal, or as a regulative idea, while Arendt is more likely to be struck by the fact that, its universality aside, the idea of justice will mean something different to every people in accordance with the distinct hues of the paradigmatic examples (or stories) by means of which it comes to grasp the idea of justice in the first place. It might be noted that, in essence, Arendt's opinion follows from the insight that lay behind her view of the importance of those authoritative stories which are archetypical for, and constitutive of, a given world view or cultural framework.[171] Such stories, on this view, are to be regarded as the "examples" which guide the reflective judgment in its employment of concepts, values, and regulative ideas.

As in the case of justice, so too with all of the other valuative criteria, ideas, and concepts that comprise the *sensus communis* of any given people. Two polities may share the same language—as do the United States and the United Kingdom—but inasmuch as they possess different political histories they will come to possess different concrete conceptions.[172] They may use the same words and hence superficially seem to employ precisely the same ideas, but inasmuch as these identical words are keyed to slightly different kinds of experiences (or examples), Arendt would hold that their concrete conceptions of justice could not possibly be the same.[173]

To grasp more fully the significance of Arendt's point, we would do well to reflect a moment upon the idea of courage and upon the way in which the tenor of its meaning so very much depends upon the particular cast of the examples with which it is associated and by which it is taught. Thus, what it means to be courageous will be one thing where Achilles is presented as the paradigm, and something quite different where it is Gandhi who figures as the exemplary case. Later in life when we think "courage" what we really think is "courageous as *X*" and it will make a difference whether we fill in the missing blank with hero A or hero B.[174]

Even if we assume that the essence of courage is the same in every case, the process of abstraction required to get to this essence suggests the practical irrelevance of so pure an essence. Moreover, if Arendt is right, the pure idea is useless from a pedagogical standpoint. Take the idea of courage: Where no concrete example is given at the same time as the idea is taught, it is clear that both the capacity to recognize it, and the capacity to embody it, will be stunted.[175]

But if only the concrete example, which possesses exemplary validity, can impart a virtue or idea then it should be observed as well that one can never merely impart a virtue or idea without imparting some sort of substantive value commitment beyond the virtue or idea itself.[176] Thus, it can be seen that any example by means of which one would give life to the idea of courage necessarily conveys some "on behalf of *X*" for the sake of which courage is being manifested. Whether this end be honor, faith, country, or self matters immensely, for the end is as much conveyed by the example as is the virtue itself. Those who would try to teach a virtue in-itself or an idea in-itself without imparting a substantive end, a "for the sake of which," have no recourse but to skip the example altogether or critique it to such a degree as to undermine its exemplary status. The net result, however—if Arendt is correct—will be a failure to impart anything at all.[177]

The lesson to be drawn is clear. The dependency of the reflective judgment upon historically contingent, concrete examples serves to buttress Arendt's non-Kantian conception of the *sensus communis*. Were the reflective judgment's operations less grounded upon localized and context-dependent elements, then perhaps it would be appropriate to construe the *sensus communis* along universalist lines. While Arendt would hardly deny that there will be certain relatively universal elements within the *sensus communis*—elements which follow from generic aspects of the human condition and from similarly generic aspects of the "existential" of political action—she would nonetheless insist that much of what comprises a given people's common sense will be particular to it alone and very much a product of its own unique history.

In sum, Arendt borrows much from Kant's conception of judgment, but at a crucial point she prefers to follow a different tack. Kant was most helpful inasmuch as he indicated the norms and procedures whereby a synchronic consensus might be attained from among a host of conflicting opinions and differing perspectives. Yet from the start, Arendt had conceived of this process as occurring in relation to a common sense that was irreducibly grounded "out there" on the concrete terrain of a particular culture with a particular conception of its ends. Thus in her essay on the "Crisis in Culture," wherein Arendt first brings the Kantian conception to the fore, she situates the Kantian process-norms within a context bounded by a common sense which is clearly conceived as containing two elements which markedly depart from what one would expect on the basis of the Kantian paradigm alone. Thus, on the one hand, common sense is identified as a web of shared understandings, a *cultura animi*, that has been imparted through contact with the exemplars of one's own culture.[178] On the other hand common sense is depicted as having implicit within itself an orientation toward that kind of judgment that insures cultural continuity.[179] It is within the frame bounded by such a common sense, which insures communicability and entails a shared action orientation, that Arendt expects the Kantian deliberative process ideals to hold sway. Though Arendt never explicitly notes where—or even that—she goes beyond Kant in the ways just delineated, she continues to do so through all the writings in which her Kantian paradigm appears.[180]

From the Judging Spectator to the Judging Actor

Genius and Taste. At length we have considered Arendt's neo-Kantian conception of spectator judgment, her conception of its functioning, and the extent to which it depends upon rather un-Kantian presuppositions. At this juncture, however, we are interested in discovering how Arendt turns her analysis of spectator judgment into a vehicle for conceptualizing the judgment that is exercised by the actor. That such a transition can be readily navigated is, perhaps, counterintuitive. After all, on first glance, the differences between acting and spectating—and between the modes of judgment they entail—do seem to be quite large. And yet, though there are real differences between these two modes of judgment, in Arendt's view, they are not as significant as their commonalities.

In the *Lectures on Kant's Political Philosophy* the shift of focus from the judgment of the spectator to that of the actor comes in the context of Arendt's consideration of Kant's analysis of the relationship between the artist and his audience who, like the actor and the spectator in politics, stand at structural antipodes of an essentially symbiotic relationship.[181] In Kant's initial formulation of the relationship, he places genius on the side of the artist and taste, or judgment, on the side of his audience, a schematization not so very different from Arendt's own initial formulation in *The Human Condition*.[182] Kant, then, asks which of the two is to be seen as more "noble."[183] Given Kant's own preference for that which is universal over that which is not, that he awards the rose to taste on account of its universality (that is, we demand it from all persons), can hardly be surprising. More substantively, it could be argued that since genius presupposes the genius's own ability to communicate, genius presupposes taste which contains within itself the criterion of communicability.[184] In other words, if there is something I would communicate to you I cannot just blurt it out; rather, I must mediate my inner impulsion according to the rules of language use, the nature of the situation, and my sense of what you are capable of understanding.[185] In short, I must exercise good judgment, which means I must respect your judgmental situation and the bounds of common sense which, at any given point in time, serve as the more or less fixed criteria of communicability. Cross the limit and what otherwise might have been dubbed genius is labeled idiocy, which is the fate of all who too regularly transgress the borders of the comprehensible.[186] Note also that the facticity of this horizon accounts for what has been described as the "spectator-effect" whereby out of a prudential interest the artist or actor is constrained to respect the taste of those whose understanding and attention he seeks.

As illuminating as it may be to contrast genius and taste, or the artist and his audience, in this way, there is something not altogether satisfying about the formulation. In a Hegelian sense, it suffers from one-sidedness and abstraction as a consequence of an essentially falsifying dichotomization. What is lost in setting the artist against his audience and genius against taste—and creates the erroneous impression that the relationship between the terms of each pair is external and oppositional—is the fact that even if he did not have it in mind to please this or that audience the artist would necessarily exercise his taste or judgment out of a need imposed by the laws governing the interrelations of his own mental faculties.[187]

Indeed, in the next stage of Arendt's presentation, she turns *with* Kant away from the external relationship between the artist and his audience to focus upon the internal mediation of taste and genius as it proceeds in the mind of the artist. For Kant, what differentiates the artist from those who are not is genius, or productive imagination, which Arendt, following Kant, defines as inspiration combined with the capacity to communicate "the subjective feeling associated with the representation," an ability which entails taste or judgment.[188] Note also that Arendt goes on to liken the inspirational element in genius, and indeed genius itself, to the capacity for giving rise to the novel in politics—which has the interesting effect of investing all persons with a "genius" for politics.[189]

In her *Lectures on Kant's Political Philosophy*, however, more important to Arendt than the inspirational side of artistry, or action, is the component which comes from judgment, or taste. Indeed, it is quite likely that the artist will censor himself not merely for the sake of the spectators by whom his work shall eventually be seen but for his own sake as well. The *sensus communis* which judgment activates belongs to the artist as a member of the community just as much as it belongs to members of his prospective audience. The pain or pleasure they will take in his work, insofar as it satisfies or offends their taste, the artist too will presumably experience in his own contemplation of the object.[190] Thus the artist too is a spectator, and not merely vicariously or by virtue of his anticipation of his audience's reaction.

This doubleness of the artist, or actor—who combines within himself both a productive, and a self-reflexive contemplative dimension—ought not to be understood in an overly mechanical way. It is not that the artist or actor must first "do his thing" before he can look upon it to judge it. The two moments are, of course, internal. In the first moment, an image of a possible object, or action, appears in his mind's eye. In the second moment, he places this image under the scrutiny of "his" common sense which is brought into play by stepping outside himself—as it were—in order to look upon his mental object as it would appear to some disinterested member of the judging community to which he belongs.[191] Where this contemplative moment gives pleasure, then, the image merits realization or communication; where it does not, the artist or actor properly keeps it to himself.[192] The important point here is to see that the artist—or actor—has effectively adopted the standpoint of the spectator who, at a later point, will come to judge the deed or object if the artist or actor chooses to place it before him.

Some readers will have been struck by Arendt's apparent departure from the position she takes in *The Human Condition*, a position which clearly differentiates between the activity of the artist and that of the actor. There, it will be recalled, Arendt contrasts the instrumental rationality of the artist with the entelechy of action, and elucidates the former by thematizing the method of the artist who first envisions before his mind's eye what only afterwards he proceeds to make.[193] Were the actor to act in a manner directly analogous to the manner in which the artist performs his craft, one might describe such action as the production of affect as effect. But presumably, were this the case, this would rout the possibilities of authentic self-disclosure, just as the production of effects is alleged by Arendt to do in the case of the artist. And yet in Arendt's lectures on Kant, she seems to liken the activity of the actor to that of the artist in just the manner we have indicated. Does this mean that Arendt has done away with the earlier distinction she so sedulously maintained?

Though the contrast with the mode of approach to action taken in *The Human Condition* is undeniable, I would suggest that the approach taken in the lectures on Kant is not essentially incompatible with it. In particular, I would note that in Arendt's account of instrumental rationality the division between ends and means is more essential than the distinction between envisioning and doing. Though both the artist and the actor may be said to do in accordance with the image they have contemplated and approved, the doing in the one case stands in a different relationship to the image that "guides" it than does the doing in the other. In the case of the artist, the image looms as the last effect that is to be produced through a series of instrumental steps; in the case of the actor, by contrast, the image denotes a state of activity that can only be personified directly and not an end that can be produced through means that are distinct from the end (or, more pointedly, from the activity) itself. Thus it should be clear that though both the actor and the artist may contemplate an image prior to doing, only in the latter case is this doing of the instrumental kind that, Arendt believes, necessarily blocks self-display.[194]

The Specificity of Action-Oriented Judgment. Treated in this manner not only the differences between the actor's and the artist's modes of activity, but more importantly the differences between the judgment exercised by the actor and that exercised by the spectator, have become blurred. To focus upon the latter pair, on the side of congruence we have found that judgment is, in the case of the actor as in the case of the spectator, always contemplative. Whether that which we must judge arises in the world of sense, or whether it arises in our minds in the moment of judging, our perspective is contemplative and properly scrutinizes whatever the object may be from the standpoint of the community, or common, sense. At one moment, then, the inner mental processes of the retrospective judge, the spectator of the present, and the actor who acts into the future are the same.

The significance of this confluence of judgmental modes in the debate over whether Arendt's Kant lectures represent a fundamental shift of emphasis is clear. The more akin the types are, the less significance ought to be attributed to the fact that Arendt has, in the context of lectures on Kant's thought, had occasion to focus upon his conception of the judgment exercised by the spectator. In this same context, I would suggest that Beiner's characterization of Arendt's "shift" from a concern with prospective judgment in her early work to a concern with retrospective judgment in her late is more than a little misleading.

On the one hand, the late work (post 1967) which consists of only a relatively small number of texts is hardly as one-sidedly concerned with retrospective judgment as Beiner would suggest. On the other hand, and more importantly, there is the fact that Arendt's concern with retrospective judgment was a long-standing one, as is evidenced in no uncertain terms by its presence in her "Understanding and Politics" (1953), *The Human Condition* (1958), and *On Revolution* (1963). Thus, that this concern turns up again in her 1970 Kant lectures is hardly surprising. It was, after all, not in 1970 but in 1958 that Arendt first had occasion to meditate at length upon storytelling—the exemplary form of retrospective judgment—as well as upon the nature of the judgment exercised by the spectator (albeit in a less than fully developed form). In support of our counterthesis, it should also be noted that in "Understanding and Politics," which Beiner sees as indicative of Arendt's "early" concern for prospective or actional judgment, a discussion of retrospective judgment figures almost as prominently. Indeed, this "tandem-treatment" of both action and retrospective judgment is paradigmatic for Arendt's way of handling these issues. What differentiates *The Lectures on Kant's Political Philosophy* from what preceded it is the fact that in the lectures Arendt comes closer than ever before to clarifying the *precise nature* of the relationship between the two kinds of judgment which she had long treated as correlative and mutually entailing. While it must be admitted that the Kant lectures are themselves far from unambiguous, there seems to be little evidence within them to justify Beiner's claim that they constitute a "break" with her long-standing concerns and conceptions. In light of the spin that Beiner places on Arendt's work in his *Political Judgment*, it would seem that he was misled because he failed to distinguish Arendt's Kant from Kant's Kant.[196] If Arendt had, in fact, embraced the "third critique" in an uncritical and unambiguously Kantian way, then Beiner would be on surer ground. For years, however, she had bent Kant to suit her ends. The effort to employ Kant's conception of spectator judgment as the basis for a theory of prospective political judgment was already of long-standing years before she delivered her Kant lectures.[197] In my view, this effort continues in these lectures as well.

In light of Arendt's overarching goal of establishing grounds for likening political judgment proper, and the deliberative aspect of that process, to the neo-Kantian, collective-process model of aesthetic judgment, Arendt's discernment of the contemplative moment that is common to judgment's various modes is very important. This commonality having been duly noted, we must underscore the differences between these modes as well lest the specificity of political judgment proper be elided.

Of the three forms of judgment which have held our attention, two can clearly be marked off as having more in common with one another than they do with the third. The spectator who judges what is before him and the retrospective storyteller who sits in judgment upon the past have as the object of their judgment something concrete which is, or was, out there in the world. Perhaps the caliber of their judgment will vary depending upon the vividness of their conception of the object, but the object itself preexists their judging of it. With regard to the judgment at the heart of action, however, this is not the case.

Action, it will be recalled, rises up out of the will, the organ of futurity. Action brings forth into the world what has never been seen or done before. In short, action produces itself as its object. That this might pose a problem for Arendt's effort to envision action as including a moment of contemplative judgment within itself seems clear. After all, what object is the actor to contemplate, given that the prospective deed that concerns him has yet to be brought into being?

To answer this question—as we noted a few pages back—Arendt refers to the simple fact that the actor first raises in his imagination the image of what he intends to do or propose, before he actually proceeds to do or propose it. This image, or a whole sequence of images, appears before his mind's eye in such a way as enables him to judge what his imagination delineates as *if he* was a spectator viewing that which is present, or a storyteller viewing what is past. Thus, even *before* embarking upon a particular project, the object becomes available for scrutiny according to the various criteria, from moral and aesthetic to pragmatic and utilitarian, which the actor possesses as a private person and as a citizen. Such is the nature of the deliberations that are necessarily prior to any course of action one chooses to pursue. Of course, where the action involved is a political action to be undertaken in one's civic capacity, the judgmental criteria of relevance are those of the community, or public, sense.[198] Though Arendt herself only occasionally extrapolates in this way from the case of the artist, given that her guiding interest is not in aesthetic but in political judgment, such an extrapolation is hardly surprising.[199]

In passing, it should be noted that the equivalence in modes of judgment—insofar as in each variety the imagination posits an object which the judgment then contemplates and judges according to the criteria available to it—should not be understood as implying an equivalence in the nature of the *objects* thus contemplated. Ontologically, from Arendt's perspective, that which has actually occurred has more reality than that which has not. Moreover, especially with respect to a possible action contemplated in the mind's eye, Arendt would be the first to note the gap between intention and execution, and the possibility of the actor's self-deception. In addition, as we saw in chapter 1, the actor acts into an environment which takes over his deed, a world which will, by what it does with it, ultimately determine its meaning. Hence, Arendt leaves it to the historians who go to work only after an event has run its course to determine the true meaning of what has transpired.[200]

Recall also that, for Arendt, the cogency of one's judgment hinges to a large degree upon the impartiality and disinterest one brings to bear in judging.[201] The more disinterested the judgment, the more likely it will be grounded on nothing but the community, or public, sense.[202] From this perspective, it might be suggested that the actor and the historian stand at opposite ends of a continuum, with the actor's proleptic assessments of his own future actions most likely to be corrupted by self-interest, and the historian's judgments of completed stories—especially as his temporal distance from them increases—least likely to be thus corrupted. The citizen-spectator of the present would presumably stand at some point in between. (Of course, one would not expect this schema to hold true in every instance, and yet as an indication of tendencies, its general validity can be assumed.) In sum, then, it can be said that in Arendt's view, though *all* types of judgment under consideration share the same essential form, the differences in the generic conditions under which they come into play will affect their relative cogency.

In a Deliberative Space. On the basis of what has been established to this point, we are able to take that step which was anticipated when it was suggested that the Kantian process model of aesthetic judgment might be treated as paradigmatic for the process of political judgment generally. It is the definitive specification of the moment of judgment internal to action that justifies this move. And I suggest that Arendt herself was moving in, and wanted her readers to follow her by moving in, this direction.

Thus, as there is an inherent parallel between the process internal to an individual's aesthetic judgment and the process of collective aesthetic judgment, Arendt seems to presuppose a parallel between the nature of the internal deliberative process prior to any particular action and the collective deliberative process prior to any collective judgment that some action or other ought to be undertaken. In the one case, there is the object and the appeals made to common sense as one person seeks to garner the assent of others to his own particular judgment. In the other case, there is the proposal for action which emanates from one citizen and the appeals made to common sense on behalf of (or against) this same proposal made by this same (or by other) citizen/s as each seeks to garner the assent (or opposition) of the rest to one position or another. In short, what naturally goes on in the mind of one person in a less procedurally systematic fashion should transpire in the collective body as well. The key difference between the two lies not so much in the difference of numbers as much as in the fact that in the collective process all appeals must be framed as appeals to common sense whereas in the individual case they need not be.

This analogy is surely sound as far as it goes. The attentive reader may have already noted, however, that the process described as being prior to political judgment contains moments which are strikingly akin to the judgment exercised by the spectator. Indeed, once one actor has placed a proposal before the rest, it is up to them to judge the "object" which he has produced, which they do by testing it against the criteria of common sense. Thus while their concern is with a future action, their procedure hardly differs from that which holds for assessing a present object.

Further reflection upon the substance of political deliberation reveals that the actors, though their main business be about arriving at a judgment regarding a prospective action, are in fact making judgments of all three kinds along the way to this decision. For example, a proposal to undertake any particular course of action necessarily presupposes an assessment of the current situation which in itself can become a contentious matter calling for the collective exercise of spectator judgment. At a different point in the same debate an outcome may hinge upon the question of whether or not the right lessons have been learned from history. At such a moment the actors will be called upon to exercise their skill in making retrospective judgments and in resolving the disputes which gather around such questions as whether in the Balkans or in the Persian Gulf we are applying or misapplying the right (or the wrong) lessons of Vietnam.

The implications of Arendt's Kantian turn should by now be clear. From the standpoint emergent in this chapter thus far, she would have us envision the political process as one of collective deliberation in which various policy proposals—each of which has already passed their author's inward test of political rectitude—are offered up for collective consideration. In this process, each proposal would presumably be tested against the various evaluative criteria which comprise a large part of the *sensus communis*, as one citizen or another brings one criterion or another to bear upon the policy recommendation. Arguments on behalf of the proposal would suggest its commensurability with the community's standards, just as arguments against it would stress the opposite. It is assumed, of course, that all citizen-deliberators will have adopted an appropriately disinterested stance, and that in their deliberations they will aim to frame good policy. The latter, in turn, is defined as policy which satisfies the publicly validated criteria of the *sensus communis*. Given

Arendt's concern for insuring the continuity of political identity, good policy should also be defined as being in conformity with the principles of action enshrined in the polity's constitution and political history.

Admittedly, the criteria that are denominated here are rather empty or formal in nature. To be more definitive, however, would be contrary to Arendt's conception of the *sensus communis* as a culturally contingent and historically emergent construct. In a substantive sense, then, what is accounted to be good policy will vary with time and place. What properly remains constant, however, is that argumentative appeals are made to publicly validated grounds and never to private feelings, for it is only in relation to the former that consensus and continuity may be repeatedly and reliably secured.[203]

Also assumed to be part of the *sensus communis* within any polity that might receive Arendt's imprimatur is a respect for the process-norms that follow from isonomy and *humanitas* which secure the status of the public space as a site of political equality and self-revelatory action. Public policy positions commensurate with these constraints and productive of long-term continuity presumably meet Arendt's formal criteria of legitimacy.

More to the point, at this juncture, than such observations is the question of how we should envision this "testing-process" as unfolding in relation to, what Arendt describes as, "representative thinking."

Representative thinking, as already observed, aims at establishing a continuity-preserving consensus on the basis of common sense. Should some policy "x" be proposed by some citizen or some group of citizens, following Arendt's conception of the political process, we should envision the process of "testing" to ensue. This was suggested in the previous paragraph. What representative thinking entails, however, is a willingness to move beyond the initial step of giving an opinion that is both disinterested and commonsensical. In this second step, Arendt would hope that each citizen will surrender his attachment to his own opinion in order to look upon the policy proposal from the alternative commonsensical perspectives, and in terms of the equally valid opinions, which his fellow citizens have brought to the fore.[204] That the citizens be willing to do this is demanded by the maxim of impartiality.

The product of such representative thinking, and of the process of discursive back and forth by means of which each citizen elucidates his own perspective for the sake of the rest, would be what Arendt calls an "enlarged mentality."[205] In particular, Arendt would imagine that the process will enlarge the mental horizon of those citizens who, despite their best intentions, had articulated points of view that were less born of the *sensus communis* than of their own narrow self-interest or bias. More generally, Arendt would imagine that the process should enlarge the mental horizon of even the least selfish or self-interested citizen inasmuch as it is inevitable that in the first moment of the process he will consider and articulate only such commonsensical perspectives as are most congenial to his nature while equally valid though less congenial commonsensical perspectives will likely not be considered at all. The enlargement of mind comes for such citizens in the second moment of the process as a result of imaginatively entering into the equally valid standpoints of others.[206]

One might then envision a process of give and take wherein each citizen properly endeavors both to test the legitimacy of his fellow citizens' various standpoints, that is, to insure they represent valid public, and not invalid private, perspectives—and to look upon the policy question proper from each of the standpoints that passes muster.[207] Where the majority of the citizenry has taken this path, Arendt would imagine that the likelihood of attaining a continuity-fostering policy consensus that is well grounded upon common sense will be much enhanced, especially on the assumption that the value of attaining this end is itself broadly acknowledged.

It seems fair to observe, however, that while the process I have detailed thus far seems likely to produce an enlarged mentality, it remains questionable whether this alone will be enough to make a policy consensus very likely.

Let us assume, for example, that the citizenry of some small country "A" has before it the recommendation that it invade country "B" in order to take control of certain natural resources which country "B" arbitrarily refuses to sell it despite the fact that these natural resources are of vital importance to country "A's" well-being. Let us further assume that in the past country "A" has acted in accordance with various principles of action ranging from the naked pursuit of its short-term material self-interest to a concern for the principle of noncoercion in international affairs. At still other times the country has acted with an eye to the court of world public opinion and national reputation. Thus, as each of these potentially incommensurable principles has played an important part in the nation's political history, each would have fair standing as a plank of common sense.

As the debate over the question of whether or not to invade country "B" begins, it seems reasonable to imagine that the citizens, in accordance with their individual natures, will tend to frame their recommendations in terms of one or another of these planks. Citizen "W" sees the issue in terms of short-term national interest and supports the invasion, while citizen "X" sees the issue in terms of the nation's standing in the world community and opposes it. Citizen "Y," however, views the matter from the same perspective as citizen "W" but disagrees with his conclusion; while citizen "Z," who is concerned with the principle of noncoercion in politics, opposes the invasion as well.

Through the process of discussion it should become clear to all that each opinion has a certain political legitimacy. Moreover, one might imagine that those citizens who never thought in terms of the morality of coercion come to do so, while those who were hitherto insensitive to practical need and the material bases of national survival become more so. Let us further assume that conflicts such as the one between citizens "W" and "Y" have been resolved, and that all agree as to where the country's narrowly conceived material interest lies. Let us also assume there is agreement that the invasion would bring glory though at the price of trampling upon the moral principle of noncoercion. Thus an enlarged mentality takes hold and enlightenment reigns. But are the citizens of country "A" any closer to resolving the policy question?

Arendt would have us place our faith in the process and in the primacy of the valuative norms of the *sensus communis*. These should suffice to produce consensus. But do they? If each of the evaluative norms were held to be of intrinsically equal importance, then the ensemble or norms encompassed by the *sensus communis* could only serve to limit the potential range of applicable principles. Just how wide the range of norms encompassed by the common sense of any given polity might be would vary from one polity to the next but within the bounded range no principle for choosing between norms—aside from majority rule perhaps—would be given. Conversely, however, we might envision a *sensus communis* which, in addition to bounding a range of valuative criteria of action, goes on to rank these criteria in relation to one another, and to provide principles for mediating conflicts between values which are on the same level of significance.

In truth, while Arendt herself does not specify one way or the other, her faith in the potential consensus-building impact of the *sensus communis* tends toward the highly systematized or maximalist conception, while her concern for not undermining the public sphere's viability as a site of self-display points in the direction of a more minimalist conception. In the case of the citizens of country "A," it could be argued that the *sensus communis* was loose and expansive enough to facilitate self-display while failing to facilitate consensus. At the opposite end of the spectrum, we might envision a *sensus communis* delimiting a very narrow range of permissible principles and giving clear rules regarding the handling of conflicts between them. On first glance, it might appear that in such a system the possibilities of self-disclosure through action are severely truncated, while the production of a policy consensus would seem to be optimized. It could be argued, however, that the chances for self-display are greater than one might expect, inasmuch as there remains an irreducibly subjective and hence self-disclosive moment in the application of even the most comprehensive system. Indeed, I shall frame an argument along such lines when we come to scrutinize the problem of self-manifestation more closely in a later section. More to point, it should be observed that the latter is no real ideal for Arendt inasmuch as it approaches the status of a closed system not so different from the ideological systems that she loathed for their radical suppression of the self-disclosive dimension of political existence. Thus, while at times Arendt finds the idea of assured consensus to be attractive, she never fails to draw back from the consequences which she instinctively felt would follow wherever this consensus was actually guaranteed. Thus she draws back as well from any conception of the sensus consensus that would be so systematized as to produce it unfailingly.

What Arendt apparently did have in mind was a kind of *sensus communis* that lay somewhere between these two poles. Born out of a collective new beginning and its interpretation, it would necessarily reflect something of that heterogeneity and openness that characterize the products of people who come together out of their differences to construct something which at once transcends and contains these same differences. From out of the plethora of motivations which brought individuals together in the act of beginning, Arendt would hope that a community sense would arise that was capacious enough to accommodate the differences present at the origin (and sure to be present subsequently) while pointed enough to facilitate the resolution of differences in the face of the need to frame coherent, and continuity-engendering, policy. A citizenry engaged in political deliberation while standing upon such a ground would, in Arendt's view, have conceptual scaffolding enough to bring their debates to a sound conclusion.

At this point, we are equipped to bring the conception of the process of political judgment developed in this chapter to bear upon the problematic with which this chapter began. Moreover, we are in a position to assess whether our treatment of political judgment and common sense can facilitate the desired rectification of the action-ideal.

Before turning to consider this question, however, it behooves us to pause and consider one of the singularly important implications of our analysis, an implication which follows from the discovery of the moment of judgment that is internal to political action. At issue at this juncture is the role of the various mental faculties in causing action to be undertaken.

Judgment, Action and the Will: An Interlude

It will be recalled from chapter 1 that, in Arendt's quest to discern the ground of action's freedom, she came upon the will which was free with respect to the pleading of reason on the one hand and with respect to the impulses of desire on the other. The will, in its essential freedom, or spontaneity, was singled out, moreover, as the source of that capacity for authoring the novel which she so much extolled. At the same time, however, this absolute freedom of the will, which made it such a marvel, was seen in a less flattering light as the source of much that is evil in the world as well. The problem with the will lay in its seeming arbitrariness, its lawless and radically contingent freedom, which, indifferently, could make it a source of either evil or good. In consequence, Arendt's attitude toward the will was fundamentally ambivalent.

That action could not be reduced to mere will was made clear in our first effort to trace action to its root. By itself the will seemed as likely to be an agency of destruction as one conducive to the upkeep of a community. Indeed, a politics of untempered will would likely be undone by the assertiveness it unleashed; and the picture it would probably present as it ran the road to ruin, tyranny, or both would hardly be a pleasant one. That Arendt's beloved Greek polis was in many ways just such a place is something Arendt seems to have only vaguely and occasionally glimpsed.[209] Nor, in light of this, is it surprising that many saw in her political ideal a none too pale reflection of the harsher side of agonal existence.[210]

For Arendt herself, of course, this aspect of Greek life was more than offset by the rich communal ethos and public spirit which, theoretically, should have served to restrain the likelihood that the darker forces would prevail. Yet within Arendt's original vision of a paradigmatic political community she fails to indicate what besides promising and forgiveness would emerge to counteract the entropic potentiality of the willful elements.

In chapter 2, of course, we explored what might be characterized as a sociological response to the problem. By means of a common culture not only would the political community be preserved over time, but also one could say that this culture—subsequent to the polity's beginning—acts to preform the community by imparting to the citizens the predisposition to regard themselves as a people sharing a common life and a common fate. The psychological effect of such an ethos in checking action's potential errancy is not to be underestimated.

At a theoretical level, however, it was not clear how the effects of a common culture were to be understood. In crucial respects, Arendt's analysis of action was hardly transformed by the introduction of the elements discussed in chapter 2. Indeed, as already noted, the dichotomized conception of the actor-spectator relationship, as formulated in *The Human Condition*, is merely transposed onto the new actor-authority dichotomy of *On Revolution*. Though judgment implicitly appears in *On Revolution*, it figures only as a function exercised by those in authority to keep in check the body of actors whenever its propensity for errancy threatens to break the bonds of continuity. That action and judgment might stand in an organic relationship to one another is never considered. That the new premium placed upon the intergenerational transmission of cultural content would affect the tenor and direction of action is clearly assumed but never really explained. Doing so would have required that Arendt introduce a fully articulated conception of the relationship between culture, common sense, and judgment on the one hand, and a fully articulated conception of the relationship between judgment and action on the other. Despite the steps Arendt takes in this direction in the work done prior to and just after writing *The Human Condition*, she fails to capitalize on it in *On Revolution* and, perhaps as a result, seeks refuge in the arms of authority.[211]

We, however, are in a position to see better than she the theoretical presuppositions at work (though hardly worked out) in *On Revolution*. In light of the conception of the relationship between common sense, judgment, and action developed in this chapter, we can see that *On Revolution* represents an effort to move toward a conception of action which overcomes the problems born of a conception (and a praxis) which is too will-dependent.

From our current vantage point we can see that by the time Arendt delivered her *Lectures on Kant's Political Philosophy* she had arrived at a conception of action rooted in more than will alone. Though action derives its original impetus and its capacity for spontaneity and novelty through the will, it has become clear that it is only action in the proper sense when whatever has originated in the unfathomable ground has been passed through the prism of reflective judgment before it makes its entry into the world. That judgment can save the will from its arbitrariness and the individual from the abyss of freedom owes, however, not to some absolutely transcendent ground towards which judgment points, but to the fact that judgment links the actor to the world by virtue of its own linkage to common sense (which is the sense of the community within which the actor lives). Only when his impulsions and ideas are thus purified will it be the case that every action, every utterance, and every deed will be congruent with the communal essence and, indeed, continuously serve to reproduce it.

In this context, it should be noted that Arendt's view of the will, and of its relation to action and to judgment, remains a subject of dispute in the secondary literature. Moreover, for reasons that will become clear presently, this dispute bears upon the controversy over the significance of

Arendt's *Lectures on Kant's Political Philosophy* for our understanding of
action.

From chapter 1, the reader will recall the question of the relationship
between action and the will. Unmentioned at that earlier point was
Arendt's statement in "What Is Freedom?" in which she suggests "that the
faculty of will and will power *in and by itself, unconnected with any other
faculties* is an essentially non-political and even anti-political capacity."[212]
According to one view, the import of this statement is to disassociate
absolutely the will from political action.[213] For those who read Arendt's
early essay along these lines, the significance of *Willing*, Arendt's last completed work, and one in which the issues adumbrated in the earlier essay
again arise, is clear. *Willing* is read as confirming Arendt's earlier rejection
of the will as a contaminant of action. In the view of these critics, Arendt's
rejection of the will renders her account of action "bizarre," problematic,
or incoherent.[214] What these critics fail to see is that Arendt never rejects
the will; she only rejects any conception which would hold it to be the
absolute and exclusive ground of action. The will, in Arendt's view, is not
fit to be the root of action until it is tempered by judgment.

Beiner's conception of how *Willing* ought to be understood differs
from the conception just adumbrated and from the view I have argued for.
Beiner is struck by the fact that, with Nietzsche and Heidegger, Arendt
finds it hard to be "pleased" with the will on account of its inherent arbitrariness on the one hand and its proclivity for wanton destructiveness on
the other. That the will might be "pleasing" to behold only where
redeemed by judgment is, in fact, obscurely perceived by Beiner. In his
view, however, the kind of judgment that redeems the will for Arendt is
not political or prospective judgment, but retrospective and reconciliatory
judgment which supervenes upon the site of action to redeem it after the
fact, that is, through the pleasure of judging what may have been horrid in
the moment of its occurrence. Hence the thrust of his reading of the *Lectures on Kant's Political Philosophy*.

Thus, like the critics mentioned above, Beiner fails to see that Arendt
never rejected the will; nor does he grasp that she never rejected action
either. That the will, in Arendt's view, grounds action is unmistakably
clear on almost every page of *Willing*. That the will—and action—are
hard to be pleased with (for the reasons stated above) leads her, however,
not to their rejection, but, as always, to search for means of making them
more "pleasing." Retrospective judgment of what has transpired is hardly
likely, in itself, to facilitate this end. As Arendt herself points out, such retrospective contemplation of the past is more likely to fill the onlooker
with revulsion and despair than to "please by the very act of judging."
Had not the tableaux of horror envisioned in the glance toward the past

led Heidegger to reject the will which he had once idealized? In sum, where there is no beauty to behold, the mere act of judging is hardly likely to convey pleasure.

To escape the abyss of freedom, then, Arendt sought to provide the will, and hence action, with a ground, with a nonarbitrary, nonsolitary source of direction which might make action itself something with which we might be more pleased in contemplation. But to this end, action itself and the will also must be made more pleasing in practice by being made less destructive, less ruinous of the world, and less dangerous to mankind. The means to this end are, in the view being propounded in this chapter, the prospective judgment and the *sensus communis* upon which it is grounded. Together they might overcome the will's arbitrariness and reck- lessness, and hence might free man from "the abyss of freedom" as well. Such, in my opinion, is the direction Arendt would have likely taken in the unwritten third section of *The Life of the Mind*. It is the direction implicit in her *Lectures on Kant's Political Philosophy*.[215]

A NEW LOGOS OF POLITICS

In order to assess the value of Arendt's conceptualization of judg- ment and political judgment from the standpoint of her larger project, it is necessary first to delineate how the consequent conception of the political process is to be mapped upon Arendt's topographical model of political space.[216] From *The Human Condition* onward, the dichotomy of chief rel- evance in this regard has been Arendt's distinction between public and pri- vate spheres; and within the former the dichotomy between actors and spectators has been of central importance. The public sphere, alone, has been conceived as being "where the action is" and action itself has been conceptualized as being governed by performative norms—at least implic- itly. This dramaturgic conception of action, and of the public space as well, is itself suggestive of that cleavage within the public space that dichotomizes between citizen-actors and citizen-spectators, that dichotomizes, in other words, between those who truly act (and directly determine policy) and those whose attention is engaged by the action, who by their praise and blame influence the quality and direction of that which unfolds before them.[217] Thus the political process is resolved into two or three distinct processes depending on whether one focuses upon actor- actor, actor-spectator, or spectator-spectator interactions. With respect to these processes, however, a certain vagueness had characterized Arendt's account of them in the works considered in the previous chapters. With the conception of political judgment set forth in this chapter, this lack of specificity, which has caused problems for us throughout, is largely over-come.

Most directly clarified by Arendt's neo-Kantian conception of spec-tator judgment is the precise nature of the process ongoing within the cir-cle of citizen-spectators and the nature of the effect that this process has upon the assemblage of citizen-actors.[218] Arendt's analysis of the judging spectator is of relevance here. Of particular importance in this context is the communal dimension of the process which Arendt's treatment serves to clarify. Thus the citizen-spectator has been depicted: as one who judges on behalf of the community; as one who seeks to gain the assent of the community to his judgment; as one who seeks a community-sustaining consensus; and as one whose public judgments are grounded upon the *sensus communis*. The judging process itself, as a consequence of the prominence given to an "exemplary" past by the *sensus communis*, emerges as essentially conservative. In the inward comparative movement at the heart of every act of judgment, something of the present is mea-sured against something exemplary from the past which constitutes the norm. Perhaps, it is not inevitable that the process of judging will tend to make of continuity a primary virtue, but in Arendt's view this is the likely result. Hence the nature of the "spectator-effect."

From a functional perspective, the role of the ring of citizen-specta-tors is to judge the policies and performances of the citizen-actors and to award praise or blame accordingly. The prominence of the *sensus commu-nis* in the minds of the citizen-spectators, in effect, makes their judgments equivalent to a judgment emanating from the *sensus communis* itself. In practice, then, the role of the citizen-spectators is to insure that the citizen-actors do not depart from the time-tested norms of the *sensus communis*. Of course, the very possibility of the citizen-spectators playing this role at all presupposes that the citizen-actors care about, and are structurally dependent upon, their good opinion. That political actors are so orientat-ed is something which Arendt's analysis of action presupposes.[219] Insuring that this is actually the case is a constitutional matter on the one hand and a matter of ethos on the other. Any broadly participatory political arrangement which makes the political fate of leading citizens a conse-quence of public opinion should suffice, so long as the ethos of the citizen-ry at large serves to insure attentiveness to politics and the prominence of the criteria of meritorious public service that are inherent in the *sensus communis*.

Should it be argued that Arendt's ideal of pure (that is, non-repre-sentative) participatory politics, by doing away with the electoral mecha-nisms of representative democracy, does away as well with the implicit division between actors and spectators, I would note the following: Clearly Arendt believes in the existential importance of political participation; nonetheless, this never leads her to doubt that political talent and interest are unevenly distributed.[220] As a result, it is not contradictory for Arendt to expect that even within the most perfectly participatory politics political prominence will vary to such a degree as to warrant the maintenance of the distinction between citizen-actors and citizen-spectators.[221] In addition, Arendt would surely point out that even within a polity in which political equality was so perfectly realized as to render all citizens equally active and prominent, the exigencies of the parliamentary, or deliberative, process itself are such as to transform into spectators the majority of those who are present in the deliberative chambers at any given point in time. Not only are these citizen-actors recurrently cast in the role of spectators vis à vis the actions and events that emanate from, and call attention to, a world beyond the relatively narrow confines of their own. More continuously—indeed, every time one of their number stands forth before them to recommend that this or that policy or project be undertaken or not—the rest of them are so cast vis à vis the one who commands their attention and seeks to persuade them of one thing or another.

More important, however, than the question of who spectates—since arguably all do—is the significance of spectatorship for the good functioning of the polity as a whole. So long as spectatorship remains grounded upon the *sensus communis* and transpires along the lines that have already been indicated, it should constitute a force that is likely to be engaged on behalf of the long-term continuity of the polity's identity. As I have already noted, had Arendt thought to secure this continuity by building upon the conceptions of the *sensus communis* and of spectator judgment that she had developed in her 1961 "The Crisis in Culture," then she might not have felt it necessary to beat a path of retreat from the isonomy of "the many" to the authority of "the few" in her 1963 *On Revolution*. That a few citizens vested with great authority over the rest might do better in this respect than the collective body of the whole political community cannot be denied with any certainty. What is clear, however, is that vesting authority in the hands of a few—even if they are only meant to personify the authority of the past for the present more generally—constitutes an affront to the basic principle of political equality Arendt espouses in *The Human Condition*. Better then to vest authority in the power of collective spectatorship for the sake of preserving isonomy since no threat to continuity is necessarily entailed thereby.[222]

So much, then, for the role played by citizen-spectators. Doubtless, spectatorship entails mental activity of a not undemanding kind; yet it is also true that spectatorship is an essentially reflective and secondary activity inasmuch as it presupposes another kind of activity that produces the object, idea, or proposal upon which the spectator's gaze is focused. What political spectatorship presupposes is political action; the political spectator, in other words, presupposes the political actor.

For Arendt, the political actor is the political artist, the political creator, the political genius who "produces" the political object, idea, or proposal which becomes grist in the political spectator's mill.[223] Alternatively, Arendt might describe the political actor as one whose existential fulfillment comes about within a life of public political activity, that is, within a life of words and deeds, of deliberation and debate, which together constitute a public life. Since this existential dimension has been treated fully in chapter 1, it need only be touched upon here. Let it suffice, then, to observe that everything posited in chapter 1 with regard to the existential structure of action, applies much more so to the political actor than to the citizen-spectator.

That the assemblage of actors determines public policy and that by means of this policy it must insure the longevity of the polity's existence and the continuity of its particular identity are matters of no small importance; and yet, Arendt fails to take any cognizance of these issues in *The Human Condition*. There, as already noted, the close treatment of existential issues is matched by the neglect of the more conventional aspects of the political process. In particular, a veil of opacity obscures the process of collective deliberation to such a degree as to render it most questionable whether individuals bent upon political self-realization of the kind Arendt espouses could ever come to an agreement regarding a question of policy. Nor are actor-actor interactions, and their status within the political process as a whole, clarified to a much greater degree in either *Between Past and Future* or *On Revolution*. It is only with her return to Kant that Arendt finds ready to hand the resources that enable her to set forth how she understands the process of collective deliberation that stands at the center of political life.[224]

As we have unpacked the implications of Arendt's lectures on Kant, it has become clear that Arendt conceives of the process of public policy formation as a collective and deliberative process of political judgment that is oriented toward the achievement of a consensus. What was loosely termed action in *The Human Condition* is thus reconceptualized. The emphasis has shifted from the existential accomplishment of the individual actor to the process of collective political deliberation whereby a policy consensus is to be secured from the midst of a multitude of actors. But, in the course of effecting this transition, Arendt has discovered and elucidated a crucial moment of political judgment that is prior to the words and deeds of the actor who, in *The Human Condition*, came into focus only as he strode upon the public stage. And while Arendt is primarily concerned with turning this discovery in a direction that will serve to elucidate the collective dimension of the political process, her understanding of the existential aspect becomes refined as well.

Perhaps, the most striking aspect of Arendt's analytic of political judgment is the degree to which it parallels her conceptualization of spectator judgment. Like the latter, it is presented as essentially contemplative in its orientation—which appears rather paradoxical in light of the differences that otherwise distinguish the function of the citizen-actor from that of the citizen-spectator. Nonetheless, Arendt discerns a moment of spectator-like contemplative judgment at the very heart of action. Arendt's analytic of genius, and her discovery of a moment of spectatorship internal to it, makes this clear.

It is important to keep in view, however, that the transformed conception of political action that follows from Arendt's discovery does not entail the complete rejection of her earlier conception. Nor can it be said that only the husk, that is, Arendt's high estimation of action as a medium of self-revelation, remains intact while the kernel has been replaced. Rather, it should be seen that the heart of action remains the same as it was in Arendt's earlier conception. Action remains the source of the novel, of the unprecedented, and of the unexpected; and it retains this capacity because it is still conceived as something that mediates between the world and the dark procreative ground of Being. All action begins in the latter depth; the idea that bursts into consciousness to take form as a proposal, a project, or a new principle emanates from this depth, and its emergence from darkness to light constitutes the beginning of action. The contemplative moment and the corresponding testing of the object by the criteria of the *sensus communis* come into play only afterwards.

In *The Human Condition* the problem with Arendt's conception of action lay in her almost exclusive attention to the primordial moment and to what it signified. With the Kant lectures, this shortcoming is repaired as Arendt's attention shifts to the second, or contemplative, moment which mediates between the articulate possibility that appears before the mind's eye of the individual—or before the assembly of citizens in the case of the polity—and its actualization as word or deed or policy. Admittedly, Arendt does not delineate very clearly how the moment of contemplative judgment stands in relation to action's originary ground and it is understandable that some readers have read the Kant lectures as implying that the reflective moment of political judgment is meant to stand on its own. But such is not Arendt's intent. Rather, the contemplative moment is comprehended as a vital component of action though never as the whole of it. The contemplative moment of judgment and the conception of the political process modeled on it do explain how action can be continuously productive of continuity and consensus but they do not explain nor even pertain to what constitutes the ground of action's very possibility.

The depth from which the possibility of action springs is both hidden and inexplicable. We know of this depth because we find evidence of it in the unprecedented actions and novel ideas which humans are continuously sending forth into the world. Some would fancy that the depth is somehow Divinity itself and Arendt herself speculates along such lines on occasion.[225] Were every new beginning that was culled from the depth a manifestation of beauty and goodness, it would be easier to assent to such propositions. Unfortunately, the course of history and the newspaper stories of contemporary life belie any such assessment. What springs freshborn from the depth is as often as not ugly, immoral, and malevolent. Better, then, to describe the depth as the ground of *all* possibility than to posit a particular cast to its moral character. It is the former after all that accounts for the nature of the relationship in which it stands to the contemplative moment of judgment.

It is the role of judgment, then, to distinguish the demonic from the angelic beginnings and to declare what is fit and not fit for entry into the public realm—as word or deed in the case of the individual—or as public principle or public policy in the case of the polity. But for the role played by judgment, the actor would be incapable of differentiating between those creatures of the depth that should and those that should not be sent forth into the world—and the world would surely be a darker more dangerous place as a result. But for the depth, however, the actor would have nothing whatsoever to send forth and judgment would have nothing to contemplate. Political action, the vocation of the citizen-actor, requires both elements, and a will to join them together in a manner that is conducive to consensus, continuity, and world order.

For the sake of these various political goods both the individual and the aggregate political wills must be properly oriented. It is not that only the possessor of a properly directed will judges before he acts—since in a certain sense an act of judgment is necessarily antecedent to every act. Rather, what marks the possessor of a properly directed will as such is that he will judge what comes before his mind's eye—whether it arises from the depths of the imagination or from the daily newspaper—by the criteria of the *sensus communis* which have been made his own intimate possession through long tutelage in culture. And the same holds true for the polity as a whole.

Rightly governed and "world-broken" is the will that submits itself to the guidance of the *sensus communis*. It is in the contemplative moment of judgment that this submission occurs. For the individual, this inward process of testing and comparison proceeds in a largely unconscious manner. For the polity as a whole there are fora, rules, and procedures to facilitate this process and to insure that it unfolds in a highly articulate and self-expressive manner.

THE ACTION IDEAL AS CRITERION: DOES THE NEW LOGOS MEASURE UP?

So much then for the topography and for the close conceptualization of the process. At this juncture, the significance of what has emerged in this chapter must be assessed. We want to know two things. First: Does this newly emergent conception overcome world alienation and thus lay the basis for a post-Cartesian common sense? And second: Does this conception satisfy the two-sided demands of the action-ideal? It was, after all, in the hope that both of these ends might be secured that we undertook to explore the writings considered in this chapter.

Arendt's concern with world alienation is articulated as such in *The Human Condition*, but it is present in her earlier work as well.[226] For Arendt, as we have seen, world alienation is meant to denote specifically the modern experience of the loss of trust in the evidence of the senses and the increasingly attenuated sense of the world's objective reality which she traces to the advent of the modern age and, more particularly, to the rise of modern science and modern philosophy.[227] More generally, world alienation connotes for her the experience of anomie, the associated sense of having lost one's place in the world, and the feeling that the common world itself has disintegrated.

The philosophical product, and equivalent, of world alienation is solipsism and the dissolution of common sense. This may lead to a kind of hypersubjectivism and to a wild proliferation of incommensurate private worlds—which on the political level may be manifest as a radicalized atomic egoism in which force alone can decide the outcome. But this is not the only imaginable outcome.[228] It is also possible that, as in the case of Descartes, the dissolution of the common world may lead the ego to seek stability in the arms of the mighty cogito and to reconstruct its inner world on the basis of the truths of pure reason that the cogito provides. Should the ego also believe that the truths of its private cogitations are meant to provide a basis for the reformation of the political order, this may engender an effort to remake the world in the image of the one truth that has been perceived. Thus solipsism may lead to a kind of rationalism and eventually to a political monism such as Arendt associates with Plato on the one hand and with totalitarianism on the other.[229]

In her endeavor to overcome world alienation Arendt takes direct aim at solipsism and at its implicit repudiation of worldly common sense. Though Arendt's frontal assault on solipsism is most evident in *Thinking*, it is important to observe that her critique of solipsism is also implicit in almost everything she says about worldly common sense in her other writings. Because we have already considered this matter at some length, I will only touch upon a few of the most important points at this time.

As we earlier noted, Arendt rejects the claims that have been made on behalf of introspection and, in particular, denies that the cogito offers privileged access to truth or reality. On the one hand, Arendt argues that introspection is as beset by the inherent limitations of *dokei moi* as any other private sense experience; on the other hand, she argues that introspection lacks the corrective capacity that only an orientation toward the intersubjective confirmation of our perceptions can provide. Another name for this process of intersubjective validation is the test of common sense, a test which entails discourse with the other and, by extension, community and community sense, as well.

In Arendt's view, this regular dependence on intersubjective validation that is implicit throughout the realm of the senses is rendered methodologically explicit in scientific inquiry. It should, however, be noted that where generic human capacities are concerned (such as logic or vision), the test of common sense is largely negative, that is, it functions as a check on corrigible error. But in the broad domain of disputable human meanings, a domain that includes politics within its purview, this is hardly so. For meanings, as we have seen, are originally products of pure thought, and, in contrast to truth, there is nothing self-evident about them.[230] Rather, meanings are necessarily private until shared, and of merely private validity until others are persuaded of their significance. In this context, where it is meaning that is at issue, common sense provides not so much a test as a medium by means of which the *dokei moi* (it-seems-to-me) of judgment can be transformed into "it-seems-to-*us*" of intersubjective validity. Not only does common sense facilitate this transformation of idiosyncratic private meanings into shared public meanings, common sense also signifies that body of meanings that have already acquired public standing.

As we have seen, world alienation is symptomatic of the loss of a common world. Common sense, by contrast, signifies a common world and acts to produce and reproduce this world. But common sense can only function in this way, and act to overcome world alienation as well, if it is already the common sense of some people.[231] From this it should not be inferred that, because common sense is always common to a particular people, every particular people will possess common sense. Indeed, Arendt makes clear that common sense (qua *Gemeinsinn*) can only come into being among people who are together in a fully discursive and properly public manner. The members of mass society, for example, lack common sense, in Arendt's view, because they are outside of this fully discursive condition and lack access to the kind of public realm that alone can fully actualize it.

The transcendence of modern world alienation depends, then, upon more than a formal refutation of Descartes' philosophical errors. Shared meanings and public agreements—be they ever so contingent—are possible only where public spaces and the requisite discursive conditions exist. It is necessary, then, to constitute such spaces and to insure that the appropriate discursive conditions come into effect. As if she had this in mind, in *On Revolution* Arendt focuses upon the problem of constituting a public space and upon the problem of transmitting the relatively constant elements of a people's common sense across the ages. By contrast, as if she were addressing the second presupposition, Arendt endeavors in "The Crisis in Culture" and in her lectures on Kant to elucidate the regulative principles that are capable of sustaining the appropriate discursive situation. Of course, it should hardly need to be pointed out that the possibility of transcending world alienation only exists for those persons who are granted a "place" in the common world, that is, for those alone who are granted the right of actively participating in the deliberations that are ongoing in the public space.

In the final analysis, then, Arendt frames a conception of a world-rooted common sense that facilitates the transcendence of world alienation and steers clear of the post-Cartesian either/or of repressive (quasi-Platonic) monism and solipsistic (quasi-Nietzschean) fragmentation. Over against these standpoints that are so destructive of the kind of "being-with" (*Mitsein*) that Arendt wants to foster, Arendt posits the kind of common sense, or community sense (*Gemeinsinn*), that can help to engender islands of shared meaning and policy agreements from out of the interstices of human difference. Such a common sense should make possible a common public life, and thus a commonality that transcends—without utterly nullifying—both inter- and intragenerational differences of opinion. To extirpate difference to any greater degree would hardly be desirable since this could only be achieved by ruining the human plurality that Arendt wants so much to foster. Nonetheless, while significant differences of public opinion will continue to be manifest, the likelihood that such differences will remain irreconcilable should be greatly reduced. More importantly, the promise of more extensive agreement is hardly necessary for achieving the end of overcoming world alienation. Does this newly emergent conception overcome world alienation and thus lay the basis for a post-Cartesian common sense? To this question the answer is, surely, yes.

How then do matters stand regarding our second query: Does the conception of action that has been developed in this chapter satisfy the two-sided demands of the action-ideal?

From the outset, I have argued, Arendt was impelled by a two-headed agenda. On the one hand, she sought to articulate a politics of self-realization and human actualization, an endeavor most fully apparent in *The Human Condition*. On the other hand—as was demonstrated at length (in chapter 2)—Arendt was almost as strongly driven to envision a mode of political action capable of sustaining the long-term continuity of any given (essentially humane) political order. In succession, however, as one or the other emphasis has come to the fore, the tenor of the antecedent configuration has shifted back and forth. Ideally the action-ideal entails the simultaneous realization of both aspects within a single construction. Unfortunately, the long sought-after balance has proven elusive. To the beginning of the present chapter, the texts considered along the way have tilted very much in one direction or the other. At issue at the present moment is whether the model of the political process elaborated in this chapter fares any better. That it fills a lacuna in Arendt's earlier work, and thus obviates an earlier point of criticism, are matters of no small importance. Of much greater concern to us, however, is the question of whether it constitutes that theoretical keystone-in-the-arch without which the action-ideal will remain an unrealized ideal.

Of the two emphases, it is easier to begin our analysis with the one which came to the fore in *Between Past and Future*. In the last chapter, I traced the manner in which Arendt's concern for the maintenance of political continuity had led her to attend to the mechanisms of social and cultural reproduction. By overdetermining the tenor and telos of action these mechanisms would help to secure continuity. In addition, we saw that Arendt was ready to rely upon anti-isonomic agents of authority to insure what cultural conditioning could only imperfectly guarantee. Under the model of the political process that has been developed in this chapter, the end of political continuity would appear to be no less likely to be attained. In large measure this is so because much of the earlier conception has been retained. Analytically, however, there has been an increase in terminological precision. What had been attributed in a general way to the effect of cultural conditioning has now been recast in terms of the role of the *sensus communis* in its several paradigmatic modes of manifestation.

From one angle, it has become clear that the *sensus communis* operates through the spectator-effect which radiates into the public space via the attention of the citizen-spectators who are gathered along its perimeter. From another angle, it has become clear that the *sensus communis* constitutes a kind of gestalt or Weltanschauung that acts to prefigure the political perceptions of the citizen-actors proper who stand within the public space. Operating, then, at both the center and periphery of the public space, the *sensus communis* traces, as it were, the boundary of permissible public discourse and does so in such a manner as generally ought to facilitate the emergence of a continuity-productive consensus. Continuity itself is to be anticipated on account of the past-rootedness of the ensemble of concepts, values, and principles which constitutes the substance of the *sensus communis*.

In chapter 2, the price paid for securing world-continuity was the sacrifice of self-actualization and uniqueness. At issue, then, is whether the conception developed in this chapter fares any better in this respect. If it does not, then all our spadework in this chapter will have been for nought.

Were the *sensus communis* only operative through the workings of the spectator-effect, then, one might want to argue that in effect Arendt divides citizens into two categories: those who act in the self-revelatory manner conceptualized in *The Human Condition* and those who spectate in the self-effacing manner that is naturally consequent upon making one's judgment the vehicle of community standards. The problem with this view is twofold. First, it conveniently overlooks the fact that from childhood onward the citizen-*actor* is raised to be a citizen-*spectator*. Second, it fails to take any cognizance of the fact that, in Arendt's view, the mode of judgment exercised by the actor and that exercised by the spectator are in essence the same. Moreover, as we have seen in detail, the role of the *sensus communis* is central for both. Thus the question of how the self-revelatory pole of the action-ideal will fare when those who must act into the future have been bred to vigilance on behalf of the past must be grappled with at this juncture just as it was necessary to do so at the end of chapter 2. At issue is whether the conception of the judging process which I have delineated will enable us to arrive at a more favorable conclusion than was obtained when the question was last considered.

To render the problem most vivid, it ought to be recalled that the citizen-spectator who judges best is the one whose judgment arises out of the *sensus communis* and accords with the most authoritative taste.[232] The best spectator rightly aims not at self-expression but at the proper application of that which is prior and general to that which is present and particular. Thus, he who stands out from the pack for the excellence of his judgment will most emphatically not be the source of new standards, but will display instead the most refined and most catholic facility in applying the authoritative criteria of the past to whatever comes before him in the present. In whatever epoch such a judge steps forward, his contribution will always be to resuscitate the authoritative standards of the past, to inject them with new vitality, and to infuse the present with a renewed sense of their timeless validity. From him, then, should come not the new but the old, which if seemingly new, is new as the gleaming gold-orange luster of polished copper is "new" when it has replaced the whitish green patina of an old and long unpolished kettle. Thanks to his efforts the old kettle is made to look like new. What had, perhaps, begun to look like an old thing ready for the dump thus receives a new lease on life.

But if such constitutes excellence in spectatorship, and if the judging process internal to civic action is understood along similar lines, then, it must be asked whether action can still be regarded as the fount of uniqueness, novelty, and originality. Or, is it the case that the Arendtian ideal in world-sustaining judgment necessarily entails a self-obfuscating traditionalism in action?

On behalf of uniqueness, novelty, and originality coming to the fore, and over against the negative inference which this stylization of the problem would seem to entail, it is necessary to recall that in rendering the inner structure of action a crucial distinction was maintained between the several moments of the process. The originary moment of spontaneous self-manifestation, in particular, was distinguished from the second inward moment of self-scrutiny in which the product of the first moment was measured against the criteria of the *sensus communis*. At issue, then, is whether the contemplative prism of the second moment will permit the light of uniqueness to pass over into the world.

In defense of the proposition that, *sensus communis* based circumspection notwithstanding, the actor's uniqueness will nonetheless be manifest in the world, Arendt would likely single out three factors for our consideration. Of these three, of utmost importance is the fact that the generative root of the individual's singularity (that is, the wellspring of uniqueness and novelty) has been neither covered over nor repressed by the newly prominent moment of inward reflection. That the latter will not extirpate what is fresh in the former owes, however, to both the character of the *sensus communis* and to the character of the politico-historical world, the second and third factors, respectively.

Thus, regarding the *sensus communis*, Arendt would likely remind us of its inherent indeterminacy and polysemous character, both of which become apparent in the moment of contemplative application and owe in large measure to the obdurate opacity and irreducible contingency of the politico-historical realm within which actions are taken. Were the politico-historical realm thoroughly law-governed or unchanging, then, over time, the paradigmatic elements of the *sensus communis* and the recursive elements of the politico-historical realm might come to conform to one another in a relation of perfect correspondence.[233] Thus might a totalizing system of rules and a totalizing knowledge of the world come to constitute a whole from within which all indeterminacy and polysemy were extruded. Formally, even in such a world, the "moment" of action would remain inwardly dirempted, and the moment of spontaneous upwelling would remain distinct from the moment of inward scrutiny. Nonetheless, it seems apparent that, to the degree the *sensus communis* achieved an imperious and absolute univocity, the likelihood of uniqueness achieving worldly expression would be severely reduced. Action would be as overdetermined and regularized as the world into which it was sent forth, while the prospects for self-revelation would be diminished quite as effectively as, in Arendt's view, they were under the hegemonic weight of totalitarian ideologies—and for reasons which are not dissimilar.[234]

Lucky for action's self-revelatory capacity, then, that neither the world nor the *sensus communis* are as rigidly structured as the "totalizers" and structuralists might claim. Instead, on Arendt's view, at the nexus between the world and the *sensus communis* there lies a moment of indeterminacy, a moment of freedom, in which the uniqueness of the self cannot help but insinuate itself.

Thus we might envision that at the end of some veiled, inchoate, spontaneous process there flashes upon the screen of consciousness an idea, a notion, or a proposal which bears the imprint of the singular identity of the one whose utterance it aspires to be. To send it forth into the world or not, becomes the question. It is at this point that judgment's contemplative moment comes into play as inwardly the actor asks himself whether or not his prospective utterance accords with time and place and all manner of circumstance. Historical precedents of equally authoritative standing likely come to mind as well as this process of reflection continues—some favorable, some unfavorable, to the course he contemplates recommending. Were we enabled somehow to record this dialogue of the actor with himself, in a given hypothetical instance the following might be heard: "A crisis looms in a far-away place. Troops must be sent at once and we cannot shy away from using them. Force must be met with force. Aggression cannot be appeased." Thus, in the contemplative gaze, the Munich paradigm comes into focus and the appropriate arguments are mustered. But wait, another paradigm is then recalled: A murky, ill-defined and unending conflict producing tens of thousands of casualties and ruinous division at home. Thus Vietnam comes to the fore as an argument against the commitment of force and against the proposal which at this point has not yet been made.

To articulate publicly the original notion would be, in effect, to appeal to the example of Munich as highly relevant. The example has public standing as a ready reference point for it is a component of the *sensus communis*. The community of listeners, in other words, would have no difficulty in understanding even a vaguely allusive reference to what by now has become a part of the collective wisdom. Conversely, however, were our representative citizen to espouse the contrary position and to frame his appeal upon a Vietnam-based analogy, this too would be popularly accessible.

Apparently, in the case I have envisioned, there are elements of worldly circumstance which call to mind both of these historical reference points. Hence the contemplative judgment must cast a glance toward the world as well in order to assess which paradigm is most fitting.

Were it the case that the world itself wore a fixed and nonpolysemous face, and that political change within it proceeded in an orderly and thoroughly predictable manner, then indeed it might be possible to read the text of reality as directly and unambiguously disclosive, for example, as a text that would tell us whether a given situation is to be understood on the model of 1938 or 1965. That the world refuses to wear such a readable face is, of course, an Arendtian axiom. Nor in her view—as we have repeatedly seen—is this a failure to be recouped by a more capable political science.

Only the transformation of man into a thoroughly predictable creature might make the fluid politico-historical medium amenable to such an "improved" science.[235] What precludes such a science—and thankfully so in Arendt's view—is the datum of human freedom which in this context should be understood as signifying that history is "made" by individuals who remain forever free to do the unpredictable and unprecedented. And thus the course of future events—and what differentiates the Munich-based from the Vietnam-based analysis are differences in the anticipated course of future events—can never be known with certainty until the chronology of historical happenings has become a part of the past.[236] Action, however, is always of the present and as such must be cloaked in uncertainty because the freedom of other actors—that is, their freedom of initiative and response—cannot be discounted.[237]

In the context of our current interest, the significance of this conception of historical reality is clear. As the contemplative judgment endeavors to test the proposal before it for its appropriateness to a given set of circumstances, it finds that the world is shot through with ambiguity and contradictory prospects. To take refuge in the arms of some method or ideology that denies the significance of the surface ambiguity and pretends to infallible comprehension of the underlying historical logos is of course always possible. Only one heady draught of such snake oil is required and all the ambiguities drop away. Of more immediate relevance, however, are the workings of the contemplative judgment which has *not* thus cashiered its uncertainty.

Arendt would hardly argue that there exists the possibility of some pure, unmediated encounter with reality as it truly is. Rather, she suggests that the contemplative judgment, which takes its bearings from the contents of the *sensus communis*, takes its bearings from a conceptual lexicon that is inwardly fragmented and nontotalizing. Thus in a given instance of analysis, one will typically have a range of reality-constitutive paradigms from which to choose, paradigms which are keyed to roughly similar fact patterns but carry radically dissimilar implications. For instance, the fact pattern which for one observer conjures forth the Vietnam example conjures forth for another the case of Munich. The significance of this stems from the fact that where a range of equally possible alternative constructions are arrayed, a choice must be made, a choice that cannot be directly determined by either the fact pattern or the *sensus communis*, inasmuch as both are polysemous. In fact, the choice will tend to be unconscious: one person *sees* a fact pattern suggestive of another Vietnam, while the other person *sees* a fact pattern suggestive of 1938. But this only serves to underscore the notion that a judgment made on the *basis* of common sense is at the same moment a judgment *determined* by something neither reducible to common sense, nor reducible to the fact pattern of the world. This determining ground must be the self, the singular root, the irreducible point of uniqueness whose manifestation had been called into question by the hegemony of the *sensus communis*. Were the *sensus communis* a closed, univocal, and totalizing construct—and thus more akin to the conceptual simulacrum projected by ideological thinking—there would be good reason to anticipate the utter annihilation of the self's effective manifestation, but the *sensus communis* does not constitute such a barrier to self-display, and apparently not even in the moment of contemplative self-reflective judgment.[238]

The train of reflection just completed began with our query as to whether, given the current paradigm, action could serve as a vehicle of self-manifestation. Internal to action, two moments had been discerned: the first spontaneous and self-revelatory, the second contemplative and self-reflective. Our concern was focused upon the second moment and its gatekeeper function. What we have discerned is that the polysemy and internal fragmentation of the *sensus communis* suffices to insure that the moment is neither mechanical nor depersonalized. Behind the veil of apodictic catholicity we have espied the self, that point of uniqueness which on first glance had seemed to be absent. What makes this discovery so significant, however, is simply this: The self, whose presence has been discerned at the root of the contemplative moment, is none other than the self whose spontaneous originary capacity figures so large in Arendt's discussion of the first moment. The author and the critic, in other words, are one and the same—which is not meant to suggest that the two moments are really one, but rather to suggest that the likelihood is strong that the first moment will be favorably reviewed in the second, and that the decision to go ahead with publication or public utterance will be taken. Thus it can be expected that the uniqueness of the self—albeit a uniqueness that is mediated by and translated into the idiom of the *sensus communis*—will see the light of day.

Not only should it be expected that the self shall *shine* through—it should also be expected that a public that has been trained to attend to the "who" as much as to the "what" will be particularly attentive to the dimension of self-display. A trained eye, in other words, is not merely more capable *generally* but is more capable of discerning those particular facets of things which it has been trained to see. Thus it becomes Arendt's position that a political culture can be created that gives as much attention to the "who" (or self-revelatory dimension of politics) as to the "what" (or issue-specific dimension). By training citizens—or future citizens—to attend to what Arendt calls the dimension of appearance and to the beauty, greatness, and virtue which are manifest within it, Arendt would hope to correct the imbalance of our current political culture, an imbalance which on Arendt's reading tends to occlude the self-revelatory dimension in its entirety. Such well-trained citizen-spectators should prove to be particularly attentive to the manifestation of that uniqueness which neither the contemplative judgment nor the *sensus communis* can thwart.

Surely some readers are still unconvinced that self-manifestation shall occur where every aboriginally self-revelatory utterance is made to pass through the prism of the *sensus communis*. For, as these readers well mark, this obligatory act of self-translation that is performed in the name of disinterest and impartiality, and for the sake of fostering intersubjective agreement, necessarily entails, at least to some degree, the diminution of the self's given alterity. After all—it will be argued—neither disinterest nor impartiality are natural attitudes of the self; nor is it natural for the self to prefer the commonweal to its own; nor is it natural for the self to express itself in the aseptic language of the public space. In effect, it is alleged that this act of translation is an act of self-mutilation if not of utter self-occlusion.

Although it may seem that such criticism is altogether to the point, in fact it is essentially misplaced. Quite simply, Arendt does not espouse the *thorough* normalization of the self. For Arendt, only the comportment of the *public* self is in question. The readiness to persuade or to be persuaded, the deference to the commonweal, and the role played by the norms of impartiality and disinterest are normative for the self only while it is acting in its civic deliberative capacity as a member of the public/ political realm. In this realm alone, where not the self but the world is what matters, these norms are essential.[239] In the private realm, by contrast, the self is free to pursue its self-interest in whatever manner—and as articulately or inarticulately—as it chooses. In the private realm, then, what the disciplinary dimension of the *sensus communis* might censor in public is allowed to become fully manifest.

But of much greater importance in this context is Arendt's argument that the normalizing requirements of public discourse serve not to occlude the *public* manifestation of human plurality, but to insure both that this manifestation occurs and that it occurs in a mode that can be understood by the others with whom one shares the world. As we have seen, Arendt expects the actor will achieve public self-manifestation because, even as an agent of the *sensus communis* and world-continuity, how he chooses to apply the one and seek the other depends upon more than that which the *sensus communis* alone provides. In other words, at the point where the protean opacity of the world meets the polyphony and heterogeneity of the *sensus communis,* Arendt discerns an irreducible moment of free application in which the actor will be guided by—and thus come to manifest—his own unique nature. This of course is Arendt's essential response to the challenge that was posed two paragraphs ago.

In addition, Arendt points out that the intersubjective validation which the actor seeks from his fellow citizens depends upon the discursive normalization of his self-presentation, at least to the degree that is necessary to facilitate his being understood. Admittedly, the latter criterion alone imposes a less stringent normalization requirement than becomes required once the concern for continuity has been added to the equation, but even the latter, Arendt insists, will not occlude self-manifestation altogether. Despite discipline and normalization, the essential self should be able to shine through.

In our assessment of the works considered in chapter 2, we had concluded that the conception of the cultural and political world envisioned in those works would quite likely hinder the manifestation of self that had been so important to Arendt in *The Human Condition.* By analogy we also reasoned that nonhegemonic subcultures were not likely to fare much better in a public world that had been thus conceived. Now, however, in light of our reassessment of the fate of the former, it seems appropriate for us to reconsider the latter conclusion as well. Thus the question arises of whether the conception of the *sensus communis* that has been developed in this chapter can legitimate a greater public role for nonhegemonic subcultures than seemed possible in relation to the construct developed in chapter 2.

The first point to be made is that like the highly particularist aspects of the self that find no legitimate public role but enjoy full freedom in the *private* realm, the private standing of the nonhegemonic cultures is assured and is regarded by Arendt as properly inviolable.[240] Yet this assurance hardly reaches to the heart of the matter which bears not upon the private but upon the public and political standing of nonhegemonic cultures and, more particularly, upon the status of nonhegemonic master narratives and principles in public debate.

As will become clear presently, how this matter is understood may depend upon whether Arendt is thought to construe the *sensus communis* "thickly" or "thinly." Had we employed this terminology in chapter 2, it would have been seen that our solicitude for the public standing of nonhegemonic master narratives and principles was occasioned by Arendt's rather "thick" conception of the substantive, as distinguished from the procedural, aspects of the *sensus communis*. Our fear was that the conjunction between the normative hegemony of a single master narrative (which was to be secured by the agency of culture, tradition, and education) and the erection of an authority, to insure this narrative's primacy, would serve to squelch the articulation of alternative political principles and contrary narratives. We worried, in other words, that the *sensus communis* was too "thick" for adequate cultural pluralism.

In Arendt's late work on judgment—especially in the most Kantian works—this concern for insuring the hegemony of a single master narrative has been less in evidence and has been displaced to a significant degree by an emphasis upon the procedural dimension of the *sensus communis*. Hence Arendt's attention to, and insistence upon, disinterest, impartiality, and the procedural mechanics of representative thinking. We have also attended to her conception of democratic validity and to her conception of the politics of opinion both of which are prominent in the late work. In large measure, these emphases seem to be compatible with the validity of alternative nonhegemonic principles and narrative standpoints. After all, if there are no privileged political (or metapolitical) standpoints—as would seem to follow from Arendt's critique of political foundationalism—then, there would seem to be no basis for obstructing the articulation of any particular perspectives.

If the earlier, "thicker," and more substantive conception of the *sensus communis* had merely been dropped by the wayside then we might conclude that the late work readily facilitates what the earlier conception seemed to preclude. But the former has not occurred. Arendt's fear of solipsistic fragmentation and political disintegration, which originally engendered the "thick" conception of *On Revolution*, continues unabated and leads her to combine her late procedural focus with her earlier conception of common sense as that common platform that serves to facilitate synchronic consensus and diachronic continuity. Thus in the late work, the *sensus communis* comes to denote both the Kantian procedural emphases and the common possession of, and fidelity to, a master narrative and a common vocabulary.

Of course, the latter elements in particular can be more or less monolithic (or "thick") and consequently more or less hostile to nonhegemonic narratives and principles.[241] On balance, however, in the works considered in this chapter, we have seen that Arendt's concern to frame conditions conducive to self-display leads her to conceive of the substantive elements of the *sensus communis* as being rather heterogeneous and loosely structured. Thus we have found that, even under the aegis of the hegemonic master narrative, a range of contrary interpretations are always possible. Indeed, it almost seems more accurate to speak not of a single master narrative but of a bounded range of authoritative narratives that are embedded within the *sensus communis* and are legitimately called into play in any given instance.

It appears, then, that a relatively expansive realm has been opened for the expression of individual and even cultural difference. Indeed, as measured against *On Revolution*, the room for the display of difference does seem vast.[242] But it must be underscored that the range of possibility is not as boundless as it may first appear. Fidelity to the origin, to the constitution, to the principles grounded in the origin, and to the range of shared elements that make the *sensus communis* the only public basis for political agreement limits the range of valid political expression. Fidelity to the procedural principles of (for example) disinterest, impartiality, and public-spiritedness should also be understood as limiting the range of legitimate discourse. That despite these constraints, there remains ample room for the public realization and public display of human plurality follows from our earlier analysis. But the limits are real: some principles and some alternative master narratives are beyond the pale and without standing. For example, at the very least, it seems Arendt would require that participants in public debate be pledged to the continuance of the polity's constitutional order. By contrast, the expression of differences of opinion regarding the meaning of this order, or regarding the proper application

of its inherent principles, is expected and indeed desirable; but the repudiation of this order would be illegitimate. A properly constituted *sensus
communis* would rightly permit the one and censure the other.

In light of Arendt's professed antifoundationalism, this continued
fidelity to a relatively thick conception of the *sensus communis* is,
arguably, problematic. By Arendt's own account, the holy origin, the
sacred constitution, and the hoary principles are arbitrary, conventional,
and lacking in ultimacy. So too, the preference for the public good, continuity, disinterest, and impartiality. Thus there is no logically or metaphysically valid reason to privilege them. And if Arendt is inclined to value
consensus nonetheless, then, in light of the conception of democratic
validity that she articulates, she ought to have privileged the consensus of
the present, whatever its grounds, instead of espousing a consensus that
favors the dead and is restricted to the essentially arbitrary principles of
the origin.[243]

In the final analysis, what accounts for Arendt's embrace of a construct that she herself admits to be arbitrary is something that has been
made clear from the beginning of this study. It is her acute sense for the
abyss of otherness (or plurality) that essentially separates one person from
the next and her equally acute sense that human individuation and well-
being depend upon the privileging of a common term that can bind us
together in, and through, time. Despite its ultimate groundlessness, a
properly appointed *sensus communis*—and the principles and institutions
that it embraces—constitutes this common term; it is our ground, the
ground of our common world, and the scaffolding of our common life. It
possesses pragmatic validity; without it our world would crumble, and all
that is of worth would be lost.

This said, it need only be reiterated that for Arendt the worth of the
world, and of the *sensus communis* that sustains it, is penultimate. Of
greater worth is human plurality and the moment of its manifestation.
However, without a stable world within which men can feel themselves to
be at home—and there can be no such world without a relatively thick
sensus communis—human plurality will be bereft of that which stimulates
its manifestation and secures its remembrance. Of course, if the *sensus
communis* is too thick, and too overdetermining, the range of human self-
manifestation will be excessively constricted. The Arendtian preference,
then, is for a *sensus communis* that is neither so capacious to be utterly
impotent and indeterminate nor so sclerotic and mechanical as to render
action utterly martinet-like. The community that possesses such common
sense will only frown upon the expression of those opinions that might do
it grave harm while permitting the expression of all the rest. Surely, from

a libertarian perspective this is problematic, but it is what follows from Arendt's conception of the *sensus communis*.

Partisans of a rational and unconstrained consensus who would like to claim Arendt as one of their own may prefer to conceive of the *sensus communis* of Arendt's late work as entailing only the neo-Kantian process norms, on the grounds that anything more substantive would illicitly overdetermine the outcomes of the political process. Postmodern partisans of difference-politics, on the other hand, who prefer to celebrate Arendt's early agonal vision, will find even the neo-Kantian norms, by themselves, to be excessively normalizing, and will tend to dismiss Arendt's conception of the *sensus communis* as an inessential and ill-conceived digression from the main lines of her work. Legitimately, each takes from Arendt only that which they find most serviceable and disregards the rest. Yet if one wants to do justice to Arendt's own project then neither characterization can be accepted.

Returning to our main theme, I will close this section by asserting the following: Upon reflection, it appears that the conception of judgment unfolded in this chapter and the revised conception of action entailed thereby, together answer to the two-sided requirements of the action-ideal. On the one hand, from the side of the self's search for meaning, a form of action has been conceptualized that is fully adequate to the criteria of uniqueness, lastingness, and freedom. On the other hand, from the side of the need to insure the durability and continuity of the public space, Arendt has produced a conception of the *sensus communis*, and of the sociological and cultural means of its inculcation, which, when conjoined to her theory of contemplative judgment, combine to produce a vehicle capable of bringing us within sight of her desired destination.

In fairness, however, before bringing this study to a close, it seems incumbent upon us to look again upon Arendt's conception of political judgment and in particular to scrutinize more critically the tenability of the correlation that has been posited between the moment of judgment internal to political action and the moment of judgment internal to political spectatorship.

BEYOND THE NEW LOGOS: A CRITIQUE

Inasmuch as the testing process whereby policy alternatives are measured against the criteria of the *sensus communis* is an essential part of the political process that is prior to the moment of political decision, Arendt is surely right to emphasize the parallel between the judgment of the spectator and that exercised by the actor. But, having granted this, it can still be asked whether Arendt is right to suggest that an adequate normative conception of political judgment can be worked out on the basis of this aspect alone.[244]

By Arendt's description, the judging process includes two analytically distinct moments. In the first, the individual citizen is expected to exercise his faculty for rendering public judgment by coming to his own disinterested opinion as to where the public interest lies in a given situation. In the second moment, each citizen is expected to offer up his opinion for the consideration of his fellow citizens and to engage in common deliberation with them. From out of the welter of disparate opinions a consensus is to be forged on the basis of common regard for the norm of impartiality and for the authoritative standing of the *sensus communis*.

Thus, in our earlier example of country "A," each citizen was depicted as coming to an opinion of his own and as stepping forth before his fellow citizens to proclaim whether and why he believed it to be proper or improper to invade country "B." Individually, and then collectively, the citizenry was depicted as engaging in the testing process by means of which, in the end, the best decision, that is, that decision that best conformed to the *sensus communis*, would come to the fore and be adopted as policy. On this view, then, the political reasoning process is essentially construed as the testing of already extant opinions. What seems to one citizen to be the policy which is most compatible with the *sensus communis*, and as such the most reasonable policy as well, is tested by his fellow citizens to see whether this is truly so.[245] Presumably, a civic consensus will coalesce behind that opinion or proposal which appears to be most fully compatible with it, and hence most reasonable as well. Where a number of opinions or proposals are before the public, the one that conforms more closely than the rest should prevail, though, as already noted, Arendt provides scarcely any glimpse of how the citizenry ought to proceed when faced with the challenge of choosing between contradictory policy proposals that are equally well-grounded upon the *sensus communis*.[246] More important at this juncture, however, is the fact that Arendt's account of this process explains not the origination of the opinions or proposals but their testing and the movement from welter to consensus. The *origination* of opinions or policy proposals is taken for granted and the moment of political judgment is treated as if it came into play only subsequently.

What accounts for this view of the matter is the dichotomy Arendt posits between the procreative depth of consciousness from out of which all actions arise and the critical vantage of the reflective judgment whose second-order function is to test by the criteria of the *sensus communis* whatever emerges from the depths and seeks the light of publicity. The problem with this approach is that, by means of it, one cannot understand the utterance that rises from the depths as already being a kind of judgment, albeit that it is neither reflective, contemplative, nor in any other way spectator-like.

If not a form of judgment, what then is it that brought the idea of invasion (for example) to the consciousness of citizen "X" of country "A" in the first place, before his good judgment led him to formulate the felt imperative in the form of the parliamentary question of whether or not country "B" ought to be invaded? If not judgment, what then? Could it be a form of reasoning? One might like to think so, but judgment and reasoning are correlative and if judgment is not entailed here, then, neither can reasoning be. Arendt seems to want us to locate the genesis of the parliamentary question in the hidden depths of the individual soul of the one who first articulated it. From there in the depths, wherein the irreducible uniqueness of the person and the forces of cultural conditioning are admixed with telluric and transcendent elements, did this question arise. Not by reasoning, not through judgment, but through something ineffable, veiled, inexplicable, and unpredictable. In Arendt's opinion, to hold otherwise would be to reduce action to *techne*, thus jeopardizing action's status as a fount of novelty while coming perilously close to a kind of determinism that is inimical to action's role as a vehicle of existential self-creation and manifestation. Judgment, method, and self-distancing come into play, on this view, only subsequent to the original moment of upwelling from the primordial depths.

The problem with this construction is that it construes the purview of judgment far too narrowly. By elevating the contemplative judgment of the spectator to paradigmatic status for political judgment generally, Arendt in effect denies that the latter has any productive or procreative role to play. Clearly Arendt fears that any conception of political judgment which intruded upon the pure spontaneity of the originary moment would undercut action's standing as a vehicle of selfhood.[247] More particularly, she fears that this standing would be undermined if the procreative ground of action were construed in terms of instrumental or practical reason.[248] For once this was allowed, action would surely come to be regarded—by actors and by everybody else—as a vehicle for the actualization of certain practical, hypothetical, or ideological imperatives and, as a result, would be incapable of manifesting a "who" in addition to a "what" which the action is about. The human, and saving, dimension of action would thus disappear. While sympathizing with Arendt's motives for vesting all originary and productive power in the veiled inner processes of the soul's dynamic uniqueness, the resulting conception is hardly tenable.

Bracketing for the moment the question of whether Arendt is right to regard these forms of instrumental and practical rationality as antithetical to the manifestation of plurality, it should be observed that in contrast to the contemplative rationality of the spectator these excluded forms of rationality are neither derivative, reflective, or critical in their first moment. Rather, by means of one method or another, each is productive of imperatives and hence directive of action as the contemplative judgment can never be. Thus, in the case of the parliamentary question of whether country "A" should invade country "B," it is not hard to imagine that what was earlier depicted as a deeply felt imperative to invade that stirred the breast of citizen "X" and arose from the depths of his being, was rather the product of a rational process and wholly deliberate. To deny this possibility and to insist instead upon construing this moment as sheer self-manifestation strains credulity. By extension, moreover, it seems clear that a large part of the public dimension of the political process will consist of the public and deliberative testing of opinions for the cogency of the reasoning employed in their formulation. Normative testing of the kind paradigmatically engaged in by the contemplative judgment will presumably occur as well. Inasmuch as a given opinion necessarily entails certain premises, goals, and principles, these can be made explicit and tested for normative adequacy against the criteria of the *sensus communis*, but such testing is hardly likely to constitute the whole of the collective and deliberative process.

On neither count, then, is Arendt's conception altogether satisfying. Neither is the originary moment void of judgment, nor can the critical and reflective moment be adequately elucidated in terms of the kind of normative testing for compatibility with the *sensus communis* which Arendt depicts as being paradigmatic for political judgment. To suggest that practical reason and instrumental rationality are potentially hostile to human plurality, and hence "intrinsically" antipolitical, is one thing. To attempt to conceptualize a politics—or a form of political judgment—that altogether excludes such forms of rationality is another. The former is a point well taken; the latter, however, is essentially false to the nature of political reality.

Indeed, even if we were to accept Arendt's truncated conception of political content, we should still imagine that politics would continue to be focused upon that most basic political question of what is to be done in a given situation—a question which necessarily calls for an exercise of moral or instrumental judgment. Contemplative and critical reflection oriented to the normative testing of policy recommendations will surely have a role to play as well, but that which is to be tested must first be conceived, and the contemplative model does not adequately account for how this occurs.

It should also be observed that Arendt's fear of the antipolitical impact of practical and instrumental reason is overdrawn and presupposes a rather caricatured conception of how the individual who would act in accordance with either is overdetermined, and thus effectively negated, by the system of reasoning he would employ. This caricatured conception hearkens back, of course, to Arendt's portrait of ideological thinking which she depicts as ruthlessly logical and radically depersonalized.[249]

Surely, Arendt's account of ideological thinking does bring out something essential in its nature. In particular, she apprehends most clearly those aspects which account for its appeal to those persons for whom refuge in a system is in the same instance a flight from freedom, contingency, and uncertainty. As Arendt rightly observes, the inherent appeal of ideology lies in its claim to function as a master key to comprehending historical reality. Ideology thus presents itself as a science capable of providing objective knowledge and complete certainty. Not only does it claim to comprehend the past and the present, but it claims to comprehend the future as well and to provide infallible guidance for the actor who would secure—or secure a place within—this future. It claims, in other words, to be a totalizing logic of the totality. Accept the system and you will henceforth be freed from the mire of incomprehension, uncertainty, and indecision.

Arendt believes that ideologies eclipse the manifestation of selfhood by the weight of the sheer self-evidence of their logic, an impersonal self-evidence which Arendt likens to that of the equation: $2+2=4$. The problem with Arendt's account, however, is that she takes the claims of the ideologies at face value and elaborates a model of ideological thinking which assumes that ideologies actually meet the expectations that are presupposed by their psychological appeal. But what ideology has ever met these expectations?

Were it the case that ideologies delivered all that they promise, then, the relevance of the human factor—and of plurality in particular—would be as thoroughly extirpated as Arendt fears. But it is not because they do not. Even within the purview of the most perfect ideological science, differences of opinion—presumably reflecting human plurality, at least in part—are continuously manifest, albeit that, as befits a true science, these differences are stylized in terms of truth and error, orthodoxy and heresy. Taking Marxism as an example, it becomes immediately evident that the broad conceptual schema which makes being a Marxist synonymous with believing, among other things, that the class struggle is the motor of history, and that communism constitutes the end of history—has hardly been capable of insuring unanimity of Marxist reckoning. Not even among the most orthodox and most economistic of Marxists is there anything like complete agreement when it comes to applying the science. Differences of opinion arise both in the retrospective application of the science as a master key to comprehending the past and in the prospective application of the science as a guide to strategy and tactics in the present. What Arendt fails to apprehend is that at the point where the pure theory of ideology meets the world of concrete facts there lies an ineluctable moment of freedom, a point of application in which the uniqueness of the individual will tend to insinuate itself no matter how much the system itself guards against it. In this respect, the application of ideological science is not so very different from the application of the *sensus communis*, as Arendt herself has depicted it. The same, I would argue, holds for the moment of application of practical or instrumental reason. In sum, I would argue that Arendt's fear is overblown and rooted in a caricatured conception of ideology and of the human "sciences," more generally. In short, what facilitates the revelation of selfhood vis à vis the "application" of the *sensus communis* should allow for it as well in the "application" of practical and hypothetical judgment.

It is perhaps not altogether surprising to find that Arendt's exclusion of necessitating—and thus "antipolitical"—modes of judgment from political legitimacy parallels her exclusion of potentially necessitating—and thus "antipolitical"—subject matter from the purview of public deliberation. In each instance, Arendt fears for the viability of freedom and for the manifestation of uniqueness, and would overcome the danger by an act of theoretical and practical triage. Thus Arendt would exclude both matters of necessity and the modes of judgment entailed by such matters, that is, such practical and instrumental *logoi* as come into play when such matters are on the table. By eliminating from politics either the necessitating content or the necessitating modes of judgment, Arendt eliminates the other as well, inasmuch as the two are mutually entailing. Although Arendt herself never draws explicit attention to the linkage that exists between the political content and the modes of political judgment which she would reject as antipolitical, the substance of the connection is clear, as is the motivation behind her decision to exclude these antipolitical elements. In my view, however, the radical nature of Arendt's solution—as it is premised upon an unnecessarily sharp, theoretical dichotomization—is uncalled for and, in a practical sense, far from cost-free. Moreover, as earlier I argued that self-manifestation would not be obscured even in the presence of the content Arendt would extrude from political life, so I am now arguing that it will not be obscured even if the regnant forms of political judgment include technical, instrumental, and ideological modes.

My point here is hardly to suggest that Arendt ought to have made room for ideology in her conception of political judgment. Rather, I mean to suggest that her rationale for viewing noncontemplative modes of judgment as necessarily antipolitical, a rationale implicitly based upon an analogy with a caricatured conception of ideological thinking, is flawed, and that their consequent exclusion from political life ought not to stand. Earlier, I suggested that the contemplative conception of political judgment could not fully account for the concrete proposals for action that constitute the real content of politics. Where national goals, principles, or priorities are a historical given—as they would be within an Arendtian polity as a consequence of the hegemony of its founding moment—political reasoning is very much a matter of trying to fit means to ends. In a given situation, the nature of the end to be secured may be clear to all, or it may not be, and the parliamentary proceedings will be shaped accordingly. Where the end is clear, the question of means will come to the fore. Connecting ends and means is not, however, the forte of contemplative reasoning but, depending on the nature of the end involved, requires some kind of practical or instrumental judgment. Of course, it is possible that the means which appear to be conducive to one end may be repellant to other ends esteemed by the polity. Testing the proposed means for normative compatibility with the range of ends encompassed by the *sensus communis* thus becomes necessary, and this is a task which calls for the exercise of judgment of the contemplative kind.

In addition, I have suggested that these other kinds of judgment—which in my view must necessarily come into play—are not inherently antithetical to the self-revelatory dimension of action that Arendt wants so much to safeguard. In arguing thus, however, it is important not to obscure the truth at the heart of Arendt's conception which pertains not to the operational reality of employing such models of judgment but to the consequences that will follow when those who believe themselves to be in possession of an absolutely infallible system of political reckoning come to power. For those who have come to power and have believed themselves to be in possession of "the key" to history have hardly hesitated before taking steps that are meant to insure their absolute ability to make history, steps which have invariably included the destruction of the public space, and of the self-realization and self-display that are intrinsic to it.

This destruction of the public space—or its shrinkage to the point of encompassing only the few members of the "guardian" class—has been justified on the assumption that knowledge of absolute truth, and only such knowledge, creates a right to wield political power. Analogous to this justification of the power of the few is the political situation in which a single criterion of valid political argument is made supreme, for example, as in the case of a polity in which moral arguments are ruled out a priori, and all arguments must be framed in terms of the increase or decrease of material wealth or relative power. Arendt's insistence that political issues must be construed as matters of opinion (or meaning) and not as questions of truth is meant to counter both of these tendencies, one of which destroys the public space directly and one of which destroys it indirectly but just as effectively by radically limiting the range of acceptable kinds of political argument.[250]

Against a politics grounded upon such monological conceptions of truth, and upon an analogously absolutist conception of political validity, Arendt opposes her own brand of politics, one that derives its legitimacy from the democratic and participatory character of a political process that she grounds upon the *sensus communis* and defines in terms of the dialectic between individual judgment and consensus formation. One particularly important implication that follows from Arendt's conception is her redefinition of foundational political axioms, or "truths," as mere contingent propositions which are supported by nothing more than a polity-wide consensus of opinion.[251] Arendt's recourse to Kant's conception of aesthetic judgment that has so much occupied our attention in this chapter was born of her perception that Kant could provide her with the means for conceptualizing how her new politics and the criterion of validity entailed by it should be understood.

As we have seen, Arendt's appropriation of Kant does point the way towards a conception of the political process which vests validity in the process itself rather than in any extrapolitical criteria. In itself this goal hardly seems problematic, and given Arendt's conception of what politics is really about, achieving this goal is of utmost importance inasmuch as the elevation of any other criterion would likely lead to the de-emphasis of participation and to the diminution of self-manifestation. Let absolute truth, moral perfection, or general welfare be made the purpose of political life or the standard of political judgment, and it is highly probable that eventually the polity will opt for that level of political participation that is commensurate with the maximal realization of the prior value. Only where the existential fruits of political participation are themselves regarded as the absolute value in politics will no effort be made to restrict the extent of participation. By vesting validity in the process, and in its own intrinsic orientation toward consensus, Arendt means to safeguard this value which she considers to be so important.

Had Arendt followed Kant no further, then the problems inherent in her construction would be insignificant. Trouble comes, however, as a consequence of her endeavor to understand political judgment as essentially contemplative, and as being, in this respect, strictly analogous to aesthetic judgment. If it were only the judgment of the citizen-spectator that Arendt meant to elucidate thereby, the analogy would be nonproblematic and indeed most illuminating. But Arendt would go further and, for reasons that we have already canvased in detail, Arendt develops a conception of the actor's judgment that obviates many of the important differences between the judgment that is exercised by the citizen-actor and that exercised by the citizen-spectator. As I have already indicated, the equation Arendt wants to posit is neither tenable in itself nor theoretically mandated.

More plausible would it have been, had Arendt only argued on behalf of the primacy, and not on behalf of the exclusive sway, of the moment of spectator-like judgment. Then, spectator-like judgment, and the normative testing by recourse to examples at which it excels, could have found their proper place within an essentially pluralistic conception of political judgment in which practical and technical judgments, and the forms of rationality associated with each, would have found their place as well. On behalf of such a pluralist conception, I have already observed that neither of the forms of rationality Arendt seeks to exclude from the political sphere is necessarily antithetical to self-manifestation or contrary to the eruption of novelty into the world. That a "who" always transcends a "what" is after all an Arendtian first principle, and it should be expected that this continues to be the case even in the face of moral and instrumental logics which Arendt regards as antagonistic to self-display.[252] To this observation I would only add what was intimated earlier: The modes of judgment Arendt would dispense with are indispensable. No theoretically adequate conception of political judgment can be imagined that does not allot to them a legitimate place.

The solution I advocate lies, then, in giving prominence *in the last instance* to the mode of spectator judgment and, more particularly, to the role of the *sensus communis* and to the disinterest and impartiality which Arendt (following Kant) regards as concomitants of valid political judgment. By means of such prominence, and by means of the prominence of the process-norms that are commensurate with such values, it could be insured that the political process will never be utterly subordinated to (for example) the true, the right, or the good as these might be defined from any of the partial and extrapolitical standpoints which Arendt decries as antipolitical and as antagonistic to human difference. Rather, the prominence of the norms and values Arendt associates with the judgment of the spectator should suffice to insure that the "antipolitical" modes of judgment will remain subordinated to the plurality-validating mode that aims to forge a consensus of opinion upon grounds which are to be distinguished from those which compel assent to truth. Prominence, then, not exclusivity is the watchword. Let every relevant form of judgment find its place within the political process but insure that in the final moment the *standpoint* of the spectator—which relativizes all truth claims as it transforms every truth into an opinion—holds sway. This alone should be enough to insure the longevity of a participatory and self-revelatory politics. In short, I would press Arendt to accept a pluralistic conception of political judgment that better accords with both the realities of politics and with her own endorsement of plurality as a cardinal political value.[253]

Some indication that Arendt herself might have been receptive to the kinds of modifications I have recommended can be inferred from her attempt—albeit inchoate and incomplete—to combine her neo-Kantian conception of spectator judgment with a neo-Aristotelian conception of *phronesis*.[254] Of course, what makes this proposition so very intriguing is the fact that *phronesis*, like the forms of rationality she would exclude from politics, is oriented toward the fitting of means to ends, albeit without introducing the kinds of validity claims that Arendt finds so troubling. In *phronesis*, the virtue, principle, or end is given, but the precise manner in which it is to be achieved is not. Determining how to proceed in a given situation thus becomes a matter of complex reckoning: much depends upon how one assesses the nature of the situation into which one proposes to act. Not only objective factors must be considered: The intentions and perceptions of other actors and their potential responses to any contemplated action must be weighed as well since these subjective elements are just as constitutive of the nature of the situation.

Were it possible to determine with precision these subjective elements and to know with absolute certainty how every potential respondent would respond to a given act, then, politics could be reduced to a form of rationality akin to the conceptions which Arendt means to delegitimate and exclude from political life. What differentiates *phronesis* from these other *logoi*, however, is that for all the emphasis that is placed upon determining the nature of the situation prior to acting, *phronesis* methodologically presupposes that the situation can only be imperfectly known, and thus presupposes as well that action will be void of the rational certitude or self-evidence that is inherent in the validity claims of the alternative *logoi*.[255] In Arendt's view, that political judgment is at best an imperfect science is, of course, a very good thing, for it is human plurality and human freedom that make it so. These factors are by now undoubtedly quite familiar. On the one hand, because every person is unique he can only be imperfectly known: thus how the other perceives the situation and what the other intends to do lies behind a veil of opacity which can never be penetrated with absolute certainty.[256] On the other hand, because every person is free, Arendt would argue that the tenor and telos of action and reaction must be shrouded in uncertainty up until the moment of its occurrence: what a person will do and how a person will respond is not something which can be infallibly determined in advance by extrapolation from past behavior.[257] Were it otherwise, nothing could ever surprise us; the unpredicted and unprecedented would never come to pass.[258] *Phronesis* both reflects these realities and takes them into account as the alternative *logoi* do not: it takes these realities into account by producing judgments that are framed by an awareness that among the factors with which it must reckon are the possible actions and opinions of others, neither of which can be predicted with any certainty. It reflects these same realities inasmuch as the judgment at which it arrives will also be colored by the subjective elements which necessarily cling to every exercise of *phronesis*, elements that—as Arendt herself was quite well aware—make every exercise of *phronesis* a manifestation of character. What especially differentiates phronesis from the alternative *logoi*, however, are the epistemological assumptions upon which it is grounded, assumptions that are compatible with the assumptions that underlie Arendt's neo-Kantian conception of the political process.

As we have seen, most problematic about the *logoi* which Arendt wants to exclude from politics is what she regards as their theoretical and practical antipathy towards the datum of human plurality, an antipathy which, in *The Human Condition*, Arendt finds symbolized in the Platonic opposition of truth to opinion.[259] Only the former, which is one, provides unmediated access to "the Real" which is also one. That opinions are many while truth is one explains why, on this view, opinion ought to be completely disregarded. The assumption is that opinions constitute erring, second-order approximations of a primary reality which opinions are "about." On the assumption that differences of opinion owe to the distorting effect of "personal factors," it is necessary to remove such factors from the process if the truth is to be found. Admittedly, such an endeavor to excise "the human element" may have a legitimate place in certain areas of scientific or logical inquiry, but in Arendt's view such a project is necessarily an anathema to a politics which she regards as permeated by, and as properly permeated by, "the human element" and such idiosyncratic "surds." Woe unto us, moreover, if this element were done away with. What—Arendt might ask—would be left? Politics as mere animal behavior? A politics of species-wide law-governed uniformities? A politics devoid of action, honor, greatness, and personality? Hence Arendt's quest

for a conception of the political process grounded upon different epistemological presuppositions and productive of consequences less inimical to
the good of human difference. *Phronesis* by its very much contrasting
evaluation of opinion points in the proper direction, a direction already
indicated by the tenor of Arendt's plurality-validating reading of Kant's
analysis of spectator judgment.

Also implicit in the Platonic opposition of truth to opinion is a negative assessment of change and contingency. Not only is the truth one, it is
unchanging and necessary. In Plato's view, opinion aims at the truth but
cannot hit the mark, and, alas, there are so many ways to miss it. That the
political landscape displays the evidence of continuous change indicates
just how little truth can be secured by means of its operative logos, the
logos of opinion. Were this logos more capable of securing its end, then
the fixity of truth would have been achieved long ago. With the purpose
of securing this end, which has hitherto been pursued by imperfect means,
Plato recommends that the logos of opinion be replaced by the logos of
truth. Only by such a transformation can politics be rid of the mutability
and contingency which signify its imperfection.

In Aristotle's opinion, Plato's solution to the "problem" of mutability is thoroughly misguided as a consequence of what might be described
as a category mistake.[260] No less than Plato, Aristotle believed that there
are fixed, immutable truths and that there is a specific mental activity by
means of which these truths can be ascertained. For Aristotle, however,
such truths are inherently metaphysical and metapolitical. By contrast, the
realm of physics and politics—the sublunary realm as it used to be
called—is ordered along different lines. Mutability and contingency are
necessarily characteristic here, and more so of politics than of physics. For
Aristotle, Plato's ambition is contrary to the order of Being itself: the difference between the nature of the realms must be respected. Indicative of
this necessary difference is the distinction Aristotle draws between *noesis*
and *phronesis*, the former being the mental activity that is oriented
towards the apprehension of timeless metaphysical truths and the latter
being the mental activity of "the calculative part" that is oriented towards
the realm of mutability and contingency. On this view, it is only the latter
which is of relevance to politics, constituting both the faculty that facilitates our coming to an opinion where mutables and contingencies are concerned and the faculty that helps us to be at home in a realm within which
opinion is the common currency.

Just how much influence Aristotle's conception of the distinction
between *noesis* and *phronesis* had upon Arendt's critique of antipolitical
forms of rationality cannot be established with any certainty since she
never makes reference to it.[261] It should be observed, however, that

Arendt's conception of what accounts for the inherent contingency and mutability of human affairs is very much sui generis, as is the moral thrust of her critique of the excluded *logoi*.[262] For Arendt, of course, the sources of mutability and contingency are human plurality and the human capacity for novelty, neither of which are apprehended as such by Aristotle. Nor ought it to be thought that Arendt's rejection of *noesis*'s application to politics is motivated by a moral concern of the same cast as Aristotle's. Arendt's own moral urgency arises from her fear that *noesis*'s latter-day counterparts could destroy the human plurality she wants so much to protect. Aristotle's moral impetus, by contrast, seems to follow from his belief that restricting political participation to a gnostic elite would effectively and unnecessarily deprive the majority of freeborn citizens of the opportunity to achieve that high level of ethical realization that such participation could foster among them. Admittedly, even the latter sounds very much like Arendt's underlying concern. But for Aristotle, the moral reason for encouraging political participation on the broadest possible scale follows from his conception of the *generic* human actualization that is achievable through living the political life. What differentiates Arendt's conception, however, is her insistence that it is not man qua man but the individual qua unique being that is actualized through this experience. In her view, Aristotle was no less unaware of this facet of human reality than was Plato. Neither had yet glimpsed the reality or importance of human uniqueness. In Arendt's opinion, had Aristotle come to this insight and grasped the connection between political participation and uniqueness's actualization he would not have ranked contemplation—which actualizes a generic human capacity—above it.[263]

What many find problematic with *phronesis*, namely its uncritical groundedness in traditional norms, could hardly have been so for Arendt given her own conception of the *sensus communis* as the proximate ground of political judgment.[264] Differences between neo-Arendtian and neo-Aristotelian conceptions of political judgment do remain of course, especially regarding Arendt's historicist and even relativist understanding of the contents of the *sensus communis*. Nor can it be said that the Aristotelian account of *phronesis* pays sufficient attention to the plurality-preservative and collective aspects of the political process which Arendt undertook to clarify by means of her recourse to the Kantian conception. Nonetheless, I would maintain that the epistemological complementarity between Arendt's rejection of totalizing rationality and Aristotle's rejection of a Platonic version of the same offers a sufficient basis upon which a marriage of the two positions might have been effected. Closer attention to *phronesis* might also have provided Arendt with a more tenable template for conceptualizing a mode of political rationality which is at once capable of attending to matters of necessity without being necessitated by them, and of realizing moral values through policy without ceasing to value the moral and existential achievement of those citizens who act on behalf of these values. Alas, for all it might have facilitated, Arendt's halting movement in this direction never comes to anything. It is nonetheless important to see that a synthesis between Arendt's neo-Kantian conception and the Aristotelian paradigm stands well within the bounds of possibility and that, if it were pursued, it could well prove to be the vehicle by means of which to achieve what Arendt took to be most important while permitting the formulation of a conception of political judgment that is more adequate to the imperatives of putative political reality. Finally, on behalf of such a synthesis, it should be observed that as *phronesis* in Aristotle's conception is dependent upon and derivative of a prior understanding of the virtues which *phronesis* actualizes anew in every present, so one might expect that an Arendtian *phronesis* would remain dependent upon, and derivative of, a temporally prior *sensus communis* which it would actualize anew in every present—thereby securing, and resecuring, the end of political continuity perpetually.

CONCLUSION

Both at the end of the first part, and now at the end of the second, I have called attention to certain weaknesses in Arendt's conceptualization. And while my criticisms are hardly insubstantial, none of the flaws that I have discerned are beyond remedy. Not only have I indicated the appropriate remedies, but I have also tried to demonstrate that these remedies are not incompatible with the ends which Arendt sought to promote by means of the particular formulations which seem so problematic. Thus I would argue that the changes I recommend remain true to Arendt's own project while bringing it into closer conformity with the dictates of putative political reality.

In drawing this work to its conclusion, however, I should like to leave aside the consideration of flaws and remedies, lest the significance of Arendt's achievement be overshadowed by that which is of lesser importance. For with greater force than many other contemporary theorists, Arendt contributes to the rediscovery of the world-redemptive and humanly fulfilling dimensions of political life. And, in the final analysis, it is this accomplishment, and not her works' weaknesses, that should be underscored.

That politics had destroyed the world of Arendt's youth did not lead her to abandon either politics or the world. Rather, it inspired her to envision a redeemed politics capable of helping both the world and the individual to achieve a condition commensurate with their potential dignity. In particular, Arendt develops, what I have called, the action-ideal as the specific form of the political revival she espouses: ideal action will at once meet the human need for a meaningful individuated existence, as well as the need to dwell within a worldly order characterized by continuity and stability. But ideal action can only meet these needs once world alienation and the political pathologies engendered by it have been overcome. To this end, over against the anarchistic tendencies of difference politics and the epistemological authoritarianism of the partisans of order, Arendt develops her conception of judgment and common sense and marries this conception to her conception of action in a manner which, in practice, should overcome world alienation and the associated pitfalls of solipsistic fragmentation and monism.

Central to my account of Arendt's action-ideal are the three axiological dyads which together comprise the structural grid upon which the action-ideal is plotted. By recourse to this underlying grid, we have been able to elucidate the basis for Arendt's belief that human endeavor becomes meaningful to the degree that it is at once free, individuating, and facilitating of self-transcendence vis à vis something of long or everlasting duration. Convincingly, Arendt argues that political action is well capable of being such a mode of endeavor.

That political action can bequeath such fulfillment is brought out by Arendt in several ways. As we have seen, one part of Arendt's argument depends upon the coloring she gives to the spatial and conceptual dichotomy of the public and private spheres.[265] Central to the rhetorical function of this dichotomy is the strong association she posits between privacy as a state of privation and the private sphere as a sphere deprived of the light of publicity.[266] Against this backdrop, the revelation of selfhood that occurs in the movement from the private to the public spheres entails the self's emergence from darkness to light and, thus, from privation to fulfillment. Conceptually, of course, the privation entailed by the private realm owes not to a lack of light but to a lack of others, that is, to a lack of others before whom to act and speak, and, more particularly, to a lack of those others who might tell the story which enables the actor to attain the mortality-transcending objectification of his singular identity.

As previously noted, in certain respects, Arendt's characterization of the private life is overwrought and rather tendentious in its bleakness. And, at the end of part one, I took issue with some of the prescriptive inferences Arendt derives from her conception of the public/private dichotomy: A politics free of matters of necessity, I argued, would be an unnecessary politics. I observed, moreover, that such a politics might be largely devoid of that existentially significant dimension of heroic self-display which Arendt hoped to engender by narrowly framing the bounds of legitimate political content.

The importance of such points of criticism notwithstanding, I would nonetheless maintain that the sharp contrast that Arendt draws between the public and private realms does capture an essential truth and accounts in large measure for the appeal that the public space has always held for those impelled to enter its precincts. Similarly, I would argue, Arendt is correct when she characterizes the public space as a sphere of freedom and correct too when she calls attention to that special mode of existence that has been known by those who have dedicated their lives to the perpetuation of an entity that has the chance of outlasting a multitude of passing generations. For we do seek a connection to that which endures as surely as we seek the actualization of our own potential uniqueness.

We have seen that Arendt conceives of political questions as questions not of truth but of opinion. We have also seen that for Arendt the political order is ultimately an order of meaning. But if, as Arendt tells us, all meanings are in their essence and origin subjective and without ultimate truth-value, then, by defining the political order in this way, Arendt, in effect, must accept that the political order itself lacks absolute or necessary transcendental foundations. As Arendt's analysis of political origins and of the *sensus communis* makes clear, this does not mean that foundations are altogether lacking, nor does it mean that what begins as a merely individual experience of meaning cannot come to be broadly shared, but it does serve to underscore that such beginnings and shared understandings are contingent and lack absolute validity.

Arendt's own vision of the political life and her apprehension of its meaning draw their inspiration chiefly from her understanding of the political experience of the ancient Greek polis but also from her appropriation of Roman foundationalism and from her neo-Kantian conception of the political realm as a realm of opinion. Hoping that we readers will find this vision to be so clear and meaningful as to make it our own, Arendt frames her work as an appeal to our collective imagination and, at least implicitly, as a call to the task of making this vision a reality by transforming the conditions of our living and doing. Such was the hope that inspired Arendt's theoretical practice and life's work.

Notes

INTRODUCTION

1. See, for example, OT, pp. 306–26, 474–79.

2. Ibid.

3. See OT, pp. 474–79.

4. See in OT, pp. 305–26, 474–79. More particularly, see Arendt's discussion of the imperialist character, a discussion which well illustrates the way in which the combination of ideology and "movement" are capable of filling the gnawing, nihilistic emptiness that characterizes the experience of the modern masses (OT, pp. 207–21).

5. See OT, pp. 207–21.

6. See OT, pp. 267–302 and pp. 290–302 more particularly regarding Arendt's development of the concept of worldlessness.

7. Ibid.

8. See OT, pp. 290–302.

9. See OT, p. 296.

10. See OT, pp. 296–97.

11. See OT, p. 297.

12. See OT, pp. 299–300.

13. See OT, pp. 301–2.

14. See OT, pp. 300–02.

15. Ibid.

16. ibid.

17. Indeed Arendt describes the condition of the masses in terms that are equally descriptive of the stateless (and hence worldless). Writing of the masses' "uprootedness" and "superfluousness," she declares: "To be uprooted means to

have no place in the world, recognized and guaranteed by others; to be superfluous means not to belong to the world at all. (OT, p. 475).

18. See OT, pp. 474–79.

19. See OT, pp. 475–76.

20. Of course neither promise is fulfilled.

21. Though in THC it will be seen that the essence of ideological thinking is traceable to Platonism while its modern primacy is traceable to Cartesian foundationalism and to the dawn of the modern age.

22. See OT, pp. 457–74. These themes are picked up again and again throughout the body of Arendt's work. At the moment, however, our concern is only to point to their originary locus in OT. All particulars in the following paragraph can be substantiated by reference to the pages mentioned at this note's beginning.

23. See OT, pp. 351–53, for example. The commonsense construction of the world is declared preferable for its "measured insight into the interdependence of the arbitrary and the planned, the accidental and the necessary. . . ." (OT, p. 352).

24. See OT, pp. 351–53.

25. Ibid.

26. This point is only implicit in OT. For a clear statement see Arendt's discussion of the sovereignty and plurality in THC, pp. 220–30, 234–35.

27. The locus classicus for Arendt's conception of the clash between truth and opinion in political life is to be found in BPF, "Truth and Politics," pp. 227–64.

28. This is not to deny the historical specificity of the conditions that gave rise to "the age of ideology." Nonetheless, along the dimension that has been thematized, the family resemblance with Platonism cannot be denied.

29. That is, common sense can only be restored when the stability and lastingness of the worldly frame have been restored as well.

30. In this text when I speak of Arendt's search for a new logos of the political space I do not mean to suggest that she seeks to discern an eternal or transcendental ordering principle of the political space, as the term "logos" might suggest to those familiar with its traditional usage. Rather, I mean to signal Arendt's quest to articulate a paradigm of collective deliberation and of political reckoning more generally that will be compatible with her emphases upon human plurality and the world's durability and stability.

31. As will become clear as we proceed (especially in chapter 3), Arendt's late turn to judgment is more of a return than a first visit and more of a fresh encounter than a first encounter. Indeed, through the years, Arendt attends to political judgment on at least several occasions. Nonetheless, it seems to me that in her late work on judgment she is specifically animated by the need to mediate between the two poles of the action-ideal, a need which for obvious reasons could not have been felt in quite the same way in earlier years.

32. To this point, now almost fifteen years since her death, only a few book-length treatments of Arendt's thought have appeared. Leaving aside both those texts which are more concerned with the woman than with the thinker and those texts which treat a single facet of her thought rather than the whole, the number of texts of a scope comparable to this one dwindles to three—one published while Arendt was still alive and two published subsequently. Of the three, Bikhu Parekh's excellent book addresses largely methodological concerns and belongs in a category by itself. Of the remaining two, Margaret Canovan's text is a better introduction to Arendt's work than is George Kateb's, though the latter is surely the more thought-provoking.

Neither Canovan nor Kateb has chosen to approach Arendt's thought in a manner comparable to the way in which it will be considered here. Canovan's approach is topical and stays close to the surface contours of Arendt's texts. In quick succession, she synopsizes Arendt's reflections upon totalitarianism, the human condition, and the modern world without, however, seeking to situate these thematic overviews within any supertextual architectonic.

By contrast, Kateb provides us with a less uniformly synoptic and less disinterested account. The problem with Kateb's "strong" reading, a "problem" which at the same time is the source of its strength, stems from his strategy of making Arendt speak to *his* prior theoretical concerns as if they were her own. At times this strategy has the effect of illuminating various facets of Arendt's thought—her conception of civil disobedience, for example—which would in no other circumstance have received such close attention. Conversely, however, this approach also has the effect of distorting the inner coherence of Arendt's thought, for Kateb often paints her into a corner that is not her own in order that she may become the perfect foil against which he may elucidate his own concerns. In consequence, a number of elements of Arendt's thought, which for Arendt might have been of only minor significance, achieve a new prominence, and though a thematic unity is imposed upon her work, it is not her own.

33. While I do not think there is any room for debate here, it must be acknowledged that it is hard to provide definitive evidence for concluding one way or the other. One bit of evidence for suggesting that Arendt believed that women might come to manifest these traits as readily as men may be inferred from Arendt's essay on Rosa Luxembourg whom she praises for possessing the panoply of political virtues.

34. Specific evidence for the notion that Arendt thought herself to be describing aspects not of the male nor of the female but of the human condition is also hard to come by. Some evidence for this notion may be inferred from the role that Isak Dinesen's conception of storytelling plays in the development of Arendt's thinking about the relation between politics and the quest for an immortal name. Following Dinesen, Arendt holds that this desire for immortal renown, which some feminist theorists (e.g., Dorothy Dinnerstein) have held to be a specifically male desire, is common to all persons by virtue of being cognizant of their mortality. In sum, as I hope the reader will discern as we proceed, though Arendt holds by the masculine pronominal conventions of her day, when she writes "man" she usually means not male nor female but human. In suggesting that this is Arendt's view, I do not mean to comment either way upon the question of whether or not Arendt equates "man" and "human" in a way that is insufficiently cognizant of sexual difference. At this juncture I am only concerned with discerning whether Arendt understood her linguistic practice as exclusive or inclusive.

CHAPTER ONE

1. While our focus will be upon THC, there will be times when reference will be made to other works by Arendt (especially in the notes) because sometimes an alternative formulation will more precisely state—or more fully elaborate—a position which, though present in THC, is less clearly enunciated there.

2 . Thus of the text's six parts, only the sixth directly pertains to the problem of man's being in the world which is discussed under the rubric of world alienation and in terms of the breakdown of common sense that is associated with the rise of Cartesianism. Just how this discussion is meant to bear upon the matters considered in the parts one through five of the text is left unclear. Indeed it is only by means of the hindsight available to one in possession of Arendt's later works that the relationship between parts one through five and part six—as well as the significance of *part three* for the subsequent development of Arendt's oeuvre—becomes clear.

3. See THC, pp. 50–58. See also, BPF, p. 156.

4. See THC, pp. 22–28, 48–58, 175–81.

5. Regarding the points raised in the paragraph more generally, see THC, pp. 17–19, 36, 53–59, 175–99.
That there is some degree of tension between the end of actualizing one's unique selfhood in a public manner in the present and that of cutting the kind of figure which is likely to be long (and favorably) remembered after one is dead and buried is apparent. Just how Arendt deals with this will be considered further on.

6. That these dichotomies play such a pivotal role in Arendt's thought is not something which she ever called to her reader's attention. That her work may be better understood in relation to these implicit dyads is the burden of argument

to be borne by this first chapter. Our immediate attention will be upon the dyads of uniqueness and uniformity, lasting and passing, and freedom and necessity. Our consideration of public and private will follow.

7. It should also be pointed out that Arendt's occasional reflections upon the dyads are scattered throughout her works and hence it is necessary to attend to these discussions wherever they are found. Nonetheless, this does not pose a problem of interpretation with respect to our current emphasis upon THC because Arendt's orientation toward the dichotomies upon which we are focusing is relatively invariant across the whole of her oeuvre.

8. See THC, pp. 8–9, 177–78; OR, pp. 211–13; and LMW, pp. 108–09, 212-217.

9. See OR, p. 211; and LMW, pp. 108–9, 212–17.

10. See THC, pp. 176–78.

11. Ibid.

12. References to the polarity between uniqueness and uniformity are manifest in one form or another in most of Arendt's works. In THC this polarity determines Arendt's conception of the political space as a site wherein man can achieve this essential revelation of his uniqueness in contrast to the uniformity which is his lot outside of it. See THC, pp. 40–43, 175–81 213–15.

13. See Martin Heidegger, *Being and Time*, trans. John Macquarrie and Edward Robinson (New York: Harper & Row, 1962), pp. 149–68.

14. See THC, pp. 8–9.

15. See THC, p. 179.

16. See THC, pp. 212–15.

17. See THC, pp. 39–41, 57.

18. See THC, pp. 212–15, 322.

19. The "who" transcends all forces. See THC, pp. 174–83, 211.

20. By contrast, it is the private and social spheres which are held to be sites of behavioral uniformities. For further consideration of Arendt's distinction between public and private spheres see "Public and Private: Spaces and Objects," towards the end of this chapter.

21. See Heidegger, *Being and Time*, pp. 279–311.

22. See THC, pp. 8–9.

23. See Heidegger, *Being and Time*, pp. 279–311.

24. See LMW, pp. 108–9, 212–17.

25. "In this world which we enter, appearing from a nowhere, and from which we disappear into a nowhere, Being and Appearing coincide . . ." (LMT, p. 19). Or: "to be alive means to be possessed by an urge to self-display, living things make their appearance like actors on a stage set for them" (LMT, p. 21).

26. See LMT, pp. 19–23.

27. Ibid.

28. Thus the "who-ness" that is objectively revealed differs from that revealed to introspection. Arendt is dubious of the worth of the latter. For this reason every adult should cleave to the public space. While Arendt acknowledges the nonprivative aspects of the private sphere, by her measure a life lived in it alone, is less than fully human. In particular, Arendt underscores that the person who never enters the public realm is "deprived of the *reality* that comes from being seen and heard by others" (THC, p. 58), a reality "which humanly and political speaking, is the same as appearance" (THC, p. 199). "To men the reality of the world is guaranteed by the presence of others, by its appearing to all; . . . [conversely] whatever lacks this appearance comes and passes away like a dream, intimately and exclusively our own, but without reality" (THC, p. 199; emphasis added).

29. See THC, pp. 182–83.

30. See THC, pp. 40–43, 57–58.

31. Political action "corresponds to the human condition of plurality, to the fact that men, not Man, live on the earth and inhabit the world. . . . This plurality is specifically the condition—not only the *conditio sine qua non* but the *conditio per quam*—of all political life" (THC, p. 7). More generally, then, plurality signifies human individuality and uniqueness.

Let it also be observed that as the community which realizes human plurality is denominated as political, the community which obliterates plurality is thus antipolitical, and the one which facilitates an interaction that contains no reference to it at all is utterly apolitical.

32. As Arendt notes in THC, the intersubjective "objectivity" man seeks can be attained in the public realm and there alone. At times Arendt equates this objectivity with the "reality" that man seeks, a reality which Arendt equates with appearance. Yet what secures this reality is not appearance per se as much as the fact that what appears in the public appears to innumerable persons simultaneously. Thus Arendt suggests that "the reality of the public realm relies upon the simultaneous presence of innumerable perspectives and aspects in which the common world presents itself for which no common denominator can ever by devised." Thus being seen and heard by others "derives significance from the fact that everyone sees and hears from a different position. . . ." (THC, p. 57). Thus, Arendt continues, the solidity of the reality men and the things of the world may achieve in the public realm "rises out of the sum total of aspects presented by one object to a

multitude of spectators." "Only where things can be seen by many in a variety of aspects without changing their identity, can worldly reality truly and reliably appear" (THC, p. 57). Thus at long last we are given Arendt's view of how it is that the public space may bestow upon man the individuality he craves.

And yet, it must be noted that the good sense of Arendt's argument aside, her belief in the likelihood of eventual agreement (regarding the nature of the intersubjectively constituted object) might be overly sanguine. What Arendt seems to overlook is the potentially irreducible incommensurability of public perspectives which is especially likely where the members of a given polity lack a common cultural paradigm.

33. THC, pp. 184–85.

34. THC, p. 184.

35. Ibid. In this paragraph, in particular, one can detect that tendency in Arendt's thought which entails a rejection of the "substantial" soul, that is, of a self which has any essence prior to, or other than, that which is phenomenally manifest in the course of a life. One consequence of this view is an implicit acknowledgement of the self's social and historical dimension. Hence, *who* one uniquely is cannot be dissociated from the circumstances of one's coming into being. Thus the import of Arendt's insistence that the proper answer to the question: "Who are you?" is only to be conveyed by the response which begins with: "Let me tell you a story." In the unique and never to be repeated concatenation of traits and circumstances a unique essence is precipitated: a life. Thus the person denied entry into the public realm is not merely denied an "outlet"; more significantly, he is denied access to the medium without which the self cannot be substantially constituted at all. Such would seem to be the implication that follows from Arendt's view.

36. "The unchangeable identity of a person, though disclosing itself intangibly in act and speech, becomes tangible only in the story of the actor's and speaker's life; but as such it can only be known, that is, grasped as a palpable entity only after it has come to its end. In other words, the human essence . . . [i.e.] the essence of who somebody is, can come into being only when life departs leaving behind nothing but a story (THC, p. 193).

37. See THC, pp. 184–92.

38. See THC, p. 190.

39. Regarding the inherent unpredictability of human affairs, its basis, and its corrective see THC, pp. 188–92, 243–47.

40. Thus in judging it is important to bear in mind that the "innermost meaning of the acted deed and the spoken word is independent of victory and defeat and must remain untouched by any eventual outcome, by their consequence for better or worse" (THC, p. 205).

41. On the surface, this view seems to be a dangerous one which would countenance all forms of political irresponsibility vis à vis foreseeable consequences. This, however, is hardly Arendt's intention. For a more plausible view of what she means to accomplish by asserting that action be judged without an eye to the consequences, see the following section.

42. THC, p 234.

43. Ibid.

44. Ibid.

45. See THC, pp. 184–91.

46. See THC, pp. 188–92.

47. "Because the actor always moves among equals and in relation to other acting beings, he is never merely a 'doer' but always and at the same time a sufferer. To do and to suffer are opposite sides of the same coin, and the story that an act starts is composed of its consequent deeds and sufferings. These consequences are boundless because action . . . acts into a medium where every reaction becomes a chain reaction. . . . [And] since action reacts upon beings who are capable of their own actions, reaction, apart from being a response, is always a new action that strikes out on its own and affects others. Thus action and reaction among men never move in a closed circle and can never be reliably confined to two partners" (THC, p. 190).

48. That courage is the essential virtue here follows from the character of the field of action. "The connotation of courage, which we now feel to be an indispensable quality of the hero, is in fact already present in a willingness to act and speak at all, to insert one's self into the world and begin a story of one's own[;] courage and even boldness are already present in leaving one's private hiding place and showing who one is and exposing one's self" (THC, p. 186).

49. Character and the ineffable "who," for whom we have been searching are the same. And yet, as Arendt is quick to point out, character is only truly revealed as the story of a life. An abstract catalogue of virtues and vices does not a character describe, for by such means one can only describe a type, a genera. Only the meld of story and abstraction woven into a single indissoluble skein reveals the unique person whose biography and character are uniquely his own and not to be duplicated. Thus, to the question "Who are you?" Arendt would have it that the only way to respond must be "Let me tell you a story." MDT, "Isak Dinesen 1885–1963," p. 105. On the relationship between the revelation of character and drama ("the most political of the arts") see THC, p. 182.

50. As Arendt writes toward the beginning of THC, "The task and potential greatness of mortals lie in their ability to produce things—works and deeds and words—which would deserve to be and, at least to a degree, are at home in

everlastingness, so that through them mortals could find their place in a cosmos where everything is immortal except themselves" (THC, p. 19).

51. Arendt's own formulation of this conceptual polarity is most clearly articulated in the essay "The Concept of History" (henceforth referred to as BPF/CH). Should one seek to trace its presence throughout the range of Arendt's works one could find it from the first to the last. In particular, see THC, pp. 17–21.

52. BPF/CH, pp. 42–46. See also THC, p. 18.

53. BPF/CH, pp. 46–47.

54. THC, p. 198.

55. BPF/CH, p. 72. See also BPF/CH, pp. 63–75.

56. See OT, pp. 207–21, and in particular p. 21; see also BPF/CH, pp. 64–85, and in particular p. 64.

57. See the discussion of Arendt's conception of public and private in this chapter.

58. This will become much clearer when we treat the dyad of freedom and necessity.

59. See THC, pp. 55–56. See also BPF/WF, p. 156.

60. This is one point about which Arendt is quite clear, namely, that greatness is such by virtue of "its distinction from the commonplace." See THC, p. 205, note 33.

61. See THC, pp. 205–7.

62. N. B . In this context it is interesting to note that Arendt makes a point of insisting that Eichmann was not great but *commonplace*. Hence "the banality of evil": evil is never great.

63. See THC, p. 77.

64. Also by way of justification we would call the reader's attention to THC, p. 205, note 33, in which Arendt notes in a rather off-hand way the connection Aristotle draws in his *Poetics* between action and beauty. First, Arendt notes that Aristotle found greatness to be a prerequisite of a dramatic plot because "the drama imitates acting" which is "judged by greatness, by its distinction from the commonplace." Then, as an aside, she continues, thus: "The same, incidentally, is true for the beautiful, which resides in greatness and *taxis*, the joining together of the parts." Thus action and beauty are both to be noted for their greatness; and presumably, it is this greatness, this special way in which they both transcend the commonplace, that makes them merit long remembrance.

65. For Arendt's view of the nature of the artwork and the beautiful see THC, pp. 167–74. See also BPF/CC, pp. 197–211.

66. THC, p. 167; BPF/CC, pp. 208–9.

67. THC, p. 173.

68. THC, p. 173 .

69. THC, p. 173.

70. This is true so long as men are less than 100 percent rule-governed in their behaviors, that is, so long as there is an element of freedom in their action.

71. In truth, however, most of what we adjudge by the standard of the beautiful is produced as artwork, that is, as work with no other end but to be beautiful. Similarly, Arendt seems at times to suggest that in the ideal public space men would step forward to reveal themselves for the sake of this alone. Worldly concerns would serve as props and foils to this end. Thus completing the analogy with the realm of art Arendt suggests that "in order to be what the world is always meant to be, a home for men during their life on earth, the human artifice must be a place fit for action and speech, for *activities not only entirely useless for the necessities of life,* but of an entirely different nature from the manifold activities of fabrication by which the world and all the things in it are produced" (THC, p. 174; emphasis added). Thus in their nonutilitarian *raison d'être* the beautiful and the word/deed are clearly associated, and—given that this quote is taken from the end of the section on the nature of the artwork—the inference is clear. The standard of greatness/beauty, which is the criterion by which that which seeks lasting-ness is to be measured, applies to both. For beauty, writes Arendt in BPF/CC, is the criterion of appearance.

72. For a speculative reading of Arendt's conception of "doing beauty," see J. Glenn Gray, "The Winds of Thought," *Social Research* 44 (Spring 1977). See also J. Glenn Gray, "The Abyss of Freedom—and Hannah Arendt,"in *Hannah Arendt: The Recovery of the Public World,* ed. Melvin A. Hill (New York: St. Martin's Press,1979), pp. 225–44.

73. See BPF/WF, pp. 151–54; OR, p. 98.

74. See BPF/WF, pp. 152–53.

75. "Albeit abstractly"—because the unique character of the doer, as distinguished from the character of the deed, is concretely and truly revealed only in his story.

76. On this distinction between "in order to" and "for the sake of," see THC, pp. 153–58, and BPF/CH, pp. 78–85. See also George Kateb, *Hannah Arendt: Politics, Conscience, Evil* (Totowa, N.J.: Rowman and Allanheld, 1983: pp. 11–14).

77. BPF/WF, p. 152.

78. See THC, pp. 35–36, 186.

79. Ibid.

80. By contrast, of the principle, Arendt explicitly notes that it "can be repeated time and again; [that] it is inexhaustible, and, [that] in distinction from its motive, the validity of the principle is universal" (BPF/WF, p. 152).

81. Let it also be noted that whereas previously it has been the positive poles of the dyads which have been treated extensively while the negative poles have been considered in a relatively perfunctory way, with the shift of attention to freedom and necessity this imbalance will be overcome. At the same time, in treating this truly comprehensive binary, the negative poles of the previously slighted dyads will receive their due.

82. This point is repeated over and over again across the length of Arendt's writing. See THC, p. 130, and LMW, pp. 128–45. Bearing in mind that nature and necessity are synonymous for Arendt, we note Arendt's representative assertion that "the will . . . can transcend nature, [even] suspend it" (LMW, p. 131).

83. Arendt refers again and again to the somatic basis of that which necessitates. Freedom, then, is in a strong sense freedom from the body and its imperious needs. Hence she speaks of the poor as unfree because they are placed "under the absolute dictate of their bodies [and hence] under the absolute dictate of necessity" (OR, p. 60). Note, however, that in Arendt's view not only the poor, but all men whose lives are consumed by the ceaseless process of ministering to biological and egocentric needs, are under the heel of necessity.

84. Arendt acknowledges that some, perhaps even most, men would be, content with such a happy, animal existence. But the best of men require something more. It is for the latter that political life is indispensable. See OR, pp. 275–81.

85. Arendt insists upon viewing freedom as arising in the space where the I-will coincides with the I-can. See LMW, p. 19.

86. If man lacked freedom of the will then his choices would be stripped of moral significance, for, in the truest sense, they would not be choices at all. Man would be little but a rational brute of no greater dignity than any other animal species. And, inasmuch as his choices would not be such that a man could take credit (or blame) for them, the basis for pride or shame would be stripped away as well.

87. If man were only a natural animal he could only have an unchanging species-life, but because he is more than an animal, because he is—at least to some degree—free, one person differs from the next and all men are caught in the web of contingent, and hence historical, processes.

88. Today, man retreats from freedom everywhere, taking cover under "isms" and ideologies that would relieve him of responsibility for himself, his actions, and the world. For Arendt this is bad faith of the worst kind. See her critique of the exculpatory myths of Jews and anti-Semites both (OT, pp. 3–11).

89. Arendts scorn for all "isms" which have the effect of diminishing the responsibility of the agent is poured forth time and again across the length and breadth of her writings. See, for example, EIJ, p. 297.

90. Ibid. Note also Arendt's assertion that "the conditions of human existence can never explain what we are or answer the question of who we are for the simple reason that they never condition us absolutely. This has always been the opinion of philosophy, in distinction from the sciences" (THC, p. 11).

91. See THC, p. 322.

92. Even when man acts in accordance with instinct, he must *choose* to do so. Thus, for Arendt, though man may act like an animal, he can never *be* an animal. See LMW, pp. 60–63.

93. See generally for this usage "What is Freedom?" in BPF. In THC this distinction parallels Arendt's distinction between animal and self-related matters on the one hand, and human and self-transcending concerns on the other.

94. See OR, pp. 170–73, on the Mayflower Compact.

95. See BPF/WF, pp. 152–57.

96. See OR, p. 175.

97. See THC, pp. 135–36.

98. On how hunger necessitates, and why, see OR, p. 60.

99. Arendt's reason for seeking to exclude the morally praiseworthy emotions of (for example) pity, compassion, and benevolence from a political role has been misunderstood by most commentators who have addressed this matter. To begin with it should be emphasized that Arendt, who had documented the horrors of totalitarianism, was quite well aware of the fact that there were worse emotional forces at work in modern politics than pity and compassion. Kateb's criticism on this point is gratuitous. (See Kateb, *Hannah Arendt*, pp. 22–25.) When, in OR, Arendt argues against these "good" emotions, it must be understood that she, who had experienced the impact of the "bad" emotions, is intent upon arguing against the easy view which would place future politics under the aegis of human benevolence. If, as Kateb suggests, the human prospect depends upon securing the continuous manifestation of goodness in the political realm, then, in Arendt's view, we would have no choice but to throw up our hands in despair. It can hardly be surprising, then, that Arendt, as both a German Jew and an optimist about politics, sought to tap a more reliable source than the milk of human kindness which, particularly in this century, has been in such short supply. Instead, as shall be seen

further on in this chapter, Arendt sought to construct a safe and decent politics from motivations and experiences which seemed to her to be much more generalizable, or at least potentially so. It must also be acknowledged, however, that Arendt was extremely critical of the political manifestations of the emotions she sought to exclude from political life. In her view those who have entered the political realm on the crest of such emotions have brought with them an excessiveness, an urgency, and an agenda hostile to politics generally, and inimical to plurality, in particular. Where such feelings are treated as political principles, the men who are urged on by a politicized "love of humanity" are, in her view, likely to perceive the polity as divided into opposing camps of good citizens and evil. Such humanitarians, in Arendt's view, will hardly hesitate before doing great harm. Against these divisive and destructive "good" emotions, as shall be seen further on, Arendt opposes the moral feelings which are synonymous with her conception of humaneness, namely, solidarity, political friendship, and respect. In this construct of motives and feelings Arendt finds what Kateb says she lacks, a moral limit insuring that action will not lead to atrocity.

That goodness in politics may become a source of great evil on behalf of its good ends is a lesson taught by history again and again. It is a lesson Arendt would have us remember, especially in an age in which the magnitude of evil done by truly evil men might make it easy to imagine the opposite to be the case.

On Arendt's view of compassion and its inappropriateness to the political realm see OR, pp. 71–72. On Arendt's associated view of goodness as similarly unfit for politics see OR, pp. 80–88 and THC, pp. 73–78.

100. See THC, pp. 126–35.

101. THC, p. 133.

102. See THC, pp. 213–14.

103. Ibid.

104. That the will to enter the public realm implies a willingness to set aside—or to transcend—the interest in self and in mere self-preservation, Arendt makes clear over and over again: "To leave the household, originally in order to embark upon some adventure and glorious enterprise, and later simply to devote one's life to the common affairs of the city, demanded courage because only in the household was one primarily concerned with one's own life and survival. Whoever entered the political realm had first to be ready to risk his life, and too great a love for life obstructed freedom, [and] was a sure sign of slavishness. . . . The "good life" was "good" to the extent that having mastered the necessities of sheer life . . . [and] by overcoming the innate urge of all living creatures for their own survival, it was no longer bound to the biological life process" (THC, pp. 36–37).

105. See THC, p. 135.

106. See OR, pp. 139–40.

107. Arendt's critique of reason—which is more a critique of coercive logicality and its political consequences—spans the length of her work from OT wherein it takes form as a critique of ideological thinking to LMW in which it is critiqued as the nemesis of freedom. Within OT and THC it is contrasted with the workings of common sense which Arendt regards as the type of rationality appropriate to politics. Throughout, Arendt's concern with logicality is based upon her sense that it can coerce or compel men in a way not compatible with human freedom or human plurality. Ultimately Arendt's answer to the coercive reign of one Truth is a conception of the deliberative process which emphasizes the legitimacy of a plurality of opinions, a legitimacy which she believes logicality opposes. Thus Arendt's critique of logic might also be understood as Arendt's taking the side of opinion in the age-old clash of it with truth. See, in particular, in BPF, "Truth and Politics"; see also "On Humanity in Dark Times: Thoughts about Lessing" in MDT.

108. Speaking of the coercive logicality inherent in ideology, Arendt cites Stalin regarding the power of ideological compulsion. "The power . . . was discovered to reside, not in the idea itself, but in its logical process which 'like a mighty tentacle seizes you on all sides as in a vice and from whose grip you are powerless to tear yourself away . . .'" (OT, p. 472).

109. It is interesting to note that in Orwell's *1984* the statement that 2+2=4 and only 4, is held by Winston Smith to be a proof of man's freedom and of the limits of totalitarian rule. See THC, p. 171.

110. It must be underscored that despite this critique Arendt is neither an irrationalist nor an arationalist. What Arendt is critical of is a type of logicality which, through the medium of an ideology, opposes all freedom of action. From a political standpoint, her problem with reason lies in its antidemocratic opposition of "Truth" to plurality. Her fear is that those who claim reason as their own may turn the truth into a weapon against the plurality of men.

111. See OT, p. 473.

112. Thus Arendt paraphrases the logic of ideology as deployed by Hitler and Stalin. "You can't say A without saying B and C and so on, down to the end of the murderous alphabet. Here, the coercive force of logicality seems to have its source; it springs from our fear of contradicting ourselves. . . ." (OT, pp. 472–73).

113. As Arendt so pithily puts it: "If the inmates are vermin, it is logical that they should be killed by poison gas; if they are degenerate, they should not be allowed to contaminate the population; if they have 'slave-like souls' (Himmler) no one should waste his time trying to re-educate them" (OT, p. 457).

114. See OT, pp. 460–79. See also OT, p. 458.

115. See OT, pp. 472–73.

116. See THC, p. 170.

117. Ibid.

118. Obviously reason/logic does not tell everyone the same thing; rather, what Arendt aims to emphasize is that given any one of an infinite number of starting premises the logical organon, that proceeds deductively, will churn out a comprehensive vision. Thus while all ideologies begin from differing premises, because each is a logical construct, each unfolds a totalizing vision out of itself. Give the starting premise anyone employing his logic should generate the same conclusions. Hence the formal consistency and universal comprehension of ideological systems.

119. Arendt's own sympathies on this point were more with Lessing whom she described as one who "never felt compelled by truth, be it imposed by others or by his own reasoning processes. . . . He was glad that—to use his parable—the genuine ring, if it had ever existed, had been lost; he was glad for the sake of the infinite number of opinions that arise when men discuss the affairs of the world" (MDT, p. 26).

120. Bionecessity is a neologism I have coined. Its signification is quite apparent. Under bionecessity are subsumed psychological, historical, and sociological necessities (determinisms).

121. See OT, pp. 457–74.

122. See THC, pp. 96–108, 126–35, 212–19.

123. See OR, pp. 60–114.

124. See LMW, p. 4.

125. See LMW, p. 5.

126. See LMW, pp. 125–46.

127. In conversation Professor Harvey Goldman pointed out that Plato's *thymos* functions as the will does for Augustine. It is Augustine, however, who first identifies this faculty as the will.

128. See LMW, p. 88.

129. LMW, p. 131 (emphasis added).

130. LMW, p. 131.

131. LMW, p. 132. .

132. See LMW, pp. 158–94.

133. See LMW, p. 217.

134. See in LMW Arendt's appreciation of Duns Scotus's analogous position (LMW, pp. 125–46).

135. And the reason for this lack of clarity within LM likely owes to the fact that ultimately she would have looked to the faculty of judgment as well to codetermine the will had she lived to write the last volume of her trilogy. At this juncture, however, we are only concerned with her position as it is developed in THC, which like LMW is conceived without explicit attention to the role of the judging faculty. Lest there be any suspicion to the contrary, it should be noted that even in her last works Arendt will continue to regard "the pure particle of uniqueness" as a chief determining ground of the will. What other elements shall come to be regarded by her as legitimately codeterminative of the will shall become clear in this study's subsequent chapters.

136. This may be understood as implicit in the way Arendt defines necessity as including reason, appetite, and forces of socialization. Freedom must lie beyond the depth reached by any of these forces.

137. See OT pp. 453–55, and, more generally, pp. 437–59.

138. See BPF, pp. 167–71, and THC, pp. 175–81.

139. See THC, pp. 176–80, and LMW, pp. 104–10.

140. See LMW, pp. 188–94.

141. Ibid.

142. Ibid.

143. In particular, see LMW, pp. 188–94. Note: though Arendt explicitly articulates this metaphysics only at the end of her career, the view of natality underlying it is not a late development in her thought. Indeed, such references to natality within her oeuvre are ubiquitous from her earliest to her latest writings, and they almost always point in the direction of the metaphysics that Arendt rather hesitantly proposes in LMW.

144. See LMW, pp. 108–10, 212–17.

145. Ibid.

146. See OR, p. 175. It should be noted that this is largely a path untaken by Arendt. Instead she relies upon other means for overcoming necessity.

147. Arendt conveys this impression in both THC and OR in her discussion of the activities which properly belong to public and private realms, respectively. In THC, see pp. 72–73 in particular. In OR, see pp. 54-70. N.B., in THC Arendt contrasts the matters of proper concern to the polis with those of proper concern to the *oikos* (home). The latter, she concludes, is where all mundane matters of necessity belong. As for the political realm, Arendt suggests, following the Greeks, that from it "everything merely necessary or useful is [to be] strictly excluded" (THC, p. 25). That this notion has consequences which are problematic in practice

has already been signaled. For a further consideration of these matters see the following section.

148. That is, in contrast to the other dichotomies which we have considered whose prominence is more a feature of the current analysis than a measure of their explicit significance for Arendt.

149. THC, p. 28.

150. This distinction between public and private realms becomes a distinction between "things that *should* be shown and things that *should* be hidden" (THC, p. 72; emphasis added).

151. The social is a vital but ultimately a derivative notion for Arendt. See THC, pp. 38–49.

152. See THC, pp. 18–19, 54–55, 196–99.

153. See THC, pp. 50–51, 175–80.

154. See THC, pp. 58–73.

155. See THC, pp. 55–58.

156. Ibid.

157. See THC, pp. 57–58.

158. The details, and significance, of Arendt's conception of common sense will be considered at length in chapter 3.

159. See THC, pp. 50–58.

160. See THC, pp. 50–52.

161. Ibid.

162. See THC, pp. 212–15. See also THC, pp. 25–27, regarding Arendt's meditation upon Aristotle's speech based definition of man as a *zoon politikon*; and THC, pp. 176–81 on the relationship between speech, action, and the revelation of who one is.

163. See THC, pp. 52, 57.

164. Thus Arendt would not allow that (for example) churches, eating clubs, or interest groups are inherently political institutions (See THC, pp. 214–15). These may possess a political dimension, as if by accident, but only the polity properly takes the manifestation of human difference as its prime end. Admittedly, this vision of political community might be a serious distortion of what political community really is. It might be the case that the polity is more akin to institutions like the church which emphasize only the common end of its members while placing no value whatsoever upon securing for them the opportunity to

achieve the manifestation of their uniqueness. For further consideration of this point see the conclusion to this chapter.

165. In one of her last essays Arendt marks this dichotomy between self-concern and concern for the commonweal in most unequivocal language. In "Public Rights and Private Interests: In response to Charles Frankel" she suggests that "there is an intrinsic conflict between the interests of individual mortals and the interest of the common world which they inhabit." Yet it is the height of political virtue to transcend the narrowness of these partial interests through the "impartiality" which enables one to "recognize and embrace the common good." That a moment of self-overcoming is incumbent upon the citizen who would identify himself with the public good is made quite clear as Arendt calls attention to the fact that this movement "is resisted at every turn by the urgency of one's self-interests, which are always more urgent than the common good." In exchange the polity offers a certain joy: "The necessary sacrifice of individual interests to the commonweal—in the most extreme case the sacrifice of life—is compensated for by public happiness"(Hannah Arendt, "Public Rights and Private Interests: In Response to Charles Frankel" in Michael Mooney and Florian Stuber, eds., *Small Comforts for Hard Times: Humanists on Public Policy* (New York: Columbia University Press, 1977, pp. 104–6).

166. See Arendt, "Public Rights and Private Interests," pp. 104-06.

167. Ibid.

168. Ibid.

169. Among the noble sentiments which would be ruined by being exposed in public Arendt includes love and pure goodness. See THC, pp. 73–78. Arendt's most comprehensive meditation upon the ruinous effects brought about by the inappropriate display of certain inherently lofty emotions/sentiments/motives—effects wrought upon the world as much as upon the soul of the one who publicizes his sentiments in this way—is to be found in OR, pp. 71–114, in Arendt's discussion of compassion, pity, and hypocrisy.

170. See THC, p. 242.

171. See RLR, p. 53. See Arendt's discussion of the principle of exclusiveness which underpins the basis of association in the private realm.

172. Arendt fears that, as in Crevoceur's prediction, "the man will get the better of the citizen" (OR, p. 140).

173. On the corruption of the public by the private see OR, pp. 252–53. Regarding Arendt's view on this issue generally, see her "Public Rights and Private Interests," pp. 103–08.

174. If this is reminiscent of Machiavelli on the corruption of republics this is hardly surprising, for Arendt's sources are those who we would group in the Machiavellian republican tradition. See OR, chaps. 4 and 5.

175. See chapter 2, generally. The heart of the matter lies in the inculcation of the proper civic ethos.

176. On Arendt's conception of political community see THC, pp. 27, 52–58, 175–83, 198–204. See also Hannah Arendt "Philosophy and Politics," *Social Research* 57, 1 (1990), pp. 73–103.

177. See THC, pp. 181–88. In particular see pp. 182–83.

178. Isonomy and *humanitas* together constitute the normative/ethical dimension of the action-ideal. Exegesis of Arendt's conception of the logos of the political process itself must await the discussion of political judgment in chapter 3. N.B., *humanitas* does not figure explicitly in THC though it is certainly implicit. Its explicit consideration is to be found in contemporaneous writings. See below.

179. See THC, pp. 220–35; OR, pp. 279–81.

180. See THC, pp. 220–25.

181. See THC, pp. 222–25; and OR, pp. 235–41, 279–80.

182. See M. Canovan, "The Contradictions of Hannah Arendt's Political Thought," *Political Theory* 6/1 (February 1978); pp. 21–22. Both M. Canovan and G. Kateb (*Hannah Arendt*, pp. 115–48) address the weaknesses of Arendt's conceptualization and critique of representative democracy. Of the two, however, Kateb's is the more trenchant and thoroughgoing both as a critique of Arendt's position and as a defense of the legitimacy of representative democracy. As strong as Kateb's defense is, however, it is somewhat besides the point. His defense is disproportionate to the small amount of consideration Arendt herself gives the matter. Kateb may be correct in questioning the significance of any modern political thinker who fails to consider seriously the best form of government that men have as yet constructed. But it is not clear that Kateb's defense scores any points that Arendt herself would be unwilling to concede. In the end, however, her attitude would remain dismissive. By comparison to the best form, representative democracy fails. With respect to this question Arendt's view is thoroughly revolutionary: there can be no true politics for the largest part of the population until the system is restructured to facilitate their continuous participation.

183. That Arendt argues on behalf of the *political* parity of such systems ought not to be understood as an argument on behalf of their *moral* equivalence. On moral grounds Arendt would be among the first to agree that representative democracy of the Anglo-American variety is far preferable to other antidemocratic systems. See OT, pp. 250–66 regarding the contrast between the Anglo-American and Continental party systems.

184. See THC, pp. 221–22.

185. Arendt's conception of *humanitas* must be gleaned from various writings which span the length of her career. Indeed, the most important texts include her first composed and last published, her biography of Rahel Varnhagen composed prior to 1938, and her lectures on Kant's political philosophy delivered at the New School in 1970 and only published in 1982. Between these two texts, of particular import are a number of essays to be found in her *Jew as Pariah* (JP) and several from her *Men in Dark Times* (MDT). Scattered remarks are to be found in her other works as well. It should also be pointed out that the term *humanitas* is not used in THC though it recurs time and again in the works that are both prior and subsequent to it. See also, generally, Arendt's "Philosophy and Politics," *Social Research* 57, 1 (1990).

186. See MDT/Lessing ("On Humanity in Dark Times: Thoughts about Lessing."), pp. 24–25. Regarding the way in which the world's reality arises out of our collective discourse about it, see THC, pp. 57–58, 280–84.

187. See MDT/Lessing, pp. 24–25.

188. For Arendt this emphasis on civic friendship is Greco-Roman in origin and differs from the intimacy of more modern vintage. In tracing the descent of the classical ideal to our own time, Arendt singles out Lessing as one of the few who, in more recent times, has truly understood it. Arendt characterizes his comprehension thus: "That humanness should be sober and cool rather than sentimental; that humanity is exemplified not by fraternity but by friendship; that friendship is not intimately personal but makes political demands and preserves a reference to the world—all this seems to us exclusively characteristic of classical antiquity" (MDT/Lessing, p. 23), yet such is the view Lessing takes in *Nathan der Wiese*. See also THC, p. 246.
In light of Arendt's embrace of isonomy and political equality as norms of the public space, we do well to recall from Aristotle's discussion of friendship and the constitution in the *Nicomachean Ethics* (Book VIII) his assertion that true friendship is only possible between equals.

189. These norms are most fully articulated in LKPP, pp. 70-77. See also RV, pp. 153–54 and the essays "Organized Guilt and Universal Responsibility," JP, pp. 234–36; "Karl Jaspers: Citizen of the World?" MDT, pp. 81–84, 91–94; and "On Humanity in Dark Times: Thoughts about Lessing," MDT, pp. 24–31. Finally, see "The Crisis in Culture," BPF, pp. 223–26.

190. As Arendt writes in her essay on Lessing, "We humanize what is going on in the world and in ourselves only by speaking about it, and *in the course of speaking we learn to be human*" (emphasis added) (MDT/Lessing, p. 25). To grasp more fully just what Arendt intends here see RV, pp. 153–54.

191. See THC, p. 180, and OR, pp. 88–89.

192. See THC, pp. 236–47.

193. See THC, pp. 188–92, 230–36.

194. See THC, pp. 243–47.

195. See THC, pp. 236–43.

196. For Arendt, man's linguistic rationality and sociability are mutually entailing. Analytically however she unfolds the norms of *humanitas* from each separately. The *locus classicus* regarding her derivation from the former is to be found in RV generally, and on pp. 153–54 in particular. The *locus classicus* regarding her derivation from the latter is to be found in her LKPP, generally, and on pp. 70–77 in particular.

197. See RV, pp. 118, 153–57; and LKPP, pp. 70–77.

198. See RV, pp. 152–54.

199. Ibid.

200. See THC, p. 215.

201. See RV, pp. 114–20, 153–54.

202. Ibid.

203. Note that this rational capacity for communication and mutual understanding is to be sharply differentiated from the type of rationality which, for Arendt, is synonymous with coercive logicality, that is, rational, or logical, necessity. On the nature of Arendt's conception of the former, see RV, pp. 118, 153–54; and LKPP, pp. 70–77.

204. In RV and LKPP, Arendt covers almost all of the ground that would have been necessary to do this. One might also observe that this is the approach taken by Habermas at a similar juncture in his own project. On the relation between Habermas and Arendt see Jurgen Habermas's "Hannah Arendt's Communications Concept of Power," in *Social Research* 44, 1 (Spring 1977). pp. 3–24.

205. See in JP, "The Jew as Pariah: A Hidden Tradition," JP, p. 90; regarding international solidarity, see "The Jewish State: 50 Years Later," JP, pp. 174–75; and regarding human coresponsibility for the deeds of one another, see "On Organized Guilt and Universal Responsibility," JP, pp. 234–36.

206. See all references in two preceding notes. See in particular "Karl Jaspers: Citizen of the World?" MDT, pp. 81–94.

207. See JP, pp. 90, 234–36; OT, p. 116; MDT, pp. 81–84, 93–94.
In passing, it should be noted that Kateb, in working out his theses regarding what he purports to be the essential amorality of Arendt's vision, and his contention that within Arendt's schema there is no check on potential moral atrocity, wholly overlooks the dimension of Arendt's thought signified by her emphasis upon the norms of *humanitas*, a theme which recurrently surfaces in her work

from the thirties (RV) to the seventies (LKPP). At issue here is not whether Arendt would personally countenance amorality in politics (of this not even Kateb would accuse her); rather, the question is whether within her conception of action there are any elements that might prevent it. Clearly, the norms implied by *humanitas* could check whatever potentiality exists in Arendt's theory for a slide toward the abyss of amorality, provided that these norms really do hold sway. Yet it might be suggested that *humanitas* has no necessary connection with action and that Arendt turns to it merely in order to check the otherwise amoral tendencies of her construct. To refute this line of argument I have emphasized the close internal relationship that binds Arendt's conception of action, as articulated in THC, to the ideals of *humanitas* which she adduces in other contexts. If Arendt herself had undertaken to make this linkage explicit and clear, and if, in particular, she had addressed the matter of action's norms more directly in THC, then, one can assume she would have saved her readers from the confusion generated by the surface implications of the latter text. To have said all this, however, is not to say that any necessity guarantees that the norms of *humanitas* will hold sway wherever a public space is opened to ideal action. Indeed, as shall be considered further on, in THC in particular, Arendt fails entirely to consider the issue of how the action-ideal might be institutionalized in such a way as to insure its own long-term viability, on the one hand, and the prevalence of action apposite norms, on the other. In sum, then, while it can be said that Arendt fails to protect her ideal against amoral derailment, this hardly justifies labeling her as an amoralist, a calumny which, in Kateb's case, seems to have resulted from his failure to consider the train of thought that has been discussed in this section. See Kateb, *Hannah Arendt*, pp. 25–42.

208. Common, that is, to all works written either contemporaneously with or subsequent to THC. More specifically, OT and most of the essays gathered in JP are not included in this claim.

209. In THC Arendt lays the foundation for this conception of the transformative effect of publicity when she observes that thought and, by inference, speech are world-aware "capacities of man" that can transform the worldless "attributes of the human animal like feelings, wants and needs" (THC, p. 168) into something specifically human and worldly. "Thought," Arendt continues, "is related to feeling and transforms its mute and inarticulate despondency . . . until [the latter is] fit to enter the world and to be transformed. . . . In each instance, a human capacity which by its very nature is world-open and communicative transcends and releases into the world a passionate intensity from its imprisonment within the self" (THC p. 168). If thought has this effect immediately, then public speech ought to have it all the more so. Unfortunately, Arendt neglected the implications of this insight.

210. Among social questions that would be excluded from Arendt's purified politics are issues of race, class, and gender.

211. On occasion Arendt does come tantalizingly close to the truth about human animality. See, for example, THC, p. 168 (and in particular the material quoted in note 192 above). Unfortunately, Arendt fails to take the implications of such occasional insights to heart in framing her general conception.

212. That is, as an extension of the instinct of self-preservation or as an extension of natural compassion.

213. Though, arguably, all ends from art to self-disclosure are born of bodily drives: either somatic or psychosomatic.

214. That even this end may be given by nature is a line of speculation not unfamiliar to Arendt. Thus, in LMT, Arendt calls the reader's attention to the work of the Swiss zoologist Adolf Portmann whose morphological studies pointed in the direction of such an animal drive. See LMT, pp. 27–30.

215. See THC, p. 168.

216. See OR, pp. 174–75.

217. Hence optimal issues deal with problems that will effect the next generation, which places all of this generation on even footing.

218. See THC, p. 180.

219. See OR, pp. 59–114. In Arendt's view, the entry of the social question, that is, the problem of poverty, into politics marked the advent of class politics and of the politics of compassion both of which were inimical to the politics of self-revelation.

220. In light of OT, pp. 301–2, see RLR, p. 47.

221. Ibid.

222. See OR, pp. 59–114 regarding the impact of the social question on French politics. See also Arendt's critique of the entire revolutionary tradition of compassion driven endeavors to solve the problem of poverty, also in OR.

223. See Hannah Pitkin, "Justice: On Relating Private and Public," in *Political Theory* 9/3 (August 1981), pp. 327–52.

PRELUDE

1. And while the "problem of content" never emerges for her as such, the cumulative adjustments in the original paradigm do serve to make it easier to argue that the content restrictions Arendt imposes are scarcely the only means by which her objectives may be secured.

2. See THC, pp. 248–85.

3. See THC, pp. 79–174, for Arendt's analysis of labor; see THC, pp. 212–20, regarding the laborer's worldlessness. His lack of common sense is implicit in the latter.

4. Ibid.

5. See OT, pp. 351–53, 456–58, 468–79, regarding the relation between the lack of common sense and susceptibility to totalitarian ideologies.

6. To this end, Arendt contrasts the work of "man: the worker," who is the artificer of the human world—and, by inference, of his own worldliness—with the labor of "man: the laboring animal," who produces perishable consumer goods and labors in accordance with the biological imperative which requires that all members of the animal kingdom must labor to eat. Arendt particularly emphasizes that the central reality of the laborer's experience is that of the evanescence of things and, indeed, that of the evanescence of the world itself. In the factory or on the farm he does not fabricate lasting things but only labors to produce perishable commodities; away from his job, as a member of modern consumer society, he experiences not a world of durability but only the rapid succession of evanescent commodities. Unfortunately, as Arendt observes, since the onset of the modern division of labor, the experiences of man "the laboring animal" have become normative and the experience of *homo faber* entirely rare. See THC, pp. 132–35.

It should be noted that there is a strong affinity between Arendt's account of worldlessness in OT and her account of world alienation in THC. In each case the experience of the world's instability and lack of durability plays a crucial role in precipitating a loss of the world and a retreat into the self. Of course in the one case the underlying cause of this experience is posited as social change and turbulence, while in the other it is held to be the disappearance of the stable and objective world of lasting man-made objects and the fact that the experience of fabricating such an objective world has almost vanished.

7. See THC, pp. 321–22.

8. Of course one could argue that the presuppositions of action might be constituted by transforming the conditions of laboring in such a way that labor itself might be able to impart the orientation toward plurality and the world that political action presupposes. Given Arendt's essentialist conception of labor, however, it seems unlikely that she could place much hope in this project.

9. See THC, pp. 248–85.

10. Ibid.

11. In addition Arendt points to the "shrinkage" of the globe associated with the "Age of Exploration," to the expropriation of the peasantry from the land that is associated with nascent capitalism, and to the innerworldly asceticism of the Reformation as combining with the far reaching implications of Galileo's discovery to produce the phenomena of world alienation. See THC, pp. 248–57.

12. Of course it had long been known that the senses can deceive us, but this deception was generally considered to be readily corrigible by recourse to additional sense evidence; and even the Platonists, who seemed ready to deny the truth value of perception, implicitly presupposed its essential trustworthiness for otherwise they could not have appealed to the perceptions of the mind's eye as conveying truth. Regarding the Cartesian turn see THC, pp. 273–84.

13. Of course what really saves Descartes is the conclusion that God is not some *Dieu trompeur*. Only God's goodness, in other words, gives Descartes the faith to hold that his inward perceptions are not themselves deceptive.

14. See THC, pp. 282–84.

15. Arendt bemoans the loss of the common sense that corresponded to a shared world and its replacement by that which corresponds to a worldless natural faculty: "This transformation of common sense into an inner sense is characteristic of the whole modern age; in German . . . it is indicated by the difference between the older . . . *Gemeinsinn* [community sense] and the more recent *gesunder Menschenverstand* [common human understanding] which replaced it" (THC, p. 283, note 44).

16. Ibid.

17. See THC, pp. 265–73, 296, 320–22. See also BPF/CH, pp. 54–63, 77–90.

18. See THC, pp. 289–304.

19. Ibid.

20. See THC, pp. 265–70.

21. See THC, pp. 321–22. See also BPF/CH, pp. 77–90.

22. Arendt is of course highly critical of this kind of social science and of Marx's science in particular. In OT she is equally critical of the various ideologies of the modern world for the same reasons. See THC, p. 321. See also BPF/CH, pp. 77–90.

23. Arendt's neglect of governance is total. Whether this was an oversight or a function of her rejection of the ruler/ruled distinction, the lack is significant and theoretically problematic. Where the government is the agent of the sovereign body of the people, and acts to mediate between the citizen qua member of the sovereign and the citizen qua subject, to dispose of the problem as if it were but another instance of the pernicious dichotomy of ruler and ruled is hardly adequate.

24. It is in the context of this reality that Arendt's construct comes to seem most problematic. Here, in particular, one wants to ask (as we asked before) whether the emphasis Arendt places upon the self-revelation of the actors is exces-

sive, especially when compared with her neglect of more traditional questions of political thought and practice. If nothing very serious hung in the balance, then Arendt's sins of omission would be more easily pardoned. At issue is not whether the matters that she has chosen to address are important. They are, and Arendt has done well to thematize them. What is at issue is whether she has paid adequate attention to the range of questions which any comprehensive political theory must take into consideration.

25. See Morgenthau, "Hannah Arendt on Totalitarianism and Democracy," *Social Research* 44 (Spring 1977): pp. 128–31.

26. That Arendt hardly ever has occasion to address the notorious instability of the sorts of fora which she espouses is, to say the least, rather strange. In THC, after all, her ideal is the Athenian polis which was hardly known for its stability. In OR, Arendt bodies forth a train of soviets, councils, and *Räte* which were similarly unstable and much more short lived, and while she does explain their failure as a consequence of party cabalism, she never makes clear why we should not expect a similar fate to befall any similarly constituted bodies. The question of whether such fora might be rendered lasting and stable is a matter of more than a little importance, and one that Arendt should have addressed if she really wanted her ideal to be treated as more than a critical foil to modernity's shortcomings.

27. This web of norms is not somehow *within* the dwelling place of the world so much as it *is* itself this dwelling place. Only the actor whose quest for individuation is pursued within the limits set by this immaterial—but no less objective for being intersubjective—web, acts in a way that is wholly commensurate with the perpetuation of the lasting frame of the world.

28. As Arendt shows in LMW (pp. 158–94), trains of thought analogous to this one, led Nietzsche and Heidegger to repudiate the will altogether. If Arendt is to advocate action in the face of these objections, a full response is obligatory. Indeed, she gives one, as will be seen in chapter 3.

29. See OR, pp. 232–39, 249–55.

30. OR, p. 234.

31. OR, p. 234.

32. As we proceed, this latter theme will be accorded a prominence commensurate with its continuing importance.

33. It should be noted that in the preface to BPF Arendt explicitly problematizes the contemporary relevance of the concepts treated in the essays of the book. In OR, however, as I will argue in the next chapter, the revival of these same concepts is called for.

34. As we will see in chapter 3, not all of Arendt's "middle period" works are silent regarding the nature of common sense and the basis of its reconstruction.

Part two of Arendt's 1961 "The Crisis in Culture," is very much concerned with common sense. It also indicates the conceptual link between Arendt's two stratagems for overcoming world alienation. Strangely, the concern for common sense manifest in this essay is not seen again in Arendt's oeuvre until some years after the 1963 publication of *On Revolution*.

35. Ronald Beiner, for example, regards Arendt's late work on judgment and common sense as evincing an interest that is wholly distinct from her earlier concern with action. I will attend to Beiner's argument in chapter 3.

CHAPTER TWO

1. Analogously, she suggests that *animal laborans* is rendered unfit for the world of action by his dwelling within a realm in which everything that comes into being quickly passes away; deprived of any sense for what lasts or deserves to last, he becomes alienated from the world and thus lacks the world-awareness that self-transcending action on behalf of the lasting world presupposes.

2. See THC, pp. 220–21. The world's disorder ultimately springs from plurality, and so it is plurality that is attacked by the philosophers.

3. THC, pp. 36–37.

4. THC, p. 55.

5. Though this is obviously an important component of Arendt's definition of the world. See THC, p. 52.

6. "The public world is what we have in common not only with those who live with us, but also with those who were here before and with those who will come after us" (THC, p. 55).

7. Arendt's view of the process of historical change is articulated with the end in mind of saving freedom from necessity and action from determinism. Arendt's critique of deterministic views of the historical process is thoroughgoing and oft reiterated across the span of her work. In the main she treats the "appearance" of necessity in history as an optical illusion that presents itself before the retrospective glance of the thinking ego. In retrospect every story *seems* to be governed by an inner logos, yet Arendt would insist that this appearance which is true for the backward looking spectator wholly falsifies the existential realities of choice which existed for the actor when what is now past was present. Thus Arendt is led to engage in a critique of the distortions born of the spectator's retrospective point of view. At different points in her work this critique takes various forms: the critique of ideological determinisms (OT); the critique of the use of natural science models in the social sciences (UP); the critique of the use of mechanical causal rationality in the social sciences (THC); the critique of the spectator's point of view as false to the inner experience of action (OR, LMW); and the cri-

tique of policy analysis which is based on all the above assumptions (CR, "Lying in Politics: Reflections on the Pentagon Papers"). Against all of these modern misunderstandings of action and the historical process Arendt juxtaposes her reading of the world as contingent, fluid, and open to change, that is, to changes which might be brought about by the influence of even one actor. To the grand theories of overarching necessity Arendt responds by emphasizing what she calls common sense which those who act in the world know to be valid, a common sense that comprehends the contingency, indeterminacy, and unpredictability of historical reality, and thus a common sense which guarantees respect for the potential efficacy of action.

8. Thus the basis for what would otherwise seem to be an overly critical assessment of Stefan Zweig's inaction. See in JP, "Portrait of a Period." See also in JP, "Organized Guilt and Universal Responsibility."

9. THC, p. 205.

10. Thus in EIJ Arendt makes reference to instances of resistance on the part of Germans who refused to cooperate with orders they found to be wholly inhumane. Of course most just went along, telling themselves that action congruent with the inward revulsion they ostensibly felt would be wholly pointless—that is, wholly inconsequential, futile, and forgotten. Arendt is sternly opposed to this fashionable way by which we each let ourselves off the hook. See EIJ, pp. 230–33.

11. Where the right degree of identification with one's city has been attained one should be able to say with Machiavelli that "I love my native city more than my own soul." In OR Arendt quotes Machiavelli approvingly, and goes on to explain the significance of his statement.

"We who no longer take for granted the immortality of the soul are apt to overlook the poignancy of Machiavelli's credo. At the time he wrote, the expression was no cliche but meant literally one was prepared to forfeit everlasting life or to risk the punishments of hell for one's city. The question, as Machiavelli saw it, was not whether one loved God more than the world, but whether one was capable of loving the world more than one's own self. *And this decision has always been the crucial decision for all who devoted their lives to politics*" (OR, p. 37, note 20; emphasis added).

12. Somehow the state of mind must be brought into being which makes it impossible for a man to live with himself if he has neglected the commonweal, or politics generally. As in private life we count upon the fear of conscience, guilt, or shame to motivate good behavior and the meeting of our personal responsibilities, so must this same dynamic complex of feeling come to play a similar role in checking whatever proclivities we might have that lead us to shirk our public responsibilities. The collective presumption must be inculcated that holds neglect of one's duty to pursue the public weal to be the moral equivalent of neglecting one's duty to care for one's own child.

Regarding the shame that ought to prey upon one who shirks his public responsibility, in JP, see "Organized Guilt and Universal Responsibility," pp. 231–36. See also "Civil Disobedience," CR, pp. 58–68; LMW, pp. 179–93; and "Thinking and Moral Considerations: A Lecture," *Social Research* 38, 3 (Fall 1971): pp. 38–46.

13. For a belated indication of Arendt's perception of this problem, see Hannah Arendt, "Philosophy and Politics," in *Social Research* 57, 1 (1990), pp. 73–103.

14. See BPF/WA, pp. 179–214.

15. See BPF/WA, p. 120; for a similar notion see OR, p. 196.

16. Ibid.

17. BPF/WA, p. 123.

18. As Arendt puts it: "to act without authority and tradition, without accepted, time-honored standards and models, without the help of the wisdom of the founding fathers, was inconceivable" (BPF/WA, p. 124).

19. Thus "corruption" becomes viewed as a consequence of departing from the hoary hallowed way.

20. See BPF/WA, p. 121; OR, p. 198.

21. Ibid.

22. See OR, p. 198.

23. Though unlike Heidegger Arendt opts to remain within the "archical" history of being and would espouse a new origin (or *arche*) where Heidegger would counsel us to embrace an an-archical postmodernism.

24. See THC, pp. 8–9, 177–78; LMW, pp. 108–10.

25. LMW, pp. 108–10.

26. Arguably Arendt's approach to beginnings is related to Heidegger's approach. For Arendt, however, the beginnings that are of utmost significance are political beginnings, whereas Heidegger was most concerned with the beginnings that marked critical moments in the history of metaphysics.

27. See this chapter's conclusion.

28. See BPF/Pref, pp. 3–15.

29. See OR, pp. 200–214.

30. See BPF/CE, pp. 193–94.

31. See OR, pp. 200–214.

32. See BPF/Pref, pp. 5–7; OR, pp. 215–22. See also MDT, "Walter Benjamin" (henceforth "MDT/Benjamin"), pp. 202–4.

33. See THC, pp. 173–74, 192.

34. See THC, p. 192.

35. See THC, p. 192; BPF/CH, pp. 78–79; and MDT, "On Humanity in Dark Times: Thoughts About Lessing" (henceforth "MDT/Lessing"), pp. 20–22.

36. See BPF, pp. 3–15.

37. See BPF/Pref, pp. 4–6.

38. See BPF/Pref, p. 6.

39. See UP, pp. 377–82. See also BPF/Pref, pp. 5–6.

40. This notion is implicit in UP, generally; in BPF/Pref; in OR, pp. 215–22; and in the idea of the *sensus communis* to be unfolded in chapter 3.

41. See UP, pp. 377–82. Note the relationship between new words and evolving experience. In the same essay, see also pp. 388–91.

42. See OR, pp. 204–13.

43. On the relationship between the state of public life and the status of historical narrative, see D. Luban, "Explaining Dark Times: Hannah Arendt's Theory of Theory," *Social Research* 50, (Spring 1983), pp. 215–48.

44. See BPF, "The Crisis in Education," pp. 193–95.

45. See BPF/Pref, pp. 3–15. See also OR, pp. 215–23.

46. See BPF/CE; BPF/CC, pp. 173–226 and more particularly, pp. 193–95. Note, however, at the end of THC, and in the texts to be considered in chapter 3 Arendt links political continuity to common sense and its preconditions.

47. See the essays in BPF generally, especially those pertaining to education, culture, and authority.

48. See in BPF/CE, pp. 173–96, and BPF/CC, pp. 197–226.

49. See BPF/CE, pp. 193–95.

50. See BPF/CC, pp. 213–15.

51. See THC, pp. 167–74.

52 . See MDT/Benjamin, pp. 198–99.

53. It ought not to be inferred from this that Arendt believed that a duly constituted tradition will be utterly homogeneous; rather she assumed it would be relatively so.

54. See THC, pp. 17–21.

55. See BPF/CC, pp. 210–11.

56. See BPF/CE, pp. 193–96.

57. Regarding the relation between emulation and the passion for excellence, see Arendt regarding John Adams in OR, pp. 69–70.

58. See BPF/CE, pp. 193–95, and BPF/CC, pp. 211–13.

59. Ibid.

60. See OR, pp. 201–02. See also BPF/WA, pp. 120–28.

61. See THC, pp. 50–58.

62. This is an ideal for Arendt which modernity has lost hold of. Alas, for the foreseeable future we must abide in the "gap" between past and future that has opened up with the collapse of tradition.

63. See in BPF/CC, Arendt's analysis of the Roman mentality of conservation and of spectatorship as good in itself, pp. 211–26.
I would also note that it is also likely that those who render tradition the service of being its continuators will reap a portion of the existential rewards of self-transcendence that Arendt associates with action, albeit that these rewards will probably be reaped in obscurity.

64. See BPF/CC, p. 212.

65. See prelude to part two.

66. BPF/CC, pp. 212–13.

67. BPF/CC, pp. 211–12.

68. Ibid.

69. Ibid.

70. Arendt's critique of apolitical *Bildung* and its pernicious consequences are most manifest in her works of closest proximity (temporal and conceptual) to the Second World War. While Arendt could not go so far as to claim with any certainty that had the men of culture behaved in a politically responsible manner it would have made a significant difference to the course of events in that period, she is nonetheless of the unequivocal opinion that their apolitical ethos rendered them worse than useless in the moment when European civilization began to collapse. On Arendt's critique of apolitical *Bildung* see the essays collected in JP, especially

"We Refugees," "The Moral of History," "Portrait of a Period," and "Organized Guilt and Universal Responsibility." See also RV, pp. 216–28. For a critique of the apolitical orientation of the Jews, see OT, pp. 54–88. For a critique of the same orientation of the bourgeoisie, see "Organized Guilt and Universal Responsibility" in JP. See also in OT, pp. 135–47. See also in MDT, "On Humanity in Dark Times," pp. 17–23. See also in BPF/CC, pp. 211–26, Arendt's most theoretical reflection on the relationship between culture and politics.

71. See "Portrait of a Period" in JP, p. 113.

72. See Arendt's discussion of Pericles' "Funeral Oration," BPF/CC, p. 214.

73. See BPF/CC, pp. 211-26; and especially, p. 215.

74. This acknowledgment is implicit in Arendt's conception of every political-civilizational unit as a world. Within each of these worlds—and there are, of course, at least as many of them as there are separate nations—Arendt would expect that there will be a particular national cultural tradition which contains a political component. Though Arendt makes no mention of this cultural particularity in her discussions of culture or education in BPF, it is clear from her discussion of authority, as well as from her discussion of the polis as a space of "organized remembrance," that Arendt takes it for granted that even under the umbrella of any given multinationally embracing civilization (for example, Western Christendom) that there would develop many distinct national traditions. Thus even of the Greeks, it may be noted, that their common possession of Homer did not preclude the development of particularist traditions in Athens and Sparta which claimed the loyalty of and shaped the ideals of these cities' citizens in ways which differentiated the citizens of the one from those of the other. See JP, pp. 125–78, and MDT, pp. 81–94 .

75. See BPF/WA, pp. 120–28.

76. See CR, "On Violence," pp. 142–55.

77. The essay under scrutiny is "The Crisis in Education" (BPF/CE), which I proceed to interpret in conjunction with her essays on culture and authority from the same text, and in light of the slant on these matters contained in OR.

78. Thus "The Crisis in Education" (BPF/CE) appeared in late 1958, which places it in the period immediately following the publication of THC. Already, then, we can detect a shift of emphasis.

79. "Education," writes Arendt, "is the point at which we decide whether we love the world enough to take responsibility for it and by the same token save it from that ruin which, except for renewal . . . would be inevitable"(BPF/CE, pp. 196).

80. See BPF/WA, p. 119.

81. Given Arendt's conception of the political space as a site of isonomy or political equality, authority should have no place within it. While in OR, as we shall see, she departs from this principle, in BPF/WA she still abides by it and insists that the place of authority remains outside the political realm in the pre-political realm of the home and school. Politically mature adults must meet the challenges of the day without the option of resolving their problems through an appeal to authority.

82. BPF/CE, pp. 195–96.

83. The child, writes Arendt, "is new only in relation to a world that was there before him, and will continue after his death. . . . Human parents . . . have not only summoned their children into life . . . they have simultaneously introduced them into a world. . ." (BPF/CE, p. 185).

84. See BPF/CC, pp. 211–26.

85. Again Arendt never explicitly articulates this consequence of her position. That it follows from what she does say is clear.

86. See Judith Shklar, "Rethinking the Past" (SR:44 1977) pp. 80–90 on the telos of Arendt's "monumental" history.

87. This follows from Arendt's conception of the polis as a space of organized remembrance in which the telling of such stories is granted a very important role (see THC, pp. 175–99) as well as from her conception of how an act of founding would become constitutive of an authoritative origin (see OR, pp. 200–05).

88. See OR, pp. 196–206.

89. OR, p. 204.

90. It should be noted that Arendt's endorsement of the American Constitution is more apparent than real. She esteems a number of the concepts embodied in the institutions associated with it, more than the institutions themselves. She appreciates the continuity that has been begotten by this combination of institutions and piety for the origin. Unfortunately, the gem at the center of the setting, the spirit of popular political action which alone makes the ring truly valuable, has been lost.

91. See UP, pp. 387–91; LKPP, pp. 67–71.

92. Ibid.

93. See BPF/WA, pp. 91–141.

94. See BPF/WA, pp. 92–93. More generally, regarding Arendt's analysis of the concept of authority and its Roman roots see BPF/WA, 120–28; OR, pp. 199–202. Regarding what Arendt takes to be current confusion regarding the

nature of authority see BPF/WA, pp. 91–104. On the character of the Roman experience and the associated conception of authority, see BPF/WA, and OR, pp. 196–214.

95. How indispensable is authority? "Its loss is tantamount to the loss of the groundwork of the world" (BPF/WA, p. 95). Once more, let it be noted that there are as many "worlds" as there are politico-cultural units.

96. BPF/WA, p. 93.

97. See BPF/WA, p. 122.

98. OR, p. 201; BPF/WA, p. 121.

99. OR, p. 202.

100. See BPF/WA, p. 122.

101. "By virtue of *auctoritas*, permanence and change were tied together" (OR, p . 201).

102. OR, p. 201.

103. See OR, p. 201.

104. Ibid.

105. It should be noted that Arendt's endorsement of this conceptual constellation is at variance with Heidegger's repudiation of enframing *arche*.

106. See OR, pp. 179–224.

107. See OR, pp. 194–214.

108. See OR, pp. 198–202.

109. See OR, pp. 200ff.

110. Ibid.

111. See OR, pp. 115–40, 248–55, 279.

112. See OR, pp. 141–214.

113. A clear indication of the difference between Arendt's judgment of the French and American revolutionary experiences and her favorable view of the American founders can be discerned at almost every turn. See, for example, OR, pp. 21–58.

114. See OR, pp. 248–55.

115. The reader may be disconcerted by the lack of certainty that permeates this formulation. "Likely" is hardly strong enough where important questions of

interpretation are at stake. Unfortunately I cannot do better since Arendt speaks not so much of her own ideal as of the products of the American and French revolutions. From this discussion I have inferred what pleases her and the nature of the modifications which would make that which pleases her still more pleasing.

116. See OR, pp. 248–55.

117. Ibid.

118. See OR, pp. 232–38.

119. See OR, pp. 248–55.

120. See OR, pp. 248–55, 278–79.

121. Ibid.

122. See OR, p. 279.

123. While I have argued that the ideal incipient in OR would graft a council system to a constitutional framework akin to that of the United States, it could be argued to the contrary that the ideal incipient in OR is that of a pure multi-tiered council system unaccompanied by executive or judiciary branches of government. Such a reading would no doubt draw all its plausibility from Arendt's optimistic assessment of the latter at the very end of OR (pp. 275–79). It seems to me, however, that such an unqualified embrace cannot be squared with Arendt's conception of authority as it has been developed in BPF and OR, a conception which points in the direction of the necessity of some Supreme Court–like organ of authority. Were Arendt's conception of authority to be transformed in certain ways—ways which will be considered in chapter 3—it might be possible for her to theorize how a pure council system could generate authority out of its interstices. But at this point, because her theoretical resources are insufficient, I must regard her comments on p. 278 as gratuitous and utopian. In short, the ideal that effectively informs the *entire* book is a council *graft* rather than a pure council *system.*

124. See, in particular, OR, "The Pursuit of Happiness," pp. 115–40.

125. Arendt takes these phrases from a letter written by John Adams. See OR, p. 119.

126. Ibid. See also OR, "The Social Question," pp. 59–114.

127. In OR the dyad of freedom and necessity plays a key part, with necessity connoting both biological need on the one hand and irrepressible historical necessity on the other. Both of these oppose freedom which here, as in THC, means public freedom, that is, the freedom enjoyed while participating in a public political life. Making use of this opposition, Arendt contrasts "liberation from necessity"—which in most revolutions has been the ambition of the *malheureux* and their compassion-driven leaders—with "the constitution of freedom" which was the aim of those *hommes de lettres* who, having been bred on Greco-Roman

classics, desired to create public spaces. Indicative of her employment of these terms, Arendt speaks of the consequences wrought by the entry of the poor into the French Revolution: "The result was that necessity invaded the political realm, the only realm where men can be truly free" (OR, p. 114).

Regarding the other dyads: The opposition of evanescence and perdurance figures large in the discussion of founding a political order capable of lasting forever. See OR, pp. 194–214.

The opposition of uniqueness and uniformity figures in Arendt's discussion of the motivations that made men dedicate themselves to founding public spaces. Regarding *les hommes de lettres*, who played a significant part in the French Revolution's early stage, Arendt suggests that they were animated by what John Adams described as, "a passion for distinction and the desire to excel another" (OR, p. 119). Yet in their own epoch, precisely this passion was denied an outlet. Because they lacked a public space within which to shine forth *les hommes de lettres* were consigned to "obscurity," because "the public realm was invisible to them and . . . they lacked the public space where they themselves could become visible and be of significance' (OR, p. 124). This, in Arendt's view, engendered their commitment to a revolution which they hoped would create spaces of public freedom in which these passions could be exercised.

128. Within OR Arendt's most sustained discussion of the role to be played by authority, tradition, and culture comes in a chapter entitled "Foundation II: Novus Ordo Saeclorum" (OR, pp. 179–214).

129. See OR, pp. 141–78, 196–204.

130. See OR, p. 126.

131. Ibid. See also THC, pp. 243–45.

132. See THC, pp. 243–45.

133. Ibid.

134. Thus, in THC, Arendt writes of "the force of mutual promise" as "the force that keeps [a people] together" in those moments when they are not presently engaged in action. Thus the promise, or, in effect, the constitution brings into existence "isolated islands of certainty in an ocean of uncertainty. . . ." (THC, p. 244).

135. See OR, pp. 165–78 on the relation between mutual promising and constitution making. Power, for Arendt, exists only in the moment of action, but of vital importance are the mutual agreements by which the power potential of a people is kept intact. Such agreements are exemplified for Arendt by the Mayflower Compact and the U.S. Constitution. Thus underscoring the continuities between THC and OR, she writes that "binding and promising, combining and covenanting are the means by which power is kept in existence; where and when men succeed in keeping intact the power which sprang up between them [that is, by promises and pledges] . . . they are already in the process of foundation, of consti-

tuting a stable worldly structure to house, as it were, their combined power of action. There is an element of the world-building capacity of men in the human faculty of making and keeping promises . . . which in the realm of politics, may well be the highest human faculty" (OR p. 175).

In this context, the reader should note that the constitution's rootedness in THC's conception of promise keeping further undermines the tenability of Kateb's attempt to distinguish between the "moral" and "amoral" variants of Arendtian political action (George Kateb, *Hannah Arendt: Politics, Conscience, Evil* (Totowa, N.J.: Rowman and Allenheld, 1983), pp. 33–44). In Kateb's view, Arendt's conception of political action as the defense of the constitution, as articulated in OR, is a moral conception of action which ought to be differentiated from her conception of action in THC which Kateb brands as immoral because of its egoistical emphasis. That there are significant differences between the conceptions unfolded in these two texts is a point which I would be the last to deny. At issue, however, is whether there is a difference of the kind that Kateb asserts. What is for Kateb a difference in kind is really a difference of degree. While Kateb accurately observes the reduced emphasis upon self-revelatory action in OR, what he apparently failed to see was the degree to which Arendt had conceived of action, even in THC, as action engaged in for the sake of, and in defense of, the polity. (A point well-established in chapter 1 of this text.) Thus the distinction he wants to draw will not bear close scrutiny: If Arendt's later vision (OR) ought to be denominated moral, on account of the fact that action is conceived as the defense of a way of life—a view which pays too little attention to Arendt's equal emphasis upon public happiness and the "passion for distinction"—then so too should her earlier vision (THC) *for the very same reasons.*

136. Only in OR are the foundational and world-building aspects of promises, as evidenced in the preceding note, fully developed. More generally, on the origin-centered foundational role of the constitution, see OR, pp. 195–204.

137. See OR, pp. 195–204. Note the significance Arendt attributes to American Constitution worship—and her approbation!

138. Action, as we saw in chapter 1, has something inherently arbitrary about it and yet the constitution, which action brings into being, is meant to serve as a stable ground. How can the one become the ground of the other?" "What saves the act of beginning from its own arbitrariness is that it carries its own principle within itself, or, to be more precise, that beginning and principle, *principium* and principle, are . . . coeval. . . . The way the beginner starts whatever he intends to do lays down the law of action for those who have joined him in order to partake in the enterprise and to bring about its accomplishment. As such, the principle inspires the deeds that are to follow. . . ." (OR, pp. 212–13).

139. See OR, pp. 195–204.

140. Writing of the American founding fathers' answer to the problem of "how to make the Union perpetual," but with an eye to addressing the implicit

conceptual problem, Arendt calls attention to their Roman solution: "The very concept of Roman authority suggests that the act of foundation inevitably develops its own stability and permanence, and authority, in this context, is nothing more or less than a kind of necessary 'augmentation' by virtue of which all innovations and changes remain tied back to the foundation which, at the same time, they augment and increase. Thus the amendments to the Constitution augment and increase the original foundations of the American republic. . . ." (OR, p. 202).

141. See OR, pp. 198, 204–04.

142. See OR, pp. 199–200, 228–31.

143. In passing it is important to emphasize that Arendt's high praise for many facets of the American Revolution and Constitution ought not to be understood as an unqualified endorsement of the American political order. Arendt is, in fact, highly critical of American political life. By her measure, the revolutionary promise has not been realized. While she appreciates the importance of the continuity securing mechanisms which comprise part of the American political order, she is as critical of the fact that the spirit of public happiness has gone out of the machine. Stability alone can hardly satisfy her. What America seemed to offer in the beginning—a stable house for public action and public happiness—was never achieved. Instead a different American dream—of private happiness based on material abundance—came into being and has prevailed. As one might expect, Arendt is staunchly critical of this animal happiness and the vitiated public life that accompanies it.

144. See BPF, pp. 3–15, 25–29.

145. Ibid. See BPF/TMA, pp. 17–40 generally.

146. See THC, pp. 248–57 and BPF/Pref, pp. 3–15.

147. Ibid.

148. See BPF/Pref, pp. 3–15, and LMW generally. In the latter Arendt includes herself among the ranks of the destroyers of metaphysics by virtue of her endeavor to reduce long-standing metaphysical truths to the status of thought experiences.

149. This problem occupies Arendt in OR, pp. 179–214.

150. In Arendt's essay on Walter Benjamin she suggests that, perhaps, in the wake of the repudiation of the great tradition only those fragments of the past which the doorkeepers of the tradition had excluded or repressed might still speak to us. In this context she speaks of Heidegger's search for the oldest *logoi*, Scholem's retrieval of the Kabbalah, and Benjamin's penchant for the refuse of past ages. While she makes no mention of her own predilection for long forgotten fragments, one can hardly escape the analogy between Arendt's own effort to

excavate the pre-philosophical roots of Greek political experience and the procedures of these three whose work she so much admired. See MDT, pp. 193–206.

151. See OR, "The Revolutionary Tradition and Its Lost Treasure, pp.
215–81.

152. Ibid.

153. Thus Arendt notes in OR that: "It is precisely the absence of continuity, tradition, and organized influence [between the various instances] that makes
the sameness of the phenomenon so very striking" (OR, p. 262). If the independence of these events can be thus construed, then Arendt seems more justified in
seizing upon the Greek political experience as exemplary and less vulnerable to
charges of having succumbed to a genetic fallacy.

154. See BPF/Pref, pp. 3–6. In OR this disappointment with "the revolutionary tradition," which, via Hegel, took its lead from the French Revolution
rather than from the American, is palpable. The former gave us the specter of historical necessity as paradigmatic whereas the latter, which gave us a vision of
"public happiness," on account of its nonarticulation, has remained of only local
significance. See OR, pp. 50–56. In Arendt's view the "glorious" moments of
unwritten history belong to the unwritten revolutionary tradition which ought to
have arisen after the American Revolution. See also OR, pp. 215–23.

155. As a point of view, this belief informs the whole of OR.

156. The issues that will be of ultimate concern to us in the next chapter are
those delineated in the previous paragraph that pertain to common sense and were
earlier denominated under the rubric of Arendt's "third stratagem."

157. Arendt states the problem as a paradox: "The perplexity was very simple and stated in logical terms, it seemed unsolvable: if foundation was the aim
and the end of revolution, then the revolutionary spirit was not merely the spirit of
beginning something new but of starting something permanent and enduring;
[paradoxically, however] a lasting institution, embodying this spirit and encouraging it to new achievement, would be self-defeating. . . . [Thus] it seems to follow
that nothing threatens the very achievement of revolution more dangerously and
more acutely than the spirit which brought them about." Which leads Arendt to
ask whether "freedom in its most exalted sense as freedom to act be the price to be
paid for foundation?"(OR, p. 232).

158. Thus Arendt, while sympathizing with Jefferson's various schemes for
perpetual revolution, characterizes them as "impracticabilities." Arendt's own preferred solution would entail granting a greater role to the localities within a
schema that linked them up to the federal constitution. Yet her enthusiasm for this
"solution" might be misplaced inasmuch as it is easy to imagine that the spirit of
public freedom might wither here too or display disheartening tendencies towards
routinization. See OR, p. 233.

159. See OR, pp. 232–34.

160. While this facet was not so much emphasized in my analysis of *The Human Condition*, it is important to see that the possibility of the polity's collective self-definition is implicit in Arendt's conception and is an implication of no small importance.

161. See THC, pp. 195–96, 220–30, 233–36. See also BPF/WA, pp. 104–20.

162. See also in LMW Arendt's analysis of the possible basis for the general antipathy of most philosophers toward the root of action, the will. In LMW she speculates that the thinking faculty itself might be prejudiced against the will and the contingency it engenders. See LMW, pp. 11–51.

163. See THC, pp. 195–96, 220–30, 233–36. See also BPF/WA, pp. 104–20.

164. Thus, having depicted action in the bleakest terms (THC, pp. 233–36) Arendt turns (THC, pp. 236–47) to consider whether, in the maelstrom which action threatens to become, there are any internal brakes that might militate against a perilous slide. In forgiving and in promising Arendt locates two such elements, and yet it seems most doubtful that between them there is sufficient power to render the site of action tranquil or harmonious. Nonetheless, it is Arendt's position that together they should suffice to make the chaos endemic to action bearable, and hence she recommends that we accept the burden of action for the sake of its ennobling aspect.

165. Thus Arendt criticizes the Platonic and the Aristotelian arguments on behalf of erecting authorities over the political realm, both of which she regards as inimical to political equality and as tending to divide the political community into rulers and ruled (BPF/WA, pp. 104–20). At the same time, it should be noted that in this same essay she is much more receptive to the Roman conception of the authority of the past, and of the origin, in particular, for the present (BPF/WA, pp. 120–25). That the Roman conception is potentially as problematic for isonomy as the other two receives no attention.

166. Ibid.

167. See BPF/CE, pp. 195–96.

168. Ibid.

169. Ibid. More substantially, see BPF/WA, pp. 104–20.

170. Arendt saw that in the case of the U.S. Constitution the effect of the organs of world continuity was to suppress self-display and political action generally. By grafting the council system to the constitution, Arendt likely imagined that she could overcome this problem. Yet by retaining a Supreme Court-like organ of authority within her system, the problem—and the resultant distortion of the

political process—seem likely to recur. Authority vested in an extrapolitical organ and isonomy are incompatible.

171. This may explain why, one-and-a-half pages from the end of OR, Arendt chose to raise the possibility that a pure council system could be framed that would be capable of generating authority from its interstices, presumably without ruining isonomy or sacrificing stability and permanence. How it might do this is not even touched upon, and the proposition—which flys in the face of the conception of authority developed in BPF and OR—is offered without any theoretical support. Nonetheless, the very fact that Arendt feels she must shift her ground so close to the end of the book may be indicative of her own dissatisfaction with the tenor of the text's immanent tendencies. See OR, p. 278.

172. If they are radically heterodox they may flourish as private nonpolitical cultures, but they must necessarily lack validity as grounds of public discourse. On the other hand, it is important to point out that there will always be a range of perspectives that are regarded as legitimate by the community as a whole. Thus, in the area of constitutional interpretation, for example, there will be a range of interpretive possibilities that are of equally authoritative pedigree. When I speak of the fate of subcultures, I have in mind those which are considered beyond the pale of legitimacy however broadly or narrowly this band is constituted.

173. For a more detailed consideration of Arendt's views the reader is referred to the conclusion of chapter 1 and to my discussion of Arendt's pessimistic opinion regarding the prospect for self-display on the part of persons who are marked as other in the eyes of the majority culture. See, in particular, the references to "Reflections on Little Rock."

174. Clearly, as the postmodern and communitarian critiques of liberal individualism have reminded us, something essential is lost when one reduces the problem of the rights of minority cultures to the problem of individual self-expression. But since these problems are not unrelated, and since Arendt only explicitly considers the latter, we must draw what inferences we can from the only resources we have.

175. See chapter 3, generally.

176. See, in particular, the posthumously published LKPP lectures originally delivered in 1970; see also BPF/TP, pp. 227–64.

177. Had Arendt developed her conception of the political process with an eye to *The Human Condition* alone, she would have only needed to frame a conception which was at once productive of a policy consensus while facilitating the citizen's continuous realization and manifestation of selfhood. In the wake of *On Revolution*, however, it becomes equally important that the conceptualization of judgment and common sense be adequate to the goal of maintaining the long-term continuity of the worldly frame as well. That Arendt's late conceptualization of judgment and common sense entails a conception of action capable of achieving

all these goals supports my decision to situate it vis à vis both *The Human Condition* and *On Revolution*.

178. See the beginning of the conclusion to this chapter.

CHAPTER THREE

1. This does not mean that action flourished prior to the age of Descartes, but that the epistemological preconditions of its future flourishing were undercut by the introspective and rationalistic turn his work symbolizes. It should also be pointed out that Arendt regards Platonic epistemology as equally hostile to action. As different as Platonic and Cartesian philosophies are in many respects, with respect to action Arendt regards them as quite similar. At different points in her oeuvre, one or the other figures as her chief nemesis—and the roles in which they are cast are nearly identical.

2. See: Ronald Beiner, "Hannah Arendt on Judging," in *LKPP*, pp. 89–156; Elisabeth Young-Bruehl, "Reflections on Hannah Arendt's *The Life of the Mind*," *Political Theory* 10/2 (May 1982): pp. 277–305; Peter Stern and Jean Yarbrough, "*Vita Activa* and *Vita Contemplativa*: Reflections on Hannah Arendt's Political Thought in *The Life of the Mind*," *Review of Politics* 43 (July 1981): pp. 323–54; and Seyla Benhabib, "Arendt, Politics and the Self," *Political Theory* 16/1 (February 1988): pp. 29-51.

3. See Beiner, "Hannah Arendt on Judging," LKPP, pp. 91–92. In short, Beiner argues that Arendt's early-period concern with the judgmental component of action ("practical judgment") gives way to a late-period concern for contemplative, solitary, and retrospective judgment which, in his view, is manifest in LKPP. In my view, Beiner overlooks the degree to which Arendt continues to be concerned with "practical judgment" even in the later period; in addition, I would argue that he is blind to the symbiotic dynamic which unifies contemplative and practical moments of judgment and ties them both to action. That Arendt's concern for action remains foremost to the last, will be argued in greater detail when we undertake to review the genetic evolution of Arendt's reflections upon judgment later in this chapter.

4. This is implicit in THC and is explicit in BPF/CC, pp. 211–26, and LMT, pp. 92–96.

5. Thus, not even the norms of *humanitas* are articulated there.

6. In OR passing reference is made to the U.S. Supreme Court's functioning as the organ of judgment and to the U.S. Senate's functioning as an organ of opinion; and while the significance of these matters is suggested, the analysis does not suffice to make clear the true nature of this significance. See OR, pp. 225–29.

7. See THC, pp. 25–27, 175–84.

8. Ibid.

9. These essays will be canvased in detail as we proceed.

10. Regarding the passing exception to this neglect, see OR, pp. 228-29.

11. In truth, matters of relevance are treated in all Arendt's works. The most significant texts with regard to judgment, however, are not among her better known works. In chronological order, from earliest to latest, the essays in which judgment figures most prominently are: UP, BFF/CC, and BPF/TP. In addition to these essays one other text will merit our close attention, Arendt's posthumously published lecture notes on Kant's political philosophy, LKPP.

12. Albeit that the Platonists sought to impose a fixed and eternal order whereas the ideologists sought to execute the eternal law of the historical process. The affinity between the Cartesian breakdown of common sense and the rise of neo-Platonist conceptions of politics ought not to be overlooked.

13. As previously noted, Arendt critiques Cartesian politics and Platonic politics as if they are essentially similar phenomena. Both presuppose the rejection of plurality and, in that sense, are antiworldly; both esteem the philosopher's truth over the opinion of the many; and both give rise to instrumentalist conceptions of politics. There are of course significant differences between the two standpoints, but from the perspective of Arendt's political concern, the differences are less important than the similarities.

14. *Thinking* refers to *The Life of the Mind: (vol. I) Thinking.* [Henceforth to be referred to as "LMT."]

15. See OT, pp. 351–53, 456–58, 468–79.

16. Ibid.

17. See OT, pp. 351–53.

18. Ibid.

19. Common sense provides one with a "measured insight into the interdependence of the arbitrary and the planned, the accidental and the necessary" (OT, p. 352).

20. "If for instance, all the 'confessions of political opponents in the Soviet Union are phrased in the same language and admit the same motives, the consistency-hungry masses will accept the fiction as supreme proof of their truthfulness; whereas common sense tells us that it is precisely their consistency which is out of this world and proves that they are a fabrication" (OT, p. 352).

21. This is implicit in her characterization of the preconditions of ideological predominance, among which loneliness qua the absence of communal life, fig-

ures most prominently. Note also the implicit anticipation of "world alienation." See OT, pp. 477–79.

22. Ibid.

23. See OT, pp. 477–79, where this notion is implicit. For a more complete articulation of the same idea see THC, pp. 283–84. See also UP, pp. 386–87 and "Philosophy and Politics," *Social Research* 57, 1 (1990), generally.

24. See THC, pp. 283–84.

25. This essay is henceforth referred to as UP.

26. Common sense, "the political sense par excellence," is "only that part of our mind and that portion of *inherited wisdom* which all men have in common in *any given civilization*" (UP, p. 386, emphasis added).

27. See UP, pp. 380–81.

28. Regarding the relation between action and common sense see UP, p. 391.

29. This perspective is implicit throughout whole essay. On the one hand Arendt emphasizes the rootedness of action in the web of preunderstandings which are "always consciously or unconsciously directly engaged in action" (UP, p. 391). On the other hand, retrospective judgment is necessarily grounded in this same web of preunderstandings. Only where judgment remains true to this matrix can it possibly be "true." See also UP, pp. 380–82.

30. Not only must the story be articulated in terms of that conceptual ensemble which is particular to the particular community. In Arendt's view, it is equally, or even more, vital that the story be true to the actional or phenomenal reality of the event as well. Causal explanations—which to her mind—falsify the nature of the phenomena, will not do. See UP, generally.

31. On the role of historians, political scientists, and storytellers, generally, see, UP, pp. 388–91.

32. Such is Arendt's view of the modern predicament. Following Kant she describes the inability to judge as "stupidity" and goes on to suggest that today "[s]tupidity has become as common as common sense was before" (UP, p. 384).

33. See also BPF/CC, pp. 220–26, and in LKPP, pp. 66–72.

34. Implicit throughout UP; for clearest articulation see BPF/CC, pp. 220–26, and LKPP, pp. 66–72.

35. See LKPP, pp. 72–76.

36. See THC, pp. 294–325. Regarding Arendt's critique of instrumentality, see also, THC, pp. 153–59. Regarding the critique of "process thinking" and the modern conception of history, see BPF/CH, pp. 75–86.

37. See THC, pp. 220–30.

38. See THC, pp. 220–36, especially pp. 234–35. Regarding this same concept, see also BPF/CH, pp. 77–80.

39. See chapter 1 discussion of *humanitas*.

40. Of course, as noted in chapter 2, within *The Human Condition* Arendt does not address the question of cultural production, or reproduction, in any detail.

41. The clearest formulation of this relationship comes in LMT. See LMT, pp. 19–23, 37–40, 92–98, 129–35. But also see BPF/CC, pp. 211–26.

42. See the endnotes to the following section for substantiating citations from BPF/CC and LMT.

43. Ibid.

44. See LMT, p. 94. Regarding the importance of the fact that the spectators' opinions are not private but influenced by their interaction, see LMT, pp. 94–96. See also BPF/CC, pp. 222–23.

45. Ibid.

46. See LMT, pp. 94–96.

47. The relative constancy of the spectators' point of view as distinguished from that of the actors' follows from the disinterestedness which, in Arendt's view, can be expected from the former much more than from the latter. See LMT, pp. 92–94. Regarding the presumptive disinterest of the spectator, see BPF/CC, pp. 219–20.

48. This conception seems implicit in the relationship between parts one and two of BPF/CC. From this perspective, Arendt's effort—which we traced in chapter 2—to lay bare the lineaments of an ethos of worldliness and the means by which it might be inculcated can be understood as an effort to discern how to inculcate the norms of right spectatorship. This effort is presupposed in all that follows.

49. In underscoring the reciprocal and symbiotic relationship between the actors and the spectators, which is quite apparent in THC, I take issue with Beiner's interpretation of Arendt's "evolving" orientation toward judgment (see LKPP,

p. 921). For Beiner, Arendt's turn to the spectator, and the judgment he exercises, is to be understood as a turning away from, and a "giving-up on," action. In my view, the turn to the spectator is misunderstood when understood so one-sidedly. For my part, the attention Arendt pays to the spectator pole is always to be understood in the context of how her meditations bear upon her understanding of action. That Beiner's approach is fundamentally misguided will emerge most fully when we turn to consider Arendt's LKPP.

50. *The Life of the Mind*, based on lectures delivered between 1973 and 1975, is relevant to both the second and third paths. As is well known, Arendt intended to write separate studies of thinking, willing, and judging. Only the first two were completed. It is crucial to my argument, however, that it is possible to deduce the likely content of the third study by scrutinizing Arendt's lectures on Kant's conception of judgment that were delivered in 1970. Since our goal is to treat the lectures on Kant "as if" they were delivered in 1975, it is important for us to situate these lectures in relation to *The Life of the Mind* wherever relevant. It is for this reason that we will set aside our chronological treatment of Arendt's writings in order to consider the relevant aspects of LM *prior* to discussing LKPP.

51. That disinterest and freedom from passion, which are both regulative conditions of good spectatorship, are more likely to characterize the spectator than the actor is a point made by Arendt repeatedly. See LMT, pp. 92–94, and BPF/CC, pp. 219–22.

52. See OR, pp. 200–202, 231. See BPF/WA, pp. 120–28.

53. See OR, pp. 200–202.

54. Thus the import of Arendt's discussion in OR of the relationship between the power and authority of the Supreme Court. See OR, pp. 200–202.

55. The conception developed here becomes explicit only in LKPP.

56. See OR, pp. 200–202, 231.

57. Though it is arguably implicit in BPF/CC.

58. These three works include two essays that were written prior to the composition of the Kant lectures: "The Crisis in Culture" (BPF/CC) written in 1961 and "Truth and Politics" (BPF/TP) written in 1967. The latter essay appeared in the second revised and expanded edition of BPF (1968). The true contemporaneity of the latter article and the lectures is even closer, a fact that becomes clear when one learns that the 1970 lecture series collected as LKPP was largely developed for a 1966 course on Kant's political thought. The third work that shows a strong Kantian influence is *Thinking* (LMT) which was originally delivered as the Gifford Lectures at the University of Aberdeen in 1973.

59. See BPF/CC, part 2, pp. 211–26.

60. See BPF/CC, pp. 215–19.

61. See BPF/CC, pp. 215–19.

62. See BPF/CC, pp. 220–22.

63. See BPF/CC, p. 220.

64. See BPF/CC, pp. 220–22. The phrase "representative thinking," actually comes from BPF/TP, p. 241.

65. See BPF/CC, p. 221. In short, such judgments lack the universal and necessary validity of logical judgments.

66. See BPF/CC, p. 219.

67. See BPF/CC, p. 222.

68. "For judgments of taste, the world is the primary thing, not man . . . neither the life interests of the individual nor the moral interests of the self are involved here" (BPF/CC, p. 222).

69. See BPF/CC, pp. 222–23.

70. Regarding the "politics of making," see, for example, THC, pp. 220–30. See also BPF/CH, pp. 75–90. Once again we see that for Arendt the assault upon Platonism and the assault upon Cartesianism are *in the current context* essentially the same.

71. See BPF/TP, pp. 239–49.

72. Both logical and factual truths are antipolitical in this respect. See BPF/TP, p. 239.

73. Ibid.

74. See BPF/TP, pp. 239–49.

75. Ibid.

76. See BPF/TP, pp. 246–47.

77. See BPF/TP, p. 246.

78. This view will be somewhat modified in LMT.

79. See BPF/TP, pp. 246–49.

80. See BPF/TP, pp. 246-47.

81. Ibid.

82. In the realm of politics the validity of propositions "remains a matter of opinion, not of truth" and as such "depend[s] upon agreement and consent; [these

propositions] are arrived at by discursive, representative thinking; they are communicated by means of persuasion and dissuasion" (BPF/TP, p. 247).

83. See BPF/TP, pp. 241–42.

84. See BPF/TP, p. 242.

85. See BPF/TP, pp. 241–42, 246–47.

86. See BPF/TP, p. 242.

87. See LMT, pp. 53–65.

88. See LMT, pp. 57–65.

89. Ibid.

90. Ibid.

91. Ibid.

92. In this same category should be included the action-ideal itself and Arendt's conception of the relation between action and human fulfillment. Admittedly, Arendt's tendency to speak ex cathedra may create the impression that she wants her ideas to accepted as not merely meaningful but as absolutely true, and this perception persists despite her explicit disavowal of any such intention. But her embrace of the Kantian distinction between *Vernunft* and *Verstand* ought to rectify this mistaken impression. Like other ideas that claim to be meaningful, the ultimate significance of Arendt's ideas depends upon the degree to which they come to be shared. This does not mean that a conception that is meaningful to only one person is less meaningful than a conception that is meaningful to many, but in politics the extent to which an opinion does come to be shared does matter.

93. Arendt regards Hobbesian and Benthamite political philosophies as neo-Cartesian for their being grounded in truths known by introspection.

94. LMT, pp. 69, 192–93.

95. See LMT, p. 69.

96. Arendt most often writes as if reflective judgments regarding meaning that are neither true nor false constitute the whole of politics. I disagree with this view and will argue that political judgment includes cognitions and hence reaches questions of truth and falsity as well. See the final section of this chapter.

97. See LMT, pp. 45–46.

98. Ibid.

99. See LMT, pp. 45–53.

100. See LMT, pp. 46–51.

101. See LMT, pp. 50–51.

102. See LMT, p. 50.

103. "Our certainty that what we perceive has an existence independent of the act of perceiving, depends entirely on the object's also appearing as such to others and being acknowledged by them" (LMT, p. 46).

104. See LMT, pp. 53–65.

105. See LMT, pp. 56–57.

106. It should be pointed out that in LMT Arendt only elucidates her conception of judgment to a minimal degree. In particular the relation between reflective judgment and the common sense or *sensus communis*—which Arendt elaborates in BPF/CC, BPF/TP, and LKPP—goes unarticulated. Instead, common sense and the *sensus communis* only figure in her discussion of the feeling of realness and in her discussion of scientific rationality. I trust the unarticulated relation would have been explicated in full had Arendt completed her study of judgment.

107. In THC Arendt focuses upon logic; in LMT she adds the interworking of the five senses to this category.

108. In "Truth and Politics" Arendt does seem to take this view without any qualification as she stylizes the contrast between truth's self-evidence and a communally constituted consensus of opinion.

109. In addition, Arendt notes that reason's interest in its own self-activity also motivates thinking.

110. Other texts, representative of this same Kantian moment in Arendt's thought, which help to clarify Arendt's own intent in the lectures are BPF/CC and BPF/TP. Where useful we shall refer to these texts.

111. Note that Kant's "third critique," *The Critique of Judgement*, is divided into two parts, the "Critique of Aesthetic Judgment" and the "Critique of Teleological Judgment" of which only the former is of interest to Arendt. From Kant's own point of view, neither half of the work is of direct political significance, though it is interesting to note that in the "Critique of Teleological Judgment" Kant articulates a teleological conception of history which in the hands of Hegel and Marx will come to entail a conception of politics which Arendt staunchly opposes. From this angle, in particular, Arendt's recourse to the implicit politics of the "neglected" half of the critique—in order to oppose the politics which can be traced to the conception developed in the other half—is most striking.

112. See in Immanuel Kant: *The Critique of Judgement*, trans. J.C. Meredith, (Oxford University Press, 1952), pp. 50–60, 81–89, 150–54 [henceforth referred to as Kant].

113. See BPF/TP, pp. 238–47.

114. This notion is intimated in THC, pp. 282–84; foreshadowed in BPF/CC, pp. 220–22; and fully manifest in LKPP, pp. 66–75.

115. Though a good beginning was made in BPF/CC, pp. 212–26.

116. That Arendt's reading of Kant represents a significant moment in the development of her theory of action is a proposition which many who have considered this part of her oeuvre have failed to appreciate. In fact, prevailing opinion has it that Arendt's Kant lectures represent the culmination of a turning *away* from action to judgment. In the opinion of (for example) Beiner (1982, 1983) Denneny, and Stern and Yarbrough (1981), Arendt's attention to Kant's conception of spectator judgment possesses only an obvious signification inasmuch as the spectator's contemplation of the art object is "obviously" analogous to the storyteller's retrospective contemplation of the past. Thus Stern and Yarbrough, after reviewing those parts of the Kant lectures that were published as an appendix to LM, reject the notion that Arendt's discussion of past-oriented spectatorship has any relevance for prospective judgment. With Beiner, they see Arendt's analysis of Kant's "third critique" as rooted in her endeavor to understand the kind of judgment that is involved in looking backward. In itself there is nothing objectionable in this view, for Arendt's treatment of aesthetic judgment does bear upon her understanding of the storyteller's praxis. What is objectionable, however, is the view that Arendt's meditation upon contemplative judgment is of no wider relevance and, in particular, that it is does not mark a new stage in the development of her conception of action. In the course of what follows, I will make clear where these critics were led astray. More sympathetic to the perspective to be unfolded here are Elisabeth Young–Bruehl ("Reflections on Hannah Arendt's *The Life of the Mind*," *Political Theory* 10/2 (May 1982): pp. 277–305.) and J. Glenn Gray ("The Abyss of Freedom—and Hannah Arendt," in *Hannah Arendt: The Recovery of the Public World*, ed. Melvyn A. Hill (New York: St. Martin's Press, 1979), pp. 225–244.). See also Ernst Vollrath, "Hannah Arendt's Method of Political Thinking," *Social Research* 44 (Spring 1977): pp. 160–82.

117. This too tends to be overlooked on account of the general misreading of the text. See LKPP, p. 55; LMT, pp. 92–96.

118. In other words, she adverts to Kant's conception of judgment and incorporates large parts of it into her own political philosophy. See BPF/CC, pp. 197–226, and BPF/TP, pp. 227–64. More particularly, apropos of Arendt's appropriation of Kant, see BPF/CC, pp. 212–24; BPF/TP, 239–49. See also the discussion of "Truth and Politics" in this chapter.

119. See BPF/CC, pp. 211–26 and BPF/TP, pp. 239–49.

120. To buttress our reading of LKPP we will make reference both in the text and especially in the notes to parallel formulations from elsewhere in Arendt's oeuvre.

121. These will be canvased in the notes as the discussion of Arendt's lectures on Kant proceeds.

122. See Kant, pp. 50–52.

123. Hence the antinomy of taste. See Kant, sec. 56, pp. 205–6.

124. See Kant, sec. 40, pp. 150–54, regarding the methodology by which conflicts of taste are to be resolved

125. See BPF/TP, pp. 239–49.

126. See BPF/TP, p. 242; BPFCC, pp. 222–23; and, in MDT, "On Humanity in Dark Times: Thoughts about Lessing, pp. 26–31.

127. See BPF/TP, pp. 239–46.

128. See Kant, *The Critique of Judgment*, pp. 150–54. See also LKPP, pp. 66–72, and BPF/CC, pp. 220–22.

129. See Kant, pp. 50-52; see also BPF/CC, p. 220; BPF/TP, p. 242; LKPP, p. 43.

130. According to Kant, "by the name *sensus communis* is to be understood the idea of a *public* sense, i.e. a critical faculty which in its reflective act takes account (*a priori*) of the mode of representation of everyone else" (Kant, p. 151). See also LKPP, pp. 66–72, and BPF/CC, pp. 220–21.

131. See Kant, pp. 150–54; or, as Arendt comments in LKPP: "This *sensus communis* is what judgment appeals to in everyone and it is this possible appeal that gives judgments their special validity" (LKPP, p. 72). See also BPF/TP, p. 242; LKPP, pp. 67–72. Summing up her own point of view Arendt suggests that "when one judges, one judges as a member of a community" (LKPP, p. 72).

132. See BPF/TP, pp. 241–43, and BPF/CC, p. 220.

133. See LKPP, pp. 67–68, 73–75.

134. That there are countervailing human interests is hardly to be denied by either Arendt or Kant. The point in the current context is to isolate the interests that undergird an orientation toward agreement.

135. See LKPP, p. 72 and BPF/CC, pp. 221–23. This conception is implicit throughout LKPP; explicitly Arendt notes: "when one judges one judges as a member of a community . . . one appeals to the community sense" (LKPP, p. 72).

It should be noted that, for Arendt, "being in a *common* world" refers in the last instance to the global community of men within which one lives as well, albeit that one lives in the latter in an existentially "thin" sense. Generally, however, unless otherwise noted, we will have in view—as Arendt herself usually did—the narrower rather than the broader construction. Regarding commonality and the ultimate extent of community, see LKPP, pp. 72-76. On the "thinness" of world citizenship see in MDT, "Karl Jaspers: Citizen of the World?"

136. See BPF/CC, pp. 221–23.

137. See Arendt "Public Rights and Private Interests," pp. 103–8, and BPF/CC, pp . 209–10.

138. This might also be inferred from the substance of Arendt's critique of the culture industry in mass society for consuming cultural artifacts that are supposed to signify the lasting quality of the public world. See BPF/CC, pp. 208–10.

139. See also BPF/CC, pp. 220–22, regarding the closely related notions of disinterest and impartiality.

140. Ibid.

141. Ibid. See also Arendt "Public Rights and Private Interests," pp. 103–8.

142. See LKPP, pp. 67, 73–74; and BPF/CC, pp. 220–23.

143. In the last instance the community in question is the global community, which is why, in Arendt's view, an Eichmann remains culpable for his actions even though they were in accord with the values of his own particular community. See EIJ, pp. 278–79.

144. See LKPP, pp. 67–73; BPF/CC, pp. 220–23; and BPF/TP, pp. 241–42. See also Kant, *The Critique of Judgment*, pp. 150–54.

145. See LKPP, pp. 67–73; BPF/CC, pp. 220–23; and BPF/TP, pp. 241–42.

146. See Kant, pp. 150–54; LKPP, pp. 42–44, 66–72; BPF/CC, p. 220; and BPF/TP, p. 242.

147. See LKPP, pp. 42–44, and BPF/CC, pp. 220–22.

148. For a depiction of this process, see BPF/TP, pp. 241–42. See also BPF/CC, p. 220.

149. This is implicit in Kant's entire project which aims at discerning the a priori, and hence universal, grounds of judgments of the beautiful and, in particular, at discerning the conditions of possibility of their subjective necessity, that is, of their bindingness on all men irrespective of their time and place. Only an inherent inner law of the human faculties could figure as such a basis, and, indeed, such a law is discovered by Kant. The aim in judging is to rise up to such a standpoint as will insure that one's judgment is reflective of this pure basis. See Kant, *The Critique of Judgment*, pp. 81–85, 150–54.

150. This follows from all the works canvased in chapter 2, as well as from Arendt's pre-Kantian conception of the common sense as a web of culturally and historically contingent preunderstandings. Moreover, as we will see further on,

Arendt's appropriation of Kant's conception does not engender a modification on this point. See also THC, pp. 283–84, regarding the difference between a common sense that is grounded in a shared world and a common sense like logic, an inner "common" sense.

151. This conclusion follows from our entire analysis of common sense to this point.

152. Thus Arendt emphasizes that "in matters of taste we must renounce ourselves in favor of others. . . . We must overcome our special subjective conditions for the sake of others. In other words, the nonsubjective element in the nonobjective senses is intersubjectivity," which in concrete terms means that "I judge as a member of *this* community and not as a member of a supersensible world" (LKPP, p. 67).

153. "In effect," is underscored to emphasize that in subjective actuality the members of a given culture might not understand their criteria of greatness, or beauty, to be anything other than absolutely so. In reality, however, what strikes the denizens of a given community as great may be only contingently so, that is, great for them but not great absolutely. Blind to this awareness, their subjective intentionality in seeking greatness remains pure and a real degree of self-overcoming is achieved. Hence there is no necessary contradiction between what is being asserted in this section and what was discussed in chapter 1 under the rubric of man's quest to be absolutely great.

154. See Kant, *The Critique of Judgment*, pp. 52, 150.

155. This follows from Kant's belief that, in its pure essence, the judgment of beauty permits universal imputation on account of the fact that the experience of beauty is rooted in a law-governed interplay between the imagination and the understanding which is the same for all men. Where men disagree regarding the beauty of "x" this can only be due, then, to a failure on the part of one or more of the parties to rise to this pure standpoint. Such failure engenders erring judgments.

156. See THC, pp. 7–8, 175–88, 213–15, regarding the central importance of human difference.

157. See LKPP, throughout. See BPF/CC, pp. 219–23, and BPF/TP, pp. 241–43.

158. See LKPP, pp. 80–85.

159. Ibid.

160. LKPP, p. 84.

161. LKPP, p. 82.

162. LKPP, p. 84.

163. LKPP, p. 82.

164. Ibid.

165. See LKPP, p. 83.

166. LKPP, p. 77.

167. It is interesting to note that Arendt sees Kant as making available for the reflective judgment an additional criterion besides the example, a criterion which Arendt rejects. This latter criterion is that of "progress." From this perspective, acts, events, and virtues are to be judged by the teleological standard of their conduciveness to historical betterment. Thus though Kant found the French Revolution to be morally repellent, in his reflective judgment he esteemed it on account of its value in advancing mankind toward a cosmopolitan existence. For Arendt, such an extrinsic criterion, like the standard of historical success, can only be applied at the cost of demeaning the intrinsic worth of deeds and the intrinsic dignity of the one who does them. By comparison, the judgment which refers (for example) the man, the act, or the virtue to the exemplary instance of the same, saves the intrinsic worth of human action and human character from the utilitarian measure which knows only how to weigh consequences. Thus Arendt's embrace of Kant's notion of the exemplary can be seen as hearkening back to her embrace of paradigms of greatness in THC. See LKPP, pp. 76–77.

168. LKPP, pp. 76–77, 84–85.

169. "The example is the particular that contains in itself . . . a concept or a general rule." Thus of one who spontaneously declares that "This man has courage" Arendt suggests that "if one were [for example] a Greek, one would have in the depths of one's mind the example of Achilles . . . One must have Achilles present even though he certainly is absent." Analogously Arendt suggests that if we call someone good we must have Jesus or St. Francis in mind. "The judgment [of person "x" as good in light of the example of Jesus] has exemplary validity to the extent that the example is rightly chosen" (LKPP, p. 84).

170. See previous note.

171. For example, stories of the kind considered in chapter 2.

172. See LKPP, pp. 84–85.

173. This rootedness of the *sensus communis* in concrete examples born of particular events and specific phenomena reinforces what was suggested in the last chapter regarding the culturo-historical contingency of the *sensus communis* wherever it is to be found. That the *sensus communis* will vary from community to community, and over time, follows from the nature of the concrete means by which it is conveyed to each generation. In this context it is interesting to note that Arendt is systematically using Kant's conception of the relation between concepts

and examples to underscore what has already been shown to be a distinctly un-Kantian conception of the *sensus communis*.

174. Though we are emphasizing the historical and cultural contingency of normative concepts, it should be seen that this contingency is even more marked in reference to descriptive concepts. Thus after noting the degree of contingency that attaches to the association between goodness and Jesus, Arendt goes on to cite "Bonapartism" as a concept which makes Napoleon an example and in the same moment restricts its validity to those heirs to a particular historical tradition who possess the experience of Napoleon. Commenting on both cases, but in particular reference to the latter, Arendt suggests that "[m]ost concepts in the historical, . . . political [and we would add, moral] sciences are of this restricted nature: they have their origin in some particular historical incident, and we then proceed to make it 'exemplary'—to see in the particular what is valid for more than one case" (LKPP, p. 85).

175. Of the relationship between the use of examples and the imparting of moral concepts, Arendt, having cited Achilles, Jesus, and St. Francis, notes that "these examples teach or persuade by inspiration, so that whenever we try to perform a deed of courage or of goodness it is as though we imitated someone else—the *imitatio Christi*, or whatever the case may be" (BPF/TP, p. 248).

176. Again, the intent is to call attention to value-laden concepts more than to purely descriptive ones.

177. The implications for the current debate regarding liberalism, civic virtue, and civic education that follow from Arendt's conception are apparent.

178. See BPF/CC, pp. 202–3, 208–13.

179. Ibid.

180. That is, in all her neo-Kantian essays subsequent to, and inclusive of, (BPF) "The Crisis in Culture." In this context, the reader might also note that many of the misreadings of Arendt's LKPP emanate from a failure to grasp the extent, or the nature, of the differences between her views and Kant's.

181. See LKPP, pp. 61–65 on the relationship between genius and taste. See also Kant, *The Critique of Judgment*, pp. 168–83.

182. See LKPP, p. 62. See also Kant, *The Critique of Judgment*, pp. 172–75.

183. See LKPP, p. 62. See also Kant, pp. 182–83.

184. Regarding the relationship between Taste and the criterion of communicability, see LKPP, pp. 63–75, 68–74. See also Kant, pp. 148–54.

185. See LKPP, pp. 63–75, 62–74.

186. Etymologically, as Arendt points out in THC, idiocy comes from the Greek for privacy. In LKPP she notes that Kant "remarks in his *Anthropology* that insanity consists in having lost [the] common sense that enables us to judge as spectators; and the opposite of it is a *sensus privatus*, a private sense, which he also calls 'logical *Eigensinn*' implying that our logical faculty . . . could indeed function without communication—except that then . . . it would lead to insane results precisely because it has separated itself from the experience that can be valid and validated only in the presence of others" (LKPP, p. 64). Hence the equivalence between idiocy and privacy. Note also, the mind's recourse to logicality when it has lost its rootedness in the world.

187. Theoretically, this insight is decisive in enabling Arendt to turn Kant's reflections upon the relationship *between* the actor/artist and the spectator into a meditation upon the nature of the judgment exercised by the actor/artist in the midst of his actional or creative endeavor. This crucial moment in Arendt's analysis is overlooked by all who fail to see that LKPP is of significance for understanding Arendt's theory of action.

188. See LKPP, pp. 62–63.

189. That is, if we understand this equation in the light of her earlier work (for example, *The Human Condition*). Regarding the equation between genius and politics, see LKPP, pp. 61–63.

190. See LKPP, pp. 67–69.

191. On the relationship between the imagination (that is, the faculty which enables us to represent an object or action in our mind's eye) and the common sense (which assesses the representation), see LKPP, pp. 66–72.

192. See LKPP, pp. 68–69.

193. The reader will also recall that in *The Human Condition* Arendt differentiates between the sovereignty of the artist (that is, the sovereignty of "making") and the nonsovereignty of the actor (that is, the nonsovereignty of acting).

194. Paradoxically, it would seem to be the sovereignty of the artist, which in practice becomes the sovereignty of technique, that in Arendt's view, effectively prevents the artwork from serving as a vehicle of self-disclosure. Thus, by contrast, the actor's nonsovereignty helps to insure that, notwithstanding the parallels with the activity of the artist, self-disclosure will still occur.

195. See Ronald Beiner, "Hannah Arendt on Judging," in LKPP, p. 92.

196. See Ronald Beiner, *Political Judgement*, pp. 12–19.

197. See, for example, BPF/CC, BPF/TP, MDT/Lessing.

198. The good citizen, of course, will only measure the object against publicly validated criteria of judgment. And in a wellfounded Arendtian polity surely no utilitarian criterion will be thus validated.

199. N.B. Arendt does *explicitly* note the equation we are emphasizing. In the same passage in which she asserts the consubstantiality of the artist's "originality" and the actor's "novelty," she proceeds to call our attention to the fact that "the critic and spectator . . . sits *in* every actor or fabricator"(LKPP, p. 63; emphasis added). Those who believe that LKPP has no bearing upon Arendt's conception of action should take note.

200. See UP, pp. 388–89; THC, pp. 184–92; and BPF/CH, p. 79.

201. Hence the superiority of the putative spectator's point of view over the interested actor's. See BPF/CC, pp. 220–21, and BPF/TP, pp. 241–42. In addition, I refer you to the earlier discussion of impartiality and disinterestedness that came at the end of the analysis of "The Crisis in Culture."

202. Ibid. See also in LKPP, pp. 68–72.

203. From Arendt's perspective, it is very important that the distinction between private and public modes of discourse be maintained. In part, the reason why Arendt believes that public discourse must adhere to forms, and appeal to reasons (or grounds), that possess public standing is because the possibility of securing valid agreements between citizens who are essentially unlike one another depends upon these agreements being arrived at in relation to a frame of reference which all parties share and regard as legitimate. And by Arendt's measure, the *sensus communis* is the only thing that all citizens presumptively share and can disinterestedly appeal to over against the differences which might otherwise make communication and agreement impossible. But another reason why Arendt insists upon the significance of the incommensurability between the forms of private and public discourse is her sense of the existential accomplishment that this discontinuity facilitates. For Arendt regards the challenge of overleaping the rift that divides interest from disinterest, and private reason from public reason, as the challenge that bestows great worth upon those who successfully meet it and thereby achieve the existential reorientation from self-concern to world-concern. Though this central dimension of Arendtian politics has not been much stressed since chapter 1, the reader should be mindful of its continuing importance.

204. By the reference to "equally valid" I want to indicate that in Arendt's view all opinions are equally legitimate as long as they are disinterested and as long as they are framed as appeals to public as distinguished from private grounds (that is, as appeals to the *sensus communis* as distinguished from the *sensus privatus*). See LKPP, pp. 43, 67, 71–74. See also BPF/TP, pp. 241–42. See also the previous note.

205. See LKPP, pp. 43, 72–73; BPF/TP, pp. 241–42; and BPF/CC, pp. 220–22 .

206. Ibid.

207. See LKPP, pp. 72–74.

208. In the following analysis I focus upon the will in its relation to judgment. Thinking, the third of the mental faculties, and the source of meaning, does not figure directly in this discussion. This does not mean that thinking has no bearing on action, though in general Arendt seems to remove it from any direct role. At the same time, it should be pointed out that Arendt sees a connection between thinking (as the silent dialogue between me and myself) and the scruples of the moral conscience. See LMT, pp. 179–93 and the essay "Thinking and Moral Considerations: A Lecture," *Social Research* 38, 3 (1971) pp. 417–46. More generally, and of greater relevance to the substance of daily political life, Arendt regards thinking as the root of the ideas, principles, and criteria that together comprise the *sensus communis*. Thinking, in the nontechnical sense of commonsense reasoning and in the sense that thinking necessarily accompanies the use of language, is assumed to accompany judging and willing.

209. The works published during Arendt's lifetime are generally silent on this issue. In only a single lecture that was posthumously published recently does Arendt acknowledge this problem. See Hannah Arendt, Philosophy and Politics," *Social Research* 57, 1 (1990) pp. 73–103.

210. Those who have criticized Arendt most severely on this count include Kateb (1983), O'Sullivan (1973), Pitkin (1981), and Schwartz (1970).

211. In particular I am thinking of the 1953 "Understanding and Politics," and the 1961 "The Crisis in Culture," (part II) in which Arendt's later conception of judgment is foreshadowed.

212. BPF/WF, p. 164; emphasis added.

213. See James Miller, "the Pathos of Novelty," in *Hannah Arendt: The Recovery of The Public World*, ed. Melvyn A. Hill (New York: St. Martins Press, 1979), pp. 177–208 and Barry Clarke "Beyond the Banality of Evil," *British Journal of Political Science* 10 (October 1980): pp. 417–39.

214. See Barry Clarke, "Beyond the Banality of Evil"; Robert Grafstein, "Political Freedom and Political Action,"*Western Political Quarterly* 39 (May 1986): pp. 464–79; Suzanne Jacobitti, "Hannah Arendt and The Will," *Political Theory* 16/1 (February 1988): pp. 53–76.

215. For a somewhat different view of how the abyss of freedom is to be transcended see Gray (in Hill, *Hannah Arendt*). For Gray the way out of the abyss lies in "doing beauty which would permit the will to escape its self-enclosure and arbitrariness by means of actions projected as responses, in the mode of emulation,

to the beauty of the natural world. Thus the will's arbitrariness and rootlessness could be overcome. Clearly Gray's response and my own differ in significant ways. At the same time, it should be noted that Glen Gray and I have understood the nature of the problem Arendt faced in encountering the abyss of freedom along fairly similar lines which would surely be grouped at one end of a continuum if Beiner's conception were placed at the other.

216. When we speak of "political" or "public" space in this section it should be kept in mind that within all but the simplest and smallest of polities there are a multiplicity of public spaces. In a federal republic, such as the United States, there are distinct public spaces on local, state, and national levels. In the ideal republic envisioned in OR there would be as many public spaces as there are distinct deliberative bodies. In this section, and elsewhere, then, though we speak of the public space as if there were only one per polity, this is not to be taken literally. Because Arendt's concern is not with the interrelations between public spaces but with public spaces conceived essentially, our mode of reference is not incorrect. But the reader must keep the truth of the matter in mind. Even within a single polity there are many public spaces and Arendt's analysis is meant to elucidate what transpires (or ought to transpire) in each of them. Ideally, Arendt would have paid as much attention to the interrelations between public spaces and addressed the problem of sub- and superordination that afflicts federal arrangements. Unfortunately, she does not.

217. For Arendt's clearest formulation of this dramaturgic division of the public space between actors and spectators see BPF/CC, pp. 218–22; LMT, pp. 92–96; and LKPP, p. 55.

218. Ibid.

219. See LMT, p. 94; and LKPP, p.55.

220. Regarding the uneven distribution of political talent and the consequent differences in political prominence, see OR, pp. 275–81. Within THC this dichotomy between actors and spectators is pervasive: see pp. 28–37, 50–58, 175–81, 192–99. Regarding spectatorship as a particular function and distinct activity see BPF/CC, pp. 213–26.

221. Ibid.

222. Near the end of OR (p. 278) Arendt may foreshadow this position when she suggests, in passing, that the pyramidal structure of council government might engender authority on every tier without relying upon any extraconciliar agency. How she might square this prospect with the contrary thrust of her analysis of authority is not considered. Had Arendt, at that juncture, looked to spectator judgment and its relationship to the *sensus communis*, perhaps, she would have discerned the mechanism we have elucidated.

223. As was noted earlier in this chapter, action has no end beyond itself and is thus free of the instrumentalizing dichotomy of means and ends that charac-

terizes the "production" of the artist. Nor has the actor the sovereignty that we associate with the artist who produces his work by himself. Nonetheless, it is permissible to describe the actor, by the words he speaks and the deeds he does—both by himself and in conjunction with others—as "producing" the objects of political attention.

224. That is to say a "return" to the Kant of the "third critique," that is, to the Kant of the 1961 "The Crisis in Culture" (BPF/CC).

225. See LMW, pp. 188–94.

226. See OT, pp. 351–53, 468–69.

227. See THC, pp. 248–80.

228. Force will decide because between radically incommensurate egos there is no other basis for order.

229. The truth of reason may be an eternal static truth (hence, Platonism) or the truth of an ongoing historical process (hence, Marxist Leninism).

230. Hence the "mistake' of those who conflate truth and meaning and would imagine that meanings have the same epistemological status as logical truths or truths of fact. From such conflation arises the grim politics of "truth in power."

231. In this section "common sense" should be understood to refer to *Gemeinsinn*, that is, to common sense qua community sense, as contrasted with *gesunder Menschenverstand* or common human understanding, which for Arendt signifies what is left when common sense in its true signification is destroyed.

232. See BPF/CC, pp. 220–23.

233. In Arendt's view the disjuncture between the assumptions of those who believe the politico-historical realm to be law-governed and the messy contingency-permeated world of political action was well exemplified by the inability of the Pentagon's planners to comprehend what was going on in Vietnam. See CR, "Lying in Politics: Reflections on the Pentagon Papers," pp. 3–47.

234. Ibid.

235. Ibid.

236. Ibid.

237. The reader should note that it is the very necessity that action be undertaken in a timely fashion which makes action itself the means by which man is definitively rescued from the abyss of freedom. Up until the moment of action, the judgment is free to recommend this and that, and the will is free to vacillate between willing and nilling. Assuming, however, that the would-be actor wants something from—or cares about something in—the world, the agent's realization

of his aims becomes dependent upon his attuning his action to the perpetually reconstellating flux of the worldly web.

Only the fact that the world demands that a decision be made, and that an action be undertaken *now*, insures that the will will transcend its freedom. In Arendt's parlance, freedom of the will ends the moment action begins. Because the world demands that action be timely, the will is forced to cancel its otherwise infinite freedom by giving birth to the word or deed. See LMW, pp. 101–2, 141.

238. Thus Arendt holds that even when judging authoritatively and selflessly, "the person discloses to an extent *also himself, what kind of person he is*" and does so "involuntarily," and necessarily (BPF/CC, p. 223).

239. Though it is the world that matters, the self is nonetheless manifest when it transcends itself for the world's sake. This is the essential paradox of Arendtian politics and we have encountered it over and over again in her work.

240. Of course it may well be that to deny nonhegemonic cultures public standing may have the effect of vitiating them.

241. And, I might add, more or less hostile to plurality and self-manifestation.

242. Indeed, this sense of relative expansiveness has helped to allay one of our greatest concerns regarding Arendt's approach in *On Revolution*.

243. And as the postmodernists have made clear, even this privileging of consensus could be called into question on antifoundationalist grounds.

244. Arendt's account aims to be normative. She would readily acknowledge that "bad" political judgments, that is, judgments made without reference to the *sensus communis*, are made all the time.

245. To test an opinion or a proposal is to explore the reasoning behind it. On Arendt's construction, then, this is equivalent to testing an opinion or proposal for its compatibility with the *sensus communis*.

246. Though it should be noted that from the standpoint of Arendt's concern for the maintenance of long-term continuity, where two policies are equally well-grounded upon the *sensus communis* and hence equally conducive to the perpetuation of that which is the substantive root of political continuity, the choice between them is essentially a matter of indifference.

247. This fear is prominent in Arendt's (OT) discussion of ideological thinking and in her discussion of the telos inherent in the concentration camps. See OT, pp. 437–79. See also THC, pp. 294–304.

248. See, for example, THC, pp. 153–59.

249. See "Ideology and Terror" in OT. See also the discussion of ideology in the introduction to this text; the discussion of rational compulsion in chapter 1; and the discussion of OT in the first part of this chapter.

250. See, for example, BPF/TP, pp. 239–49.

251. See Arendt regarding the principle of democratic validity inherent in Jefferson's "We *hold* these truths to be self-evident . . ." in OR, pp. 192–94. More generally, see BPF/TP, pp. 239–49.

252. But this claim on behalf of irrepressible selfhood having been duly registered, it is nonetheless important to reiterate that Arendt's fear of the totalitarian propensities inherent in the nature of the validity claims of these intrinsically antipluralist logics is not to be regarded as being without warrant. By the standards of truth or of right reckoning projected by such forms of rationality, the validity of any one form precludes the validity of any other. Each demands exclusive sway and only the relativities of power keep one form from driving all its competitors from the field.

253. Arendt wants to give plurality its due. Paradoxically, however, as Arendt would have us employ this conception, the plurality it respects would not encompass the plurality of modes of political judgment which, in my view, have a rightful place in political life.

254. Arendt's explicit discussion of *phronesis* is strikingly limited, but see in BPF/CC, p. 22 in which the Kantian and Greek conceptions are treated as roughly equivalent. In a different vein, however, see Arendt's discussion in LMW, pp. 59–62. My point in what follows is not to suggest that Arendt ever intended to constitute a synthesis of Kant's and Aristotle's conceptions of judgment, but rather to suggest that such a fusion would at once answer to Arendt's concerns and to those that have been raised in this critique of her conception of judgment.

255. See Aristotle, *Nicomachean Ethics*, 1140a24–1142a29.

256. See THC, pp. 175–88.

257. See THC, p. 244.

258. See THC, pp. 246–47.

259. See BPF/TP, pp. 232–49. In Plato's own oeuvre, the contrast between truth and opinion is a recurrent motif and deep concern. For those in search of a precis of his understanding of the essence of this distinction see *Republic*, 473d–511e. And more particularly, see his discussion of "the line" and the various levels of cognition, 509d–511b.

260. In this paragraph I am arguing on the basis of distinctions drawn by Aristotle in *Nicomachean Ethics*, 1138b18–1143b17.

261. It should be noted that Arendt does not grant the objective reality of the concepts pondered by *noesis*.

262. It should be emphasized that Arendt's opposition is not built on strictly moral grounds. Indeed, in large measure, Arendt's opposition is based upon an epistemological critique of the presuppositions of the ideologists and of the neo-Platonists as well. Thus in Arendt's view, the truth of human plurality and of the human capacity for novelty makes the excluded *logoi false* to the nature of the reality they claim to comprehend.

263. Regarding Arendt's view of the implications that follow from the decision to rank the *vita contemplativa* above the *vita activa*, see THC, pp. 12–21. See also, BPF/CH, pp. 45-47.

264. Of course Aristotle and Arendt would account for the origin and normativity of these norms in radically dissimilar ways.

265. See in chapter 1, "Public and Private: Spaces and Objects." See also THC, pp. 22–78.

266. See THC, pp. 58–60.

Bibliography

Arendt, Hannah. *Between Past and Future*. New York: Penguin Books, 1968.

Arendt, Hannah. *Crises of the Republic*. New York: Harcourt Brace Jovanovich, 1972.

Arendt, Hannah. *Eichmann in Jerusalem*. 2d ed. New York: Penguin Books, 1965.

Arendt, Hannah. "History and Immortality." *Partisan Review* 24/1 (Winter 1957): 12–35.

Arendt, Hannah. *The Human Condition*. Chicago: The University of Chicago Press, 1958.

Arendt, Hannah. *The Jew as Pariah*. Edited by Ron H. Feldman. New York: Grove Press, Inc., 1978.

Arendt, Hannah. *Lectures on Kant's Political Philosophy*. Edited by Ronald Beiner. Chicago: The University of Chicago Press, 1982.

Arendt, Hannah. *The Life of the Mind*. New York: Harcourt Brace Jovanovich, 1978.

Arendt, Hannah. *Men in Dark Times*. New York: Harcourt Brace Jovanovich, 1968.

Arendt, Hannah. *On Revolution*. New York: Penguin Books, 1963.

Arendt, Hannah. "Philosophy and Politics." *Social Research* 57/1 (Spring 1990): 73–103.

Arendt, Hannah. *The Origins of Totalitarianism*. New York: Harcourt Brace Jovanovich, 1973.

Arendt, Hannah. "Public Rights and Private Interests: In Response to Charles Frankel." In *Small Comforts for Hard Times: Humanists on Public Policy*, Edited by Michael Mooney and Florian Stuber, pp. 103–8. New York: Columbia University Press, 1977.

Arendt, Hannah. *Rahel Varnhagen: The Life of a Jewish Woman*. Rev. ed. New York. Harcourt Brace Jovanovich, 1974.

Arendt, Hannah. "Reflections on Little Rock." *Dissent* 6/1 (Winter 1959): 44–71.

Arendt, Hannah. "A Reply" [to Eric Voeglin's review of *The Origins of Totalitarianism*]." *Review of Politics* 15 (January 1953): 77–84.

Arendt, Hannah. "Thinking and Moral Considerations: A Lecture." *Social Research* 38/3 (Fall 1971): 417–46.

Arendt, Hannah. "Understanding and Politics." *Partisan Review* 20/4 (July–August 1953): 377–92.

Arendt, Hannah. "What is Existenz Philosophy?" *Partisan Review* 8/1 (Winter 1946): 34–56.

Beiner, Ronald. "Hannah Arendt on Judging." In *Lectures on Kant's Philosophy. See* Arendt 1982.

Beiner, Ronald. *Political Judgment.* Chicago: The University of Chicago Press, 1983.

Benhabib, Seyla. "Arendt, Politics and the Self." *Political Theory* 16/1 (February 1988): 29–51.

Bernstein, Richard J. "Hannah Arendt: The Ambiguities of Theory and Practice." In *Political Theory and Praxis: New Perspectives*, Edited by Terrence Ball, pp. 141–58. Minneapolis: University of Minnesota Press, 1977.

Canovan, Margaret. "Arendt, Rousseau, and Human Plurality in Politics." *Journal of Politics* 45 (May 1983): 286–302.

Canovan, Margaret. "The Contradictions of Hannah Arendt's Political Thought." *Political Theory* 6/1 (February 1978): 5–26.

Canovan, Margaret. *The Political Thought of Hannah Arendt.* New York: Harcourt Brace Jovanovich, 1974.

Clarke, Barry. "Beyond the Banality of Evil." *British Journal of Political Science* 10 (October 1980): 417–39.

Cooper, Leroy, A. "Hannah Arendt's Political Philisophy: An Interpretation." *Review of Politics* 38 (April 1976): 145–76.

Denneny, Michael. "The Privilege of Ourselves: Hannah Arendt on Judgment." In *Hannah Arendt: The Recovery of the Public World. See* Hill 1979.

Dossa, Shiraz. "Hannah Arendt on Eichmann: The Public, the Private and Evil." *Review of Politics* 46 (April 1982): 163–82.

Dossa, Shiraz. "Human Status and Politics: Hannah Arendt on the Holocaust." *Canadian Journal of Political Science* 8/2 (June 1980): 309–23.

Grafstein, Robert. "Political Freedom and Political Action." *Western Political Quarterly* 39 (May 1986): 464–79.

Glenn Gray, J. "The Abyss of Freedom—and Hannah Arendt." In *Hannah Arendt: The Recovery of the Public World. See* Hill 1979.

Glenn Gray, J. "The Winds of Thought." *Social Research* 44/1 (Spring 1977): 44–62.

Habermas, Jürgen. "Hannah Arendt's Communications Concept of Power." *Social Research* 44/1 (Spring 1977): 3–24.

Heather, Gerard, P., and Matthew Stolz. "Hannah Arendt and the Problem of Critical Theory." *Journal of Politics* 41 (February 1979): 2–22.

Heidegger, Martin. *Being and Time.* Translated by John Macquarrie and Edward Robinson. New York: Harper & Row, 1962.

Hill, Melvyn, A., ed. *Hannah Arendt: The Recovery of the Public World.* New York: St. Martin's Press, 1979. This collection contains essays by Elisabeth Young-Bruehl, Bernard Crick, Mildred Bakan, Bikhu Parekh, Kenneth Frampton, Robert W. Major, Peter Fuss, James Miller, Stan Spyros Draenos, J. Glenn Gray, Michael Denneny, and Melvyn A. Hill.

Hinchman, Lewis P., and Hinchman, Sandra, K. "In Heidegger's Shadow: Hannah Arendt's Phenomenological Humanism." *Review of Politics* 46 (April 1984): 183–211.

Jacobitti, Suzanne. "Hannah Arendt and the Will." *Political Theory* 16/1 (February 1988): 53–76.

Jay, Martin, and Botstein, Leon. "Hannah Arendt: Opposing Views." *Political Review* 45/3 (1983): 348–80.

Kant, Immanuel. *The Critique of Judgement.* Translated by J.C. Meredith. Oxford: Oxford University Press, 1952.

Kateb, George. "Death and Politics: Hannah Arendt's Reflections of the American Constitution." *Social Research* 54/3 (Fall 1987): 605–28.

Kateb, George. *Hannah Arendt: Politics, Conscience, Evil.* Totowa, N.J.: Rowman and Allanheld, 1983.

Knauer, James, T. "Motive and Goal in Hannah Arendt's Concept of Political Action." *American Political Science Review* 74 (September 1980): 721–33.

Luban, David. "Explaining Dark Times." *Social Research* 50 (Spring 1983): 215–48.

Mack, Arien, ed. *Social Research* 44 (Spring 1977). The issue consists of essays on Hannah Arendt by Jürgen Habermas, Hans Jonas, J. Glenn Gray, Robert Nisbet, Judith N. Shklar, Sheldon Wolin, Bernard Crick, Hans Morganthau, Dolf Sternberger, Erich Heller, Ernst Vollrath, and Elisabeth Young-Bruehl.

McKenna, George. "On Hannah Arendt Politics: As It Is, Was, Might Be." *Salmagundi* 10/11 (Fall 1969–Winter 1970): 104–22.

Miller, James. "The Pathos of Novelty: Hannah Arendt's Image of Freedom in the Modern World." In *Hannah Arendt: The Recovery of the Public World. See* Hill 1979.

Mooney, Michael, and Stuber, Florian, eds. *Small Comforts for Hard Times: Humanists on Public Policy.* New York: Columbia University Press, 1977.

Moors, Kent G. "Modernity and Human Initiative: The Structure of Hannah Arendt's *Life of the Mind.*" *The Political Science Reviewer* 10 (1980): 189–230.

Morgenthau, Hans. "Hannah Arendt on Totalitarianism and Democracy." *Social Research* 44/1 (Spring 1977): 127–31.

Nelson, John S. "Politics and Truth: Arendt's Problematic." *American Journal of Political Science* 22/2 (May 1978): 270–301.

O'Sullivan, Noel. "Hannah Arendt: Hellenic Nostalgia and Industrial Society." In *Contemporary Political Philosophies.* Edited by Anthony de Crespigny and Kenneth Minogue. New York: Dodd, Mead, 1975.

O'Sullivan, Noel. "Politics, Totalitarianism and Freedom: The Political Thought of Hannah Arendt." *Political Studies* 21/2 (June 1973): 183–98.

Parekh, Bikhu. *Hannah Arendt and the Search for a New Political Philosophy.* London: The Macmillan Press, Ltd., 1981.

Pitkin, Hanna Fenichel. "Justice: On Relating Private and Public." *Political Theory* 9/3 (August 1981): 327–52.

Pitkin, Hanna Fenichel. "Review of Oakeshott's Political Thought." *Dissent* 20 (Fall 1973): 496–525.

Riley, Patrick. "Hannah Arendt on Kant, Truth and Politics." *Political Studies* 35 (1987): 379–92.

Schwartz, Benjamin I. "The Religion of Politics: Reflections on the Thought of Hannah Arendt." *Dissent* 17 (April/May 1970): 144–61.

Shklar, Judith. "Rethinking the Past." *Social Research* 44/1 (Spring 1977): 80–90.

Shklar, Judith, N. "Review of *Between Past and Future.*" *History and Theory* 2/3 (1963): 286–92.

Stern, Peter and Yarbrough, Jean. "Hannah Arendt." *American Scholar* 47 (Summer 1978): 37–86.

Stern, Peter and Yarbrough, Jean. "*Vita Activa* and *Vita Contemplativa*: Reflections on Hannah Arendt's Political Thought in *The Life of the Mind.*" *Review of Politics* 43 (July 1981): 323–54.

Voegelin, Eric. "The Origins of Totalitarianism." *Review of Politics* 15 (January 1953): 68–76, 85.

Vollrath, Ernst. "Hannah Arendt and the Method of Political Thinking." *Social Research* 44/1 (Spring 1977): 160–82.

Young-Bruehl, Elisabeth. *Hannah Arendt: For Love of the World.* New Haven: Yale University Press, 1982.

Young-Bruehl, Elisabeth. "Reflections on Hannah Arendt's *The Life of the Mind.*" *Political Theory* 10/2 (May 1982): 277–305.

Index

Accountability, 93

Acculturation, 153

Action: aesthetics of, 172; analysis of, 78–79; and beauty, 243n64; beginning of, 203; boundlessness of, 59, 90, 133, 146; coercive logic in, 42; in common, 59, 83, 114, 122, 147; and common sense, 82, 85; communicative, 60; and community, 27; comprehension in, 62; consequences of, 29; contemplative judgment in, 189; contours of, 19–23; effect of storytelling on, 103; errancy in, 152, 153, 155, 156, 196; evaluative criteria of, 194; founding, 132; and freedom, 48; governing norms, 152; grand scale, 84; heroic, 29; influence of spectators on, 158; and interaction, 27; irreversibility of, 59, 90; and judgment, 148; moment of, 211, 229; and natality, 24–25; nature of, 13; and necessity, 40–44; nobility of, 84; political, 19, 58, 68, 114, 121, 140, 142, 202, 204, 208, 240n31; possibility of, 204; potential of, 86; presuppositions of, 258n8; primacy of, 153; principles of, 33–34; public, 49, 56–62, 85; relationship to judgment, 13; restorative, 86; resuscitation of, 81; revolutionary, 119, 132; self-actualizing, 131; self-interest in, 95; self-revelatory, 66–67, 82–83, 90, 130, 225; as symbolization of character, 33; and uniqueness, 25–30;

unpredictability of, 28–29, 59, 90, 146; and will, 38, 197, 198; and world continuity, 83, 84, 86, 89, 90, 91, 96, 104, 130, 132

Action-ideal, 10, 62, 71, 119, 205–219, 253n178, 282n92; architectonic structure of, 62, 63; role of education in, 111; self-revelation in, 104, 120; worldly pole of, 104, 120, 125

Actors: accountability of, 93; and common sense, 77; magnitude of acts, 34; relationship to spectators, 141, 151–154, 155, 219–220, 279n49, 184–187; self-transcendence of, 90; unpredictability of, 28, 29

Alienation, 6; from the public realm, 5; from the world, 11, 12, 81, 85, 86, 89, 90, 95, 129–130, 140, 154, 205, 206, 207, 208, 238n2, 261n34

Anomie, 9, 126

Anti-semitism, 2

Appearance, 27; as evidence, 80; and performative norms, 33; in public space, 50; and reality, 81; realm of, 175; untrustworthiness of, 167

Arendt, Hannah: analysis of totalitarianism, 1–10; conception of judgment, 141–177; concern for freedom, 38–40, 48; concern for origins, 98–118; on freedom and necessity, 36–49, 66; interpretive difficulties, 1; on lasting and passing, 30–36; and participatory